ASPEN PUBLISHERS

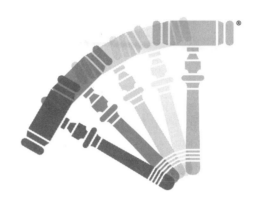

Casenote™ *Legal Briefs*

CONSTITUTIONAL LAW

Keyed to Courses Using

**Rotunda's
Modern Constitutional Law**

Eighth Edition

Wolters Kluwer
Law & Business

AUSTIN   BOSTON   CHICAGO   NEW YORK   THE NETHERLANDS

This publication is designed to provide accurate and authoritative information in regard to the subject matter covered. It is sold with the understanding that the publisher is not engaged in rendering legal, accounting, or other professional services. If legal advice or other expert assistance is required, the services of a competent professional person should be sought.

— From a Declaration of Principles adopted jointly by a Committee of the American Bar Association and a Committee of Publishers and Associates

To contact Customer Care, e-mail customer.care@aspenpublishers.com, call 1-800-234-1660, fax 1-800-901-9075, or mail correspondence to:

Aspen Publishers
Attn: Order Department
P.O. Box 990
Frederick, MD 21705

Printed in the United States of America.

1 2 3 4 5 6 7 8 9 0

ISBN 978-0-7355-7043-6

About Wolters Kluwer Law & Business

Wolters Kluwer Law & Business is a leading provider of research information and workflow solutions in key specialty areas. The strengths of the individual brands of Aspen Publishers, CCH, Kluwer Law International and Loislaw are aligned within Wolters Kluwer Law & Business to provide comprehensive, in-depth solutions and expert-authored content for the legal, professional and education markets.

CCH was founded in 1913 and has served more than four generations of business professionals and their clients. The CCH products in the Wolters Kluwer Law & Business group are highly regarded electronic and print resources for legal, securities, antitrust and trade regulation, government contracting, banking, pension, payroll, employment and labor, and health-care reimbursement and compliance professionals.

Aspen Publishers is a leading information provider for attorneys, business professionals and law students. Written by preeminent authorities, Aspen products offer analytical and practical information in a range of specialty practice areas from securities law and intellectual property to mergers and acquisitions and pension/benefits. Aspen's trusted legal education resources provide professors and students with high-quality, up-to-date and effective resources for successful instruction and study in all areas of the law.

Kluwer Law International supplies the global business community with comprehensive English-language international legal information. Legal practitioners, corporate counsel and business executives around the world rely on the Kluwer Law International journals, loose-leafs, books and electronic products for authoritative information in many areas of international legal practice.

Loislaw is a premier provider of digitized legal content to small law firm practitioners of various specializations. Loislaw provides attorneys with the ability to quickly and efficiently find the necessary legal information they need, when and where they need it, by facilitating access to primary law as well as state-specific law, records, forms and treatises.

Wolters Kluwer Law & Business, a unit of Wolters Kluwer, is headquartered in New York and Riverwoods, Illinois. Wolters Kluwer is a leading multinational publisher and information services company.

Format for the Casenote Legal Brief

Nature of Case: This section identifies the form of action (e.g., breach of contract, negligence, battery), the type of proceeding (e.g., demurrer, appeal from trial court's jury instructions) or the relief sought (e.g., damages, injunction, criminal sanctions).

Fact Summary: This is included to refresh your memory and can be used as a quick reminder of the facts.

Rule of Law: Summarizes the general principle of law that the case illustrates. It may be used for instant recall of the court's holding and for classroom discussion or home review.

Facts: This section contains all relevant facts of the case, including the contentions of the parties and the lower court holdings. It is written in a logical order to give the student a clear understanding of the case. The plaintiff and defendant are identified by their proper names throughout and are always labeled with a (P) or (D).

Palsgraf v. Long Island R.R. Co.

Injured bystander (P) v. Railroad company (D)

N.Y. Ct. App., 248 N.Y. 339, 162 N.E. 99 (1928).

NATURE OF CASE: Appeal from judgment affirming verdict for plaintiff seeking damages for personal injury.

FACT SUMMARY: Helen Palsgraf (P) was injured on R.R.'s (D) train platform when R.R.'s (D) guard helped a passenger aboard a moving train, causing his package to fall on the tracks. The package contained fireworks which exploded, creating a shock that tipped a scale onto Palsgraf (P).

🏛 RULE OF LAW
The risk reasonably to be perceived defines the duty to be obeyed.

FACTS: Helen Palsgraf (P) purchased a ticket to Rockaway Beach from R.R. (D) and was waiting on the train platform. As she waited, two men ran to catch a train that was pulling out from the platform. The first man jumped aboard, but the second man, who appeared as if he might fall, was helped aboard by the guard on the train who had kept the door open so they could jump aboard. A guard on the platform also helped by pushing him onto the train. The man was carrying a package wrapped in newspaper. In the process, the man dropped his package, which fell on the tracks. The package contained fireworks and exploded. The shock of the explosion was apparently of great enough strength to tip over some scales at the other end of the platform, which fell on Palsgraf (P) and injured her. A jury awarded her damages, and R.R. (D) appealed.

ISSUE: Does the risk reasonably to be perceived define the duty to be obeyed?

HOLDING AND DECISION: (Cardozo, C.J.) Yes. The risk reasonably to be perceived defines the duty to be obeyed. If there is no foreseeable hazard to the injured party as the result of a seemingly innocent act, the act does not become a tort because it happened to be a wrong as to another. If the wrong was not willful, the plaintiff must show that the act as to her had such great and apparent possibilities of danger as to entitle her to protection. Negligence in the abstract is not enough upon which to base liability. Negligence is a relative concept, evolving out of the common law doctrine of trespass on the case. To establish liability, the defendant must owe a legal duty of reasonable care to the injured party. A cause of action in tort will lie where harm,

though unintended, could have been averted or avoided by observance of such a duty. The scope of the duty is limited by the range of danger that a reasonable person could foresee. In this case, there was nothing to suggest from the appearance of the parcel or otherwise that the parcel contained fireworks. The guard could not reasonably have had any warning of a threat to Palsgraf (P), and R.R. (D) therefore cannot be held liable. Judgment is reversed in favor of R.R. (D).

DISSENT: (Andrews, J.) The concept that there is no negligence unless R.R. (D) owes a legal duty to take care as to Palsgraf (P) herself is too narrow. Everyone owes to the world at large the duty of refraining from those acts that may unreasonably threaten the safety of others. If the guard's action was negligent as to those nearby, it was also negligent as to those outside what might be termed the "danger zone." For Palsgraf (P) to recover, R.R.'s (D) negligence must have been the proximate cause of her injury, a question of fact for the jury.

▶ ANALYSIS
The majority defined the limit of the defendant's liability in terms of the danger that a reasonable person in defendant's situation would have perceived. The dissent argued that the limitation should not be placed on liability, but rather on damages. Judge Andrews suggested that only injuries that would not have happened but for R.R.'s (D) negligence should be compensable. Both the majority and dissent recognized the policy-driven need to limit liability for negligent acts, seeking, in the words of Judge Andrews, to define a framework "that will be practical and in keeping with the general understanding of mankind." The Restatement (Second) of Torts has accepted Judge Cardozo's view.

Quicknotes
FORESEEABILITY A reasonable expectation that change is the probable result of certain acts or omissions.

NEGLIGENCE Conduct falling below the standard of care that a reasonable person would demonstrate under similar conditions.

PROXIMATE CAUSE The natural sequence of events without which an injury would not have been sustained.

Party ID: Quick identification of the relationship between the parties.

Concurrence/Dissent: All concurrences and dissents are briefed whenever they are included by the casebook editor.

Analysis: This last paragraph gives you a broad understanding of where the case "fits in" with other cases in the section of the book and with the entire course. It is a hornbook-style discussion indicating whether the case is a majority or minority opinion and comparing the principal case with other cases in the casebook. It may also provide analysis from restatements, uniform codes, and law review articles. The analysis will prove to be invaluable to classroom discussion.

Issue: The issue is a concise question that brings out the essence of the opinion as it relates to the section of the casebook in which the case appears. Both substantive and procedural issues are included if relevant to the decision.

Holding and Decision: This section offers a clear and in-depth discussion of the rule of the case and the court's rationale. It is written in easy-to-understand language and answers the issue presented by applying the law to the facts of the case. When relevant, it includes a thorough discussion of the exceptions to the case as listed by the court, any major cites to the other cases on point, and the names of the judges who wrote the decisions.

Quicknotes: Conveniently defines legal terms found in the case and summarizes the nature of any statutes, codes, or rules referred to in the text.

Aspen Publishers is proud to offer *Casenote Legal Briefs*—continuing thirty years of publishing America's best-selling legal briefs.

Casenote Legal Briefs are designed to help you save time when briefing assigned cases. Organized under convenient headings, they show you how to abstract the basic facts and holdings from the text of the actual opinions handed down by the courts. Used as part of a rigorous study regimen, they can help you spend more time analyzing and critiquing points of law than on copying bits and pieces of judicial opinions into your notebook or outline.

Casenote Legal Briefs should never be used as a substitute for assigned casebook readings. They work best when read as a follow-up to reviewing the underlying opinions themselves. Students who try to avoid reading and digesting the judicial opinions in their casebooks or on-line sources will end up shortchanging themselves in the long run. The ability to absorb, critique, and restate the dynamic and complex elements of case law decisions is crucial to your success in law school and beyond. It cannot be developed vicariously.

Casenote Legal Briefs represents but one of the many offerings in Aspen's Study Aid Timeline, which includes:

- *Casenote Legal Briefs*
- *Emanuel Law Outlines*
- *Examples & Explanations* Series
- *Introduction to Law* Series
- Emanuel *Law in a Flash* Flashcards
- Emanuel *CrunchTime* Series

Each of these series is designed to provide you with easy-to-understand explanations of complex points of law. Each volume offers guidance on the principles of legal analysis and, consulted regularly, will hone your ability to spot relevant issues. We have titles that will help you prepare for class, prepare for your exams, and enhance your general comprehension of the law along the way.

To find out more about Aspen Study Aid publications, visit us on-line at *http://lawschool.aspenpublishers.com* or e-mail us at *legaledu@aspenpubl.com*. We'll be happy to assist you.

Get this Casenote Legal Brief as an AspenLaw Studydesk eBook today!

By returning this form to Aspen Publishers, you will receive a complimentary eBook download of this Casenote Legal Brief in the AspenLaw Studydesk digital format.* Learn more about AspenLaw Studydesk today at *www.AspenLaw.com.*

Name	Phone ( )

Address	Apt. No.

City	State	ZIP Code

Law School	Year (check one) ☐ 1st ☐ 2nd ☐ 3rd

Cut out the UPC found on the lower left corner of the back cover of this book. Staple the UPC inside this box. Only the original UPC from the book cover will be accepted. (No photocopies or store stickers are allowed.)

Attach UPC
inside this box.

Email (Print legibly or you may not get access!)
Title of this book (course subject)
ISBN of this book (10- or 13-digit number on the UPC)
Used with which casebook (provide author's name)

Mail the completed form to:

Aspen Publishers, Inc.
Legal Education Division
130 Turner Street, Bldg 3, 4th Floor
Waltham, MA 02453-8901

* Upon receipt of this completed form, you will be emailed a code for the digital download of this book in AspenLaw Studydesk format. The AspenLaw Studydesk application is available as a 60-day free trial at *www.AspenLaw.com.*

For a full list of print titles by Aspen Publishers, visit *lawschool.aspenpublishers.com.*
For a full list of digital eBook titles by Aspen Publishers, visit *www.AspenLaw.com.*

(Make a photocopy of this form and your UPC for your records.)

A. Decide on a Format and Stick to It

Structure is essential to a good brief. It enables you to arrange systematically the related parts that are scattered throughout most cases, thus making manageable and understandable what might otherwise seem to be an endless and unfathomable sea of information. There are, of course, an unlimited number of formats that can be utilized. However, it is best to find one that suits your needs and stick to it. Consistency breeds both efficiency and the security that when called upon you will know where to look in your brief for the information you are asked to give.

Any format, as long as it presents the essential elements of a case in an organized fashion, can be used. Experience, however, has led *Casenotes* to develop and utilize the following format because of its logical flow and universal applicability.

NATURE OF CASE: This is a brief statement of the legal character and procedural status of the case (e.g., "Appeal of a burglary conviction").

There are many different alternatives open to a litigant dissatisfied with a court ruling. The key to determining which one has been used is to discover *who is asking this court for what*.

This first entry in the brief should be kept as *short as possible*. Use the court's terminology if you understand it. But since jurisdictions vary as to the titles of pleadings, the best entry is the one that addresses who wants what in this proceeding, not the one that sounds most like the court's language.

RULE OF LAW: A statement of the general principle of law that the case illustrates (e.g., "An acceptance that varies any term of the offer is considered a rejection and counteroffer").

Determining the rule of law of a case is a procedure similar to determining the issue of the case. Avoid being fooled by red herrings; there may be a few rules of law mentioned in the case excerpt, but usually only one is *the* rule with which the casebook editor is concerned. The techniques used to locate the issue, described below, may also be utilized to find the rule of law. Generally, your best guide is simply the chapter heading. It is a clue to the point the casebook editor seeks to make and should be kept in mind when reading every case in the respective section.

FACTS: A synopsis of only the essential facts of the case, i.e., those bearing upon or leading up to the issue.

The facts entry should be a short statement of the events and transactions that led one party to initiate legal proceedings against another in the first place. While some cases conveniently state the salient facts at the beginning of the decision, in other instances they will have to be culled from hiding places throughout the text, even from concurring and dissenting opinions. Some of the "facts" will often be in dispute and should be so noted. Conflicting evidence may be briefly pointed up. "Hard" facts must be included. Both must be *relevant* in order to be listed in the facts entry. It is impossible to tell what is relevant until the entire case is read, as the ultimate determination of the rights and liabilities of the parties may turn on something buried deep in the opinion.

Generally, the facts entry should not be longer than three to five *short* sentences.

It is often helpful to identify the role played by a party in a given context. For example, in a construction contract case the identification of a party as the "contractor" or "builder" alleviates the need to tell that that party was the one who was supposed to have built the house.

It is always helpful, and a good general practice, to identify the "plaintiff" and the "defendant." This may seem elementary and uncomplicated, but, especially in view of the creative editing practiced by some casebook editors, it is sometimes a difficult or even impossible task. Bear in mind that the *party presently* seeking something from this court may not be the plaintiff, and that sometimes only the cross-claim of a defendant is treated in the excerpt. Confusing or misaligning the parties can ruin your analysis and understanding of the case.

ISSUE: A statement of the general legal question answered by or illustrated in the case. For clarity, the issue is best put in the form of a question capable of a "yes" or "no" answer. In reality, the issue is simply the Rule of Law put in the form of a question (e.g., "May an offer be accepted by performance?").

The major problem presented in discerning what is *the* issue in the case is that an opinion usually purports to raise and answer several questions. However, except for rare cases, only one such question is really the issue in the case. Collateral issues not necessary to the resolution of the matter in controversy are handled by the court by language known as *"obiter dictum"* or merely *"dictum."* While dicta may be included later in the brief, they have no place under the issue heading.

To find the issue, ask *who wants what* and then go on to ask *why did that party succeed or fail in getting it*. Once this is determined, the "why" should be turned into a question.

The complexity of the issues in the cases will vary, but in all cases a single-sentence question should sum up the issue. *In a few cases,* there will be two, or even more rarely, three issues of equal importance to the resolution of the case. Each should be expressed in a single-sentence question.

Since many issues are resolved by a court in coming to a final disposition of a case, the casebook editor will reproduce the portion of the opinion containing the issue or issues most relevant to the area of law under scrutiny. A noted law professor gave this advice: "Close the book; look at the title on the cover." Chances are, if it is Property, you need not concern yourself with whether, for example, the federal government's treatment of the plaintiff's land really raises a federal question sufficient to support jurisdiction on this ground in federal court.

The same rule applies to chapter headings designating sub-areas within the subjects. They tip you off as to what the text is designed to teach. The cases are arranged in a casebook to show a progression or development of the law, so that the preceding cases may also help.

It is also most important to remember to *read the notes and questions* at the end of a case to determine what the editors wanted you to have gleaned from it.

HOLDING AND DECISION: This section should succinctly explain the rationale of the court in arriving at its decision. In capsulizing the "reasoning" of the court, it should always include an application of the general rule or rules of law to the specific facts of the case. Hidden justifications come to light in this entry; the reasons for the state of the law, the public policies, the biases and prejudices, those considerations that influence the justices' thinking and, ultimately, the outcome of the case. At the end, there should be a short indication of the disposition or procedural resolution of the case (e.g., "Decision of the trial court for Mr. Smith (P) reversed").

The foregoing format is designed to help you "digest" the reams of case material with which you will be faced in your law school career. Once mastered by practice, it will place at your fingertips the information the authors of your casebooks have sought to impart to you in case-by-case illustration and analysis.

B. Be as Economical as Possible in Briefing Cases

Once armed with a format that encourages succinctness, it is as important to be economical with regard to the time spent on the actual reading of the case as it is to be economical in the writing of the brief itself. This does not mean "skimming" a case. Rather, it means reading the case with an "eye" trained to recognize into which "section" of your brief a particular passage or line fits and having a system for quickly and precisely marking the case so that the passages fitting any one particular part of

the brief can be easily identified and brought together in a concise and accurate manner when the brief is actually written.

It is of no use to simply repeat everything in the opinion of the court; record only enough information to trigger your recollection of what the court said. Nevertheless, an accurate statement of the "law of the case," i.e., the legal principle applied to the facts, is absolutely essential to class preparation and to learning the law under the case method.

To that end, it is important to develop a "shorthand" that you can use to make margin notations. These notations will tell you at a glance in which section of the brief you will be placing that particular passage or portion of the opinion.

Some students prefer to underline all the salient portions of the opinion (with a pencil or colored underliner marker), making marginal notations as they go along. Others prefer the color-coded method of underlining, utilizing different colors of markers to underline the salient portions of the case, each separate color being used to represent a different section of the brief. For example, blue underlining could be used for passages relating to the rule of law, yellow for those relating to the issue, and green for those relating to the holding and decision, etc. While it has its advocates, the color-coded method can be confusing and time-consuming (all that time spent on changing colored markers). Furthermore, it can interfere with the continuity and concentration many students deem essential to the reading of a case for maximum comprehension. In the end, however, it is a matter of personal preference and style. Just remember, whatever method you use, underlining must be used sparingly or its value is lost.

If you take the marginal notation route, an efficient and easy method is to go along underlining the key portions of the case and placing in the margin alongside them the following "markers" to indicate where a particular passage or line "belongs" in the brief you will write:

N   (NATURE OF CASE)
RL   (RULE OF LAW)
I   (ISSUE)
HL   (HOLDING AND DECISION, relates to
      the RULE OF LAW behind the decision)
HR   (HOLDING AND DECISION, gives the
      RATIONALE or reasoning behind the
      decision)
HA   (HOLDING AND DECISION, APPLIES
      the general principle(s) of law to the facts
      of the case to arrive at the decision)

Remember that a particular passage may well contain information necessary to more than one part of your brief, in which case you simply note that in the margin. If you are using the color-coded underlining method instead of margin notation, simply make asterisks or checks in the margin next to the passage in question in the colors that indicate the additional sections of the brief where it might be utilized.

The economy of utilizing "shorthand" in marking cases for briefing can be maintained in the actual brief writing process itself by utilizing "law student shorthand" within the brief. There are many commonly used words and phrases for which abbreviations can be substituted in your briefs (and in your class notes also). You can develop abbreviations that are personal to you and which will save you a lot of time. A reference list of briefing abbreviations can be found on page xii of this book.

C. Use Both the Briefing Process and the Brief as a Learning Tool

Now that you have a format and the tools for briefing cases efficiently, the most important thing is to make the time spent in briefing profitable to you and to make the most advantageous use of the briefs you create. Of course, the briefs are invaluable for classroom reference when you are called upon to explain or analyze a particular case. However, they are also useful in reviewing for exams. A quick glance at the fact summary should bring the case to mind, and a rereading of the rule of law should enable you to go over the underlying legal concept in your mind, how it was applied in that particular case, and how it might apply in other factual settings.

As to the value to be derived from engaging in the briefing process itself, there is an immediate benefit that arises from being forced to sift through the essential facts and reasoning from the court's opinion and to succinctly express them in your own words in your brief. The process ensures that you understand the case and the point that it illustrates, and that means you will be ready to absorb further analysis and information brought forth in class. It also ensures you will have something to say when called upon in class. The briefing process helps develop a mental agility for getting to the *gist* of a case and for identifying, expounding on, and applying the legal concepts and issues found there. The briefing process is the mental process on which you must rely in taking law school examinations; it is also the mental process upon which a lawyer relies in serving his clients and in making his living.

Abbreviations for Briefs

acceptance	acp	offer	O
affirmed	aff	offeree	OE
answer	ans	offeror	OR
assumption of risk	a/r	ordinance	ord
attorney	atty	pain and suffering	p/s
beyond a reasonable doubt	b/r/d	parol evidence	p/e
bona fide purchaser	BFP	plaintiff	P
breach of contract	br/k	prima facie	p/f
cause of action	c/a	probable cause	p/c
common law	c/l	proximate cause	px/c
Constitution	Con	real property	r/p
constitutional	con	reasonable doubt	r/d
contract	K	reasonable man	r/m
contributory negligence	c/n	rebuttable presumption	rb/p
cross	x	remanded	rem
cross-complaint	x/c	res ipsa loquitur	RIL
cross-examination	x/ex	respondeat superior	r/s
cruel and unusual punishment	c/u/p	Restatement	RS
defendant	D	reversed	rev
dismissed	dis	Rule Against Perpetuities	RAP
double jeopardy	d/j	search and seizure	s/s
due process	d/p	search warrant	s/w
equal protection	e/p	self-defense	s/d
equity	eq	specific performance	s/p
evidence	ev	statute of limitations	S/L
exclude	exc	statute of frauds	S/F
exclusionary rule	exc/r	statute	S
felony	f/n	summary judgment	s/j
freedom of speech	f/s	tenancy in common	t/c
good faith	g/f	tenancy at will	t/w
habeas corpus	h/c	tenant	t
hearsay	hr	third party	TP
husband	H	third party beneficiary	TPB
in loco parentis	ILP	transferred intent	TI
injunction	inj	unconscionable	uncon
inter vivos	I/v	unconstitutional	unconst
joint tenancy	j/t	undue influence	u/e
judgment	judgt	Uniform Commercial Code	UCC
jurisdiction	jur	unilateral	uni
last clear chance	LCC	vendee	VE
long-arm statute	LAS	vendor	VR
majority view	maj	versus	v
meeting of minds	MOM	void for vagueness	VFV
minority view	min	weight of the evidence	w/e
Miranda warnings	Mir/w	weight of authority	w/a
Miranda rule	Mir/r	wife	W
negligence	neg	with	w/
notice	ntc	within	w/i
nuisance	nus	without prejudice	w/o/p
obligation	ob	without	w/o
obscene	obs	wrongful death	wr/d

Table of Cases

Judicial Review

Quick Reference Rules of Law

Marbury v. Madison

Justice (P) v. Secretary of State (D)

5 U.S. (1 Cranch) 137, 2 L.Ed. 60 (1803).

NATURE OF CASE: Writ of mandamus to compel delivery of commission.

FACT SUMMARY: President Jefferson's Secretary of State, Madison (D), refused to deliver a commission granted to Marbury (P) by former President Adams.

🏛 RULE OF LAW
The Supreme Court has the power, implied from Article VI, § 2 of the Constitution, to review acts of Congress and, if they are found repugnant to the Constitution, to declare them void.

FACTS: On March 2, 1801, the outgoing President of the United States, John Adams, named 42 justices of the peace for the District of Columbia under the Organic Act passed the same day by Congress. William Marbury (P) was one of the justices named. The commissions of Marbury (P) and other named justices were signed by Adams on his last day in office, March 3, and signed and sealed by the Acting Secretary of State, John Marshall. However, the formal commissions were not delivered by the end of the day. The new President, Thomas Jefferson, treated those appointments that were not formalized by delivery of the papers of commission prior to Adams leaving office as a nullity. Marbury (P) and other affected colleagues brought this writ of mandamus to the Supreme Court to compel Jefferson's Secretary of State, James Madison (D), to deliver the commissions. John Marshall, then Chief Justice of the Supreme Court, delivered the opinion.

ISSUE: Does the Constitution give the Supreme Court the authority to review acts of Congress and declare them, if repugnant to the Constitution, to be void?

HOLDING AND DECISION: (Marshall, C.J.) Yes. The government of the United States is a government of laws, not of men. The President, bound by these laws, is given certain political powers by the Constitution which he may use at his discretion. To aid him in his duties, he is authorized to appoint certain officers to carry out his orders. Their acts as officers are his acts and are never subject to examination by the courts. However, where these officers are given by law specific duties on which individual rights depend, any individual injured by breach of such duty may resort to his country's laws for a remedy. Here, Marbury (P) had a right to the commission, and Madison's (D) refusal to deliver it violated that right. The present case is clearly one for mandamus. However, should the Supreme Court be the court to issue it? The Judiciary Act of 1789 established and authorized United States courts to issue writs of mandamus to courts or persons holding office under U.S. authority. Secretary of State Madison (D) comes within the Act. If the Supreme Court is powerless to issue the writ of mandamus to him, it must be because the Act is unconstitutional. Article III of the Constitution provides that the Supreme Court shall have original jurisdiction in all cases affecting ambassadors, other public ministers and consuls, and where a state is a party. In all other cases, the Supreme Court shall have appellate jurisdiction. Marbury (P) urged that since Article III contains no restrictive words, the power to assign original jurisdiction to the courts remains in the legislature. But if Congress is allowed to distribute the original and appellate jurisdiction of the Supreme Court, as in the Judiciary Act, then the constitutional grant of Article III is form without substance. But no clause in the Constitution is presumed to be without effect. For the Court to issue a mandamus, it must be an exercise of appellate jurisdiction. The grant of appellate jurisdiction is the power to revise and correct proceedings already instituted; it does not create the cause. To issue a writ of mandamus ordering an executive officer to deliver a paper is to create the original action for that paper. This would be an unconstitutional exercise of original jurisdiction beyond the power of the Court. It is the province and duty of the judicial department to say what the law is. And any law, including acts of the legislature, which is repugnant to the Constitution is void. Mandamus was denied.

▶ ANALYSIS

Judicial review of legislative acts was a controversial subject even before the Constitution was ratified and adopted. Alexander Hamilton upheld the theory of judicial review in the Federalist Papers. He argued that the judiciary, being the most vulnerable branch of the government, was designed to be an intermediary between the people and the legislature. Since the interpretation of laws was the responsibility of the judiciary, and the Constitution the supreme law of the land, any conflict between legislative acts and the Constitution were to be resolved by the court in favor of the Constitution. But other authorities have attacked this position. In the case of *Eakin v. Raub*, Justice Gibson dissented, stating that the judiciary's function was limited to interpreting the laws and should not extend to scrutinizing the legislature's authority to enact them. Judge Learned Hand felt that judicial review was inconsistent with the separation of powers. But history has supported the authority of judicial review of legislative acts. The United States survives on a tripartite government. Theoret-

Continued on next page.

ically, the three branches should be strong enough to check and balance the others. To limit the judiciary to the passive task of interpretation would be to limit its strength in the tripartite structure. *Marbury* served to buttress the judiciary branch making it equal to the executive and legislative branches.

■===■

Quicknotes

JUDICIAL REVIEW The authority of the courts to review decisions, actions or omissions committed by another agency or branch of government.

ORIGINAL JURISDICTION The power of a court to hear an action upon its commencement.

WRIT OF MANDAMUS A court order issued commanding a public or private entity, or an official thereof, to perform a duty required by law.

■===■

Cooper v. Aaron

Parties not identified.

358 U.S. 1 (1958).

NATURE OF CASE: Review of suspension of plan to desegregate.

FACT SUMMARY: The Governor and Legislature of Arkansas refused to obey a federal court order to desegregate the public schools in Little Rock based on the Brown v. Board of Education case pending further challenges to the Brown decision.

🏛 RULE OF LAW
State officials may not refuse to obey federal court orders resting on constitutional grounds.

FACTS: The Governor and Legislature of the State of Arkansas acted upon the premise that there was no duty on state officials to obey federal court orders resting upon U.S. Supreme Court interpretations of the U.S. Constitution. The actions consisted of the suspension of a desegregation plan for the public schools in Little Rock. The state officials claimed that they had the right to disobey the order until the decision in *Brown v. Board of Education*, 344 U.S. 1 (1952), was further challenged. The U.S. Supreme Court reviewed the actions.

ISSUE: May state officials refuse to obey federal court orders resting on constitutional grounds?

HOLDING AND DECISION: (Warren, C.J.) No. The Constitution of the United States is the "supreme law of the land." The federal judiciary is supreme in the exposition of the law of the Constitution. No state legislature or executive or judicial officer can refuse to obey a federal court order based upon a federal interpretation of the Constitution without violating the duty to support the Constitution. If such refusal were permitted, the fiat of the official would be the supreme law instead of the Constitution. State officials may not refuse to obey federal court orders resting on constitutional grounds.

▌ *ANALYSIS*

The Supremacy Clause of the U.S. Constitution, Article VI, requires that federal court decisions based on U.S. Supreme Court interpretations of constitutional language govern the states' legislative, judicial, and executive branches. However, where the federal court asserts power based on anything other than the Constitution or constitutional interpretations, the doctrine announced in *Erie R. Co. v. Tomkins*, 304 U.S. 64 (1938), may permit the state law, if applicable, to govern.

Quicknotes

SUPREMACY CLAUSE Art. VI, Sec. 2, of the Constitution, which provides that federal action must prevail over inconsistent state action.

Martin v. Hunter's Lessee

Heir (P) v. Landowner (D)

14 U.S. (1 Wheat.) 304, 4 L.Ed. 97 (1816).

NATURE OF CASE: Appeal by a state from a U.S. Supreme Court decision.

FACT SUMMARY: The Virginia Supreme Court contested the authority of the U.S. Supreme Court's authority to decide local land matters on appeal.

🏛 RULE OF LAW
The U.S. Supreme Court has appellate jurisdiction to review state court decisions.

FACTS: The Virginia Legislature passed an act confiscating all land owned by loyal British subjects. Lord Fairfax's land was given to Hunter (D). The U.S. entered into two treaties with Great Britain which guaranteed that the land would remain with the British subjects/sympathizers. Martin (P), Fairfax's heir, brought suit in state court to recover the land from Hunter (D) based on these treaties. The court refused to abide by the treaties holding that the U.S. had no authority to bind it in such matters. The U.S. Supreme Court reversed. The Virginia Supreme Court refused to comply with the order and appealed, alleging that the U.S. Supreme Court had no appellate jurisdiction over state court decisions.

ISSUE: Does the U.S. Supreme Court have appellate jurisdiction over state court decisions?

HOLDING AND DECISION: (Story, J.) Yes. The Constitution granted the authority to Congress to define the jurisdiction of the judiciary of the United States. In § 24 of the Judiciary Act of 1789, the U.S. Supreme Court was clearly granted the authority to review state court decisions where appropriate. Deciding the reach of treaties entered into by the U.S. is clearly a federal question which may be reviewed and interpreted by the U.S. Supreme Court regardless of whether the action was begun in a state court. Both the Constitution and the appellate authority granted under the Judiciary Act mandate such a finding. Judgment of the Court of Appeals reversed and judgment of the District Court affirmed.

CONCURRENCE: (Johnson, J.) While the authority of the Court is supreme over persons and cases, it has no authority to compel state tribunals' actions. Our writ of mandate was not intended to offend state tribunals.

▌*ANALYSIS*

The federal courts have the power to review through appeals when: (1) the validity of a federal statute has been challenged by a state court; (2) the constitutionality of a state statute has been sustained. Such appeals are a matter of right. Review by certiorari is discretionary and may be granted where: (1) the validity of a federal statute has been challenged in state court; (2) a state statute is challenged as unconstitutional; (3) the litigation involves privileges, immunities, or rights under the Constitution or treaties.

Quicknotes

APPELLATE JURISDICTION The power of a higher court to review the decisions of lower courts.

FEDERAL QUESTION The authority of the federal courts to hear and determine in the first instance matters pertaining to the federal Constitution, federal law, or treaties of the United States.

TREATY An agreement between two or more nations for the benefit of the general public.

Ex parte McCardle

Prisoner (P) v. Court (D)

74 U.S. (7 Wall.) 506, 19 L.Ed. 264 (1869).

NATURE OF CASE: Appeal from denial of habeas corpus.

FACT SUMMARY: McCardle (P) appealed from a denial of habeas corpus to the Supreme Court, but Congress passed an act forbidding the Court jurisdiction.

🏛 RULE OF LAW
Although the Supreme Court derives its appellate jurisdiction from the Constitution, the Constitution also gives Congress the express power to make exceptions to that appellate jurisdiction.

FACTS: After the Civil War, Congress imposed military government on many former Confederate States under authority of the Civil War Reconstruction Acts. McCardle (P), a Mississippi newspaper editor, was held in military custody on charges of publishing libelous and incendiary articles. McCardle (P) brought a habeas corpus writ based on a congressional act passed on February 5, 1867. The act authorized federal courts to grant habeas corpus to persons held in violation of constitutional rights, and also gave authority for appeals to the Supreme Court. The circuit court denied McCardle's (P) habeas corpus writ, but the Supreme Court sustained jurisdiction for an appeal on the merits. However, after arguments were heard, Congress passed an act on March 21, 1868, that repealed that much of the 1867 Act that allowed an appeal to the Supreme Court from the circuit court and the exercise by the Supreme Court by jurisdiction on any such appeals, past or present.

ISSUE: Does Congress have the power, under the Constitution, to make exceptions to the appellate jurisdiction of the Supreme Court?

HOLDING AND DECISION: (Chase, C.J.) Yes. The appellate jurisdiction of the Supreme Court is not derived from acts of Congress, but is conferred by the Constitution with such exceptions and regulations as Congress shall make. And though Congress has affirmatively described in the Act of 1789 the regulations governing the exercise of the Supreme Court's appellate jurisdiction with the implication that any exercise of that jurisdiction not within the purview of the Act would be negated, the exception to the appellate jurisdiction in the present case is not to be inferred from such affirmations. The exceptions in this case are express. That part of the 1867 Act giving the court appellate jurisdiction in habeas corpus cases is expressly repealed. The effect is to take away the court's jurisdiction, dismissing the cause. When a legislative act is repealed, it is as if it had never existed except to transactions past and closed. Thus, no judgment can be rendered in a suit

after repeal of the act under which it was brought. But this does not deny forever the court's appellate power in habeas corpus cases. The Act of 1868 affects only such appeals from circuit courts brought under the Act of 1867. Appeal dismissed for lack of jurisdiction.

▶ ANALYSIS

McCardle is clearly an example of judicial restraint. The authority of Congress to control the jurisdiction of the Supreme Court is not unlimited. This was proved in *Marbury v. Madison*, 5 U.S. 137, 2 L.Ed. 60 (1803), where the Court, faced with an extension by Congress of its original jurisdiction as granted under the Constitution refused to accept the constitutionality of the congressional act. While this specifically limited the Supreme Court's original jurisdiction, it provided Marshall with the ideal arena to assert the doctrine of judicial review. But in *McCardle*, the Court backed away from confrontation with Congress due to current-day political crises that followed the Civil War. Thereafter, the Court sought to limit congressional power by the power of judicial review announced in *Marbury*. The Court held on several occasions that certain congressional attempts to delimit its jurisdiction were unconstitutional attempts to invade the judicial province. Such congressional actions were considered a violation of the separation of powers. Today, it is doubtful that *McCardle* would be sustained.

■==■

Quicknotes

APPELLATE JURISDICTION The power of a higher court to review the decisions of lower courts.

JUDICIAL REVIEW The authority of the courts to review decisions, actions or omissions committed by another agency or branch of government.

ORIGINAL JURISDICTION The power of a court to hear an action upon its commencement.

WRIT OF HABEAS CORPUS A proceeding in which a defendant brings a writ to compel a judicial determination of whether he is lawfully being held in custody.

■==■

Muskrat v. United States

Indian citizen (P) v. Federal government (D)

219 U.S. 346 (1911).

NATURE OF CASE: Constitutional challenge to federal law.

FACT SUMMARY: Congress authorized an Indian tribe to bring suit to test the validity of a federal law.

🏛 RULE OF LAW
The Constitution limits the authority of federal courts to cases and controversies and they may not issue purely advisory opinions.

FACTS: Congress enacted legislation allotting certain lands to the Cherokee Indians. The number of Indians authorized to use the lands was subsequently increased. Congress then enacted legislation permitting the original allottees to challenge the validity of the increase. Priority was to be given to the suit. Attorney fees were to be paid from government-held tribal funds if the original allottees prevailed. The validity of the increase was upheld and Muskrat (P), one of the plaintiffs, appealed. It was alleged that this was a friendly collusive suit and the U.S. (D) had no interest adverse to the Indians. Since there was no case or controversy involved, federal courts could not decide the issue since it would involve issuing an advisory opinion which was beyond its authority.

ISSUE: May federal courts issue advisory opinions as to the validity of federal laws where no actual case or controversy exists?

HOLDING AND DECISION: (Day, J.) No. The Constitution limits the judicial power of federal courts to matters involving cases and controversies. Mere advisory opinions concerning the validity of federal statutes is therefore beyond the power of the courts. Such authority may not be delegated to the courts by coordinate branches of the government. Government agencies should render such opinions and their validity is then tested in the courts when an actual case or controversy arises. The case herein involves neither law nor equity. The U.S. (D) has no adverse interest to Muskrat (P). Any controversy involved is actually between the two groups of allottees. The only question herein is whether the legislation is or is not valid. Since no jurisdiction to hear such a question existed, the judgments are reversed and the case remanded.

▌ *ANALYSIS*

There must be a definite, concrete case or controversy between the parties; there must be an adverse legal interest between them and it must be real and substantial. Without this type of adverse situation, the strongest and most complete argument may not be presented and an appropriate adjudication of the matter may be foreclosed. Some states authorize advisory opinions as to the validity of legislation. The U.S. Supreme Court will not review these decisions.

■═■

Quicknotes

ADVISORY OPINION A decision rendered at the request of an interested party of how the court would rule should the particular issue arise.

CASES AND CONTROVERSIES Constitutional requirement in order to invoke federal court jurisdiction that the matter present a justiciable issue.

COLLUSION An agreement between two or more parties to engage in unlawful conduct or in other activities with an unlawful goal, typically involving fraud.

■═■

Baker v. Carr

Parties not identified.

369 U.S. 186 (1962).

NATURE OF CASE: Review of decision declining federal court jurisdiction in reapportionment controversy.

FACT SUMMARY: The State of Tennessee failed to enact any reapportionment measures from 1901 until this suit, resulting in such wide disparity in the voting power of various counties that the majority of the state legislators were elected by a minority of voters, and this action was brought in federal court on the ground of denial of equal protection.

🏛 RULE OF LAW
A challenge by state officials of a claim based on a federal constitutional ground does not present a nonjusticiable political question.

FACTS: Between 1901 and the time of this suit, the State of Tennessee failed to enact any reapportionment measures as to the voting powers of the various counties of the state despite great population shifts. The result was that 20 of the 33 senators of the state were elected by 37% of the voters and 63 of the 99 house members were elected by 40% of the voters. The electing power of a single vote in one county was 19 times that of another in one comparison. This suit was brought to require a reapportionment and the federal district court declined to hear the controversy for lack of subject matter jurisdiction. The U.S. Supreme Court granted review of that decision.

ISSUE: Does a challenge by state officials of a claim based on a U.S. Constitutional ground present a nonjusticiable political question?

HOLDING AND DECISION: (Brennan, J.) No. The mere fact that the suit presents a question of protection of a political right does not mean that it presents a political question. The constitutional guaranty of a republican form of government (the Guaranty Clause) does not interfere with the relationship between the federal judiciary and the state governments, though it may make controversies between the federal courts and the coordinate branches of the federal government into "political questions." The "political questions" doctrine has foundations in areas of concern, but the cases in none of them support the contention that reapportionment is left to the state without guidance. "Political questions" involve a textually demonstrable constitutional commitment of the issue to a coordinate political department, or a lack of a manageable standard for resolution, or an impossibility of decision without failing to respect the coordinate branches. A challenge by state officials of a claim based upon a federal constitutional ground does not present a nonjusticiable political question. Reversed and remanded.

DISSENT: (Frankfurter, J.) This Court's authority rests upon sustained public confidence in its moral sanction. The Court must be detached from political entanglements by abstaining from clashing itself with political forces in political settlements. The claim in this case is hypothetical and the Court has given no guidelines for any specific, definite remedies.

▶ ANALYSIS

Political questions are generally those left to other areas of the government than the judiciary by specific constitutional language. The relationship of the question to the nonjudicial branch is not always easy to evaluate, especially as the bureaucracy grows.

■=■

Quicknotes

EQUAL PROTECTION A constitutional guarantee that no person shall be denied the same protection of the laws enjoyed by other persons in like circumstances.

JUSTICIABILITY An actual controversy that is capable of determination by the court.

POLITICAL QUESTION An issue that is more appropriately left to the determination of another governmental branch and which the court declines to hear.

REAPPORTIONMENT PLAN The alteration of a voting districts' boundaries or composition to reflect the population of that district.

SEPARATION OF POWERS The system of checks and balances preventing one branch of government from infringing upon exercising the powers of another branch of government.

SUBJECT MATTER JURISDICTION A court's ability to adjudicate a specific category of cases based on the subject matter of the dispute.

■=■

Powell v. McCormack

Representative-elect (P) v. Speaker of the House (D)

395 U.S. 486 (1969).

NATURE OF CASE: Appeal from exclusion from Congress.

FACT SUMMARY: Powell (P), who was excluded from the 90th Congress due to his diversion of House funds, wrongful assertion of privileges, and falsification of expenditure reports, brought this action for a declaratory judgment and for back salary after his re-election to the 91st Congress.

🏛 RULE OF LAW
A challenge to the power of Congress to exclude an elected member of Congress for misconduct is not a nonjusticiable political question.

FACTS: Adam Clayton Powell (P) was duly elected in his congressional district as a member of the House of Representatives of the 90th Congress. That Congress refused to seat Powell (P) and formed a House Select Committee to review his qualifications and to decide whether to punish him under the Constitution. Powell (P) was found to have met the standing requirements but to have wrongfully asserted privilege and immunity from state court process and wrongfully diverted House funds to himself and others and falsified expenditure reports. McCormack (D) ruled, as Speaker of the House, that a simple majority was enough to pass a resolution to exclude Powell (P) and declare his seat open. The resolution was passed, and Powell (P) brought this action for a declaratory judgment that he did occupy his seat and for back pay. The district court and court of appeals ruled against him and the Supreme Court granted review, though Powell (P) was by then seated as a member of the 91st Congress by virtue of his re-election.

ISSUE: Is a challenge to the power of Congress to exclude an elected member of Congress for misconduct a nonjusticiable political question?

HOLDING AND DECISION: (Warren, C.J.) No. Though McCormack (D) urges otherwise, the exclusion of Powell (P) is to be tested by the standards governing expulsion. Since Powell (P) seeks a declaratory judgment, a court can grant the relief here sought, and since back pay is requested, the question is not moot. The inquiry, then, is whether the conduct of Congress involved a "political question" under qualifications set forth in the Constitution, which cannot be changed without a constitutional amendment. Powell's (P) qualifications are within those set forth. The expulsion of a member for misconduct is within congressional power, but it requires the concurrence of two-thirds of the Congress and not a simple majority. Thus, a challenge to the power of Congress to exclude an elected member of Congress for misconduct is not a nonjusticiable political question.

CONCURRENCE: (Douglas, J.) If this were an expulsion case there would be no justiciable controversy after a vote of two-thirds or more of the Congress. But it is not an expulsion case, and "misconduct" may raise different questions.

DISSENT: (Stewart, J.) The events which have taken place since certiorari was granted have rendered this case moot.

▶ ANALYSIS

The Court conceded in the majority opinion that if the congressional committee made factual determinations showing that Powell (P) was lacking in any of the standing requirements to be qualified to serve, the federal courts "might" be barred from reviewing the findings. Sanctions for misconduct are not part of the Article I, § 5 qualification language however, and judicial review is not barred as to those sanctions.

■═■

Quicknotes

DECLARATORY JUDGMENT An adjudication by the courts which grants not relief but is binding over the legal status of the parties involved in the dispute.

JUDICIAL REVIEW The authority of the courts to review decisions, actions or omissions committed by another agency or branch of government.

JUSTICIABILITY An actual controversy that is capable of determination by the court.

MOOTNESS Judgment on the particular issue would not resolve the controversy.

POLITICAL QUESTION An issue that is more appropriately left to the determination of another governmental branch and which the court declines to hear.

STANDING Whether a party possesses the right to commence suit against another party by having a personal stake in the resolution of the controversy.

■═■

Nixon v. United States

Judge (D) v. Federal government (P)

506 U.S. 224 (1993).

NATURE OF CASE: Appeal of judicial impeachment.

FACT SUMMARY: Nixon (D), a district court judge who was impeached by the House of Representatives and convicted by the Senate, claimed that the Senate procedures violated the Constitution.

🏛 RULE OF LAW
The Senate holds the sole power to try impeachments, and the judiciary may not review the impeachment process.

FACTS: Nixon (D), a Mississippi federal district court judge, was convicted of making false statements before a federal grand jury and sentenced to prison. Nixon (D) refused to resign his office while serving his sentence. The House of Representatives adopted articles of impeachment which were presented to the Senate. Pursuant to Senate Impeachment Rule XI, a committee held hearings and presented the transcript to the full Senate. The Senate then voted by more than the two-thirds requirement to convict Nixon (D). Nixon (D) filed suit in district court contending that the procedures of Rule XI, particularly the committee hearings, violated the Constitution because the Senate must "try" all impeachments under Article I, § 3. The district court ruled the claim was not justiciable, and the court of appeals affirmed. Nixon (D) appealed to the U.S. Supreme Court.

ISSUE: May the judiciary review Senate impeachment procedures?

HOLDING AND DECISION: (Rehnquist, C.J.) No. The Senate holds the sole power to try impeachments, and the judiciary may not review the process. According to the language of Article I, § 3, clause 6, the Senate has the "sole" authority to try impeachments. The original interpretation of this provision was that the Senate was to have the exclusive power of impeachment. Judicial review of Senate impeachments would be inconsistent with the system of checks and balances created by the Constitution. The impeachment process is an important constitutional check on the judiciary and judicial review of the impeachment of judges would introduce a risk of bias that the Constitution sought to eliminate. Furthermore, the lack of finality to impeachments, if they were open to judicial review, would cause significant chaos for the government. Therefore, judicial review of the impeachment procedures used by the Senate is inappropriate. Nixon's (D) claim is not justiciable. Affirmed.

CONCURRENCE: (Stevens, J.) The policy of judicial restraint, respect for a coordinate branch of government, and the potential anomalies that could occur by not adhering to this policy justify the majority's position.

CONCURRENCE: (White, J.) Although the Senate has wide discretion in the impeachment process, judicial review is appropriate to ensure that the Senate adheres to a minimal set of procedural standards. However, Nixon (D) has not proven that the use of committees is an improper way of "trying" the impeachment.

CONCURRENCE: (Souter, J.) Judicial review of Senate impeachment procedures is only proper when the Senate acts so far beyond the scope of its constitutional authority that a judicial response is necessary.

▶ ANALYSIS

The decision is an example of the so-called "political question" doctrine for limiting judicial review. Under this doctrine, judicial review is inappropriate if there is a "textually demonstrable constitutional commitment of the issue" to another branch of the government. This standard was first announced in *Baker v. Carr*, 369 U.S. 186 (1962).

Quicknotes

IMPEACHMENT The discrediting of a witness by offering evidence to show that the witness lacks credibility.

JUDICIAL REVIEW The authority of the courts to review decisions, actions or omissions committed by another agency or branch of government.

JUSTICIABILITY An actual controversy that is capable of determination by the court.

Implied Powers

Quick Reference Rules of Law

M'Culloch v. Maryland

Bank cashier (D) v. State (P)

17 U.S. (4 Wheat.) 316, 4 L.Ed. 579 (1819).

NATURE OF CASE: Action arising out of a violation of a state statute.

FACT SUMMARY: M'Culloch (D), the cashier of the Baltimore branch of the U.S. Bank, issued bank notes in violation of a Maryland (P) statute providing that no bank, without authority from the state, could issue bank notes except on stamped paper issued by the state.

🏛 RULE OF LAW
(1) Certain federal powers giving Congress the discretion and power to choose and enact the means to perform the duties imposed upon it are to be implied from the Necessary and Proper Clause.
(2) The federal Constitution and the laws made pursuant to it are supreme and control the constitutions and the laws of the states, and cannot be controlled by them.

FACTS: A Maryland (P) statute prohibited any bank operating in the state without state authority from issuing bank notes except upon stamped paper issued by the state. The law specified the fees payable for the paper, and provided for penalties for violators. An Act of Congress established a U.S. Bank. M'Culloch (D), the U.S. Bank's cashier for its Baltimore branch, issued bank notes without complying with the Maryland (P) law.

ISSUE:
(1) Does Congress have the power to incorporate a bank?
(2) Does a state have the power to impose fees on the operation of an institution created by Congress pursuant to its constitutional powers?

HOLDING AND DECISION: (Marshall, C.J.)
(1) Yes. It's true that this government is one of enumerated powers. However, the Constitution does not exclude incidental or implied powers. It does not require that everything be granted expressly and minutely described. To have so required would have entirely changed the character of the Constitution and made it into a legal code. The enumerated powers given to the government imply the ordinary means of execution. The power of creating a corporation may be implied as incidental to other powers, or used as a means of executing them. The Necessary and Proper Clause gives Congress the power to make "all laws which shall be necessary and proper, for carrying into execution" the powers vested by the Constitution in the U.S. Government. Maryland (P) argues that the word "necessary" limits the right to pass laws for the execution of the granted powers to

those which are indispensable. However, in common usage "necessary" frequently means convenient, useful, essential. Considering the word's common usage, its usage in another part of the Constitution (Article I, § 10), and its inclusion among the powers given to Congress, rather than among the limitations upon Congress, it cannot be held to restrain Congress. The sound construction of the Constitution must allow Congress the discretion to choose the means to perform the duties imposed upon it. As long as the end is legitimate and within the scope of the Constitution, any means which are appropriate, are plainly adapted to that end, and which are not prohibited by the Constitution, but are consistent with its spirit, are constitutional. A bank is a convenient, useful, and essential instrument for handling national finances. Hence, it is within Congress's power to enact a law incorporating a U.S. bank.

(2) No. The federal Constitution and the laws made in pursuance thereof are supreme. They control the constitutions and laws of the states and cannot be controlled by them. Maryland (P) is incorrect in its contention that the powers of the federal government are delegated by the states who alone are truly sovereign. The Constitution derives its authority from the people, not from the states. Here, Maryland's (P) statute in effect taxes the operation of the U.S. Bank, a bank properly created within Congress's power. The power to tax involves the power to destroy. Here it is in opposition to the supreme congressional power to create a bank. Also, when a state taxes an organization created by the U.S. Government, it acts upon an institution created by people over whom it claims no control. The states have no power, by taxation or otherwise, to impede, burden, or in any manner control the operations of constitutional laws enacted by Congress. The Maryland (P) statute is, therefore, unconstitutional and void.

▶ ANALYSIS

Federalism is the basis of the Constitution's response to the problem of governing large geographical areas with diverse local needs. The success of federalism depends upon maintaining the balance between the need for the supremacy and sovereignty of the federal government and the interest in maintaining independent state government and curtailing national intrusion into intrastate affairs. The U.S. federal structure allocates powers between the nation and the states by enumerating the powers delegated to the

Continued on next page.

national government and acknowledging the retention by the states of the remainder. The Articles of Confederation followed a similar scheme. The Constitution expanded the enumerated national powers to remedy weaknesses of the Articles. The move from the Articles to the Constitution was a shift from a central government with fewer powers to one with more powers.

Quicknotes

ENUMERATED POWERS Specific powers mentioned in, and granted by, the constitution; e.g., the taxing power.

FEDERALISM A scheme of government whereby the power to govern is divided between a central and localized governments.

NECESSARY AND PROPER CLAUSE, ACT I, § 8 OF THE CONSTITUTION Which enables congress to make all laws that may be "necessary and proper" to execute its other, enumerated powers.

■≡■

State Powers in View of the Commerce Clause

Quick Reference Rules of Law

Gibbons v. Ogden

Steamboat operator (D) v. Steamboat operator (P)

22 U.S. (9 Wheat.) 1, 6 L.Ed. 23 (1824).

NATURE OF CASE: Appeal from injunction against navigation.

FACT SUMMARY: The State of New York granted Fulton and Livingston an exclusive license to operate steamboats in all New York waters, and Ogden (P), the assignee of that license, sued to enjoin Gibbons (D) from operating steamboats between New York and New Jersey through New York waters.

▥ RULE OF LAW
A state may not by its laws or acts regulate the commerce among the several states.

FACTS: Robert Fulton and Robert Livingston obtained an exclusive license from the State of New York to operate steamboats in New York waters. They assigned the license to Ogden (P). Ogden (P) then brought this suit against Gibbons (D), who was operating steamboats in New York waters between the states of New York and New Jersey. Gibbons (D) was licensed to carry on coasting trade and was enrolled under an act of Congress. The state courts granted the injunctions against Gibbons (D), and Gibbons (D) appealed to the Supreme Court.

ISSUE: May a state by its laws or acts regulate the commerce among the several states?

HOLDING AND DECISION: (Marshall, C.J.) No. It is argued that as an incident of sovereignty the states, under the Tenth Amendment, may severally regulate commerce coextensively with the federal government within their respective jurisdiction. For example, the power to lay and collect taxes granted by the states to the federal government in the Constitution does not interfere with the states' individual rights to do the same. However, the taxing power of a state is limited to taxing for state purposes, and the federal power to taxing for federal purposes. Commerce between the states is not similarly divided. The Congress is specifically authorized by the Constitution to regulate interstate commerce, and while Congress is doing so, the state may not. Congress has enacted a licensing provision, and the laws of New York must yield to it. The state may not by its laws or acts regulate the commerce among the several states. New York cannot prevent a federally enrolled, licensed vessel from enjoying all the privileges conferred by the act of Congress. Reversed.

CONCURRENCE: (Johnson, J.) The commerce power is exclusive and resides in Congress. There remains nothing for the state to act upon, even in the absence of the act of Congress.

▶ ANALYSIS

The development of the law of the Commerce Clause of the Constitution indicates that if a state regulation interferes with interstate commerce, no usurping federal statute is necessary for the federal courts to strike it down. The aim of the framers of the Constitution was to establish a free common market, unfettered by local restriction, so as to promote trade among the several states and the free access necessary to sustain it.

■■■

Quicknotes

COMMERCE CLAUSE Article 1, section 8, clause 3 of the United States Constitution, granting Congress the power to regulate commerce with foreign countries and between the states.

LICENSE A right that is granted to a person allowing him or her to conduct an activity that without such permission he or she could not lawfully do, and which is unassignable and revocable at the will of the licensor.

■■■

Cooley v. Board of Wardens

Shipowner (D) v. State agency (P)

53 U.S. (12 How.) 299, 13 L.Ed. 996 (1851).

NATURE OF CASE: Action for violation of a state local pilot law.

FACT SUMMARY: Cooley (D) violated a Pennsylvania law requiring all ships using the port of Philadelphia to engage a local pilot.

🏛 RULE OF LAW

The states may regulate those areas of interstate commerce which are local in nature and do not demand one national system of regulation by Congress.

FACTS: In 1803, Pennsylvania passed a law which required every ship entering or leaving the port of Philadelphia to use a local pilot. The law imposed a penalty of half the pilotage fee which was paid to the Board of Wardens (P) and put in a fund for retired pilots and their dependents. Cooley (D), who was a consignee of two ships which had left the port without a local pilot, was held liable under the law. Cooley (D) challenged the right of the state to impose regulations on pilots because it interfered with interstate commerce. The Board of Wardens (P) relied on an act of Congress in 1789 which stated that all pilots in the rivers, harbors, and ports of the United States shall continue to be regulated in conformity with the existing laws of the states and such laws as the states shall enact for that purpose, until Congress enacts legislation to the contrary.

ISSUE: Is the grant of power to Congress to regulate interstate and foreign commerce an exclusive grant prohibiting the states from legislating, even in areas of primarily local concern?

HOLDING AND DECISION: (Curtis, J.) No. It is evident from the congressional Act of 1789 that Congress recognized that the states can, in some areas, enact regulations that have an effect on interstate commerce. Some subjects of commerce demand a single uniform national rule and therefore Congress has exclusive jurisdiction over those areas. However, there are some subjects that are primarily local in nature and therefore require many different rules to meet the local necessities. The problem concerning pilots is local in nature and therefore Congress does not have exclusive power over this area. In the act that Congress passed allowing the states to regulate pilots, Congress has recognized that the problems involved with pilots do not demand one uniform rule and thus allowed the states to regulate pilots. The court held that the grant of the power over commerce to Congress did not imply a prohibition on the states to exercise the same power, but it is the exercise of the power by Congress that may make the exercise of the same power by the states unlawful. The court noted that its decision in this case applied only to its facts and did not attempt to delineate the dividing line between those subjects of commerce that were primarily local and those which were primarily national in scope. The decision of the lower courts upholding Cooley's (D) fine was affirmed.

▶ ANALYSIS

The local interest versus the national interest test is still used by the Court today. In applying this test the Court balances the national interest against the local interest and also determines if the local regulation discriminates against interstate commerce. If the local interest outweighs the national interest and the regulation does not discriminate against interstate commerce, the states are allowed to regulate that subject of commerce. If it appears that the state regulation has placed a burden on interstate commerce, the Court has drawn the line and refused to hold the state regulations valid even though a local subject may be involved.

■═■

Quicknotes

COMMERCE CLAUSE Article 1, section 8, clause 3 of the United States Constitution, granting Congress the power to regulate commerce with foreign countries and between the states.

INTERSTATE COMMERCE Commercial dealings between two parties located in different states or located in one state and accomplished through a point in another state or a foreign country; commercial dealings transacted between two states.

■═■

South Carolina State Highway Dept. v. Barnwell Brothers, Inc.

State agency (D) v. Truck operator (P)

303 U.S. 177 (1938).

NATURE OF CASE: Appeal from invalidation of truck size limitation.

FACT SUMMARY: After the South Carolina legislature enacted a statute prohibiting the operation on its highways of trucks wider than 90 inches and heavier than 20,000 pounds, the trial court struck down the statute as an unreasonable burden on interstate commerce.

🏛 RULE OF LAW
A limitation on interstate commerce to promote safety that does not discriminate against interstate commerce in favor of intrastate commerce does not unconstitutionally burden interstate commerce.

FACTS: The legislature of South Carolina enacted a statute prohibiting the operation of trucks on its highways if the trucks were wider than 90 inches and heavier than 20,000 pounds. The statute was designed to promote highway safety. Barnwell Brothers, Inc. (P) successfully challenged the statute, which interfered with its travel through the state, the trial court holding that the prohibition was an unreasonable restriction on interstate commerce. Much traffic that would normally pass through South Carolina while engaging in commerce was barred from the state. The Supreme Court granted certiorari.

ISSUE: Does a limitation on interstate commerce to promote safety that does not discriminate against interstate commerce in favor of intrastate commerce unconstitutionally burden interstate commerce?

HOLDING AND DECISION: (Stone, J.) No. It has been recognized that there are matters of local concern, the regulation of which unavoidably involves some regulation of interstate commerce. Since adoption of a weight or width regulation for motor vehicles is a legislative decision, its constitutionality is not to be determined because the weight of the evidence in court appears to favor a different standard. The statute here is designed to promote safety, a local concern, and no federal statute in this area has preempted South Carolina's power to regulate traffic to this extent. A limitation on interstate commerce to promote safety that does not discriminate against interstate commerce in favor of intrastate commerce does not unconstitutionally burden interstate commerce. Reversed.

▶ ANALYSIS

The Court here was persuaded by the danger, in the 1930s, of trucks wider than 90 inches traveling on local roads. Later cases indicate that even if couched in terms of

safety, a regulation impeding interstate commerce can be judicially struck down if as a matter of practical fact, it discriminates by its effect against interstate commerce.

■══■

Quicknotes

COMMERCE CLAUSE Article 1, section 8, clause 3 of the United States Constitution, granting Congress the power to regulate commerce with foreign countries and between the states.

INTERSTATE COMMERCE Commercial dealings between two parties located in different states or located in one state and accomplished through a point in another state or a foreign country; commercial dealings transacted between two states.

■══■

Southern Pacific Co. v. Arizona

Railroad company (D) v. State (P)

325 U.S. 761 (1945).

NATURE OF CASE: Action to recover statutory penalties for violation of the Arizona Train Limit Law.

FACT SUMMARY: The Arizona Train Limit Law prohibited the operation within the state of passenger trains more than 14 cars long and freight trains more than 70 cars long.

🏛 RULE OF LAW
In deciding whether a state law places an unreasonable burden on interstate commerce, and hence, cannot be sustained, the courts must balance the nature and extent of the burden which would be imposed by the statute against the merits and purposes to be derived from the state regulation.

FACTS: The Arizona Train Limit Law made it unlawful to operate within the state a train of more than 14 passenger cars or 70 freight cars. It authorized the state to recover a money penalty for each violation. Arizona (P) brought this action against Southern Pacific (D) to recover the statutory penalties for operative trains within the state in violation of the Act. The trial court decided for Southern Pacific (D) on the basis of detailed findings. The state supreme court reversed. It thought that the statute was enacted within the state's police power and that it bore some reasonable relation to the health, safety, and well-being of the state's people. Hence, the court thought, the statute should not be overturned notwithstanding its admittedly adverse effect on interstate commerce.

ISSUE: In determining whether a state law imposes an unallowable burden on interstate commerce, is it for the courts to balance the burden to be imposed against the merits and purposes to be derived from the law?

HOLDING AND DECISION: (Stone, C.J.) Yes. Wide scope has been left to the states for regulating matters of local concern, but such regulation must not materially restrict the free flow of interstate commerce or interfere with it in matters requiring national uniformity. The courts must determine the nature and extent of the burden which a state regulation would impose on interstate commerce, and then balance that burden against the benefits and merits to be derived from the regulation. In this case, the findings show that the operations of trains of more than 14 passenger cars and more than 70 freight cars is standard practice of the major U.S. railroads. If train length is to be regulated, national uniformity in regulation, such as only Congress can impose, is "practically indispensable to the operation of an efficient and economic national railway system." The findings leave no doubt that the Arizona Train Limit Law imposes a serious burden on interstate commerce. The practical effect of the law is to control train operations beyond the boundaries of the state because of the necessity of breaking up and reassembling long trains before entering and leaving the regulating state. Further, the Arizona law has no reasonable relation to safety. It in fact makes train operation more dangerous as is demonstrated by the increase in accidents due to the increase in the number of trains. The purpose of the Act was to cut down on "slack action accidents." Slack action is increased as train length is increased. However, the trial court found that such accidents occurred as frequently in Arizona as in Nevada, where train length is unregulated. Hence, the total effect of the law as a safety measure in reducing accidents is so slight as to not outweigh the national interest in keeping interstate commerce free from substantial interference and from subjection to local regulation (which does not have a uniform effect on the interstate train journey which it interrupts). Arizona (P) relies on *South Carolina v. Barnwell*, 303 U.S. 177 (1938). However, that case concerned the state's power to regulate the use of its highways, a field over which the state has a far more extensive control than over railroads. Here, Arizona's (P) safety interest is clearly outweighed by the national interest in an adequate, economical, and efficient railway system. The state supreme court's decision sustaining the statute is reversed.

DISSENT: (Black, J.) The Court decides that it is unwise governmental policy to regulate the length of trains; I note my dissent.

▶ ANALYSIS

In *Southern Pacific*, the Court employs the balancing of interests test, which, as the dissenting opinion points out, is a departure from the *Barnwell* rational basis test. The following are examples of regulations which were held not to unreasonably burden commerce (or where a national interstate commerce interest did not outweigh the state's benefits). A requirement that all persons operating trains within the state (even those in purely interstate movement) be licensed to insure their skill and fitness were upheld. Likewise, the Court upheld "full crew" laws defining the size of train crews. Laws prescribing reasonable safety and comfort devices and others limiting the speed of trains within city limits, as well as those regulating grade crossing, were also upheld.

Continued on next page.

Quicknotes

INTERSTATE COMMERCE Commercial dealings between two parties located in different states or located in one state and accomplished through a point in another state or a foreign country; commercial dealings transacted between two states.

POLICE POWER The power of a government to impose restrictions on the rights of private persons, as long as those restrictions are reasonably related to the promotion and protection of public health, safety, morals and the general welfare.

RATIONAL BASIS TEST A test employed by the court to determine the validity of a statute in equal protection actions, whereby the court determines whether the challenged statute is rationally related to the achievement of a legitimate state interest.

Baldwin v. G.A.F. Seelig, Inc.

State (D) v. Milk dealer (P)

294 U.S. 511 (1935).

NATURE OF CASE: Action seeking injunctive relief from state law.

FACT SUMMARY: New York (D) prohibited the sale of milk purchased out-of-state for less than the minimum in-state price of milk.

🏛 RULE OF LAW
A state may not seek to regulate prices by excluding foreign goods obtained at a lower price.

FACTS: New York (D) enacted a statute prohibiting the importation of out-of-state milk for a price less than that charged in-state. G.A.F. Seelig, Inc. (Seelig) (P) purchased out-of-state milk at a lower price and attempted to sell it in New York (D). New York (D) refused to license Seelig (P). Seelig (P) sought injunctive relief. The district court found that the New York (D) law was an undue burden on interstate commerce. As to milk still in its original cans it granted an injunction. Milk imported in bottles was found to be outside the stream of interstate commerce and subject to State (D) regulation.

ISSUE: May a state regulate intrastate prices by prohibiting the importation of less expensive goods?

HOLDING AND DECISION: (Cardozo, J.) No. A state may not, in any form or guise, directly burden interstate commerce. The New York (D) statute is, in reality, a duty used to erect barriers between the states. The fact that it was enacted to protect intrastate prices is immaterial. The injunction was therefore proper as to the canned milk. However, merely because goods are no longer in their original container/package is not, in itself, sufficient to find them subject to state regulation. It is a mere guideline which, in appropriate circumstances, may be ignored. The New York (D) statute places an unreasonable burden on interstate commerce and the fact that the milk is no longer in its original container is immaterial to the purpose and/or effect of the statute. New York (D) is enjoined from preventing the importation of bottles into the State (D). The secondary "health" purpose in providing pure milk could be accomplished in a far less restrictive method. Affirmed in part and reversed in part.

▶ ANALYSIS

The purpose of the Commerce Clause was of utmost importance to the unification of the states into one nation. It was designed—and so remains—so that the states "must sink or swim together, and that in the long run prosperity and salvation are in union and not division." If states could use the excuse that they must protect their merchants, farmers, and workers from out-of-state competition during hard times, here the depression, the solidarity of the union would be endangered. The decision in *Baldwin* was reaffirmed in 1964.

■■■

Quicknotes

COMMERCE CLAUSE Article 1, section 8, clause 3 of the United States Constitution, granting Congress the power to regulate commerce with foreign countries and between the states.

INTERSTATE COMMERCE Commercial dealings between two parties located in different states or located in one state and accomplished through a point in another state or a foreign country; commercial dealings transacted between two states.

LICENSE A right that is granted to a person allowing him or her to conduct an activity that without such permission he or she could not lawfully do, and which is unassignable and revocable at the will of the licensor.

■■■

Henneford v. Silas Mason Co.

State (D) v. Contractors (P)

300 U.S. 577 (1937).

NATURE OF CASE: Action to declare tax invalid.

FACT SUMMARY: Washington (D) enacted a use tax on property purchased elsewhere but which is used in the State (D).

🏛 RULE OF LAW
A use tax granting a credit for retail sales taxes paid in other states is valid.

FACTS: Washington (D) enacted a 2% use tax on goods purchased outside of the State (D) at retail and then brought into the State (D) for use. A credit was allowed for sales tax paid in the other state(s). If it were 2% or more, no use tax was assessed. If less than 2%, the amount paid was a credit. The Silas Mason Co. (Mason) (P) brought equipment into the State (D) for use on a construction project. Washington (D) assessed a use tax on the equipment being used in the State (D). Mason (P) appealed the imposition of the tax, alleging that it was an undue burden on interstate commerce which violated the Commerce Clause.

ISSUE: May a state impose a use tax on goods within the state?

HOLDING AND DECISION: (Cardozo, J.) Yes. A tax on the use of property within the state will generally be deemed valid. The tax is on goods which have come to rest and entered the stream of local commerce/use within the state. The tax is not on interstate commerce, but upon the privilege of use after the commerce is at an end. It is nondiscriminatory in that it equalizes the treatment of goods purchased within and without the State (D). A credit is granted for any taxes assessed elsewhere and it is applied only to retail sales. This is not to indicate that a use tax which did not grant such credits would be unconstitutional. That question is not before the court. The tax is imposed after the goods are at rest in the state and provides no burden to interstate commerce since it has already ended. The motive behind the statute is immaterial. It will not invalidate an otherwise lawful act regardless of whether the real reason for its enactment was to raise revenue (a valid purpose) or to protect local commerce (an invalid one). So long as a valid purpose exists, the rationale is immaterial. The tax is valid. Reversed.

▶ ANALYSIS

The Court, in subsequent cases, upheld the imposition of use taxes which allowed no credit for sales taxes paid in other states. The Court reasoned that the grounds for imposing a use and a sales tax were dissimilar. The use tax is imposed on the privilege of using or consuming goods in the state; the sales tax is on the merchant for the privilege of selling goods. No Commerce Clause problems exist because the goods have finally come to rest in the state imposing the use tax. The taxing of various attributes of ownership is a power of state sovereignty.

■=■

Quicknotes

COMMERCE CLAUSE Article 1, section 8, clause 3 of the United States Constitution, granting Congress the power to regulate commerce with foreign countries and between the states.

INTERSTATE COMMERCE Commercial dealings between two parties located in different states or located in one state and accomplished through a point in another state or a foreign country; commercial dealings transacted between two states.

USE TAX A sales tax on the use, consumption, or storage of tangible property; collectible by the seller where the purchaser is located in a different state.

■=■

Dean Milk Co. v. City of Madison

Milk company (P) v. City (D)

340 U.S. 349 (1951).

NATURE OF CASE: Action challenging the validity of a city ordinance regulating the sale of milk and milk products within the municipality's jurisdiction.

FACT SUMMARY: A Madison (D) ordinance made it unlawful to sell any milk as pasteurized unless it has been processed and bottled at an approved pasteurization plant located within five miles of the city.

🏛 RULE OF LAW
A locality may not discriminate against interstate commerce, even to protect the health and safety of its people, if reasonable alternatives exist which do not discriminate and are adequate to conserve legitimate local interests.

FACTS: Dean Milk Co. (P) was an Illinois corporation engaged in distributing milk products in Illinois and Wisconsin. Madison (D) was a city in Wisconsin. A Madison (D) ordinance prohibited the sale of any milk as pasteurized unless it had been processed and bottled at an approved pasteurization plant located within five miles of the city. Dean Milk (P) has pasteurization plants located 65 and 85 miles from Madison (D). Dean Milk (P) was denied a license to sell its milk products within Madison (D) solely because its pasteurization plants were more than five miles away. Dean Milk (P) contended that the ordinance imposed an undue burden on interstate commerce.

ISSUE: Can an ordinance, which in practical effect, prevents out-of-state sellers from competing with local producers, be upheld?

HOLDING AND DECISION: (Clark, J.) No. A locality may not discriminate against interstate commerce, even to protect the health and safety of its people, if reasonable alternatives exist which do not discriminate and are adequate to conserve legitimate local interests. The Madison (D) ordinance erects an economic barrier protecting a major local industry against competition from without the state. Hence, it plainly discriminates against interstate commerce. It must be decided whether the ordinance can be justified in view of the local interest and the available methods for protecting those interests. Reasonable and adequate alternatives do exist. Madison (D) could send its inspectors to the distant plants or it could exclude from its city all milk not produced in conformity with standards as high as those enforced by Madison (D). It could use the local ratings checked by the U.S. Public Health Service to enforce such a provision. The Madison (D) ordinance must yield to the principle that "one state, in its dealings with another, may not place itself in a position of economic isolation." Reversed.

DISSENT: (Black, J.) Dean Milk's (P) personal preference not to pasteurize within five miles of Madison (D), not the ordinance, keeps its milk out of Madison (D). The lower court found the ordinance to be a good faith attempt to safeguard public health. Never has a bona fide health law been struck down on the ground that equally good or better alternatives exist. At the very least the ordinance should not be invalidated without having the parties present evidence on the relative merits of the Madison (D) ordinance and the alternatives suggested by the Court. The Court cannot, on the basis of judicial knowledge, guarantee that the substitute methods it proposes would not lower health standards.

▌ ANALYSIS

In *Nebbia v. People of New York*, 291 U.S. 502 (1934), the Court sustained the state regulation of minimum milk prices to be paid by dealers to local producers. However, in *Baldwin v. G.A.F. Seelig, Inc.*, 294 U.S. 511 (1935), the same law was challenged as applied to out-of-state producers. The Supreme Court held that application to be an unconstitutional burden on commerce in that it "set a barrier to traffic between one state and another as effective as if custom duties, equal to the price differential (between the out-of-state price and the minimum price set by New York) had been laid upon the thing transported." *Baldwin* was heavily relied upon in *Dean Milk*.

■—■

Quicknotes

COMMERCE CLAUSE Article 1, section 8, clause 3 of the United States Constitution, granting Congress the power to regulate commerce with foreign countries and between the states.

INTERSTATE COMMERCE Commercial dealings between two parties located in different states or located in one state and accomplished through a point in another state or a foreign country; commercial dealings transacted between two states.

■—■

H.P. Hood & Sons v. Du Mond

Dairy company (P) v. State (D)

336 U.S. 525 (1949).

NATURE OF CASE: Appeal from denial of application to operate a facility to acquire and ship milk.

FACT SUMMARY: H.P. Hood & Sons (Hood) (P), a Massachusetts dairy corporation, operated plants in New York which purchased milk from local producers for shipment to Boston, and Du Mond (D) refused a license to Hood (P) to operate a third such facility on the ground that the effect of a grant would be to divert milk from the undersupplied New York markets to Massachusetts.

🏛 RULE OF LAW

A state may not deny a nonresident a license to purchase products for sale in other states solely to protect that state's own supply to the detriment of interstate commerce.

FACTS: H.P. Hood & Sons (Hood) (P) was a Massachusetts corporation engaged in the dairy business. It operated two receiving stations in New York where it purchased milk from local producers and shipped it to the Boston area for sale. Hood (P) applied for a license to operate a third station but Du Mond (D), the New York Commissioner of Agriculture and Markets, denied the application on the ground that the milk purchased by the third proposed facility would be diverted from New York to Massachusetts. The state courts upheld the denial, and Hood (P) appealed.

ISSUE: May a state deny a nonresident a license to purchase products for sale in other states solely to protect that state's own supply to the detriment of interstate commerce?

HOLDING AND DECISION: (Jackson, J.) No. The restrictions questioned in this case are those which have the impact of curtailing the volume of interstate commerce and aiding local economic interests. It has been held that when a state recognizes an article to be a subject of commerce, it cannot prohibit it from being a subject of interstate commerce. The purpose of the Commerce Clause of the Constitution is to assure every farmer and craftsman that he will have free access to every market in the nation. If the impact of a regulation by a state is to discriminate against interstate commerce so as to give advantage to local economic interests, the regulation cannot stand. Thus, a state may not deny a nonresident a license to purchase products for sale in other states solely to protect that state's own supply to the detriment of interstate commerce. Reversed and remanded.

DISSENT: (Black, J.) The language of the Act permitting Du Mond's (D) refusal is not discriminatory. The judiciary has used the Due Process and Commerce Clauses to produce a never-ending stream of challenges to governmental regulation.

DISSENT: (Frankfurter, J.) The central issue here is whether the difference between sanitation or bookkeeping regulations and destructive competition regulations is great enough to justify a different result in cases involving the latter than those involving the former.

▶ ANALYSIS

The discriminatory impact of a statute enacted by a state is relevant as well as the discriminatory language or intent in a Commerce Clause case. Here, nonresidents would be burdened by the New York statute while New York residents would be benefitted. Because this was attempted to be accomplished by regulation of interstate commerce, the statute could not stand.

■■■

Quicknotes

COMMERCE CLAUSE Article 1, section 8, clause 3 of the United States Constitution, granting Congress the power to regulate commerce with foreign countries and between the states.

DUE PROCESS CLAUSE Clauses found in the Fifth and Fourteenth Amendments to the United States Constitution providing that no person shall be deprived of "life, liberty, or property, without due process of law."

INTERSTATE COMMERCE Commercial dealings between two parties located in different states or located in one state and accomplished through a point in another state or a foreign country; commercial dealings transacted between two states.

■■■

Hughes v. Oklahoma

Buyer (D) v. State (P)

441 U.S. 322 (1979).

NATURE OF CASE: Appeal from conviction for transport of goods prohibited by statute.

FACT SUMMARY: Hughes (D) was convicted under an Oklahoma (P) statute prohibiting interstate transport of minnows seined or procured in Oklahoma (P) waters.

🏛 RULE OF LAW
A statute may not prohibit the transport of goods from one state to another to conserve that state's supply of such goods.

FACTS: Oklahoma (P) enacted a statute forbidding the transport of minnows seined or procured from the waters of Oklahoma (P). Hughes (D) purchased minnows from an Oklahoma (P) dealer, licensed to do business in that state, and Hughes (D) transported the minnows to Texas. Following his arrest, he was convicted under the statute, despite his contention that the statute violated the Commerce Clause of the Constitution. The Supreme Court granted review.

ISSUE: May a statute prohibit the transport of goods from one state to another to conserve that state's supply of such goods?

HOLDING AND DECISION: (Brennan, J.) No. A statute may not prohibit the transport of goods from one state to another to conserve that state's supply of such goods. The Commerce Clause should apply to state regulations of wild animals in the same way that it applies to regulations of other natural resources. *Geer v. Connecticut*, 161 U.S. 519 (1896), is therefore overruled. The statute in question here does not have effects upon interstate commerce that are merely "incidental"; instead, the statute overtly blocks the flow of interstate commerce. The purpose of conservation, while arguably legitimate, could be properly promoted by alternative means that would not have the discriminatory effect upon interstate commerce that this statute has. A statute may not prohibit the transport of goods from one state to another to conserve that state's supply of such goods. No provision for limits on the number of minnows that may be taken out of Oklahoma (P) is provided for in the statute. Conservation must be accomplished in a fashion consistent with the principle that "our economic unit is the Nation." Reversed.

DISSENT: (Rehnquist, J.) The statute even-handedly prevents any person from exporting Oklahoma (P) minnows outside of the state. It does not improperly protect Oklahoma (P) citizens from outside competition.

▶ ANALYSIS

In determining whether a state regulation has gone beyond its permissible scope, the courts inquire as to the existence of any less burdensome alternatives. Where a statute completely prohibits interstate commerce, there is usually something less burdensome that can be done instead.

■■■

Quicknotes

COMMERCE CLAUSE Article 1, section 8, clause 3 of the United States Constitution, granting Congress the power to regulate commerce with foreign countries and between the states.

INTERSTATE COMMERCE Commercial dealings between two parties located in different states or located in one state and accomplished through a point in another state or a foreign country; commercial dealings transacted between two states.

■■■

Reeves, Inc. v. Stake

Distributor (P) v. State (D)

447 U.S. 429 (1980).

NATURE OF CASE: Action to enjoin action taken by South Dakota as unconstitutional.

FACT SUMMARY: During a time of shortage, South Dakota promulgated a plan to confine the sale of the cement it produced in its plant to South Dakota residents.

🏛 RULE OF LAW
In the absence of congressional action, nothing in the Commerce Clause prohibits a state from being a market participant (as opposed to a regulator) and acting in that capacity to favor its own citizens over others.

FACTS: In 1919, South Dakota had built its own plant to produce cement. By the 1970s, some 40% of its output was going to out-of-state distributors. Reeves, Inc. (P) was an out-of-state distributor which had purchased almost all of its cement from the South Dakota plant for 20 years. In 1978, a nationwide cement shortage arose and the Commission running South Dakota's plant decided to reaffirm its policy of supplying all South Dakota customers first and to honor all contract commitments, with the remaining volume allocated on a first-come, first-served basis. Reeves (P) was hit hard, and brought suit against the Commission (D) challenging the constitutionality of the plant's policy favoring South Dakota buyers under the Commerce Clause. The district court enjoined the practice, but the court of appeals reversed on the grounds that *Hughes v. Alexandria Scrap*, 426 U.S. 794 (1976), held a state could freely act as a market participant, as opposed to a regulator, and in that capacity act to favor its own citizens over others.

ISSUE: When acting as a market participant rather than as a regulator, is a state free to act in that capacity to favor its own citizens over others without violating the Commerce Clause?

HOLDING AND DECISION: (Blackmun, J.) Yes. The Commerce Clause does not prohibit a state from favoring its own citizens over others while acting as a market participant rather than as a regulator. The Commerce Clause responds principally to state taxes and regulatory measures impeding free private trade in the national marketplace. There is no indication of a constitutional plan to limit the ability of a state itself to operate freely in the free market, which is what South Dakota was doing here. Affirmed.

DISSENT: (Powell, J.) The Commerce Clause was intended to prevent just this type of economic protectionism. In *Alexandra Scrap*, an exception was recognized for state action as market participant where no impermissible burden on interstate commerce was found. That exception cannot apply here, where such a burden exists.

▶ ANALYSIS

South Dakota could have steered clear of the Commerce Clause by providing that cement it produced be used only for its own public needs or that it first would go to fulfill those needs. The Clause does not reach a state's action in procuring goods and services for the operation of its government, so a state can act in that vein without regard to the effect on interstate commerce.

■▬■

Quicknotes

COMMERCE CLAUSE Article 1, section 8, clause 3 of the United States Constitution, granting Congress the power to regulate commerce with foreign countries and between the states.

MARKET PARTICIPANT DOCTRINE Allows states acting as market participants (i.e. businesses) to be exempted from the dormant clause.

■▬■

Hicklin v. Orbeck

Nonresidents (P) v. State (D)

437 U.S. 518 (1978).

NATURE OF CASE: Appeal from holding of constitutionality of the Alaska Hire Act.

FACT SUMMARY: Hicklin (P) and others challenged the constitutionality of an Alaska state statute requiring the employment of qualified Alaska residents in preference to nonresidents on oil and gas projects.

RULE OF LAW
A state may not require that state residents be hired over nonresidents in order to ease an unemployment problem.

FACTS: In 1972, the Alaska legislature passed the "Alaska Hire" Act, which required that all oil and gas leases, and other contracts dealing with the production of oil products, contain a provision "requiring the employment of qualified Alaska residents" in preference to nonresidents. The employment preference was administered by providing Alaska residents with resident cards to show to prospective employers. Hicklin (P) and other individuals desirous of securing jobs covered by the Act, but unable to qualify for the necessary resident cards, challenged the Act as violative of both the Privileges and Immunities Clause of Article IV, § 2 of the United States Constitution, and the Equal Protection Clause of the Fourteenth Amendment. The Alaska Supreme Court held that the Act's general preference for Alaska residents was constitutionally permissible.

ISSUE: May a state require that state residents be hired over nonresidents in order to ease an unemployment problem?

HOLDING AND DECISION: (Brennan, J.) No. The purpose of the Privileges and Immunities Clause is to place the citizens of each state on the same footing with citizens of other states, so far as the advantages resulting from citizenship in those states are concerned. Even assuming that a state may validly attempt to alleviate its unemployment problem by requiring private employers within the state to discriminate against nonresidents, Alaska Hire's discrimination against nonresidents cannot withstand scrutiny under the Privileges and Immunities Clause. If Alaska is to attempt to ease her unemployment problem by forcing employers within a state to discriminate against nonresidents, the means by which she does so must be more closely tailored to aid the unemployed the Act is intended to benefit. Alaska's ownership of the oil and gas that is the subject matter of the Alaska Hire Act simply constitutes insufficient justification for the pervasive discrimination that the Act mandates. Reversed.

▶ ANALYSIS

In *Baldwin v. Fish and Games Comm'n of Montana*, 436 U.S. 371 (1978), the Supreme Court upheld a system under which a nonresident of Montana was compelled to pay 25 times as much as a resident, if he wished to hunt elk. Justice Blackmun, writing for the majority, stated that "Appellants' interest in sharing this limited resource on more equal terms with Montana residents simply does not fall within the purview of the Privileges and Immunities Clause . . . Appellants . . . cannot contend that they are deprived of a means of a livelihood by the system or of access to any part of the state to which they may seek to travel."

Quicknotes

EQUAL PROTECTION CLAUSE A constitutional guarantee that no person should be denied the same protection of the laws enjoyed by other persons in like circumstances.

PRIVILEGED AND IMMUNITIES CLAUSE OF ARTICLE IV, § 2 A provision in the Fourteenth Amendment to the United States Constitution recognizing that any individual born in any of the United States is entitled to both state and national citizenship and guaranteeing such citizens the privileges and immunities thereof.

United Building and Construction Trades Council of Camden County and Vicinity v. Mayor and Council of the City of Camden

Contractors' council (P) v. City (D)

465 U.S. 208 (1984).

NATURE OF CASE: Appeal from a judgment upholding a local residency ordinance.

FACT SUMMARY: The New Jersey Supreme Court upheld the constitutionality of a state statute on the basis that the Privileges and Immunities Clause did not apply to municipal ordinances which discriminated on the basis of local residence rather than state citizenship.

🏛 **RULE OF LAW**
Municipal ordinances that discriminate on the basis of municipal residence violate the Privileges and Immunities Clause.

FACTS: Camden (D) enacted an ordinance requiring that at least 40% of the employees on its construction projects be Camden (D) residents. United (P), a council of contractors, sued, contending the ordinance discriminated in favor of municipal residents in violation of the Privileges and Immunities Clause. The New Jersey Supreme Court held that the Privileges and Immunities Clause applied only to discrimination based on state citizenship and not to discrimination based on municipal residence. United (P) appealed.

ISSUE: Does the Privileges and Immunities Clause apply to discrimination based on municipal residence?

HOLDING AND DECISION: (Rehnquist, J.) Yes. Municipal ordinances that discriminate on the basis of municipal residence violate the Privileges and Immunities Clause. A municipality gains its power to act as a political subdivision of a state. That which a state is prohibited from doing, its political subdivision necessarily is prohibited from doing. Under the ordinance, out-of-state citizens and New Jersey citizens who are not Camden (D) residents are not afforded the same privileges as Camden (D) residents in terms of pursuing a livelihood. Because the pursuit of a livelihood is a fundamental privilege protected by the Clause, the ordinance was constitutional. Reversed and remanded.

▎**ANALYSIS**

The Court in this case recognized the distinction between a Commerce Clause analysis and a Privileges and Immunities Clause analysis. If this ordinance were analyzed solely under the Commerce Clause, it would have been upheld because Camden (D), as a market participant, rather than a market regulator, could discriminate against out-of-state businesses.

Quicknotes

COMMERCE CLAUSE Article 1, section 8, clause 3 of the United States Constitution, granting Congress the power to regulate commerce with foreign countries and between the states.

MARKET PARTICIPANT DOCTRINE Allows states acting as market participants (i.e. businesses) to be exempted from the dormant clause.

PRIVILEGED AND IMMUNITIES CLAUSE OF ARTICLE IV, § 2 A provision in the Fourteenth Amendment to the United States Constitution recognizing that any individual born in any of the United States is entitled to both state and national citizenship and guaranteeing such citizens the privileges and immunities thereof.

■■■■

Silkwood v. Kerr-McGee Corp.

Estate adminstrator (P) v. Employer (D)

464 U.S. 238 (1984).

NATURE OF CASE: Appeal from denial of punitive damages in personal injury case.

FACT SUMMARY: Karen Silkwood (P) appealed from a decision reversing the trial court's award of punitive damages in a nuclear incident personal injury case, on the grounds that the Nuclear Regulatory Commission's (NRC) exclusive authority to regulate safety matters in connection with the operation of nuclear plants required the preemption of the award for punitive damages.

> ## 🏛 RULE OF LAW
> The Nuclear Regulatory Commission's exclusive authority to regulate safety matters in connection with the operation of nuclear plants does not necessarily require the preemption of awards of punitive damages under state law in nuclear incident personal injury cases.

FACTS: Karen Silkwood (P) was a laboratory analyst for Kerr-McGee (D) in its plant in Oklahoma engaged in the manufacture of plutonium rods for use as reactor fuel in nuclear power plants. In November 1974, she became contaminated while working, and the subsequent investigation showed high levels of contamination at her home. Later, she was killed in an unrelated automobile accident. Silkwood (P), her father, as administrator of her estate, brought suit against Kerr-McGee (D) based on common law tort principles under Oklahoma law, seeking to recover for the contamination injuries to his daughter and her property. The evidence indicated that although Kerr-McGee (D) did not always comply with Nuclear Regulatory Commission's (NRC) regulations, there was compliance with most federal regulations. The case was submitted to the jury on alternate theories of strict liability and negligence, and the jury returned an award for personal injuries, property damage, and a $10 million punitive damage award. On appeal, the court of appeals reversed the award for punitive damages on the grounds that the award of punitive damages was state action that competed substantially with the NRC in the regulation of safety matters in connection with the operation of nuclear plants in the same way that legislative action on the state's part would have competed, and therefore the award was preempted by federal law. From this decision, Silkwood (P) appealed.

ISSUE: Does the NRC's exclusive authority to regulate safety matters in connection with the operation of nuclear plants necessarily require the preemption of awards of punitive damages under state law in nuclear incident personal injury cases?

HOLDING AND DECISION: (White, J.) No. The NRC's exclusive authority to regulate safety matters in connection with the operation of nuclear plants does not necessarily require the preemption of awards of punitive damages under state law in nuclear incident personal injury cases. The operation of state law can be preempted in two ways. If there is congressional intent to completely occupy a certain field, any state law falling within the field is preempted. If state law has not been entirely displaced in the area in question, state law will still be preempted to the extent that it actually conflicts with the federal law. It has been concluded in previous cases that the federal government occupies the entire field of nuclear safety concerns, and Kerr-McGee (D) contends that this should be dispositive of the case. But examination of the legislative history of nuclear legislation indicates that Congress's decision to prohibit states from enacting regulations with respect to nuclear safety was premised on the belief that the NRC was better qualified to determine appropriate safety standards in the field. But there is nothing in the legislative history to indicate that Congress seriously intended to prohibit the use of state law tort remedies in nuclear accident cases. Passage of the Price-Anderson Act, which requires the operators of licensed nuclear plants to obtain private financial protection against potentially bankrupting state lawsuits arising out of a nuclear incident, seems to assume the availability of state tort remedies to persons injured in nuclear incidents. The indication is that Congress intended for the traditional principles of state tort law to apply in full force unless expressly supplanted by Congress. Punitive damages are a part of traditional state tort law. There is tension between the conclusion that the NRC has exclusive authority to regulate safety in the nuclear field, and allowing that a state may nevertheless award damages based on its own law of liability. It must be assumed, however, that Congress was aware of the tension and was willing to tolerate it. Kerr-McGee (D) has shown nothing in the legislative history or the regulations that suggests that punitive damages were not to be allowed. The award of punitive damages in this case does not create an impermissible conflict with the federal scheme of regulation, nor does it frustrate the objectives of the federal law. It must be concluded that the award of punitive damages in the present case is not preempted by federal law. Reversed.

DISSENT: (Blackmun, J.) The award of punitive damages in the present case operates to enforce a particular standard of safety in the operation of nuclear plants, the type of state action that is required to be preempted in any

Continued on next page.

field, such as this one, where federal law supplants state law. By adhering to traditional preemption analysis, state law would have been available to compensate victims for injuries caused by radiation hazards, yet would have preempted the ability to compel adherence to a particular standard of safety through the award of punitive damages.

▌▶ *ANALYSIS*

The dissent by J. Powell in the present case brings up the issue of where the presumption of preemption should be, for instead of being placed on Silkwood (P), who sought to rely on the state law, it was placed on Kerr-McGee (D), whom the Court found could show nothing in the regulations or the legislative history that would suggest that punitive damages were not to be allowed. In cases where federal law has supplanted state law in a given field, it would seem that there should be a positive presumption of preemption, if any presumption is required at all, since in those cases any action that falls within the prescribed field would be per se preempted. In most preemption cases, there is either a directly conflicting state statute, or, as was argued in the present case, a federal regulation which is said to have completely occupied the field so as to preempt operation of state law. This latter approach should be avoided, as it allows the court to dictate the result of any particular case by expanding or restricting the field occupied, and it does not focus in on whether the state law in question is administratively incompatible with the scheme of federal regulation.

■══■

Quicknotes

NEGLIGENCE Conduct falling below the standard of care that a reasonable person would demonstrate under similar conditions.

PREEMPTION Judicial preference recognizing the procedure of federal legislation over state legislation of the same subject matter.

PUNITIVE DAMAGES Damages exceeding the actual injury suffered for the purposes of punishment, deterrence and comfort to plaintiff.

STRICT LIABILITY Liability for all injuries proximately caused by a party's conducting of certain inherently dangerous activities without regard to negligence or fault.

■══■

Commerce Clause: Federal Powers

Quick Reference Rules of Law

The Daniel Ball

Federal government (P) v. Shipowners (D)

77 U.S. (10 Wall.) 557, 19 L.Ed. 999 (1871).

NATURE OF CASE: Appeal of admiralty penalty.

FACT SUMMARY: The owners of the ship the Daniel Ball (D) refused to submit to federal inspection and licensing on the ground that its activities were confined to wholly intrastate travel on the Grand River in Michigan.

🏛 RULE OF LAW

A ship or other vehicle for the transportation of commodities becomes an instrumentality of interstate commerce, subject to federal control, whenever it participates in the transportation of goods from state to state; this remains true even though such instrumentality functions wholly within a single state.

FACTS: The Daniel Ball (D) was a steamship engaged in the business of transporting goods on the Grand River in Michigan. Though it transported goods destined both from and for other states, it at all times remained in the state of Michigan; and, in fact, was not adequately constructed for travel outside (on Lake Michigan). Congress had enacted a law requiring licensing and inspection of all steamships engaged in interstate commerce; however, the owners of the Daniel Ball (D) refused to submit to it, on the ground that Congress's interstate commerce power did not extend to the wholly intrastate activities of the Daniel Ball (D). The U.S. (P) initiated an admiralty action to recover a penalty from the owners and this appeal followed.

ISSUE: Is a commercial vehicle, engaged in the business of transporting commodities traded in interstate commerce, immune from the federal commerce power merely because it limits its travel to the boundaries of a single state?

HOLDING AND DECISION: (Field, J.) No. A ship or other vehicle for the transportation of commodities becomes an instrumentality of interstate commerce, subject to federal control, whenever it participates in the transportation of goods from state to state; this remains true even though such instrumentality functions wholly within a single state. The fact that several independent instrumentalities may be employed in the transportation of commodities in interstate commerce will not alter the basic interstate nature of such activity for any one of them. Though it is true that the regulation of wholly intrastate commerce is within the province of the states, not the federal government, regulation of the transportation of goods traded in interstate commerce in any navigable waters within the United States must be included within the province of the federal government if the federal commerce power is to have any effect. Here, the Daniel Ball (D) was engaged in such transportation. That it was not itself travelling from state to state or operating in connection with any line of ships so travelling is irrelevant. The federal commerce power must prevail. Affirmed.

▶ ANALYSIS

The broadest of Congress's commerce powers is its plenary power over the channels and facilities of interstate commerce. Note, that the Grand River in *Daniel Ball* was such a channel in the eyes of the Court even back in 1871. Note, further, however, that the Court did not have to resort to the commerce power to regulate shipping. Article III, § 2 of the Constitution extends federal regulatory power to all cases of admiralty and maritime jurisdiction.

■■■

Quicknotes

ADMIRALTY That area of law pertaining to navigable waters.

PLENARY Unlimited and open; as broad as a given situation may require.

INTERSTATE COMMERCE Commercial dealings between two parties located in different states or located in one state and accomplished through a point in another state or a foreign country; commercial dealings transacted between two states.

■■■

United States v. E.C. Knight Co.

Federal government (P) v. Refineries (D)

156 U.S. 1, 39 L.Ed. 325 (1895).

NATURE OF CASE: Action to cancel sales contracts.

FACT SUMMARY: The American Sugar Refining Co. (ASR) (D) purchased four Philadelphia sugar refineries resulting in its near-complete control of the sugar industry, and the Government (P) filed this suit for cancellation of the sales as acts in restraint of trade and interstate commerce.

RULE OF LAW
The purchase of nearly all of an industry's facilities is not subject to federal regulation under the Commerce Clause of the Constitution if the facilities are all located in one state.

FACTS: The American Sugar Refining Co. (ASR) (D) purchased four Philadelphia sugar refineries by acquisition of their capital stock. After the purchases, ASR (D) owned nearly all the sugar refineries in the United States though all were located in Philadelphia. The Government (P) brought this suit seeking cancellation of the contracts of sale on the ground that the purchases constituted acts in restraint of trade and interstate commerce which could be remedied under the Commerce Clause of the Constitution.

ISSUE: Is the purchase of nearly all of an industry's facilities subject to federal regulation under the Commerce Clause of the Constitution if the facilities are all located in one state?

HOLDING AND DECISION: (Fuller, C.J.) No. The relief of the citizens of each state from the burden of monopoly and restraint of trade was left with the states to deal with. Commerce succeeds to manufacture and is not a part of it. A monopoly of manufacturing within a certain industry is not subject to the power of the federal government to regulate commerce under the Commerce Clause. The fact that an article is manufactured for export to another state does not determine the time when the article or product passes from the control of the state and belongs to commerce, for federal control purposes. The purchase of nearly all of an industry's facilities is not subject to federal regulation under the Commerce Clause of the Constitution if the facilities are all located in one state. The purchase of Philadelphia refineries bore no direct relationship to commerce between the states and is thus not subject to federal regulation.

▶ ANALYSIS

In later cases, the Supreme Court rapidly changed from a restrictive interpretation of antitrust legislation based on the "direct" or "indirect" effects of the challenged conduct to a policy of examining the practical results. Thus, the power of the Commerce Clause has been enhanced significantly since this case was decided.

Quicknotes

ANTITRUST Body of federal law prohibiting business conduct that constitutes a restraint on trade.

COMMERCE CLAUSE Article 1, section 8, clause 3 of the United States Constitution, granting Congress the power to regulate commerce with foreign countries and between the states.

MONOPOLY A privilege or right conferred upon an individual or entity granting it the exclusive power to manufacture, sell and distribute a particular service or commodity; a market condition in which one or a few companies control the sale of a product or service thereby restraining competition in respect to that article or service.

RESTRAINT OF TRADE Agreements between entities for the purpose of impeding free trade that results in a monopoly, suppression of competition, or affecting prices.

Houston, East & West Texas Railway v. United States (The Shreveport Case)

Railroad (P) v. Federal government (D)

234 U.S. 342 (1914).

NATURE OF CASE: Appeal from ruling upholding an Interstate Commerce Commission order.

FACT SUMMARY: Houston (P) charged higher rates for transport between Shreveport, Louisiana and points within Texas, than it did for transport over greater distances between points within Texas alone, and the Government (D) ordered Houston (P) to desist from this practice.

🏛 RULE OF LAW
Under the Commerce Clause of the Constitution, Congress may prevent instrumentalities of interstate and intrastate commercial intercourse from being used in their intrastate operations to the injury of interstate commerce.

FACTS: Houston (P) maintained a practice of charging a higher rate for rail transport between Shreveport, Louisiana, and points in Texas than it did for transport over even greater distances between stops within Texas alone. The Government (D) ordered Houston (P) to desist from this practice. Houston (P) then brought this suit to set aside the order to desist issued by the Interstate Commerce Commission on the ground that it exceeded the Commission's authority. The Commerce Court held that the order was authorized and that Houston (P) could comply by raising the intrastate rates to match the interstate rates. Houston (P) appealed.

ISSUE: May Congress, under the Commerce Clause of the Constitution, prevent instrumentalities of interstate and intrastate commercial intercourse from being used in their intrastate operations to the injury of interstate commerce?

HOLDING AND DECISION: (Hughes, J.) Yes. Congress has the paramount power to regulate the commerce between the states. Where the power over interstate commerce exists, it dominates. Where the regulation of intrastate carriers involves control of interstate commerce, the power of Congress controls. Thus, under the Commerce Clause of the Constitution, Congress may prevent instrumentalities of interstate and intrastate commercial intercourse from being used in their intrastate operations to the injury of interstate commerce. Congress is entitled to keep the highway of interstate communication open to interstate traffic upon fair and equal terms. Affirmed.

▶ ANALYSIS

The effect upon interstate commerce occasioned by intrastate activities is enough to ground federal regulation where the railroads are concerned, but it has not been held to be sufficient in all cases. The Tenth Amendment has been viewed in some cases as a bar to federal regulation where the effect is said to be "indirect."

Quicknotes

COMMERCE CLAUSE Article 1, section 8, clause 3 of the United States Constitution, granting Congress the power to regulate commerce with foreign countries and between the states.

INTERSTATE COMMERCE Commercial dealings between two parties located in different states or located in one state and accomplished through a point in another state or a foreign country; commercial dealings transacted between two states.

TENTH AMENDMENT The tenth amendment to the United States Constitution reserves those powers therein, not expressly delegated to the federal government or prohibited to the states, to the states or to the people.

Lottery Case (Champion v. Ames)

Government (P) v. Alleged conspirator (D)

188 U.S. 321 (1903).

NATURE OF CASE: Appeal from dismissal of a petition for a writ of habeas corpus after indictment for conspiracy to violate a lottery law.

FACT SUMMARY: The Federal Lottery Act prohibited transporting lottery tickets from one state to another.

🏛 RULE OF LAW
Under its power to regulate commerce, Congress may, for the purpose of guarding the morals of the people and protecting interstate commerce, prohibit the carrying of lottery tickets in interstate commerce.

FACTS: Champion (D) was indicted for conspiracy to violate the Federal Lottery Act. The law prohibited importing, mailing, or transporting from one state to another any lottery ticket. The indictment charged shipment by Wells Fargo Express of a box containing lottery tickets. Champion (D) challenged the constitutionality of the Act.

ISSUE: May Congress, under its commerce power, prohibit the transporting of lottery tickets in interstate commerce?

HOLDING AND DECISION: (Harlan, J.) Yes. The power to regulate commerce among the states has been expressly given to Congress. By this statute, Congress does not interfere with traffic or commerce carried on exclusively within the limits of a state. It is only regulating interstate commerce. As a state may, for the purpose of guarding the morals of its people, forbid all sales of lottery tickets within its limits, so Congress, for the purpose of guarding public morals and protecting interstate commerce, may prohibit transporting lottery tickets in interstate commerce. "We should hesitate long before adjudging that an evil of such an appalling character cannot be met and crushed by the only power competent to that end." Affirmed.

DISSENT: (Fuller, C.J.) The power to suppress lotteries belongs to the states and not to Congress. To hold that Congress has a general police power is to defeat the operation of the Tenth Amendment. The shipping of lottery tickets from state to state is not interstate commerce. Just as insurance policies create contractual relations and a means of enforcing a contract right and have been held not to be interstate commerce, so should it be with lottery tickets. Neither should a lottery ticket become an article of interstate commerce simply because it is placed in an envelope and mailed.

▶ ANALYSIS

Early twentieth century reformers seeking a constitutional basis for broader federal police measures were encouraged by the lottery decision. The decision is an example of one in which the Court treats the commerce power as analogous to a federal police power. The *Lottery Case* precedent sustained a variety of early twentieth century laws excluding objects deemed harmful from interstate commerce. Examples include the Mann Act prohibiting the transportation of women for immoral purposes, a statute banning interstate transportation of adulterated or misbranded articles, and a statute banning interstate transportation of goods made in violation of state law or possession of which violated state law.

∎━∎

Quicknotes

CONSPIRACY Concerted action by two or more persons to accomplish some unlawful purpose.

POLICE POWER The power of a government to impose restrictions on the rights of private persons, as long as those restrictions are reasonably related to the promotion and protection of public health, safety, morals and the general welfare.

TENTH AMENDMENT The tenth amendment to the United States Constitution reserves those powers therein, not expressly delegated to the federal government or prohibited to the states, to the states or to the people.

∎━∎

Hammer v. Dagenhart (The Child Labor Case)

Attorney General (D) v. Parent (P)

247 U.S. 251 (1918).

NATURE OF CASE: Appeal from a decree enjoining enforcement of the Child Labor Act.

FACT SUMMARY: Congress passed a law prohibiting the shipment in interstate commerce of any products of any mills, mines, or factories which employed children.

🏛 RULE OF LAW
The making of goods and the mining of coal are not commerce, nor does the fact that these things are to be afterwards shipped or used in interstate commerce make their production a part of such commerce.

FACTS: A congressional act prohibited the shipment in interstate commerce of the product of any mine or quarry which employed children under the age of 16. It prohibited the shipment in such commerce of the product of any mill, cannery, workshop, or factory which employed children under the age of 14 or employed children between the ages of 14 and 16 for more than eight hours a day or more than six days a week, or before 6 a.m. or after 7 p.m. Dagenhart (P) brought this action on behalf of his two minor children after being informed by the company where they worked of their impending discharge on the effective date of the Act. Hammer (D), the U.S. Attorney General, and the company which had employed Dagenhart's (P) children were named as defendants.

ISSUE: Can Congress, under its commerce power, pass a law prohibiting the transportation in interstate commerce of products of companies which employed children as laborers in violation of the terms of the law?

HOLDING AND DECISION: (Day, J.) No. It is argued that the power of Congress to regulate commerce includes the power to prohibit the transportation of ordinary products in commerce. However, in cases such as The Lottery Case, 188 U.S. 321 (1903), the power to prohibit the carrying of lottery tickets is as to those particular objects the same as the exertion of the power to regulate. In those cases, the use of interstate commerce was necessary to the accomplishment of harmful results. Regulation over commerce could only be accomplished by prohibiting the use of interstate commerce to affect the evil intended. Here, the thing intended to be accomplished by this act is the denial of interstate commerce facilities to those employing children within the prohibited ages. The goods shipped are of themselves harmless. The production of articles intended for interstate commerce is a matter of local regulation. The making of goods and the mining of coal are not commerce, nor does the fact that these things are to be afterwards shipped or used in interstate commerce make their production a part thereof. It is also argued that congressional regulation is necessary because of the unfair advantage possessed by manufacturers in states which have less stringent child labor laws. However, Congress has no power to require states to exercise their police powers to prevent possible unfair competition. The Act is unconstitutional and the decree enjoining its enforcement is affirmed.

DISSENT: (Holmes, J.) The *Lottery Case* and others following it establish that a law is not beyond Congress's commerce power merely because it prohibits certain transportation. There is no legal distinction between the evils sought to be controlled in those cases and the evil of premature and excessive child labor. The Court has no right to substitute its judgment of which evils may be controlled.

▶ *ANALYSIS*

After the *Hammer* decision, Congress sought to regulate child labor through the taxing power. That law was invalidated in *Bailey v. Drexel Furnishing Co.*, 259 U.S. 20 (1922). Subsequently, Congress submitted a proposed constitutional amendment to the states which authorized a national child labor law. The amendment has not been ratified, but the need for it has largely disappeared in view of *U.S. v. Darby*, 312 U.S. 100 (1941), which overruled *Hammer*.

Quicknotes

INTERSTATE COMMERCE Commercial dealings between two parties located in different states or located in one state and accomplished through a point in another state or a foreign country; commercial dealings transacted between two states.

POLICE POWER The power of a government to impose restrictions on the rights of private persons, as long as those restrictions are reasonably related to the promotion and protection of public health, safety, morals and the general welfare.

Carter v. Carter Coal Co.

Stockholder (P) v. Corporation (D)

298 U.S. 238 (1936).

NATURE OF CASE: Stockholder suit to enjoin company from complying with requirements of the Coal Conservation Act.

FACT SUMMARY: The Coal Conservation Act attempted to regulate certain aspects of coal production. Carter (P) brought suit to enjoin his company (D) from complying with the Act.

🏛 RULE OF LAW
Production or manufacture of goods that are later to be shipped out of state is not interstate commerce and is not subject to federal regulation.

FACTS: The Coal Conservation Act of 1935 established a tax on coal production. Producers would receive a reduction of this tax by accepting coal codes which were to be formulated. These codes would establish minimum prices for coal, wages, and hours for workers, and would require that producers recognize their employees' right to organize and bargain collectively. Carter (P) brought this action to enjoin Carter Coal Co. (D) from complying with these requirements and from paying the tax.

ISSUE: Is the production of coal that may or may not be shipped across state lines "interstate commerce" that would allow federal regulation?

HOLDING AND DECISION: (Sutherland, J.) No. The attempted federal regulation of coal production is not sustainable as within Congress's power to regulate interstate commerce or as within a more general power to regulate for the public welfare. The preamble of the Act states that the production of coal "directly affects interstate commerce" and that regulation is necessary to protect the public interest in maintaining an adequate supply of coal and promoting fair producer-employee relations. It has always been held that Congress can only exercise powers that were specifically delegated to it by the Constitution; therefore, this Act cannot be sustained merely on the ground that it promotes the general welfare. The Act, then, can only be upheld if it is within the powers granted the federal government by the Commerce Clause. In manufacturing a product which it subsequently ships into interstate commerce, a manufacturer engages in two separate activities: first, the manufacture or production of a product (which is purely local and only subject to state regulation); second, the actual shipment of the goods across state lines, which is subject only to federal regulation. Since production is purely local, and this Act purports to regulate the employer/employee relationship in production, the Act

is not a valid exercise of Congress's power to regulate interstate commerce, and cannot be sustained.

▶ ANALYSIS

The *Carter* case, like *Schecter*, is based on a strict geographical definition of interstate commerce. If the act in question, here the production of coal, takes place at all times within a single state, it cannot be interstate commerce and cannot be regulated. Although the Court admits that coal production has an effect on interstate commerce, it was only an indirect, not a direct effect. The weakness of this argument is pointed out in the dissent—intrastate acts can have such a great influence on interstate commerce, even in the absence of a direct effect, that the literalistic direct/indirect distinction serves no purpose.

■═■

Quicknotes

COMMERCE CLAUSE Article 1, section 8, clause 3 of the United States Constitution, granting Congress the power to regulate commerce with foreign countries and between the states.

INTERSTATE COMMERCE Commercial dealings between two parties located in different states or located in one state and accomplished through a point in another state or a foreign country; commercial dealings transacted between two states.

■═■

National Labor Relations Board v. Jones & Laughlin Steel Corp.

Government agency (P) v. Employer (D)

301 U.S. 1 (1937).

NATURE OF CASE: Appeal from refusal to enforce order to reinstate workers discharged.

FACT SUMMARY: The National Labor Relations Board (NLRB) (P) ordered Jones (D) to reinstate workers that Jones (D) had fired for their union activities and when Jones (D) refused to obey the order, the court of appeals refused to enforce it.

🏛 RULE OF LAW
Under the Commerce Clause of the Constitution, the National Labor Relations Board may regulate an employer's employee relations conduct that could have a direct effect upon interstate commerce.

FACTS: Jones (D) fired certain workers because of their union activities in an effort to discourage unionization of its steel works. The The National Labor Relations Board (NLRB) (P) ordered Jones (D) to reinstate the workers and pay them back wages, and Jones (D) refused to do so. The NLRB (P) brought this suit to require the remedies ordered but the court of appeals refused to order Jones (D) to comply on the ground that the order was outside of the scope of federal power. The NLRB (P) appealed.

ISSUE: Under the Commerce Clause of the Constitution, may the NLRB regulate an employer's employee relations conduct that could have a direct effect upon interstate commerce?

HOLDING AND DECISION: (Hughes, C.J.) Yes. It has been previously held that in some cases manufacturing is not commerce and is thus beyond the power of the federal government under the Commerce Clause. The National Labor Relations Board (NLRB) (P) urges, however, that the steel mill business is dependent upon the moving of ore and minerals through the various states and then sending steel through them to consumer market, which involves interstate commerce. This is true. Although activities may be intrastate in character when separately considered, if they have such a close and substantial relation to interstate commerce that their control is essential or appropriate to protect that commerce, Congress may exercise that control. Under the Commerce Clause of the Constitution, the NLRB may regulate an employer's employee relations conduct that could have a direct effect upon interstate commerce. Reversed.

▶ *ANALYSIS*

The distinction made in the early Commerce Clause cases between production and commerce is abandoned in this case. A more practical method for determining the existence of federal power and the propriety of using it was found to be a case-by-case method of viewing practical effects of the challenged conduct in relation to the economic needs of the United States.

■═■

Quicknotes

COMMERCE CLAUSE Article 1, section 8, clause 3 of the United States Constitution, granting Congress the power to regulate commerce with foreign countries and between the states.

NATIONAL LABOR RELATIONS BOARD An agency established pursuant to the National Labor Relations Act for the purpose of prohibiting unfair labor practices by employers and unions.

■═■

United States v. Darby

Federal government (P) v. Lumber manufacturer (D)

312 U.S. 100 (1941).

NATURE OF CASE: Criminal prosecution for violation of Fair Labor Standards Act.

FACT SUMMARY: Darby (D) was a lumber manufacturer, some of whose goods were later shipped in interstate commerce. He was indicted for violation of the wage and hour provisions of the Fair Labor Standards Act, and defended on the ground that as an intrastate producer he was not subject to federal regulation.

🏛 RULE OF LAW
Congress has the power to regulate the hours and wages of workers who are engaged in the production of goods destined for interstate commerce and can prohibit the shipment in interstate commerce of goods manufactured in violation of the wage and hour provisions.

FACTS: Darby (D) was a manufacturer of finished lumber, and a large part of the lumber he produced was shipped in interstate commerce. The purpose of the Fair Labor Standards Act was to prevent the shipment in interstate commerce of certain products produced under substandard labor conditions. The Act set up minimum wages and maximum hours and punished the shipment in interstate commerce of goods produced in violation of the wage/hour requirements and also punished the employment of persons in violation of those requirements. Darby (D) was arrested for both shipment of goods in violation of the Act and employment of workers in violation of the Act. The trial court dismissed the indictment on the ground that the Act was an unconstitutional regulation of manufacturing within the states.

ISSUE: Does Congress have the power to prohibit shipment in interstate commerce of goods produced in violation of the wage/hour provisions of the Fair Labor Standards Act and the power to prohibit employment of workers involved in the production of goods for interstate shipment in violation of the wage/hour provisions of the Fair Labor Standards Act?

HOLDING AND DECISION: (Stone, J.) Yes. Both prohibitions are a constitutional exercise of Congress's commerce power. Although manufacturing itself is not interstate commerce, the shipment of goods across state lines is interstate commerce and the prohibition of such shipment is a regulation of commerce. Congress has plenary power to exclude from interstate commerce any article which it determines to be injurious to public welfare, subject only to the specific prohibitions of the Constitution. In the Fair Labor Standards Act, Congress has determined that the shipment of goods produced under substandard labor conditions is injurious to commerce, and therefore has the power to prohibit the shipment of such goods, independent of the indirect effect of such prohibition on the states. The prohibition of employment of workers engaged in the production of goods for interstate commerce at substandard conditions is also sustainable, independent of the power to exclude the shipment of the goods so produced. The power over interstate commerce is not confined to the regulation of commerce among the states, but includes regulation of intrastate activities which so affect interstate commerce as to make regulation of them an appropriate means to the end of regulating interstate commerce. Here, Congress has determined that the employment of workers in substandard conditions is a form of unfair competition injurious to interstate commerce, since the goods so produced will be lower priced than the goods produced under adequate conditions. Such a form of competition would hasten the spread of substandard conditions and produce a dislocation of commerce and the destruction of many businesses. Since Congress has the power to suppress this form of unfair competition, and the Act is an appropriate means to that end, the wage/hour provisions are within Congress's power. It is irrelevant that only part of the goods produced will be shipped in interstate commerce; Congress has power to regulate the whole factory even though only a part of the products will have an effect on interstate commerce. Reversed.

▶ ANALYSIS

Darby, like *Jones & Laughlin*, is an example of the application of the affectation doctrine. It had long been the law that Congress had the power to exclude from interstate commerce harmful objects or immoral activities, such as mismarked goods or lottery tickets. This case extends the power to exclude articles produced under conditions which Congress considered harmful to the national welfare. Even though production of lumber was an entirely intrastate activity, it was a part of an economic process that led to the eventual sale of lumber across state limits, affecting interstate commerce. The federal commerce power extends to purely intrastate transactions; the effect on commerce, not the location of the regulated act, is the basis for the exercise of the federal power. This case overruled the earlier case of *Hammer v. Dagenhart*, 247 U.S. 251 (1918), which held unconstitutional an attempt

Continued on next page.

by Congress to exclude articles made by child labor from interstate commerce.

■■■■

Quicknotes

FAIR LABOR STANDARDS ACT Enacted in 1938, the statute establishes a minimum wage applicable to all employees of covered employers and provides for mandatory overtime payment for covered employees who work more than 40 hours a week. Executive, administrative and professional employees paid on a salary basis are exempt from the statute.

■■■■

Wickard v. Filburn

Secretary of Agriculture (P) v. Farmer (D)

317 U.S. 111 (1942).

NATURE OF CASE: Action to enjoin enforcement of penalty provisions of the Agricultural Adjustment Act.

FACT SUMMARY: Filburn (D) was ordered to pay a penalty imposed by the Agriculture Adjustment Act for producing wheat in excess of his assigned quota. He argued that the federal regulations could not be constitutionally applied to his crops because part of his crop was intended for his own consumption, not for interstate commerce.

🏛 RULE OF LAW
Farm production that is intended for consumption on the farm is subject to Congress's commerce power, since it may have a substantial economic effect on interstate commerce.

FACTS: The purpose of the Agriculture Adjustment Act was to control the volume of wheat moving in interstate commerce to avoid surpluses and shortages which would result in abnormally high or low prices and thereby obstruct commerce. Under the Act, the Secretary of Agriculture would set a national acreage allotment for wheat production, which would be divided into allotments for individual farms. Filburn (D) was the owner and operator of a small farm. In the past he had grown a small amount of wheat of which he sold part, fed part to poultry and livestock (some of the livestock were later sold), used part in making flour for home consumption, and kept the rest for seeding the next year. In 1940, his wheat production exceeded the maximum he was allowed under the Agriculture Adjustment Act and he was assessed a penalty for the excess. Filburn (D) refused to pay on the ground that the Act was unconstitutional in that it attempted to regulate purely local production and consumption which, at most, had an indirect effect on interstate commerce. The government argued that the Act regulates not production and consumption, but only marketing (which was defined in the Act to include the feeding of the wheat to livestock which is later sold), and even if interpreted to include production and consumption, it was a legitimate exercise of the Commerce Clause and the Necessary and Proper Clause.

ISSUE: Does Congress, under the Commerce Clause, have the power to regulate the production of wheat which is grown for home consumption purposes rather than for sale in interstate commerce?

HOLDING AND DECISION: (Jackson, J.) Yes. A local activity, such as production, may be reached under the Commerce Clause if it exerts a substantial economic effect on interstate commerce. The Act was enacted because of the problems of the wheat market: there had been a decrease in export in recent years, causing surpluses which in turn caused congestion in the market and lower prices. It has been repeatedly held that the commerce power of Congress includes the power to regulate prices and practices affecting prices. Wheat destined for home consumption has an effect on the interstate price of wheat and is, therefore, subject to regulation. As the market price of wheat climbs, farmers will sell more of their crop which was intended for home consumption on the market causing a decrease in prices. Even if the wheat is never sold, there still is a substantial effect on interstate commerce because it reduces demand for wheat; that wheat which Filburn (D) produces for his own use means that he will buy less wheat on the market. Although the actual effect of Filburn's (D) overproduction will be small, the combination of all such producers does cause a substantial effect on commerce. Reversed.

▶ ANALYSIS

Wickard is yet another application of the "affectation doctrine." The Court focuses not on the nature of the regulated activity (e.g., whether it is local) but on the final economic effect of that activity. Here, although the effect of Filburn's (D) excess wheat production was insignificant on the national market, there still was some effect, at least in theory, so regulation was allowed. The Court in *Wickard* expressly rejected the old formulas for determining the extent of the commerce power such as direct/indirect and production/commerce.

■■■

Quicknotes

COMMERCE CLAUSE Article 1, section 8, clause 3 of the United States Constitution, granting Congress the power to regulate commerce with foreign countries and between the states.

NECESSARY AND PROPER CLAUSE, ACT I, § 8 OF THE CONSTITUTION Which enables congress to make all laws that may be "necessary and proper" to execute its other, enumerated powers.

■■■

Child Labor Tax Case (Bailey v. Drexel Furniture Co.)

Collector of Internal Revenue (D) v. Furniture company (P)

259 U.S. 20 (1922).

NATURE OF CASE: Constitutional challenge to federal law.

FACT SUMMARY: Congress enacted a bill imposing a special tax on those employing children under a certain age.

🏛 RULE OF LAW
Congress may not enact laws under certain of its enumerated powers to achieve ends beyond its authority.

FACTS: Congress enacted the Child Labor Act, which applied a percentage of profit tax to any company employing children under a certain age. The Act also restricted the number of days per week and hours per day which could be worked. Both the Internal Revenue Service and the Department of Labor could enter and inspect the businesses covered under the Act. Drexel Furniture Co. (P) was assessed a tax for employing a factory boy under the age of 14 in violation of the Act. Drexel (P) appealed the tax assessment on the ground that this was not a tax act and that Congress had no authority to regulate purely local conduct which was reserved to the states. Drexel (P) alleged that the Act was merely a sham to accomplish an end outside of Congress's power.

ISSUE: May Congress, under the guise of one of its enumerated powers, attempt to achieve an end which is beyond its power?

HOLDING AND DECISION: (Taft, C.J.) No. Congress may not, under the pretext of enacting laws pursuant to its legitimate powers, pass laws to accomplish ends beyond its authority. The Act herein is not a tax law. It is not designed to raise revenue, but to coerce businesses into abiding by national child labor laws. It excuses innocent conduct while punishing willful violations of the Act. The tax is not proportioned on the degree or frequency of violations. It is a penalty not a tax. The point herein is to order conduct, not raise revenue. The conduct sought to be regulated is local in nature and is beyond the power of Congress. The tax is unconstitutional. Affirmed.

▶ ANALYSIS

The taxing and spending powers have close functional and doctrinal ties to the commerce power, since the manner in which taxes are imposed can have significant regulatory impacts. As with commerce laws, taxing measures have been used to deal with "police" as well as economic problems. Regulation through taxing has been resorted to when the need for legislation seemed great and the direct regulatory authority through the Commerce Clause was

"under constitutional clouds," such as in the cases of child labor and of New Deal legislation in the 1930s.

Quicknotes

COMMERCE CLAUSE Article 1, section 8, clause 3 of the United States Constitution, granting Congress the power to regulate commerce with foreign countries and between the states.

ENUMERATED POWERS Specific powers mentioned in, and granted by, the constitution; e.g., the taxing power.

SPENDING POWER The power delegated to Congress by the Constitution to spend money in providing for the nation's welfare.

TAXING POWER The authority delegated to Congress by the Constitution to impose taxes.

United States v. Butler

Federal government (P) v. Receivers (D)

297 U.S. 1 (1936).

NATURE OF CASE: Action challenging the constitutionality of the Agricultural Adjustment Act of 1933.

FACT SUMMARY: The Agricultural Adjustment Act of 1933 states that there is a national economic emergency arising from the low price of agricultural products in comparison with other commodities. To remedy this situation, a tax will be collected from processors of an agricultural product. The revenue raised will be paid to farmers who curtail their production of that product.

🏛 RULE OF LAW
Congress may not, under the pretext of exercising the taxing power, accomplish prohibited ends, such as the regulation of matters of purely state concern and clearly beyond its national powers.

FACTS: The Agricultural Adjustment Act of 1933 declared that a national economic emergency had arisen due to the disparity between the prices of agricultural and other commodities, resulting in the destruction of farmers' purchasing power. To remedy this situation, a tax will be collected from processors of agricultural products. The revenue raised thereby will be paid to farmers who voluntarily curtail their production of those crops used by the processors. The Secretary of Agriculture is to determine the crops to which the Act's plan shall apply. In July 1933, the Secretary determined that the Act's plan should be applied to cotton. A tax claim was presented to Butler (D) as receivers of the Hoosal Mills Corp., as cotton processors. The district court held the tax to be valid.

ISSUE: Is a tax on the processing of agricultural products valid where the revenue raised by the tax is to be paid to farmers who voluntarily curtail their production of crops?

HOLDING AND DECISION: (Roberts, J.) No. First of all, Butler (D) has standing to question the validity of the tax because it is but a part of the unconstitutional plan of the Agricultural Adjustment Act. A tax, as the term is used by the Constitution, is an exaction for the support of the government. It has never been thought to mean the expropriation of money from one group for the benefit of another, as is attempted by the Act in question here. The Act is unconstitutional in that it invades the rights of the states. It is a statutory plan to regulate and control agriculture production, a matter beyond the power of the federal government. The government, in attempting to defend the Act, places great reliance on the fact that the Act's plan is voluntary. However, the farmer who chooses not to comply with the plan loses benefits. "The power to confer or

withhold unlimited benefits is the power to coerce or destroy." Even if the plan were truly voluntary, it would not be valid. "At best, it is a scheme for purchasing with federal funds submission to federal regulation of a subject reserved to the states." Contracts for the reduction of acreage and the control of production are not within Congress's power. Congress has no power to enforce the ends sought by this Act onto the farmer. Hence, it may not indirectly accomplish those ends by taxing and spending to enforce them. If this Act is valid, Congress could exercise its power to regulate all industry. It could extract money from one branch of an industry and pay it to another branch. Congress may not under the pretext of exercising the taxing power, accomplish prohibited ends. Affirmed.

DISSENT: (Stone, J.) Courts are to be concerned only with the power to enact statutes, not with their wisdom. The constitutional power of Congress to tax the processing of agricultural products is not questioned. The present tax is held to be invalid because the use to which its proceeds are to be put is disapproved. The tax is held to be invalid because it is a step in a plan to regulate agricultural production. The Court states that state powers are infringed by the expenditure of the proceeds of the tax to compensate farmers for the curtailment of their crop production. Such a limitation is contradictory and destructive of the power to appropriate for the public welfare, and is incapable of practical application. Congress's spending power is not subordinate to its legislative powers. This independent grant of power presupposes freedom of selection among diverse ends and aims and the capacity to impose such conditions as will render the choice effective. It is contradictory to say that there is a power to spend for the national welfare, while rejecting any power to impose conditions reasonably adapted to the end which justifies the expenditure. "If appropriation in aid of a program of curtailment is constitutional, and it is not denied that it is, payment to farmers on condition that they reduce their crop acreage is constitutional."

▶ ANALYSIS

The *Butler* decision contributed greatly to the pressure that produced the Court-packing plan a few months later. It is called the landmark case in the area of federal regulation of local matters through taxation. However, if the tax and the appropriation provisions had not been so closely tied together, it is doubtful that the Court would have invalidated the tax. The tax appeared to have a valid revenue-raising purpose, and once separated from the

Continued on next page.

taxing provisions, there would have been no one with standing to attack the appropriation.

■═■

Quicknotes

SPENDING POWER The power delegated to Congress by the Constitution to spend money in providing for the nation's welfare.

TAXING POWER The authority delegated to Congress by the Constitution to impose taxes.

■═■

Chas. C. Steward Machine Co. v. Davis

Corporation (P) v. Commissioner of Internal Revenue (D)

301 U.S. 548 (1937).

NATURE OF CASE: Action challenging the constitutionality of a federal tax statute.

FACT SUMMARY: The Social Security Act required Steward Machine Co. (P), an Alabama corporation, to pay a tax as an employer of eight or more people, but Steward Machine (P) brought a suit for a refund on the ground the Act constituted an unlawful invasion of the reserved powers of the states.

🏛 RULE OF LAW
The federal unemployment insurance tax levied against employers of eight or more people under the Social Security Act is not an unconstitutional invasion of the reserved powers of the state.

FACTS: Individual states were unable to provide the massive relief needed by the large number of people unemployed during the Depression. When Congress passed the Social Security Act in 1935, it imposed an excise tax on employers of eight or more people based on the wages paid. An employer's contribution to a state unemployment fund could be credited against the federal tax if the particular state plan complied with specific minimum requirements. The federal tax funds went into the General Treasury. After paying the tax due, Steward Machine (P), an Alabama employer of more than eight people, filed suit for a refund. It charged that the aforementioned tax plan was unconstitutional because, inter alia, it attempted to coerce states to abandon their governmental functions and adopt unemployment compensation plans fashioned by federal criteria. The argument was that the purpose of the Act was not revenue, but an unlawful invasion of the reserved powers of the states. The district court and court of appeals found the Act constitutional, and Steward Machine (P) appealed.

ISSUE: Does the tax levied against employers of eight or more people under the Social Security Act represent an unconstitutional invasion of the reserved powers of the states?

HOLDING AND DECISION: (Cardozo, J.) No. There is no unconstitutional invasion of the reserved powers of the states to be found in Social Security Act provisions regarding the levying of an excise tax on employers of eight or more people. The Act does not attempt to coerce the states in contravention of the Tenth Amendment or of restrictions implicit in our federal form of government. There has been no showing that the tax and credit provisions at issue in this case operate in combination as weapons of coercion, destroying or impairing

the autonomy of the states. There is a vast difference between an inducement and coercion, and in this case the federal government merely offered an inducement to states to adopt unemployment compensation plans to meet the needs of the people. The states remain free to act as they see fit, to adopt a plan or not, or to repeal a plan once it has been adopted. The federal government acted to safeguard the national treasury in a time of crisis and did not act in a coercive fashion. The provisions at issue are constitutional. Affirmed.

▶ ANALYSIS

Congress has continued using its spending power to "influence" the states in the exercise of their sovereign powers. There are, of course, limitations on such use of the spending power. One is constitutional in nature. Congress cannot tie federal funding to a state's accepting federally imposed conditions which violate other provisions of the Constitution that protect individual rights. Another is practical. There is a "cost" involved in exerting influence on state decisions, i.e., the federal government must be willing to spend the money in order to achieve its particular goal.

Quicknotes

EXCISE TAX A tax imposed on the performance of an act, engagement in an occupation, or the enjoyment of a privilege.

RESERVED POWER A power specifically withheld because it is not mentioned or otherwise implied in powers conferred by a constitution or statute.

SPENDING POWER The power delegated to Congress by the Constitution to spend money in providing for the nation's welfare.

TENTH AMENDMENT The tenth amendment to the United States Constitution reserves those powers therein, not expressly delegated to the federal government or prohibited to the states, to the states or to the people.

Heart of Atlanta Motel, Inc. v. United States

Motel (P) v. Federal government (D)

379 U.S. 241 (1964).

NATURE OF CASE: Constitutional challenge to federal act.

FACT SUMMARY: Heart of Atlanta Motel, Inc. (Motel) (P) discriminated against Negroes allegedly in violation of Title II of the Civil Rights Act of 1964.

RULE OF LAW
Congress may prohibit discrimination in public accommodations under its authority under the Commerce Clause.

FACTS: Heart of Atlanta Motel, Inc. (Motel) (P) was located within easy access to state and interstate highways. Motel (P) solicited patronage through national advertising. Much of its patronage came from conventions and approximately three-quarters of its guests were from out-of-state. Motel (P) discriminated against Negroes. Motel (P) brought a declaratory judgment action to declare that Title II of the Civil Rights Act of 1964 was unconstitutional or had no effect on it. Title II prohibited discrimination or segregation in any place of public accommodation, including motels. Motel (P) alleged that the Act was beyond the power of Congress. The court upheld the Act.

ISSUE: May Congress prohibit discrimination in public accommodations under its Commerce Clause power?

HOLDING AND DECISION: (Clark, J.) Yes. Congress has the power to regulate interstate travel. Under this power it may reach purely local activities which may have a significant and harmful effect on travel. Millions of people travel each year. Negroes are often subject to discrimination around the country. The inability to find accommodations has become acute. This has the effect of restricting the individual's right to travel. While the actions of a single motel may have no appreciable effect, cumulatively the effect on the right to interstate travel may be profound. The Commerce Clause covers both commercial and noncommercial travel. The Act does not deprive Motel (P) of a property right under the Fifth Amendment. Having made use of the products of interstate commerce and activities, Motel (P) cannot complain of its regulation under the Commerce Clause. Affirmed.

CONCURRENCE: (Black, J.) The question of whether particular operations affect interstate commerce sufficiently to be subject to Congress's commerce power is one for this Court. Here the Act is a valid exercise of congressional power since Motel's (P) record of discrimination tended to directly interfere with interstate commerce.

▶ ANALYSIS

In *Maryland v. Wirtz*, 392 U.S. 183 (1968), the Court conclusively settled the issue of whether Congress's power under the Commerce Clause extends to purely local activity. The Court held that Congress has the authority to declare that an entire class of activity affects commerce. The only question which the court must decide is whether the class is within reach of federal power. The Court has no right to go beyond such a finding excising "trivial" activities.

Quicknotes

COMMERCE CLAUSE Article 1, section 8, clause 3 of the United States Constitution, granting Congress the power to regulate commerce with foreign countries and between the states.

FIFTH AMENDMENT Provides that no person shall be compelled to serve as a witness against himself, or be subject to trial for the same offense twice, or be deprived of life, liberty, or property without due process of law.

Katzenbach v. McClung

Parties not identified.

379 U.S. 294 (1964).

NATURE OF CASE: Action seeking injunctive relief and attacking the validity of Title II of the Civil Rights Act of 1964 as applied to a restaurant.

FACT SUMMARY: Ollie's Barbecue refused sit-down service to Negroes. The lower court found that a substantial portion of the food served in the restaurant had moved in interstate commerce.

🏛 RULE OF LAW
Although an activity is local and may not be regarded as commerce, it may still be reached by Congress if it exerts a substantial economic effect on interstate commerce.

FACTS: Ollie's Barbecue was a family-owned restaurant situated on a state highway, 11 blocks from an interstate highway and a somewhat greater distance from railroad and bus stations. It had a take-out service for Negroes, but refused to serve them in its dining rooms. The lower court found that a substantial portion of the food served in the restaurant had moved in interstate commerce. It was argued that Congress legislated a conclusive presumption that a racial discrimination in restaurants serving food, which had been transported in interstate commerce, affects such commerce. Congress made no formal findings on this issue.

ISSUE: Can Congress, pursuant to its commerce power, prohibit racial discrimination in a restaurant which serves food that was transported in interstate commerce?

HOLDING AND DECISION: (Clark, J.) Yes. Although an activity is local and may not be regarded as commerce, it may still, whatever its nature, be reached by Congress if it exerts a substantial economic effect on interstate commerce. Further, although an individual defendant or plaintiff's own effect on commerce may be slight, if his contribution taken together with that of many others similarly situated is substantial, then that individual's activity may be regulated. Hence, although the amount of food served at Ollie's may be insignificant when compared with the amount of food transported in interstate commerce, and although Ollie's may appear to be local, Congress may still regulate it if there is a rational basis for its finding the Civil Rights Act to be necessary to the protection of commerce. It is true that Congress did not make any formal findings as to the effect upon commerce of racial discrimination in restaurants. However, Congress did conduct prolonged hearings on the Act, and the record is replete with testimony of the burdens placed on commerce by discrimination in restaurants. Diminutive spending by Negroes springing from discrimination

practiced by restaurants, and the total loss of such people as customers has, regardless of the absence of direct evidence, a close connection to interstate commerce. Also there was testimony that discrimination in restaurants had a direct and restrictive effect upon interstate travel by Negroes. This testimony afforded ample basis for the conclusion that restaurants practicing discrimination sold less interstate food, that travel was obstructed, and business in general suffered due to the practice of racial discrimination in restaurants. Hence, Congress had a rational basis for finding that such discrimination had a direct and adverse effect on the free flow of interstate commerce. The Act, as applied to restaurants, and to Ollie's, is constitutional. Reversed.

▶ *ANALYSIS*

Prior to the 1964 Act, the Court had found that general provisions of the Interstate Commerce Act prohibited racial discrimination by interstate carriers. *Henderson v. U.S.*, 339 U.S. 816 (1950), held that these provisions prohibited segregation in railroad dining cars. In *Boynton v. Virginia*, 364 U.S. 454 (1960), the Court reversed a trespass conviction of a black interstate bus passenger who had been refused service at a bus terminal restaurant. Like the Interstate Commerce Act, the National Labor Relations Act and the Railway Labor Act contain no provisions specifically addressed to racial discrimination, and interpretations have made them applicable to the civil rights area. In *Steele v. Louisville and N.R.R.*, 323 U.S. 192 (1944), it was held that a union's status as exclusive bargaining agent under the Railway Labor Act carried the implied duty to represent all members in the bargaining unit without discrimination.

■■■

Quicknotes

INTERSTATE COMMERCE Commercial dealings between two parties located in different states or located in one state and accomplished through a point in another state or a foreign country; commercial dealings transacted between two states.

RATIONAL BASIS REVIEW A test employed by the court to determine the validity of a statute in equal protection actions, whereby the court determines whether the challenged statute is rationally related to the achievement of a legitimate state interest.

■■■

United States v. Lopez

Federal government (P) v. Bearer of gun (D)

514 U.S. 549 (1995).

NATURE OF CASE: Review of order reversing federal firearms conviction.

FACT SUMMARY: A federal law that prohibited possession of a gun near a school was challenged as not authorized under the Commerce Clause.

🏛 RULE OF LAW
A federal law enacted under Commerce Clause authority must substantially affect interstate commerce.

FACTS: In 1990, Congress enacted the Gun-Free School Zones Act (GFSZA), which made it a federal offense to possess a firearm within a school zone. Lopez (D) was convicted under the statute. He appealed, contending that the law, adopted under Commerce Clause authority, exceeded such authority. The Fifth Circuit agreed and reversed. The Supreme Court granted review.

ISSUE: Must federal laws enacted under Commerce Clause authority substantially affect interstate commerce?

HOLDING AND DECISION: (Rehnquist, C.J.) Yes. Federal laws enacted under Commerce Clause authority must substantially affect interstate commerce. As an initial proposition, it must be remembered that the federal government is a government of enumerated powers, not general powers. The extent of legislative power under the Clause must be analyzed under this proposition. The best view of the limits of Commerce Clause power under this standard is that a law passed thereunder must substantially affect interstate commerce to be valid. Under this standard, the GFSZA cannot pass constitutional scrutiny. Simply because education affects interstate commerce, Congress cannot enact all legislation relating thereto. If this standard were used, the powers of the federal government would quickly assume those of a general police power. This is not how the federal government was designed. Consequently, the GFSZA is unconstitutional. Affirmed.

CONCURRENCE: (Thomas, J.) This Court must at some point modify its Commerce Clause jurisprudence, but this case does not require such analysis to be decided.

DISSENT: (Stevens, J.) Commerce is vitally dependent on the education of our nation's children. Accordingly, the GFSZA is constitutional since it relates to interstate commerce.

DISSENT: (Breyer, J.) The power to regulate interstate commerce encompasses the power to regulate local activities that significantly affect interstate commerce.

▶ ANALYSIS

It is textbook constitutional law that state governments possess general powers, and the federal government possesses only enumerated powers. In practice, beginning with the New Deal, the reach of the federal government has grown to something not far from a general power, with the Commerce Clause being the main vehicle for such growth. By the early 1990s, a backlash had begun against increasing federalization, and, as it is well known, the Supreme Court often reads election results.

Quicknotes

COMMERCE CLAUSE Article 1, section 8, clause 3 of the United States Constitution, granting Congress the power to regulate commerce with foreign countries and between the states.

ENUMERATED POWERS Specific powers mentioned in, and granted by, the constitution; e.g., the taxing power.

POLICE POWER The power of a government to impose restrictions on the rights of private persons, as long as those restrictions are reasonably related to the promotion and protection of public health, safety, morals and the general welfare.

United States v. Morrison

Federal government (P) v. Students (D)

529 U.S. 598 (2000).

NATURE OF CASE: Suit alleging sexual assault in violation of the Violence Against Women Act.

FACT SUMMARY: Brzonkala (P) brought suit against two football-playing male students (D) and Virginia Polytechnic Institute under the Violence Against Women Act.

RULE OF LAW
Commerce Clause regulation of intrastate activity may be upheld only where the activity being regulated is economic in nature.

FACTS: Brzonkala (P), a student at Virginia Polytechnic Institute, (Virginia Tech) complained that football-playing students Morrison (D) and Crawford (D) assaulted and repeatedly raped her. Virginia Tech's Judicial Committee found insufficient evidence to punish Crawford (D), but found Morrison (D) guilty of sexual assault and sentenced him to immediate suspension for two semesters. The school's vice president set this aside as excessive punishment. Brzonkala (P) then dropped out of the university and brought suit against the school and the male students (D) under the Violence Against Women Act, 42 U.S.C. § 13981, providing a federal cause of action of a crime of violence motivated by gender.

ISSUE: May Commerce Clause regulation of intrastate activity be upheld only where the activity being regulated is economic in nature?

HOLDING AND DECISION: (Rehnquist, C.J.) Yes. Commerce Clause regulation of intrastate activity may only be upheld where the activity being regulated is economic in nature. The Court considered whether either the Commerce Clause or the Fourteenth Amendment authorized Congress to create this new cause of action. There are three main categories of activity Congress may regulate under its Commerce Clause power: (1) the use of channels of interstate commerce; (2) regulation or protection of the instrumentalities of interstate commerce or persons or things in interstate commerce, though the threat may come from intrastate activities; and (3) the power to regulate those activities having a substantial relation to interstate commerce. Brzonkala (P) argued that § 13981 falls under the third category. In *Lopez*, this Court concluded that those cases in which federal regulation of intrastate activity (based on the activity's substantial effects on interstate commerce) has been sustained have included some type of economic endeavor. Gender motivated crimes of violence are not economic activities. While § 13981 is supported by numerous findings regarding the serious impact that gender-motivated violence has on victims and their families, the existence of congressional findings is not sufficient in itself to sustain the constitutionality of Commerce Clause legislation. Whether a particular activity affects interstate commerce sufficiently to come under the constitutional power of Congress to regulate is a judicial question. The Court also rejects the argument that Congress may regulate noneconomic, violent criminal conduct based solely on that conduct's aggregate effect on interstate commerce. The regulation and punishment of intrastate violence that is not directed at the instrumentalities of interstate commerce is reserved to the states. Brzonkala (P) also argued that § 5 of the Fourteenth Amendment authorized the statutory cause of action. This argument is based on the assertion that there is pervasive bias in various state justice systems against victims of gender-motivated violence. While sex discrimination is one of the objects of the Fourteenth Amendment, the amendment only prohibits state action. Affirmed.

CONCURRENCE: (Thomas, J.) The notion of a substantial effects test is inconsistent with Congress's powers and early Commerce Clause jurisprudence, perpetuating the federal government's (P) view that the Commerce Clause has no limits.

DISSENT: (Souter, J.) Congress has the power to legislate with regard to activities that in the aggregate have a substantial effect on interstate commerce. The fact of the substantial effect is a question for Congress in the first instance and not the courts. Here Congress assembled a mountain of data demonstrating the effects of violence against women on interstate commerce.

DISSENT: (Breyer, J.) Congress, in enacting the statute, followed procedures that work to protect the federalism issues at stake. After considering alternatives, Congress developed the federal law with the intent of compensating for documented deficiencies in state legal systems, and tailored federal law to prevent its use in areas traditionally reserved to the states. This law represents the result of state and federal efforts to cooperate in order to resolve a national problem.

ANALYSIS

The primary issue here is that the federal government is seeking to regulate areas traditionally regulated exclusively by the states. The majority concludes that the regulation and punishment of intrastate violence that is not directed to the instrumentalities of interstate commerce is the

Continued on next page.

exclusive jurisdiction of local government. What the dissent argues here is that Congress in this case has amassed substantial findings to demonstrate that such intrastate violence does have an effect on the instrumentalities of commerce.

■■■

Quicknotes

COMMERCE CLAUSE Article 1, section 8, clause 3 of the United States Constitution, granting Congress the power to regulate commerce with foreign countries and between the states.

INTRASTATE ACTS For purposes of Commerce Clause analysis, refers to activities constituting commerce within a state, as opposed to interstate commerce.

■■■

National League of Cities v. Usery

Cities (P) v. Labor Secretary (D)

426 U.S. 833 (1976).

NATURE OF CASE: Action for declaratory judgment.

FACT SUMMARY: Congress, in 1974, extended the minimum wage and overtime provisions of the Fair Labor Standards Act to cover all state and municipal employees.

🏛 RULE OF LAW

The Tenth Amendment prohibits Congress from enacting any legislation designed to "operate to directly displace the states' freedom to structure integral operations in . . . traditional government functions," and, as such, Congress may not employ the commerce power to interfere with any state activity, the performance of which can be characterized as an "attribute of sovereignty."

FACTS: In 1938, Congress passed the Fair Labor Standards Act to regulate minimum wage and overtime pay in private industry. Commencing in 1961 and culminating in 1974, Congress began to pass amendments to the act extending its provisions to public employees. By 1974, the act had been expressly extended to all public employees of "a state or a political subdivision of a state" among others. Thereupon, the National League of Cities (P) as well as several cities and states, filed this action for a declaratory judgment that such amendments, though theoretically within the commerce power, were unconstitutional violations of the Tenth Amendment. From judgment for Labor Secretary Usery (D), this appeal followed.

ISSUE: May Congress, acting pursuant to the commerce power, regulate the labor market insofar as it concerns state and municipal government employees?

HOLDING AND DECISION: (Rehnquist, J.) No. The Tenth Amendment prohibits Congress from enacting any legislation designed to "operate to directly displace the states' freedom to structure integral operations in traditional governmental functions," and, as such, Congress may not employ the commerce power to interfere with any state activity, the performance of which can be characterized as an "attribute of sovereignty." Though the commerce power is correctly characterized as plenary it is not without other constitutional limitations. One such limitation, the Tenth Amendment, protects the states against any intrusion into sovereign state activities. There can be little doubt that the amendments challenged here interfere with "attributes of sovereignty" of the states. The increased costs to the states coupled with the necessary interference in the delivery of service (which will certainly be occasioned by the work adjustments which these amendments will cause) clearly interferes with the right of the states to manage their own affairs. Reversed.

CONCURRENCE: (Blackmun, J.) The virtual balancing approach adopted today for determining when the commerce power must give way to the Tenth Amendment is essential to federalism.

DISSENT: (Brennan, J.) The majority decision is a great blow to Congress's power under the Commerce Clause. There is no support for this decision in either the Constitution nor in precedent. This Court should practice judicial restraint in this area since this decision upsets the political balance between Congress and the states.

DISSENT: (Stevens, J.) Congress's power to regulate the labor market under the commerce power must extend to state and municipal employees to be effective.

▶ ANALYSIS

This case points up one more example of the Burger Court's policy of restricting federal power while expanding the "sovereign" powers of the states. Note that it overrules the 1968 case of *Maryland v. Wirtz,* 392 U.S. 183 (1968), in which early 1960s amendments to the Fair Labor Standards Act (dealing with extensions of the act to public employees "engaged in commerce" and/or, working in state hospitals, schools, and other institutions) were sustained by the Court under the commerce power. Note also that the rationale of the Court is identical to the later discredited rationale of the early 1930s Court which invalidated much of the early New Deal legislation (*Carter v. Carter Coal Co.,* 298 U.S. 238 (1936), *Hammer v. Dagenhart,* 247 U.S. 251 (1918), *U.S. v. Butler,* 297 U.S. 1 (1936), etc.).

■■■

Quicknotes

FAIR LABOR STANDARDS ACT Enacted in 1938, the statute establishes a minimum wage applicable to all employees of covered employers and provides for mandatory overtime payment for covered employees who work more than 40 hours a week. Executive, administrative and professional employees paid on a salary basis are exempt from the statute.

SOVEREIGNTY The absolute power conferred to the state to govern and regulate all persons located, and activities conducted, therein.

Continued on next page.

TENTH AMENDMENT The tenth amendment to the United States Constitution reserves those powers therein, not expressly delegated to the federal government or prohibited to the states, to the states or to the people.

Garcia v. San Antonio Metropolitan Transit Authority

Federal agency (P) v. Municipal transit authority (D)

469 U.S. 528 (1985).

NATURE OF CASE: Appeal from denial of application of federal labor standards to state operations.

FACT SUMMARY: Garcia (P) appealed from a decision for San Antonio Metropolitan Transit Authority (SAMTA) (D) holding that municipal ownership and operation of a mass transit system is a traditional governmental function and thus, according to the test laid down in National League of Cities v. Usery, 426 U.S. 833 (1976), its system was immune from the requirements of the Fair Labor Standards Act (FLSA).

🏛 RULE OF LAW
The test for determining state immunity from federal regulation under the Commerce Clause is not whether the state activity sought to be regulated is a traditional state function, but rather whether the regulation as applied to the state activity is destructive of state sovereignty or violative of any constitutional provision.

FACTS: San Antonio Metropolitan Transit Authority (SAMTA) (D) is the public mass transit authority that provides transportation in the San Antonio metropolitan area. The Wage and Hour Administration of the Department of Labor (P) found that SAMTA's (D) operations were not immune from the application of the minimum wage and overtime requirements of FLSA. SAMTA (D) filed an action for declaratory judgment, seeking a ruling that pursuant to the earlier decision in *National League of Cities v. Usery*, its activities comprised a traditional governmental function and were thus immune from the requirements of the FLSA. During the appeals of this case, the Supreme Court decided a case that found that the provision of a commuter rail service was not a traditional governmental function and thus did not enjoy constitutional immunity from congressional regulation under the Commerce Clause. The case was remanded to the district court in light of this case, which adhered to its original view and entered judgment in favor of SAMTA (D). From this decision, Garcia (P) appealed.

ISSUE: Does the test for determining whether a state activity is immune from federal regulation under the Commerce Clause continue to include a determination of whether the activity is a traditional state governmental function?

HOLDING AND DECISION: (Blackmun, J.) No. The test for determining state immunity from federal regulation under the Commerce Clause is not whether the state activity sought to be regulated is a traditional governmental function, but rather whether the regulation as applied to the state activity is destructive of state sovereignty or violative of any constitutional provision. The prerequisite for governmental immunity under *National League of Cities v. Usery*, that the federal statute tread on traditional governmental functions, has proved to be an unworkable standard. The *National League* case gave no indication of how to determine whether a function was a traditional or nontraditional one. The decisions of the lower courts, which have made elusive constitutional distinctions in order to find some functions traditional and others nontraditional, indicate the difficulty in applying the standard. This Court has previously rejected the notion that a governmental function could be determined to be traditional on a purely historical basis since this basis does not allow accommodating changes in the historical functions of states. Any distinction that purports to separate out important governmental functions is inconsistent with the role of federalism in a democratic society, which allows states to engage freely in any activity not forbidden to them under the Constitution, since allowing unelected federal judiciaries to determine which functions may be important disserves the principles of democratic self-government. The manner in which the states are insulated from congressional regulation under the Commerce Clause is found in the limitations imposed by the Constitution under Article I and in the structure of the federal government itself, which in giving the states considerable influence over both branches of the Congress and the executive branch, affords the states protection against the unbridled regulation of the federal government under the Commerce Clause. The constitutional scheme developed to protect the "states as states" is thus one of process, not one of result. It is sufficient to say that in the present case the application of the minimum wage and overtime requirements of the FLSA to SAMTA (D) is not destructive of state sovereignty or violative of any constitutional provision, and that therefore SAMTA (D) is not immune from the application of the FLSA. *National League of Cities v. Usery* is overruled. Reversed and remanded.

DISSENT: (Powell, J.) The Court in the present case works a substantial alteration of the federal government and the states, allowing Congress to assume a state's sovereign power free from judicial review.

DISSENT: (O'Connor, J.) State autonomy should be weighed as a factor in the balance when determining whether the means chosen by Congress to regulate the states as states is appropriate. By abandoning *National*

Continued on next page.

League, state sovereignty has been left at the mercy of Congress's as of yet undeveloped capacity for self-restraint.

DISSENT: (Rehnquist, J.) Either approach suggested by the dissents is preferable to the Court's actions in the present case, and under either approach, the judgment of the district court should be affirmed.

▶ *ANALYSIS*

The continuing validity of *National League of Cities v. Usery* had always been in doubt, and the scope of that particular opinion had uncertain limits. For example, it was not clear that Congress would be prohibited from affecting traditional governmental function of the states under various powers delegated to Congress, such as the war power or the civil rights enforcement power, and it was not clear whether that decision would apply to regulatory conditions attached to federal grants disbursed through the spending power.

■━━■

Quicknotes

COMMERCE CLAUSE Article 1, section 8, clause 3 of the United States Constitution, granting Congress the power to regulate commerce with foreign countries and between the states.

FAIR LABOR STANDARDS ACT Enacted in 1938, the statute establishes a minimum wage applicable to all employees of covered employers and provides for mandatory overtime payment for covered employees who work more than 40 hours a week. Executive, administrative and professional employees paid on a salary basis are exempt from the statute.

FEDERALISM A scheme of government whereby the power to govern is divided between a central and localized governments.

IMMUNITY Exemption from a legal obligation.

SOVEREIGNTY The absolute power conferred to the state to govern and regulate all persons located, and activities conducted, therein.

■━━■

New York v. United States

State (P) v. Federal government (D)

505 U.S. 144 (1992).

NATURE OF CASE: Appeal of dismissal of complaint to invalidate a radioactive waste disposal act.

FACT SUMMARY: Instead of complying with the Low-Level Radioactive Waste Policy Act's mandate to enter into a regional compact, New York (P) enacted legislation, providing for the siting and financing of a disposal facility in the state, and challenged the three incentives of the amended Act as violative of the Tenth Amendment.

🏛 RULE OF LAW
While Congress has substantial power under the Constitution to encourage the states to provide for the disposal of the radioactive waste generated within their borders, the Constitution does not confer upon Congress the ability to compel the states to do so.

FACTS: In 1980, Congress (D) enacted the Low-Level Radioactive Waste Policy Act, holding each state responsible for providing for the availability of capacity either within or outside the state for the disposal of low-level radioactive waste generated within its borders. The Act authorized states to enter into regional compacts that would have the authority to restrict the use of their disposal facilities to waste generated within member states. Congress (D) amended the Act in 1985, providing three types of incentives, monetary, disposal site access, and taking title, to encourage the states to comply with their statutory obligation. Rather than join a regional compact, New York (P) enacted legislation, providing for the siting and financing of a disposal facility in the state, and then challenged the three incentives on several grounds. The district court dismissed the complaint, and the court of appeals affirmed. On this appeal, New York (P) claimed only that the Act was inconsistent with the Tenth Amendment and the Guarantee Clause.

ISSUE: While Congress has substantial power under the Constitution to encourage the states to provide for the disposal of the radioactive waste generated within their borders, does the Constitution confer upon Congress the ability to compel the states to do so?

HOLDING AND DECISION: (O'Connor, J.) No. While Congress has substantial power under the Constitution to encourage the states to provide for the disposal of the radioactive waste generated within their borders, the Constitution does not confer upon Congress the ability to compel the states to do so. The Framers chose a Constitution that confers upon Congress (D) the power to regulate individuals, not states. The Act's first set of incentives, in which Congress (D) has conditioned grants to the states upon the states' attainment of a series of milestones, is well within the authority of Congress (D) under the Commerce and Spending Clauses and is therefore not inconsistent with the Tenth Amendment. In the second set of incentives, Congress (D) offered states the choice of regulating private activity, within the scope of the Commerce Clause, according to federal standards, or having state law preempted by federal regulation. This represents a conditional exercise of Congress's (D) commerce power within its authority and thus does not violate the Tenth Amendment. In the third set of incentives, the take title provision offers state governments a choice of either accepting ownership of waste or regulating according to the instructions of Congress (D). Either way, the Act commandeers the legislative processes of the states by directly compelling them to enact and enforce a federal regulatory program, an outcome that does not lie within the authority conferred upon Congress (D) by the Constitution, which only gives Congress (D) the authority to either regulate matters directly or to preempt contrary state regulation. Furthermore, neither of the Act's two acceptable sets of incentives denies any state a republican form of government under the Guarantee Clause. The take title provision may be severed from the rest of the Act, which is still operative and serves Congress's (D) objective of encouraging the states to attain local or regional self-sufficiency in the disposal of low-level radioactive waste. Affirmed in part; reversed in part.

CONCURRENCE AND DISSENT: (White, J.) The take title provision is not unconstitutional, but Congress (D) could adopt a similar measure through its powers under the Spending or Commerce Clauses.

CONCURRENCE AND DISSENT: (Stevens, J.) The notion that Congress (D) does not have the power to issue a simple command to state governments to implement legislation enacted by Congress (D) is incorrect and unsound. There is no such limitation in the Constitution.

▶ ANALYSIS

The Court identifies two methods, short of outright coercion, by which Congress (D) may urge a state to adopt a legislative program consistent with federal interests. First, under its spending power, Congress (D) may attach conditions on the receipt of federal funds. If a state's citizens view federal policy as sufficiently contrary to local interests, they may elect to decline a federal grant.

Continued on next page.

Second, Congress (D) has the power to offer states the choice of regulating private activity according to federal standards or of having state law preempted by federal regulation.

■■■■

Quicknotes

COMMERCE CLAUSE   Article 1, section 8, clause 3 of the United States Constitution, granting Congress the power to regulate commerce with foreign countries and between the states.

SPENDING CLAUSE   The power delegated to Congress by the Constitution to spend money in providing for the nation's welfare.

TENTH AMENDMENT   The tenth amendment to the United States Constitution reserves those powers therein, not expressly delegated to the federal government or prohibited to the states, to the states or to the people.

■■■■

Printz v. United States

Law enforcement officers (P) v. Federal government (D)

521 U.S. 898 (1997).

NATURE OF CASE: Review of judgment upholding the constitutionality of the Brady Act.

FACT SUMMARY: Two chief law enforcement officers (CLEOs) (P) filed actions challenging the constitutionality of several interim provisions of the Brady Act which required that they perform background checks on prospective gun purchasers.

🏛 RULE OF LAW
The federal government may neither issue directives requiring the states to address particular problems, nor command the states' officers, or those of their political subdivisions, to administer or enforce a federal regulatory program.

FACTS: The Gun Control Act of 1968 (GCA) established a detailed federal scheme governing the distribution of firearms. In 1993, Congress amended the GCA by passing the Brady Act, which required the attorney general to establish a national instant background check system by November 30, 1998, and immediately put into place certain interim provisions. The interim provisions required that any firearms dealer who proposed to sell a handgun must receive identifying information from the buyer and provide that information to the chief law enforcement officers (CLEOs) of the buyer's residence. The CLEOs must make a reasonable effort to ascertain within five business days whether receipt or possession of the firearm would be in violation of any local, state, or federal law. Printz (P) and Mack (P), the CLEOs for counties in Montana and Arizona, respectively, filed separate actions challenging the Brady Act's interim provisions. They argued that the congressional action compelling state officers to execute federal laws and pressing them into service was unconstitutional. The Government (D) countered that Congresses have been enacting statutes since the country's formation that required the participation of state officials in the implementation of federal laws. The district courts held that although the provisions were unconstitutional, they were severable from the remainder of the Act. On appeal, the holdings were reversed and all of the interim provisions were found to be constitutional. The Supreme Court granted review.

ISSUE: May the federal government issue directives requiring the states to address particular problems, or command the states' officers, or those of their political subdivisions, to administer or enforce a federal regulatory program?

HOLDING AND DECISION: (Scalia, J.) No. The federal government may neither issue directives requiring

the states to address particular problems, nor command the states' officers, or those of their political subdivisions, to administer or enforce a federal regulatory program. Although early congresses may have been empowered to impress state judges into service, there is no evidence that they commanded the states' executive officers absent a particularized constitutional authorization. More recent federal statutes requiring the participation of state or local officials have been linked with federal funding measures unlike the one at issue here. Furthermore, the structure of the Constitution explicitly confers upon Congress the authority to regulate individuals, not the states. Finally, this Court, as well various circuit and appellate courts, have consistently concluded that Congress may not compel the states to enact or enforce a federal regulatory program. Neither may Congress circumvent this prohibition by issuing directives to conscript state officers directly. Reversed.

CONCURRENCE: (O'Connor, J.) The Court has appropriately refrained from deciding whether other purely ministerial reporting requirements imposed by Congress on state and local authorities pursuant to its Commerce Clause powers are similarly invalid. However, the provisions invalidated in this case utterly fail to adhere to the design and structure of the Constitution.

DISSENT: (Stevens, J.) The Brady Act was passed in response to what Congress described as an "epidemic of gun violence," in essence, a national emergency. When Congress exercises the powers delegated to it by the Constitution, it may impose affirmative obligations on executive and judicial officers of state and local governments as well as ordinary citizens. This conclusion is firmly supported by the text of the Constitution, the early history of the nation, decisions of this Court, and a correct understanding of the basic structure of the federal government.

DISSENT: (Souter, J.) Justice Stevens's dissent was correct in most aspects, but subject to the following qualification. In interpreting Alexander Hamilton's writings in The Federalist No. 27, it seems clear that the state governmental machinery and its officers have always served the auxiliary function of supporting federal law.

▶ ANALYSIS

The majority and dissent both found numerous justifications, from mostly similar sources, of why the Brady Act's provisions should or should not stand. Justice Stevens perhaps brought up the most current and compelling argument: the necessity of addressing a

Continued on next page.

serious and growing national problem. When evaluating a solution to a "national epidemic" it would seem that finding a workable remedy would be most imperative.

■━━■

Quicknotes

COMMERCE CLAUSE Article 1, section 8, clause 3 of the United States Constitution, granting Congress the power to regulate commerce with foreign countries and between the states.

■━━■

The President and Congress

Quick Reference Rules of Law

United States v. Curtiss-Wright Export Corp.

Federal government (P) v. Arms dealer (D)

299 U.S. 304 (1936).

NATURE OF CASE: Appeal from conspiring to sell arms in violation of a Presidential proclamation.

FACT SUMMARY: Curtiss-Wright Export Corp. (Curtiss-Wright) (D) was indicted for conspiracy to sell arms to Bolivia in violation of a Presidential proclamation authorized by a congressional resolution.

🏛 RULE OF LAW
The President of the United States has the power to regulate trade between the United States and foreign nations by proclamation.

FACTS: After both the Senate and the House of Representatives passed a joint resolution to permit the President to prohibit the sale of arms to foreign nations by Presidential proclamation "as he may deem necessary," President Roosevelt issued a proclamation forbidding arms sales to a group of countries including Bolivia. Curtiss-Wright Export Corp. (Curtiss-Wright) (D) arranged to sell 15 machine guns to Bolivia and continued such plans after the proclamation. Thereupon, Curtiss-Wright (D) was indicted for conspiracy to sell arms in violation of the proclamation, despite the fact that Roosevelt had later revoked the proclamation. The revocation contained a provision that liabilities and penalties incurred before the revocation were not extinguished. Curtiss-Wright (D) challenged the power of the President to issue the proclamation on the ground that it was an improper delegation of legislative power to give the President authority to prohibit the gun sales, and that the revocation, despite its language, ended all liability incurred under the proclamation. The court dismissed the indictment.

ISSUE: Has the President of the United States the power to regulate trade between the United States and foreign nations by proclamation?

HOLDING AND DECISION: (Sutherland, J.) Yes. The matter of arms sales to foreign nations is entirely external to the United States and is a matter of foreign affairs. The proposition that the federal government has only those powers enumerated in the Constitution and the implied powers necessary to carry them out is applicable to internal affairs. In matters of foreign affairs, the President is the sole organ of the federal government and speaks for the nation as a whole. His power is not conditioned in this area upon any act of Congress, but is a plenary power, exclusive to him. When the Congress, by resolution, authorizes the President to exercise such a power, further support is lent to the acts of the President, though he may act in the absence of such support from the legislature. The President

of the United States has the power to regulate trade between the United States and foreign nations by proclamation. Reversed.

▶ ANALYSIS

The President has powers in the realm of foreign affairs that he is without in the area of internal affairs. This is the expected and obvious result of the necessity of the country's speaking with one voice to other countries. In internal matters, where the President and the Congress have no constitutionally granted power, the Tenth Amendment reserves the power for the states.

■━■

Quicknotes

CONSPIRACY Concerted action by two or more persons to accomplish some unlawful purpose.

ENUMERATED POWERS Specific powers mentioned in, and granted by, the constitution; e.g., the taxing power.

IMPLIED POWERS Powers impliedly delegated to the various branches of government that, while not expressly stated in the Constitution, are necessary to effectuate the enumerated powers.

PLENARY Unlimited and open; as broad as a given situation may require.

PROCLAMATION A public announcement, written or otherwise presented, that gives notice of a governmental act that has been or is being done; a declaration usually made by a bailiff or other governmental authority.

■━■

Youngtown Sheet & Tube Co. v. Sawyer

Steel company (P) v. Secretary of Commerce (D)

343 U.S. 579 (1952).

NATURE OF CASE: Suit for declaratory and injunctive relief from a presidential order.

FACT SUMMARY: Faced with an imminent steel strike during the Korean War, the President ordered governmental seizure of the steel companies to prevent the strike. The companies challenged his power to take such action as being without constitutional authority or prior congressional approval.

RULE OF LAW
The President, as leader of the Executive Branch, is bound to enforce the laws within the limits of the authority expressly granted to him by the Constitution and he cannot usurp the lawmaking power of Congress by an assertion of an unspecified aggregation of his specified powers.

FACTS: As a result of long, but unsuccessful, negotiations with various steel companies, the United Steel Workers of America served notice of an intent to strike in April, 1952. Through the last months of the negotiating the President had utilized every available administrative remedy to effect a settlement and avert a strike. Congress had engaged in extensive debate on solutions but had passed no legislation on the issue. By order of the President, the Secretary of Commerce (D) seized the steel companies so that steel production would not be interrupted during the Korean War. The steel companies (P) sued in federal district court to have the seizure order declared invalid and to enjoin its enforcement. The Government (D) asserted that the President had "inherent power" to make the order and that it was "supported by the Constitution, historical precedent, and court decisions." The district court granted a preliminary injunction which was stayed the same day by the court of appeals. The Supreme Court granted certiorari and ordered immediate argument.

ISSUE: May the President, relying on a concept of inherent powers, and in his capacity as Commander-in-Chief, make an order which usurps the lawmaking authority of Congress on the basis of a compelling need to protect the national security?

HOLDING AND DECISION: (Black, J.) No. There is, admittedly, no express congressional authority for these seizures, and so, if any authority for the President's act can be found, it must come from the Constitution. In the absence of express authority for the President's act, it is that the power can be implied from the aggregate of his express powers granted by the Constitution. This order cannot be justified by reliance on the President's role as Commander-in-Chief. Even though

the term "theater of war" has enjoyed an expanding definition, it cannot embrace the taking of private property to prevent a strike. The President's powers in the area of legislation are limited to proposing new laws to Congress or vetoing laws which he deems inadvisable. This order is not executive implementation of a congressional act but a legislative act performed by the President. Only Congress may do what the President has attempted here. The Constitution is specific in vesting the lawmaking powers in Congress and we, therefore, affirm the district court's decision to enjoin the enforcement of this order.

CONCURRENCE: (Frankfurter, J.) This decision does not attempt to define the limits of presidential authority. The President cannot act in contravention of an express congressional act nor may he act where Congress has done nothing. Were this a case of a long history of congressional acquiescence to presidential practice our decision might be different, but no such showing has been made.

CONCURRENCE: (Douglas, J.) It is unquestioned that the situation produced by the suspension of steel production bore heavily upon the country, but it did not create the power that the President sought to exercise. While the President may act and obtain the later ratification of Congress so as to validate that action, the act is not lawful unless and until Congress has so ratified.

CONCURRENCE: (Jackson, J.) When the President acts with the authority expressly granted by Congress he has all the power of the Presidency plus all that Congress has delegated to him. Without congressional sanction, however, he acts on his own independent powers only, the boundaries of which must be tested by the imperatives of the contemporary events rather than abstract legal theories. When he acts inconsistently with the express or implied will of Congress, the President has the least power. It is with this level of power only that the President acted in this case. The need for steel for the efforts of the United States in the Korean conflict did not give the President mastery over the internal affairs of the country.

CONCURRENCE: (Clark, J.) Congress has prescribed the measures necessary to meet the emergencies of this nature and I cannot find any justification to sanction deviation from those measures.

ANALYSIS

Justice Black's broad language was criticized by many scholars as being overly expansive for the case presented.

Continued on next page.

However, other authorities pointed out that the broad arguments advanced by the government required a broad response. During oral argument before the Court, the government counsel stated that while the Constitution imposed limits on congressional and judicial powers, no such limits were imposed on the presidency. While supplemental briefs were filed modifying this position, the damage may already have been done. The Court was faced with a paucity of judicial precedents. The President and Congress have traditionally preferred political rather than judicial solutions to their conflicts. This practice avoids the limitations imposed on future actions by binding judicial precedents. And, as can be seen by the cases of *Marbury v. Madison*, 5 U.S. 137 (1803), and *United States v. Nixon*, 418 U.S. 683 (1974), the executive branch has not fared well when it has submitted to judicial jurisdiction.

■══■

Quicknotes

INHERENT POWERS Authority originating from a government or sovereign source, beyond those explicitly granted in the Constitution; power that is necessary for the proper administration of official duty.

TAKING A governmental action that substantially deprives an owner of the use and enjoyment of his or her property, requiring compensation.

■══■

Rasul v. Bush

Foreign-national detainee (P) v. President of the United States (D)

542 U.S. 466 (2004).

NATURE OF CASE: Appeal from the dismissal of petitions for habeas corpus for lack of jurisdiction.

FACT SUMMARY: U.S. military forces captured 14 foreign nationals during military operations in Afghanistan following the terrorist attacks of September 11, 2001. U.S. forces then held the foreign nationals for more than two years, without charging them or permitting them access to either counsel or courts, at the U.S. naval base at Guantanamo Bay, Cuba.

🏛 **RULE OF LAW**
Federal courts have jurisdiction under 28 U.S.C. 2241 to hear habeas petitions filed by foreign nationals who are being held outside the sovereign territory of the United States if the United States nonetheless exercises exclusive jurisdiction over the site of the detention.

FACTS: U.S. military forces invaded Afghanistan after the terrorist attacks on the United States on September 11, 2001. During the military operations in Afghanistan, U.S. forces captured some 640 foreign nationals and transported them, for purposes of detention, to the U.S. naval base at Guantanamo Bay, Cuba. U.S. forces at Guantanamo Bay then held the foreign nationals, including the 14 petitioners (P) in these consolidated cases, for more than two years; the detentions did not permit detainees access to formal charges, consultation with counsel, or any tribunal that could decide the legality of the detentions. Although Guantanamo Bay obviously was not within the sovereign territory of the United States, U.S. forces occupied the naval base there pursuant to a 1903 lease agreement and a 1934 treaty that, together, granted the United States exclusive jurisdiction over the naval base potentially in perpetuity. Relatives of 14 detainees (P) filed suit on behalf of the 14 detainees (P) in the U.S. District Court for the District of Columbia, alleging that the detainees (P) were being held in violation of U.S. law. The trial court dismissed all petitions, treating them as petitions for habeas corpus that were controlled by *Johnson v. Eisentrager*, 339 U.S. 763 (1950). The court of appeals affirmed, also holding that *Eisentrager* required dismissal for lack of jurisdiction. The 14 detainees (P) sought further review in the U.S. Supreme Court.

ISSUE: Do federal courts have jurisdiction under 28 U.S.C. 2241 to hear habeas petitions filed by foreign nationals who are being held outside the sovereign territory of the United States if the United States nonetheless exercises exclusive jurisdiction over the site of the detention?

HOLDING AND DECISION: (Stevens, J.) Yes. Federal courts have jurisdiction under 28 U.S.C. 2241 to hear habeas petitions filed by foreign nationals who are being held outside the sovereign territory of the United States if the United States nonetheless exercises exclusive jurisdiction over the site of the detention. *Eisentrager* differs from this case in several important respects. First, *Eisentrager* decided constitutional rights, whereas 28 U.S.C. 2241 squarely governs this case. Furthermore, the detainees (P) here differ substantially from their counterparts in *Eisentrager*: these detainees (P) are not nationals of countries with whom the United States is at war, these petitioners deny that they have engaged in any form of aggression against the United States, these petitioners have had no access to any tribunal, and the United States exercises exclusive jurisdiction over the site of these detainees' (P) detention. Since Bush (D) concedes that U.S. citizens in Guantanamo Bay could file habeas petitions like those at issue in this case, and since the habeas statute does not distinguish between citizens and noncitizens, foreign nationals detained outside the United States at a site under the exclusive control of the United States also may invoke the jurisdiction of federal courts under 28 U.S.C. 2241. Reversed.

CONCURRENCE: (Kennedy, J.) Two key distinctions remove this case from *Eisentrager*: the site of the detentions here is for all practical purposes the territory of the United States, and the detentions are for an indefinite duration. The argument for such detentions based on military need only weakens with the passage of time. This more flexible approach is consistent with *Eisentrager* while also avoiding finding an automatic statutory grant of jurisdiction for claims filed by foreign nationals who are held outside the United States.

DISSENT: (Scalia, J.) The Court's unprecedented ruling ignores the plain text of 28 U.S.C. 2241, which clearly requires that a court hearing a habeas petition have territorial jurisdiction over the detainee who files the petition. No federal district court has territorial jurisdiction over Guantanamo Bay, and the petitions in this case were therefore correctly dismissed. Further, *Eisentrager* itself distinguished the portion of the majority's rationale that is based on the possibility of U.S. citizens filing habeas petitions in similar circumstances. Today's holding will have apparently unlimited consequences: now, any foreign national captured overseas can legitimately challenge his detention in any federal district court. One strange result of this case is that wartime prisoners have greater rights than do domestic detainees—because domestic detainees

Continued on next page.

must sue in the district in which their detentions occur. Such a countertextual decision, especially when it is rendered in a time of war, represents the worst abuse of judicial restraint.

▶ *ANALYSIS*

As excerpted in the casebook, Justice Scalia's dissent in *Rasul* misses the key point of contact between Justice Stevens's opinion for the majority and Justice Kennedy's concurrence. The common basis for the majority and Justice Kennedy was the fact that the naval base at Guantanamo Bay was within the exclusive jurisdiction and control of the United States, even though the base clearly was not within the sovereign territory of the United States. Contrary to Justice Scalia's expressed fears, that common rationale seems to place a significant limitation on similar suits: such suits will lie under *Rasul* only if the site of the detention is within the exclusive jurisdiction and control of the United States.

■══■

Quicknotes

HABEAS CORPUS   A proceeding in which a defendant brings a writ to compel a judicial determination of whether he is lawfully being held in custody.

■══■

Hamdi v. Rumsfeld

Alleged enemy combatant (P) v. Secretary of Defense (D)

542 U.S. 507 (2004).

NATURE OF CASE: Appeal from the denial of right to challenge enemy-combatant status.

FACT SUMMARY: Hamdi (P), an American citizen designated as an enemy-combatant, argued that he was entitled to contest such designation in court.

🏛 RULE OF LAW
Due process requires that a citizen held in the United States as an enemy combatant be given a meaningful opportunity to contest the factual basis for that detention before a neutral decisionmaker.

FACTS: Hamdi (P), an American citizen, was designated by the Government (D) an "enemy combatant" and placed into indefinite detainment. The federal court of appeals held the detention to be legally authorized and that Hamdi (P) was entitled to no further opportunity to challenge his enemy-combatant label. Hamdi (P) appealed to the United States Supreme Court.

ISSUE: Does due process require that a citizen held in the United States as an enemy combatant be given a meaningful opportunity to contest the factual basis for that detention before a neutral decisionmaker?

HOLDING AND DECISION: (O'Connor, J.) Yes. Due process requires that a citizen held in the United States as an enemy combatant be given a meaningful opportunity to contest the factual basis for that detention before a neutral decisionmaker. It is vital not to give short shrift to the values that this country holds dear or to the privilege that is American citizenship. At the same time, the exigencies of the circumstances may demand that, as here, aside from certain core elements, enemy combatant proceedings may be tailored to alleviate their uncommon potential to burden the Executive Branch at a time of ongoing military conflict. Hearsay, for example, may need to be accepted as the most reliable available evidence from the government (D) in such a proceeding. Furthermore, even a burden-shifting scheme in which credible government evidence is presumed true would not offend the Constitution so long as such presumption remains a rebuttable one and fair opportunity for rebuttal is provided. The parties agree that initial captures on the battlefield need not receive the full range of constitutional guarantees. While the Court accords the greatest respect and consideration to the judgments of military authorities in matters relating to the actual prosecution of a war, and recognizes that the scope of that discretion is necessarily wide, it does not infringe on the core role of the military for the courts to exercise their own time-honored and constitutionally

mandated roles of reviewing and resolving claims such as those present here. A state of war is not a blank check for the President when it comes to the rights of the nation's citizens. Vacated and remanded.

CONCURRENCE AND DISSENT IN PART: (Souter, J.) The government (D) has failed to demonstrate that the Force Resolution authorizes the detention complained of here, even on the facts the government (D) claims. If the government (D) raises nothing further than the record now shows, the Non-Detention Act entitles Hamdi (P) to be released. The branch of government asked to counter a serious threat is not the branch on which to rest the Nation's entire reliance in striking the balance between the will to win and "the cost in liberty on the way to victory."

DISSENT: (Scalia, J.) If civil rights are to be curtailed during wartime, it must be done openly and democratically, as the Constitution requires, rather than by silent erosion through an opinion of the Court. Whatever the merits of the view that war silences law or modulates its voice, such view has no place in the interpretation and application of a Constitution designed precisely to confront war and, in a manner that accords with democratic principles, to accommodate it.

DISSENT: (Thomas, J.) The Executive Branch, acting pursuant to powers vested in the President by the Constitution and by explicit congressional approval, has determined that Hamdi (P) is an enemy combatant and should be detained. This detention falls squarely within the war powers of the federal government, and the Court lacks the expertise and capacity to second-guess such decision. Accordingly, Hamdi's (P) habeas challenge should fail, and there is no reason to remand the case.

▶ ANALYSIS

As made clear in the *Hamdi* decision, in cases of this type the Court must balance two vital yet competing interests: on the one hand, respect for separation of powers and the fundamental importance of the nation to be able to protect itself during time of war; on the other hand, the critical and deep-seated individual constitutional interests at stake.

■═■

Quicknotes

DUE PROCESS CLAUSE Clauses found in the Fifth and Fourteenth Amendments to the United States

Continued on next page.

Constitution providing that no person shall be deprived of "life, liberty, or property, without due process of law."

SEPARATION OF POWERS The system of checks and balances preventing one branch of government from infringing upon exercising the powers of another branch of government.

■═■

Missouri v. Holland

State (P) v. Game warden (D)

252 U.S. 416 (1920).

NATURE OF CASE: An action in equity to enjoin the enforcement of the Migratory Bird Treaty Act.

FACT SUMMARY: Missouri (P) claimed that the Bird Treaty Act was an unconstitutional interference with the rights reserved to the states by the Tenth Amendment.

🏛 RULE OF LAW
Congress can constitutionally enact a statute under Article I, § 8, to enforce a treaty created under Article II, § 2, even if the statute by itself is unconstitutional.

FACTS: On December 8, 1916, the United States entered into a treaty with Great Britain to protect birds that migrated between Canada and the United States. Congress passed a statute to enforce the Migratory Bird Treaty which allowed the Secretary of Agriculture to formulate regulations to enforce the treaty. The State of Missouri (P) filed a bill in equity to prevent Holland (D), the game warden of the United States, from enforcing the treaty. Missouri (P) claimed that the statute was an unconstitutional interference with the rights reserved to the states by the Tenth Amendment and that it had a pecuniary interest as owner of the wild birds which were being interfered with. Before the treaty had been entered into, Congress had attempted to regulate the killing of migratory birds within the states and that statute, standing by itself, had been declared unconstitutional. The United States contended that Congress had the power to enact the statute to enforce the treaty and that the statute and treaty were the supreme law of the land.

ISSUE: Can Congress validly enact a statute to enforce a treaty if the statute standing by itself would be unconstitutional because it interfered with the rights reserved to the states by the Tenth Amendment?

HOLDING AND DECISION: (Holmes, J.) Yes. Article II, § 2 grants the President the power to make treaties and Article VI, § 2 declares that treaties shall be part of the supreme law of the land. If a treaty is a valid one, Article I, § 8, gives Congress the power to enact legislation that is a necessary and proper means to enforce the treaty. While acts of Congress are the supreme law of the land only when they are made in pursuance of the Constitution, treaties are valid when made under the authority of the United States. The Court stated that there were qualifications to the treaty-making power, but felt that the qualifications must be determined by looking at the facts of each case. There are situations that require national action which an act of Congress could not deal with, but which a treaty enforced with a congressional act could. Because Missouri (P) did not have the power to adequately control the problem connected with the migratory birds (nor did any other state acting alone), this was a situation which required national action. Therefore, even though Missouri (P) would have been able to establish regulations pertaining to the birds if Congress had not already done so, Congress could establish regulations in conjunction with the treaty without infringing on the rights reserved to the states by the Tenth Amendment. The Court rejected Missouri's (P) claim that it had a pecuniary interest as an owner when the birds were in the state. There is no ownership until there is possession and the birds never came into the possession of the State of Missouri (P). Congress can, therefore, constitutionally enact a statute under Article I, § 8, to enforce a treaty even if the statute by itself would be unconstitutional. Affirmed.

▶ ANALYSIS

Many people were upset with the decision in this case because they feared that the Court had interpreted the treaty power so broadly that all constitutional limitations could be overridden by the use of treaties and accompanying congressional legislation. In 1954, the Bricker Amendment was narrowly defeated which required that a treaty could only become effective as internal law in the United States through legislation which would be valid in the absence of the treaty. This would have, in effect, overruled the decision in this case, because the congressional act was not valid when standing by itself. Several other similar proposals were made during the following three years, which also failed.

Quicknotes

EQUITY Fairness; justice; the determination of a matter consistent with principles of fairness and not in strict compliance with rules of law.

TENTH AMENDMENT The tenth amendment to the United States Constitution reserves those powers therein, not expressly delegated to the federal government or prohibited to the states, to the states or to the people.

TREATY An agreement between two or more nations for the benefit of the general public.

Whitney v. Robertson

Merchant (P) v. Customs officer (D)

124 U.S. 190 (1888).

NATURE OF CASE: Action to recover customs duties.

FACT SUMMARY: Whitney (P), a merchant, claimed that sugar he imported from the Dominican Republic should have been free from customs payments.

🏛 RULE OF LAW
Treaties, like acts of legislation, are the supreme law of the land.

FACTS: In August 1882, Whitney (P) imported a large quantity of molasses sugars from the Dominican Republic. These goods were similar in kind to sugars produced in the Hawaiian Islands, which were admitted free of duty under a treaty with the King of those islands and an act of Congress, passed to carry the treaty into effect. Whitney (P) claimed that by a treaty with the Dominican Republic, the goods should have been admitted free of duty. Robertson (D), who was at the time Collector of the port of New York, refused to allow the claim, treated the goods as dutiable articles under the acts of Congress, and exacted duties on them in the amount of $21,936.

ISSUE: Are treaties, like acts of legislation, the supreme law of the land?

HOLDING AND DECISION: (Field, J.) Yes. By the Constitution, a treaty is placed on the same footing, and made of like obligation, with an act of legislation. Both are declared by that instrument to be the supreme law of the land. When the two relate to the same subject, the courts will always endeavor to construe them so as to give effect to both, if that can be done without violating the language of either; but if the two are inconsistent, the one last in date will control the other, provided always the stipulation of the treaty on the subject is self-executing. Here, the act of Congress under which the duties were collected authorized their exaction. It is of general application, making no exception in favor of goods of any country. It was passed after the treaty with the Dominican Republic, and, if there is any conflict between the stipulations of the treaty and the requirements of the law, the latter must control.

▶ ANALYSIS

The Restatement view is contrary to the position taken in this case. It provides that "the superseding of (a self-executing treaty) as domestic law of the United States by subsequent act of Congress does not affect the international obligations of the United States under the (treaty)."

See, Restatement (Second), Foreign Relations Law of the United States, § 145(2) (A.L.I. 1965).

Quicknotes

CUSTOMS Federal agency responsible for assessing imported goods collecting duties.

TREATY An agreement between two or more nations for the benefit of the general public.

Goldwater v. Carter

Senator (P) v. President (D)

444 U.S. 996 (1979).

NATURE OF CASE: Abrogation of treaty.

FACT SUMMARY: Goldwater (P) challenged the authority of President Carter (D) to unilaterally terminate a mutual defense treaty with Taiwan.

🏛 RULE OF LAW
The abrogation of a treaty is a nonjusticiable political question.

FACTS: President Carter (D) gave unilateral notice of the termination of the mutual defense treaty to Taiwan, to be effective on January 1, 1980, pursuant to the termination clause contained in the treaty allowing either party to terminate with one year's notice. Several senators, including Goldwater (P), and several members of the House sued for declaratory and injunctive relief, claiming that the President (D) may not terminate the treaty without legislative participation. The circuit court reversed the district court, which had held that the President's (D) notice of termination was ineffective unless two-thirds of the Senate, or a majority of both Houses, approved.

ISSUE: Is the abrogation of a treaty a nonjusticiable political question?

HOLDING AND DECISION: (Rehnquist, J.) Yes. The basic question presented by Goldwater (P) in this case is "political" and therefore nonjusticiable because it involves the authority of the President (D) in the conduct of our country's foreign relations, and the extent to which the Senate or Congress is authorized to negate the action of the President (D). Because the Constitution is silent as to the Senate's participation in the abrogation of a treaty, the instant case must be controlled by political standards. Accordingly, the prior proceedings in the federal courts must be vacated. Vacated and remanded with directions to dismiss the complaint.

CONCURRENCE: (Powell, J.) The present dispute between Congress and the President (D) is not ripe for judicial review, because Congress has not yet taken any official actions to assert its constitutional authority. Further, the present case is not a political question, because there is no lack of judicially discoverable and manageable standards for resolving this case; nor is a decision impossible without an initial policy determination of a kind clearly for nonjudicial discretion.

DISSENT: (Blackmun, J.) The present case should have been fully adjudicated, because it is indefensible, without further study, to pass on the issues of presidential power to terminate a treaty, justiciability, standing, and ripeness.

DISSENT: (Brennan, J.) The issue of decision-making authority must be resolved as a matter of constitutional law, not political discretion. It is well established that the Constitution commits to the President (D) alone the power to recognize, and withdraw recognition from, foreign regimes.

▶ ANALYSIS

The majority holds that the issues presented constitute a political question because the Constitution makes no provision for Senate participation in the abrogation of treaties. This view stems from an earlier case, where the issue of rejection of constitutional amendments by state legislatures was held to be a political question. See, *Coleman v. Miller*, 307 U.S. 433 (1939).

■=■

Quicknotes

JUSTICIABILITY An actual controversy that is capable of determination by the court.

POLITICAL QUESTION An issue that is more appropriately left to the determination of another governmental branch and which the court declines to hear.

RIPENESS A doctrine precluding a federal court from hearing or determining a matter, unless it constitutes an actual and present controversy warranting a determination by the court.

STANDING Whether a party possesses the right to commence suit against another party by having a personal stake in the resolution of the controversy.

TREATY An agreement between two or more nations for the benefit of the general public.

■=■

United States v. Pink

Federal government (P) v. Superintendent of Insurance (D)

315 U.S. 203 (1942).

NATURE OF CASE: Review of state court order directing disposition of assets.

FACT SUMMARY: While Pink (D), the Superintendent of Insurance for New York, held assets of the First Russian Insurance Co. deposited by First Russian in order to do business in New York, the Russian government nationalized all Russian property. Pink (D), who paid off certain claims of American citizens against First Russian, was ordered by the New York Court of Appeals to pay the remainder to the Board of Directors of First Russian despite an assignment to the United States (P) of certain unpaid claims by the newly recognized Russian government.

RULE OF LAW
When the President of the United States enters into an international agreement with a recognized foreign government, the agreement is given effect despite any order from any state court to the contrary.

FACTS: Pursuant to a New York statute, First Russian had deposited certain assets with Pink (D) in order to do business in New York. First Russian had claims outstanding against it held by both Americans and foreign entities. While First Russian was in operation in its New York branch office, the Russian government nationalized all Russian property wherever situated. The President of the United States entered into an agreement with the Russian government known as the "Litvinov Assignment," whereby certain claims were assigned to the Government (P). After Pink (D) had paid First Russian's American creditors, the court of appeals ordered the remainder to be paid to the Board of Directors of First Russian. The Government (P) brought this action to enjoin such payment and to claim the assets assigned by the international agreement, and then appealed the New York Court of Appeals ruling in favor of Pink (D).

ISSUE: When the President of the United States enters into an international agreement with a recognized foreign government, is the agreement given effect despite orders from state courts to the contrary?

HOLDING AND DECISION: (Douglas, J.) Yes. Recognition of a foreign sovereign conclusively binds the courts, and in this case, the Russian government was so recognized and the Litvinov Assignment was drawn up as one transaction. The assignment was an international compact. The power of the Government (P) in matters of external or foreign affairs may be exercised without regard to state laws or policies. The agreement reached here gave no right to First Russian to collect any part of the assets held by Pink (D) and furthermore assigned those assets to the Government (P). Since the President had the power to make the agreement, and the states have no power to override it, the New York Court of Appeals was without power to make its orders. When the President of the United States enters into an international agreement with a recognized foreign government, the agreement is given effect despite any order from any state court to the contrary. Reversed and remanded.

► ANALYSIS

The aftermath of the Russian Revolution did not inspire much faith in the Russian government in the minds of many Americans, nor in the courts of the State of New York. However, when President Roosevelt and the Russian government completed the Litvinov Assignment, this attitude became irrelevant. The President's power to engage the nation in executive international agreements is superior to any policy of any state.

Quicknotes

ASSIGNMENT A transaction in which a party conveys his or her entire interest in property to another.

Dames & Moore v. Regan

Assignee (P) v. Secretary of Treasury (D)

453 U.S. 654 (1981).

NATURE OF CASE: Appeal from denial of injunction against enforcement of Executive Order.

FACT SUMMARY: Dames & Moore (Dames) (P) was the assignee of a contract with Iran's government under which Iran owed Dames (P) nearly $3.5 million secured by a prejudgment attachment of Iranian assets located in the United States. Upon the release by Iran of American hostages, President Reagan ratified an Executive Order by President Carter to free Iranian assets from all attachments for submission to a Claims Tribunal, and the sheriff thus refused to execute on Iranian assets securing Dames' (P) claim.

> 🏛 **RULE OF LAW**
> The President may nullify attachments on foreign assets and can authorize the suspension of claims against such assets pending in the American courts.

FACTS: Dames & Moore (Dames) (P) was the assignee of certain contract rights held by one of its subsidiaries. These rights were pursuant to a contract with the Iranian government for work performed toward the building of a nuclear power plant there. Under the contract, Iran owed Dames (P) some $3.5 million. Dames (P) filed suit in federal district court and obtained an attachment of Iranian assets in the United States to secure its claim. After the attachment, but before judgment or execution, the American embassy officials being held as hostages by Iran were released, prompting an Executive Order by President Carter and later ratified by President Reagan, to release Iranian assets from all attachments for submission to a Claims Tribunal. The sheriff then refused to execute on the assets securing Dames' (P) claim, even though Dames (P) had obtained summary judgment against Iran in the district court. Dames (P) filed a suit in the district court for a preliminary injunction against the United States and the Secretary of the Treasury (D) to prevent enforcement of the Executive Order. The petition was denied and Dames (P) appealed.

ISSUE: May the President nullify attachments on foreign assets and authorize the suspension of claims against such assets pending in the American courts?

HOLDING AND DECISION: (Rehnquist, J.) Yes. While no statutory congressional authority gave the President the power to suspend the claims against Iranian assets pending in the American courts, the general tenor of the measures enacted by Congress (the Hostage Act and the International Emergency Economic Powers Act) make it clear that the President was acting with the acceptance of

Congress. Congress is not able to enact legislation on every act it contemplates that the President will do to enforce the laws. But here Congress has implicitly approved the President's action by enacting the International Claims Settlement Act and amending it in 1980 in the wake of the Iranian crisis. This Act permits the settlement of claims against foreign assets in situations of this type. Thus, the President may nullify attachments on foreign assets and authorize the suspension of claims against such assets pending in the American courts. Since Congress has acquiesced in the President's action, he may settle the claims. Affirmed.

CONCURRENCE: (Stevens, J.) There is only a remote chance that requiring Dames (P) to litigate his claim in another forum will constitute a "taking" and so this question need not be reached. The rest of the majority opinion is correct.

CONCURRENCE IN PART: (Powell, J.) The nullification of attachments on assets securing Dames' (P) claim may constitute a taking of property. However, the majority is correct in holding that the President has the power to further the interest of the nation's foreign policy in the manner here implemented.

▶ *ANALYSIS*

Part of the "deal" which led to the release of the American hostages was the freeing of Iranian assets frozen by President Carter. It was essential to the integrity of the government's promise that it not "loophole" its way out of the promise by what might be considered by Iran as a legal technicality. Note that the claims were not destroyed or impaired, but simply moved for adjudication to another forum. Nonetheless, the possibility that the full claim in each case might not be paid, the administrative inconvenience of suing elsewhere, and the fact that Dames (P) had already completed its litigation successfully, all raised a question of fairness under this plan.

■=■

Quicknotes

ATTACHMENT The seizing of the property of one party in anticipation of, or in order to satisfy, a favorable judgment obtained by another party.

EXECUTIVE ORDER An order issued by the President, or another executive of government, which has the force of law.

Continued on next page.

TAKING A governmental action that substantially deprives an owner of the use and enjoyment of his or her property, requiring compensation.

Galvan v. Press

Resident alien (D) v. Government (P)

347 U.S. 522 (1954).

NATURE OF CASE: Appeal from dismissal of petition for writ of habeas corpus.

FACT SUMMARY: Galvan (D), a resident alien, was ordered deported for past membership in the Communist Party.

🏛 RULE OF LAW
Congress has broad powers over the admission and deportation of aliens.

FACTS: Galvan (D), an alien of Mexican birth who had resided in the United States since 1918, admitted during questioning by the Immigration and Naturalization Service in March 1948, that he had been a member of the Communist Party from 1944 to 1946. Pursuant to the Internal Security Act of 1950, which was enacted by Congress, Galvan (D) was ordered deported for past membership in the Communist Party. During the period of his membership, the Communist Party functioned as an active political organization, and no federal law then forbade Communist Party political activities. The Ninth Circuit Court of Appeals sustained the denial by the district court of Galvan's (D) petition for a writ of habeas corpus.

ISSUE: Does Congress have broad powers over the admission and deportation of aliens?

HOLDING AND DECISION: (Frankfurter, J.) Yes. The power of Congress over the admission of aliens and their right to remain is necessarily very broad, touching as it does upon basic aspects of national security. An alien, however, does have the same protection for his life, liberty, and property under the Due Process Clause as is afforded to a citizen. Even though deportation is a drastic measure, Congress has the exclusive authority to formulate the policies governing its use. Because of the wide powers given to Congress, and the fact that the ex post facto clause does not apply to deportation, the judgment below must be affirmed.

DISSENT: (Black, J.) For joining a lawful political group years ago—an act which he had no possible reason to believe would subject him to the slightest penalty—Galvan (D) now loses his job, his friends, his home, and maybe even his children, who must choose between their father and their native country. And this is to be done without proof or finding that Galvan (D) knew that the Communist Party had any evil purposes, or that he agreed with any such purposes that it might have had.

▶ ANALYSIS

In the present case, the Court held that the Internal Security Act of 1950 did not violate due process. The Act penalized aliens merely for joining the Communist Party. Under the Act, support or even demonstrated knowledge of the Communist Party's advocacy of violence was not intended to be a prerequisite for deportation.

Quicknotes

DUE PROCESS CLAUSE Clauses found in the Fifth and Fourteenth Amendments to the United States Constitution providing that no person shall be deprived of "life, liberty, or property, without due process of law."

EX POST FACTO After the fact; A law that makes criminal activity or increases the punishment for a crime that occurred, or eliminates a defense that was available to the defendant, prior to its passage.

WRIT OF HABEAS CORPUS A proceeding in which a defendant brings a writ to compel a judicial determination of whether he is lawfully being held in custody.

Fiallo v. Bell

Parent (P) v. Government (D)

430 U.S. 787 (1977).

NATURE OF CASE: Action challenging provisions of the Immigration and Nationality Act (INA).

FACT SUMMARY: Fiallo (P), an unwed natural father, and his illegitimate offspring challenged provisions of the INA, denying him preferential treatment as a parent.

RULE OF LAW
Congress has broad powers to expel or exclude aliens.

FACTS: The INA granted special preference immigration status to aliens who qualified as the children or parents of United States citizens or lawful permanent residents. The definition did not extend to an illegitimate child seeking preference by virtue of his relationship with his natural father. The natural father of an illegitimate child who is either a United States citizen or permanent resident alien is not entitled to preferential treatment as a parent. Fiallo (P), an unwed natural father, and his illegitimate offspring, contending that these provisions of the INA were unconstitutional, sought to enjoin permanently enforcement of the challenged statutory provisions to the extent that the statute precluded them from qualifying for the special preference accorded other parents and children.

ISSUE: Does Congress have broad powers to expel or exclude aliens?

HOLDING AND DECISION: (Powell, J.) Yes. The power to expel or exclude aliens as a fundamental sovereign attribute exercised by the government's political departments is largely immune from judicial control. The conditions of entry for every alien, the particular classes of aliens that shall be denied entry altogether, the basis for determining such classification, the right to terminate hospitality to aliens, the grounds on which such determination shall be based, have been recognized as matters solely for the responsibility of the Congress, and wholly outside the power of the Supreme Court to control. Here, Congress exercised its discretion for a facially legitimate and bona fide reason, and its determination must be upheld.

▶ ANALYSIS

In an earlier case which illustrates the broad congressional powers in the field of immigration and nationality, the United States sought to exclude without a hearing the alien wife of a citizen who had served honorably in the United States armed forces during World War II, solely upon a finding by the Attorney General that her admission would be detrimental to United States interests. The

Supreme Court excluded judicial review, finding that the congressional statutory scheme authorized such action. See, *U.S. ex rel. Knauff v. Shaughnessy*, 338 U.S. 537 (1950).

Quicknotes

IMMIGRATION AND NATIONALITY ACT, 8 U.S.C. § 1101 Defines a refugee eligible for asylum as anyone who is outside their country of origin and who is unwilling to return because of a well-founded fear of persecution on account of race, religion, nationality, membership in a particular social group, or political opinion.

JUDICIAL REVIEW The authority of the courts to review decisions, actions or omissions committed by another agency or branch of government.

Afroyim v. Rusk

Citizen (P) v. Government (D)

387 U.S. 253 (1967).

NATURE OF CASE: Declaratory judgment action.

FACT SUMMARY: Afroyim (P), a naturalized American citizen, left the U.S. and voluntarily voted in an Israeli election, and as a result pursuant to the Nationality Act of 1940 was deemed to have lost his American citizenship.

🏛 RULE OF LAW
Congress cannot, consistent with the Fourteenth Amendment, enact a law stripping an American of his citizenship that he has never voluntarily renounced or given up.

FACTS: Afroyim (P), born in Poland, became a naturalized American citizen in 1926. In 1950 he went to Israel and in 1951 he voluntarily voted in an Israeli election. In 1960 he applied for a renewal of his U.S. passport; his request was denied based on the fact that he had lost his American citizenship by virtue of § 401(e) of the Nationality Act of 1940, which provides that a U.S. citizen shall lose his citizenship if he votes in a political election in a foreign state. Afroyim (P) contested this action on constitutional grounds.

ISSUE: Can Congress, consistent with the Fourteenth Amendment, enact a law stripping an American of his citizenship that he has never voluntarily renounced or given up?

HOLDING AND DECISION: (Black, J.) No. Congress cannot, consistent with the Fourteenth Amendment, enact a law stripping an American of his citizenship that he has never voluntarily renounced or given up. The Fourteenth Amendment does not grant Congress the power to take away citizenship once it has been acquired, nor can this power be implied from this provision. The Fourteenth Amendment is designed to protect every citizen of this nation from forcible destruction of his citizenship and gives him a constitutional right to remain a citizen unless he voluntarily relinquishes that citizenship. Here Afroyim (P) never voluntarily relinquished his American citizenship although he voted in an Israeli election, and no act of Congress could deprive him of his citizenship involuntarily. Reversed.

DISSENT: (Harlan, J.) There is nothing in the history of or the Fourteenth Amendment itself which forbids Congress from withdrawing the citizenship of an unwilling citizen. Rather Congress is at liberty to expatriate a citizen if the expatriation is an appropriate power of Congress otherwise given to them by the constitution. When one votes in an election of a foreign state, expatriation would seem proper.

▶ ANALYSIS

The decision was 5-4. The majority overruled the *Perez v. Brownwell*, 356 U.S. 44 (1957), case decided only 10 years prior to the present case. That too was a 5-4 decision holding that Congress did have the right to involuntarily expatriate an American citizen. The issue of expatriation has always been subject to heated debate in Congress as well as the Supreme Court.

■═■

Quicknotes

EXPATRIATION The voluntary renunciation of one's country and becoming a citizen or subject of another.

FOURTEENTH AMENDMENT 42 U.S.C. § 1983 Defamation by state officials in connection with a discharge implies a violation of a liberty interest protected by the due process requirements of the U.S. Constitution.

■═■

Rogers v. Bellei

Government (D) v. Citizen (P)

401 U.S. 815 (1971).

NATURE OF CASE: Appeal from holding of unconstitutionality of immigration statute.

FACT SUMMARY: Bellei (P) was born in Italy at a time when his mother's status as an American citizen conferred citizenship upon Bellei (P) at his birth despite his father's sole citizenship in Italy. In 1952 the Immigration and Nationality Act removed Bellei's (P) citizenship because he never remained in the United States for five continuous years between his fourteenth and twenty-eighth years.

🏛 RULE OF LAW
A person neither born nor naturalized as a citizen in the United States is not entitled to protection from removal of a prior statutory grant of citizenship by Congress under the Fourteenth Amendment.

FACTS: Bellei (P) was born in Italy. His father was an Italian citizen and not an American citizen. His mother was an American citizen. Bellei (P) was granted citizenship in the United States at his birth by a statute existing at that time. In 1952, Congress passed the Immigration and Nationality Act, § 301(b) of which removed Bellei's (P) citizenship because he had not spent five continuous years in the United States between his fourteenth and twenty-eighth years. After notification of his loss of citizenship, Bellei (P) brought this action and the district court held the statute unconstitutional under the Fourteenth Amendment prohibition against deprivation of citizenship. The Supreme Court granted review.

ISSUE: Is a person neither born nor naturalized as a citizen in the United States entitled to protection from removal of a prior statutory grant of citizenship by Congress because of the Fourteenth Amendment?

HOLDING AND DECISION: (Blackmun, J.) No. The Fourteenth Amendment has no application to a citizen born abroad and not naturalized in the United States. While the first sentence of that amendment prohibits removal of citizenship without consent, it applies only to citizens born or naturalized in this country. A person neither born nor naturalized as a citizen in the United States is not entitled to protection from removal of a prior statutory grant of citizenship by Congress because of the Fourteenth Amendment. The imposition of the requirement of § 301(b) is not unreasonable, arbitrary, or unlawful. Reversed.

DISSENT: (Black, J.) The Constitution cannot rise and fall with this Court's passing notions of what is "fair" or "reasonable." It has been held that no American can be deprived of his citizenship without his assent, but the Court overrules that decision here.

▶ ANALYSIS

Naturalization within the United States according to the applicable statutes at the time would have prevented this deprivation. Bellei (P) was not so naturalized, though he would have no reason to think he should be after his grant of citizenship at the time he received it, at birth.

■═■

Quicknotes

FOURTEENTH AMENDMENT 42 U.S.C. § 1983 Defamation by state officials in connection with a discharge implies a violation of a liberty interest protected by the due process requirements of the U.S. Constitution.

NATURALIZATION The process pursuant to which a person becomes a citizen of the United States.

■═■

United States v. Helstoski

Federal government (P) v. Congressman (D)

442 U.S. 477 (1979).

NATURE OF CASE: Appeal from denial of motion to dismiss indictments.

FACT SUMMARY: Helstoski (D), a former Congressman, was indicted on various criminal acts resulting from political corruption.

🏛 RULE OF LAW
A member of Congress may be prosecuted under a criminal statute provided that the government's case does not rely on legislative acts or the motivation for legislative acts.

FACTS: In June 1976, a grand jury returned a multiple-count indictment charging Helstoski (D) and others with various criminal acts, including allegations that aliens had paid money for the introduction of private bills which would suspend the application of the immigration laws so as to allow them to remain in this country. Helstoski (D) moved to dismiss the indictment, contending that the indictment violated the Speech or Debate Clause. Although the district court denied Helstoski's (D) motion, it did order that "the United States (P) may not, during the presentation of its case-in-chief, at the trial . . . introduce evidence of the performance of a past legislative act" by Helstoski (D). This ruling was affirmed by the court of appeals and then appealed by the United States (P).

ISSUE: May a member of Congress be prosecuted under a criminal statute provided that the government's case does not rely on legislative acts or the motivation for legislative acts?

HOLDING AND DECISION: (Burger, C.J.) Yes. A member of Congress may be prosecuted under a criminal statute provided that the Government's (P) case does not rely on legislative acts or the motivation for legislative acts. A legislative act has been defined as an act generally done in Congress in relation to the business before it. Although references to past legislative acts of a member of Congress may not be introduced, a promise to deliver a speech, to vote, or to solicit other votes at some future date may be introduced because a promise to do an act in the future is not "speech or debate." Further, Helstoski (D) has not waived any protections under the clause. Waiver can be found only after explicit and unequivocal renunciation of that protection. Affirmed.

CONCURRENCE AND DISSENT: (Stevens, J.) The Speech or Debate Clause does not require rejection of evidence that merely refers to legislative acts when that evidence is not offered for the purpose of proving the legislative act itself. If the evidentiary reference to legislative acts is merely incidental to a proper purpose, the judge should admit the evidence and instruct the jury as to its limited relevance.

DISSENT: (Brennan, J.) A corrupt agreement to perform legislative acts, even if provable without reference to the acts themselves, may not be the subject of a general conspiracy prosecution.

▶ ANALYSIS

In the majority opinion, the Chief Justice states that "The Speech or Debate Clause was designed to preclude prosecution of members for legislative acts. The clause protects against inquiry into acts that occur in the regular course of the legislative process and into the motivation for those acts."

■=■

Quicknotes

CONSPIRACY Concerted action by two or more persons to accomplish some unlawful purpose.

SPEECH/DEBATE CLAUSE Art. 1, § 1, cl. 1 of the Constitution grants congressmen immunity "for any speech or debate in either House." The courts have extended this privilege to matters beyond pure speech and debate, but only when necessary to prevent indirect impairment of such deliberations.

■=■

Hutchinson v. Proxmire

Scientist (P) v. Senator (D)

443 U.S. 111 (1979).

NATURE OF CASE: Appeal from summary judgment denying damages for defamation.

FACT SUMMARY: Hutchinson (P), a research behavioral scientist, sued Senator William Proxmire (D) for defamation arising out of the presentation of a "Golden Fleece" award.

🏛 RULE OF LAW
The Speech or Debate Clause protects only those communications that are an integral part of the deliberative and legislative process.

FACTS: Ronald Hutchinson (P), a research behavioral scientist, sued Senator William Proxmire (D) and his legislative assistant for defamation arising out of Proxmire's (D) giving what he called his "Golden Fleece" award to the federal agencies that had sponsored Hutchinson's (P) research. The "Golden Fleece" award, which was presented for the most egregious examples of wasteful governmental spending, was given for Hutchinson's (P) research, which concentrated upon the behavior patterns of certain animals, such as the clenching of jaws when they were exposed to various aggravating stressful stimuli. Proxmire (D) referred to Hutchinson (P) and the award in a speech and two subsequent newsletters. Hutchinson (P) filed suit on April 16, 1976, alleging that Proxmire's (D) actions had subjected him to a loss of respect and to humiliation. The court of appeals affirmed the action of the district court in granting Proxmire's (D) motion for summary judgment, holding that the Speech or Debate Clause protected the statements made in a press release, and in the newsletters.

ISSUE: Does the Speech or Debate Clause protect only those communications that are an integral part of the deliberative and legislative process?

HOLDING AND DECISION: (Burger, C.J.) Yes. The Speech or Debate Clause protects only those communications that are an integral part of the deliberative and legislative process. Nothing in the history or in the explicit language of the clause suggests any intention to create an absolute privilege from liability or suit for defamatory statements made outside of the congressional chambers. Neither the newsletters nor a press release were essential to the deliberations of the Senate, and neither was part of the deliberative process. Valuable and desirable as it may be in broad terms, the transmittal of information about individual member's activities, in order to inform the public and other members is not a part of the legislative function or the deliberations that make up the legislative process. Reversed and remanded.

CONCURRENCE AND DISSENT: (Stewart, J.) Because telephone calls to federal agency officials are a routine and essential part of the congressional oversight function, such activity is protected by the Speech or Debate Clause.

DISSENT: (Brennan, J.) Public criticism by legislators of unnecessary governmental expenditures, whatever its form, is a legislative act shielded by the Speech or Debate Clause.

▶ *ANALYSIS*

The speech in which Proxmire (D) presented the "Golden Fleece" Award contained the following comments: "The funding of this nonsense makes me almost angry enough to scream and kick or even clench my jaws . . . Dr. Hutchinson's studies should make the taxpayers as well as his monkeys grind their teeth. In fact, the good doctor has made a fortune from his monkeys and in the process made a monkey out of the American taxpayer."

Quicknotes

DEFAMATION An intentional false publication, communicated publicly in either oral or written form, subjecting a person to scorn, hatred or ridicule, or injuring him or her in relation to his or her occupation or business.

SPEECH/DEBATE CLAUSE Art. 1, § 1, cl. 1 of the Constitution grants congressmen immunity "for any speech or debate in either House." The courts have extended this privilege to matters beyond pure speech and debate, but only when necessary to prevent indirect impairment of such deliberations.

United States v. Nixon

Federal government (P) v. President (D)

418 U.S. 683 (1974).

NATURE OF CASE: Appeal from denial of a motion to quash a third-party subpoena duces tecum.

FACT SUMMARY: A subpoena duces tecum was issued by the special prosecutor directing Nixon (D), the President of the United States, to turn over taped presidential conversations and transcripts.

RULE OF LAW

Neither the doctrine of separation of powers nor the need for confidentiality of high level communications alone can sustain an absolute, unqualified presidential privilege of immunity from judicial process under all circumstances.

FACTS: A grand jury indicted seven presidential advisors of conspiracy to defraud the United States (P) and to obstruct justice. Nixon (D), the President of the United States, although not indicted, was named as a co-conspirator. Upon motion of the special prosecutor, a third-party subpoena duces tecum was issued ordering Nixon (D) to turn over tape recordings and transcripts of certain presidential conversations relating to certain precisely identified meetings between Nixon (D) and others. Nixon (D) appealed specially seeking to quash the subpoena on grounds relating to a claim of absolute executive privilege. The motion to quash was denied, and this appeal followed.

ISSUE: Can either the doctrine of separation of powers or the need for confidentiality of high level communications alone sustain an absolute, unqualified presidential privilege of immunity from judicial process under all circumstances?

HOLDING AND DECISION: (Burger, C.J.) No. Neither the doctrine of separation of powers nor the need for confidentiality of high level communications alone can sustain an absolute, unqualified presidential privilege of immunity from judicial process under all circumstances. The court is the final arbiter of executive privilege. First, the courts had jurisdiction over the question because the district court's order was final. Second, the matter was justiciable because the mere assertion of a claim of an "intrabranch dispute" (the Special Prosecutor, an Executive appointive, against the Chief Executive), without more, has never operated to defeat federal jurisdiction. Here, the executive was required to enforce its own regulation, which had the force of law, giving the Special Prosecutor his unique independence within the Executive Branch itself. Turning to the claim of privilege that doctrine of separation of powers does not preclude judicial review of a President's claim of privilege, it is for the Court to interpret claims with respect to powers alleged to derive from enumerated powers. While the sovereign power of federal government has been divided amongst three coequal branches, the separate powers were not intended to operate with absolute independence. The legitimate needs of judicial process may outweigh presidential privilege. It is not denied that the shaping of government policy requires confidentiality which, in turn, requires a presumptive privilege of confidentiality for presidential communications. While this privilege has received utmost deference when based upon military or diplomatic secrecy, no case has given such deference to a president's generalized interest in confidentiality. Thus, "when the ground for asserting privilege as to subpoenaed materials sought for use in a criminal trial is based only on the generalized interest in confidentiality, it cannot prevail over the fundamental demands of due process of law in the fair administration of criminal justice." Affirmed.

ANALYSIS

This case can be summed up in the well-known saying, "no man is above the law." The President's resignation from office followed shortly after announcement of this decision relating and arising out of the Watergate scandal. While the President argued a claim of confidentiality, nowhere in the constitution is there any explicit reference to such a privilege. However, "to the extent (confidentiality) relates to the effective discharge of a President's powers, it is constitutionally based." Here, that privilege clashed with the specific constitutional rights of a defendant in a criminal trial "to be confronted with the witnesses against him" and "to have compulsory process for obtaining witnesses in his favor" and was overcome by those rights.

■■■■

Quicknotes

EXECUTIVE IMMUNITY Immunity of the president from suit for decisions made pursuant to his official duties.

JUSTICIABILITY An actual controversy that is capable of determination by the court.

SEPARATION OF POWERS The system of checks and balances preventing one branch of government from infringing upon exercising the powers of another branch of government.

SUBPOENA DUCES TECUM A court mandate compelling the production of documents under a witness' control.

■■■■

Nixon v. Administrator of General Services

President (P) v. Executive Branch official (D)

433 U.S. 425 (1977).

NATURE OF CASE: Action challenging the constitutionality of the Presidential Recordings and Materials Preservation Act.

FACT SUMMARY: Nixon (P) asserted that the Act was unconstitutional because it violated the separation of powers, Presidential privilege doctrines, and other constitutional doctrines.

RULE OF LAW
Congress may prescribe reasonable means for the screening of presidential materials.

FACTS: The Presidential Recordings and Materials Preservation Act directed the Administrator of General Services (D), an official of the Executive Branch, to take custody of the Presidential papers and tape recordings of former President Richard M. Nixon (P), and promulgated regulations that (1) provided for the orderly processing and screening by executive branch archivists of such materials for the purpose of returning to Nixon (P) those that were personal and private in nature, and (2) determined the terms and conditions upon which public access may eventually be had to these materials that were retained. Nixon (P) filed suit, asserting that the Act was unconstitutional because it violated the separation of powers doctrine, Presidential privilege doctrines, and other constitutional doctrines. The district court rejected Nixon's (P) claims.

ISSUE: May Congress prescribe reasonable means for the screening of Presidential materials?

HOLDING AND DECISION: (Brennan, J.) Yes. In determining whether the Act disrupts the proper balance between the coordinate branches, the proper inquiry focuses on the extent to which it prevents the Executive Branch from accomplishing its constitutionally assigned functions. Here, nothing contained in the Act renders it unduly disruptive of the executive branch, and therefore, unconstitutional on its face. The Executive Branch remains in full control of the Presidential materials, and the Act facially is designed to ensure that the materials can be released only when release is not barred by some applicable privilege inherent in that branch. Further, the mere screening of the materials by archivists will not impermissibly interfere with candid communication of views by Presidential advisors. Congress can legitimately act to protect the substantial public interest in reconstructing their history by entrusting Nixon's (P) materials to expert handling by trusted and disinterested professionals. By preserving these materials, the Act may be thought to aid the legislative process, because they provide a source for facilitating a full airing of the events leading to Nixon's (P) resignation, and thus are within the scope of Congress's broad investigative powers. Affirmed.

▶ ANALYSIS

In a dissenting opinion not published in the text of the case, Justice Rehnquist argued: "Today's decision countenances the power of any future Congress to seize the official papers of an outgoing President as he leaves the inaugural stand. In so doing, it poses a real threat to the ability of future Presidents to receive candid advice and to give candid instructions."

Quicknotes

PRESIDENTIAL POWERS Authority vested in the exexutive branch of the U.S. federal government to execute laws.

SEPARATION OF POWERS The system of checks and balances preventing one branch of government from infringing upon exercising the powers of another branch of government.

Nixon v. Fitzgerald

President (D) v. Government employee (P)

457 U.S. 731 (1982).

NATURE OF CASE: Appeal from decision denying absolute immunity.

FACT SUMMARY: Nixon (D), the former President of the United States, contended that he was entitled to absolute presidential immunity for official actions taken during his term of office.

🏛 RULE OF LAW
The President of the United States is entitled to absolute immunity from damages liability predicated on his official acts.

FACTS: In January 1970, Fitzgerald (P) lost his job as a management analyst for the Department of the Air Force, when he was dismissed from his position after testifying before the Subcommittee on Economy in Government of the Joint Economic Committee of the United States Congress, regarding cost overruns on the C-5A transport plane project. At a subsequent news conference, Nixon (D), then President, asserted that he had approved of Fitzgerald's (P) discharge from his position, although the White House press office issued a retraction of the statement the next day. After hearing over 4,000 pages of testimony, the Chief Examiner for the Civil Service Commission found that Fitzgerald's (P) termination had been the result of purely personal and impermissible reasons. Subsequently, Fitzgerald (P) filed this action in the United States district court for damages for wrongful termination. After the district court held that Nixon (D) was not entitled to claim absolute presidential immunity, this appeal followed.

ISSUE: Is the President of the United States entitled to absolute immunity from damages liability predicated on his official acts?

HOLDING AND DECISION: (Powell, J.) Yes. The President of the United States is entitled to absolute immunity from damages liability predicated on his official acts. The President occupies a unique position in the constitutional scheme, and is the chief constitutional officer of the Executive Branch, entrusted with supervisory and policy responsibilities of utmost discretion and sensitivity. Because of the singular importance of the President's duties, diversion of his energies by concern with private lawsuits would raise unique risks to the effective functioning of government. In view of the visibility of his office and the effect of his actions on countless people, the President would be an easily identifiable target for suits for civil damages. Here, Fitzgerald (P) argues that Nixon (D) would have acted outside the outer perimeter of his duties by ordering the discharge of an employee who was lawfully

entitled to retain his job in the absence of such cause as would promote the efficiency of the service. However, it clearly is within the President's constitutional and statutory authority to prescribe the manner in which the Secretary will conduct the business of the Air Force. Because this mandate of office must include the authority to prescribe reorganizations and reductions in force, Nixon's (D) alleged wrongful acts lay well within the outer perimeter of his authority. Reversed.

CONCURRENCE: (Burger, C.J.) The presidential immunity here derives from and is mandated by the constitutional doctrine of separation of powers.

DISSENT: (White, J.) Attaching absolute immunity to the office of the President, rather than to particular activities that the President might perform, places the President above the law. It is a reversion to the old notion that the king can do no wrong.

▎*ANALYSIS*

The majority opinion quoted Justice Story's analysis of presidential immunity in support of its argument. That analysis reads in part: "There are . . . incidental powers, belonging to the executive department, which are necessarily implied from the nature of the functions, which are confided to it. Among these, must necessarily be included the power to perform them . . . The President cannot, therefore, be liable to arrest, imprisonment, or detention, while he is in the discharge of the duties of his office; and for this purpose his person must be deemed, in civil cases at least, to possess an official inviolability." J. Story, Commentaries on the Constitution of the United States, § 1563, at 418-419 (1833 ed.).

■■■

Quicknotes

EXECUTIVE IMMUNITY Immunity of the president from suit for decisions made pursuant to his official duties.

SEPARATION OF POWERS The system of checks and balances preventing one branch of government from infringing upon exercising the powers of another branch of government.

■■■

Clinton v. Jones

Presidential (D) v. Employee (P)

520 U.S. 681 (1997).

NATURE OF CASE: Appeal of order reinstating trial in suit for damages against the president.

FACT SUMMARY: President Clinton (D), who was sued by Jones (P) following an alleged incident that occurred in 1991 before his election to the office of president, sought to have all litigation on the matter suspended until after his term has concluded.

⚖ RULE OF LAW

The doctrine of separation of powers does not require federal courts to stay all private actions against the President until he leaves office.

FACTS: Clinton (D) was elected to the presidency in 1992, and re-elected in 1996, with his term of office expiring on January 20, 2001. In May 1991, while serving as the Governor of Arkansas, he delivered a speech at an official conference held at the Excelsior Hotel in Little Rock, Arkansas. Paula Jones (P), a state employee working at the registration desk of the conference, alleged that she was persuaded by a state police officer named Ferguson to leave her desk and visit Clinton (D) in a business suite at the hotel where he made "abhorrent" sexual advances that she vehemently rejected. In May 1994, two days before the three-year period of limitations to file the complaint would have expired, Jones (P) filed a suit for damages against Clinton (D) and Ferguson. Jones's (P) allegations against Clinton (D) included conspiracy to deprive her of federal civil rights under color of state law, and state-law torts of intentional infliction of emotional distress and defamation. Clinton (D) filed a motion to dismiss on grounds of presidential immunity, and requested the court to defer all other pleadings and motions until after the immunity issue was resolved. The district court denied the motion to dismiss on immunity grounds and ruled that discovery could proceed, but ordered any trial stayed until the end of Clinton's (D) presidency. Jones (P) and Clinton (D) appealed, and the appellate court affirmed the denial of the motion to dismiss, but reversed the order postponing the trial, stating that it was the functional equivalent of a grant of temporary immunity. Clinton (D) appealed, and the Supreme Court granted certiorari.

ISSUE: Does the doctrine of separation of powers require federal courts to stay all private actions against the President until he leaves office?

HOLDING AND DECISION: (Stevens, J.) No. The doctrine of separation of powers does not require federal courts to stay all private actions against the President until he leaves office. The principal rationale for affording certain public officials immunity from suits for money damages arising out of their official acts is inapplicable to unofficial conduct. Although Clinton (D) argues that the doctrine of separation of powers places limits on the authority of the Judiciary to interfere with the Executive Branch, it does not follow that these principles would be violated by allowing Jones's (P) action to proceed. There is no suggestion that the Judiciary is being asked to perform any function that might in some way be described as executive, or that this decision will curtail the scope of official powers of the Executive Branch. Additionally, a lengthy stay of trial would violate the rights of Jones (P), who filed her complaint within the statutory period and is entitled to a timely disposition of her claims. Only three sitting presidents have been subjected to suits for their private actions, and it is unlikely that this decision will result in a deluge of such litigation. If Congress deems it appropriate to afford the President stronger protection, it may respond with appropriate legislation. Affirmed.

CONCURRENCE: (Breyer, J.) The majority was correct in finding that the Constitution does not automatically grant the President an immunity from civil lawsuits based on his private conduct. However, if the President sets forth and explains a conflict between a judicial proceeding and his public duties, the Constitution permits a judge to schedule a trial in an ordinary civil damages action only within the constraints that forbid a federal judge from interfering with the President's discharge of his duties.

▶ ANALYSIS

The President is absolutely immune from civil damages liability for his official acts in office. See *Nixon v. Fitzgerald*, 457 U.S. 731 (1982). In *Fitzgerald*, the Court noted that because of the singular importance of the president's duties, diverting his energies by concern about private lawsuits would raise unique risks to the effective functioning of the government. Clinton (D) argued, albeit unsuccessfully, that he too would be distracted from his public duites by participation in Jones's (P) lawsuit. But the *Fitzgerald* court's central concern was not the distraction of actually participating in a trial, but the worry and caution attendant to the possibility of damages actions stemming from any particular official decision.

■==■

Quicknotes

DEFAMATION An intentional false publication, communicated publicly in either oral or written form, subjecting a

Continued on next page.

person to scorn, hatred or ridicule, or injuring him or her in relation to his or her occupation or business.

INTENTIONAL INFLICTION OF EMOTIONAL DISTRESS Intentional and extreme behavior on the part of the wrongdoer with the intent to cause the victim to suffer from severe emotional distress, or with reckless indifference, resulting in the victim's suffering from severe emotional distress.

SEPARATION OF POWERS The system of checks and balances preventing one branch of government from infringing upon exercising the powers of another branch of government.

STAY An order by a court requiring a party to refrain from a specific activity until the happening of an event or upon further action by the court.

■═■

Immigration and Naturalization Service v. Chadha

Government agency (D) v. Alien (P)

462 U.S. 919 (1983).

NATURE OF CASE: Appeal of a decision holding a statute unconstitutional.

FACT SUMMARY: Chadha (P) claimed that the House of Representative's unilateral veto of the Attorney General's recommendation to suspend his deportation was unconstitutional.

🏛 RULE OF LAW
All acts of a legislative nature must be passed by both houses of Congress and presented for presidential approval to be constitutionally valid.

FACTS: Chadha's (P) deportation for remaining in the United States after the expiration date of his student visa was suspended by the Attorney General under the Immigration and Nationality Act, yet such suspension was unilaterally vetoed by the House of Representatives under authority of another section of that Act. Chadha (P) appealed to the Board of Immigration Appeals and the Ninth Circuit Court of Appeals which held the section allowing the one-house veto was severable from the Act and unconstitutional.

ISSUE: Must all acts of a legislative nature be passed by both houses of Congress and presented for presidential approval to be constitutionally valid?

HOLDING AND DECISION: (Burger, C.J.) Yes. All acts of a legislative nature must be passed by both houses of Congress and presented for presidential approval to be constitutionally valid. Because the veto action supplanted the need for private legislation to affect deportation proceedings, and because the action alters the rights and duties of individuals and branches of government it is an action of a legislative nature, and as such is constitutionally valid only if passed by both houses and presented for presidential approval. The Constitution requires bicameral passage and presentment as checks against the oppressive actions of any single house. Further, the Constitution specifically enumerates those areas where single house action is valid, and deportation is not among them. Therefore, the section of the Act allowing a one-house veto without bicameral passage or presentment to the President is unconstitutional and is severed from the Act. Affirmed.

CONCURRENCE: (Powell, J.) The use of the legislative veto is unconstitutional under the facts of this case, yet its extensive inclusion in congressional legislation should not be rendered unconstitutional in all cases.

DISSENT: (White, J.) Because of the extensive use of the legislative veto which is now held unconstitutional by the majority opinion, untold numbers of federal statutes are now unconstitutional. For this reason, the holding should have been based on the narrower ground of separation of powers. Further, the power of veto is not the power to pass law without the approval of both houses and the President, rather it is an action authorized by a properly passed and presented statute.

▶ ANALYSIS

The interrelationship and separateness of the legislative and the executive branches is illustrated in this case. The majority opinion stresses that valid law is not enacted without the presentment of the bill to the President as a check on congressional power. The dissent stresses the interrelationship created when Congress delegates authority to the executive branch, yet reserves the ultimate veto power. The rationale of the majority illustrates the underlying basis for the doctrine of separation of powers, yet the Court adopted the more expansive basis for the veto's unconstitutionality as its being fundamentally adverse to the legislative process.

Quicknotes

SEPARATION OF POWERS The system of checks and balances preventing one branch of government from infringing upon exercising the powers of another branch of government.

VETO A refusal by the president or a governor to sign into law a bill that has been passed by a legislature.

Clinton v. City of New York

President (D) v. State (P)

524 U.S. 417 (1998).

NATURE OF CASE: Challenge to the constitutionality of new presidential powers.

FACT SUMMARY: The Line Item Veto Act of 1996 allowed the president to cancel provisions that have been signed into law. Parties affected by President Clinton's (D) cancellation of a provision of the Balanced Budget Act of 1997 challenged the constitutionality of the Act.

RULE OF LAW

The cancellation provisions authorized by the Line Item Veto Act are not constitutional.

FACTS: President Clinton (D) used his authority under the Line Item Veto Act of 1996 to cancel a provision of the Balanced Budget Act of 1997. This forced New York (D) to repay certain funds to the federal government under the Medicaid program and removed a tax benefit to food processors acquired by farmers' cooperatives. New York City (P) and several private organizations challenged the constitutionality of the Medicaid cancellation and the Snake River Potato Growers (a farmer's cooperative) (P) challenged the food processors provision.

ISSUE: Are the cancellation provisions authorized by the Line Item Veto Act constitutional?

HOLDING AND DECISION: (Stevens, J.) No. The cancellation provisions authorized by the Line Item Veto Act are not constitutional. The Line Item Veto Act gives the President the power to "cancel in whole" three types of provisions that have already been signed into law: (1) any dollar amount of discretionary budget authority; (2) any item of new direct spending; or (3) any limited tax benefit. With respect to each cancellation, the president must determine that it will (i) reduce the federal budget deficit; (ii) not impair any essential government functions; and (iii) not harm the national interest. A cancellation takes effect upon receipt by Congress of the notification of the cancellation. However, a majority vote of both Houses is sufficient to make the cancellation null and void. Although the Constitution expressly authorizes the President to veto a bill under Article I, § 7, it is silent on the subject of unilateral presidential action that repeals or amends parts of duly enacted statues as authorized under the Line Item Veto Act. Constitutional silence should be construed as express prohibition. If there is to be a new role for the President in the procedure to determine the final text of a law, such a change must come through the amendment procedures and not by legislation.

CONCURRENCE: (Kennedy, J.) Separation of powers was designed to protect liberty, because the concentration of power in any single branch is a threat to liberty.

CONCURRENCE AND DISSENT: (Scalia, J.) If the Line Item Veto Act authorized the President (P) to "decline to spend" any item of spending rather than "canceling" it, it would have been constitutional. Given that there is only a technical difference between the two actions and that it is no different from what Congress has permitted the president to do since the formation of the Union, the Line Item Veto does not offend Article I, § 7.

DISSENT: (Breyer, J.) Given how complex our nation has become, Congress cannot divide bills into thousands or tens of thousands of separate appropriations bills, each of which the President (P) would have to veto or sign separately. Therefore, the Line Item Veto may help representative government work better.

▶ ANALYSIS

The majority did not comment on the wisdom of the Line Item Veto Act, because they found this step unnecessary given their finding that the Act was unconstitutional. Justice Kennedy did not let that stop him, since he felt that the Line Item Veto Act affected the separation of powers which in turn threatened liberty.

■■■

Quicknotes

SEPARATION OF POWERS The system of checks and balances preventing one branch of government from infringing upon exercising the powers of another branch of government.

■■■

Bowsher v. Synar

Parties not identified.

478 U.S. 714 (1986).

NATURE OF CASE: Appeal from decision invalidating reporting provision of Gramm-Rudman-Hollings Act.

FACT SUMMARY: Defendant appealed from a district court decision invalidating the reporting provisions of the Gramm-Rudman-Hollings Deficit Control Act, finding that they impermissibly allowed Congress to play a direct role in the execution of the laws in violation of separation of powers.

RULE OF LAW
Placing the responsibility for the execution of laws in the hands of an officer subject to removal only by the Legislature allows the Legislature to retain control over the execution of the laws and, thus, violates the doctrine of separation of powers.

FACTS: In 1985, the Gramm-Rudman-Hollings Deficit Control Act was signed into law. The automatic reductions contemplated by the Act were accomplished through the so-called "reporting provisions" of the Act. Under the reporting provisions, the Directors of the Office of Management and Budget and the Congressional Budget Office would make their deficit calculations and program reduction recommendations to the Comptroller General, who, after review, would report his conclusions to the President. The President was required to implement the recommendations of the Comptroller General. The Comptroller General was subject to removal only by Congress, through impeachment or joint resolution on specified grounds. The Act contained a fallback provision outlining procedures in the event that the reporting provisions were invalidated. Plaintiff challenged the constitutionality of the reporting provisions on separation of powers grounds, and the district court agreed, invalidating the reporting provisions. Defendant appealed.

ISSUE: Does placing the responsibility for the execution of laws in the hands of an officer subject to removal only by the Legislature allow the Legislature to retain control over the execution of the laws, thus violating the doctrine of separation of powers?

HOLDING AND DECISION: (Burger, C.J.) Yes. Placing the responsibility for the execution of laws in the hands of an officer subject to removal only by the Legislature allows the Legislature to retain control over the execution of the laws and, thus, violates the doctrine of separation of powers. [The Court first disposed of standing arguments.] The Constitution did not contemplate an active role by Congress in the supervision of officers charged with the execution of the laws it enacts.

An examination of the Comptroller General's removal provisions makes it clear that that officer does not act independently of, but rather subservient to, Congress. Regardless of assessments that, practically speaking, removal will not take place, the removal provisions were specifically implemented to give the Legislature control over the audit. An examination of the report made by the Comptroller General and its binding nature reveals the executive nature of the duties conducted by the Comptroller General. Striking down the removal provision need not be considered, as the Act itself provides a fallback provision. Since executive duties are being vested in an officer subject to removal only by Congress, the removal provisions violate the separation of powers. Affirmed.

CONCURRENCE: (Stevens, J.) The long-standing statutory duties of the Comptroller General clearly indicate that he is an agent of Congress. The *Chadha* decision clearly states that when Congress and/or its agents legislate, it must follow the enactment and presentment provisions of the Constitution.

DISSENT: (White, J.) The removal authority retained by Congress does not render the Comptroller an "agent" of the Congress, incapable of receiving executive power. Limitations on presidential removal power violate the separation of powers when they impair the Executive Branch from carrying out its executive duties.

DISSENT: (Blackmun, J.) Assuming constitutional infirmity, it would be preferable and consistent with congressional intent to void the congressional removal authority as opposed to the reporting provisions of the Act.

ANALYSIS

The Court's opinion in the present case gave little consideration to the alternative presented by the Blackmun dissent, to void the removal provisions. They clearly took the easy way out, since legislative history emphasized that Congress would have preferred to invalidate the removal rather than the reporting provisions. Further, the legislative history of the removal provisions shows that Congress was concerned with the Comptroller General's independence, rather than legislative control of the office.

Quicknotes

AGENT An individual who has the authority to act on behalf of another.

Continued on next page.

SEPARATION OF POWERS The system of checks and balances preventing one branch of government from infringing upon exercising the powers of another branch of government.

■═■

Morrison v. Olson

Independent counsel (P) v. Opposing counsel (D)

487 U.S. 654 (1988).

NATURE OF CASE: Appeal from reversal of denial of motion to quash subpoenas.

FACT SUMMARY: Morrison (P) appealed from a decision reversing a district court decision upholding the constitutionality of the independent counsel provisions of the Ethics in Government Act and denying Olson's (D) motion to quash subpoenas, contending in part that those provisions were not violative of the Appointments Clause of the Constitution.

RULE OF LAW

The independent counsel provisions of the Ethics in Government Act are not violative of the Appointments Clause of the Constitution.

FACTS: Sections 591-599 of the Ethics in Government Act (Act) allow for the appointment of an "independent counsel" to investigate and prosecute appropriate certain high ranking government officials for violations of criminal laws. The Attorney General conducts an initial investigation, and only if the Attorney General applies to the Special Division created by the Act for appointment of independent counsel, is independent counsel appointed. The Special Division appoints independent counsel and defines his prosecutorial jurisdiction. Within this jurisdiction, the independent counsel is granted full power and independent authority to exercise all powers of the Department of Justice. The Attorney General and the Department of Justice are required to suspend all proceedings regarding matters within independent counsel's jurisdiction. Independent counsel's tenure is governed by two provisions. The first provision allows the Attorney General, on his own personal action, to remove independent counsel for good cause. Independent counsel can seek judicial review of this decision. The other provision allows termination of independent counsel's office when he informs the Attorney General he has substantially completed his investigations or prosecutions undertaken under the Act, or when the Special Division so determines. Finally, the Act provides for congressional oversight of independent counsel's activities. In 1984, the House Judiciary Committee began an investigation into the Justice Department's role in an EPA document production controversy. The chairman requested that the Attorney General seek the appointment of an independent counsel to investigate the role of Olson (D), Schmults (D), and Dinkins (D). The Attorney General applied for appointment of independent counsel with respect to Olson (D) only. McKay (P) was appointed independent counsel, and Morrison (P) succeeded him. After unsuccessfully attempting to have the Committee's allegations against Schmults (D) and Dinkins (D) reviewed, Morrison (P) subpoenaed them and Olson (D) pursuant to the Olson (D) investigation. All three moved to quash the subpoenas, claiming the independent counsel provisions were unconstitutional, and that therefore Morrison (P) had no authority to proceed. The district court disagreed and denied the motions to quash. The court of appeals reversed, and from that decision, Morrison (P) appealed, contending in part that the independent counsel provisions of the Act were not violative of the Appointments Clause of the Constitution.

ISSUE: Are the independent counsel provisions of the Ethics in Government Act violative of the Appointments Clause of the Constitution?

HOLDING AND DECISION: (Rehnquist, C.J.) No. The independent counsel provisions of the Ethics in Government Act are not violative of the Appointments Clause of the Constitution. Since Morrison (P) is subject to removal by a higher Executive Branch official, and since her office is restricted in jurisdiction, tenure, and authorized duties, it is clear that she is an inferior officer, and not a principal officer as the court of appeals concluded. Secondly, the Appointments Clause does not on its face provide for any limitation on interbranch appointments; rather, it seems to grant Congress considerable discretion as to where to vest the power to appoint inferior officials. While congressional power to provide for interbranch appointments is not unlimited, it is not impermissible in this case for Congress to vest the power to appoint independent counsel in a specially created federal court (the Special Division). There is no actual incongruity in a court appointing prosecutorial officers where, as here, Special Division officers cannot participate in any matters handled by the appointed independent counsel. [The Court went on to conclude that these provisions did not violate Article III of the Constitution dealing with the Separation of Powers.] Reversed.

DISSENT: (Scalia, J.) The Founders declined to divide the executive power, and, therefore, the Constitution vests all of the executive power, not just some of it, in the President. Here, the Attorney General had a duty to comply with Congress's request unless he could conclude that there were no reasonable grounds to believe that further investigation was warranted. Thus, by application of the independent counsel provisions, Congress effectively compelled a criminal investigation of a high-level

Continued on next page.

presidential appointee. The statute must be invalidated on separation-of-power grounds if (1) the conduct of a criminal prosecution (and of an investigation to decide whether to prosecute) is the exercise of purely executive power, and (2) if the statute deprives the President of the exclusive control of that power. Because the majority concedes that both of these conditions are met, the inevitable conclusion must be that the statute is void. Instead, the majority greatly exaggerates the extent of control the President has through the Attorney General. The statute gives the independent counsel wide investigative and prosecutorial discretion, and even takes the decision of whether getting a conviction is worth disclosure of national security information away from the President and gives it to the independent counsel. Thus, the core prosecutorial function is taken away from the President. The majority replaces the constitutional prescription that the executive power belongs to the President with a balancing test that is not based on constitutional analysis, and merely announces that the ability to control the decision whether to investigate and prosecute the President's closest advisors, and even the President himself, is not so central to the functioning of the Executive Branch that it has to be under his control. Also, the majority is incorrect in characterizing the independent counsel as an inferior officer. First, independent counsel is removable only for "good cause" whereas principal officers may be removed by the President at will. Second, independent counsel, although performing only limited duties, nonetheless exercises great power. Finally, the independent counsel serves until she decides that her work is completed, so her tenure is not limited. And, although her jurisdiction is limited, within that jurisdiction she exercises more than the full power of the Attorney General. Moreover, the independent counsel is not even subordinate to the President. For all these reasons, independent counsel is not an inferior officer and her appointment must be made by the President with the advice and consent of the Senate; otherwise the appointment is unconstitutional. The law has been settled that the President may remove principal officers, but that his ability to remove inferior officers may be restricted. The majority's opinion, however, eliminates that distinction and now permits restriction of the removal of any executive officers. Such restriction can give rise to abuses of power that cannot be remedied through accountability of the President to the people.

▶ ANALYSIS

Other cases have upheld the federal court's power to appoint private attorneys to prosecute contempt of court orders, justifying the decision in part on the need for the Judiciary to have the power to independently vindicate its own authority. Justice Scalia, the author of the dissent, concurred in this judgment. See *Young v. United States ex rel. Vuitton et Fils S.A.*, 481 U.S. 787 (1987).

Quicknotes

APPOINTMENTS CLAUSE Article II, section 2, clause 2 of the United States Constitution conferring power upon the president to appoint ambassadors, public ministers and consuls, judges of the Supreme Court and all other officers of the United States with the advice and consent of the Senate.

INFERIOR OFFICERS Members of the executive branch having less power or authority in relation to others.

SEPARATION OF POWERS The system of checks and balances preventing one branch of government from infringing upon exercising the powers of another branch of government.

U.S. Term Limits, Inc. v. Thornton

Parties not identified.

514 U.S. 779 (1995).

NATURE OF CASE: Review of order striking down State law.

FACT SUMMARY: Arkansas voters passed an initiative imposing term limits on its congressional delegation.

RULE OF LAW

States may not impose term limits on their congressional representatives.

FACTS: In 1992, Arkansas enacted, through a ballot initiative, a law that, among other things, imposed term limits on its representatives to the U.S. House of Representatives and U.S. Senate. The mechanism for achieving this was to be limitations on ballot access. The Arkansas Supreme Court struck down this law as contrary to the U.S. Constitution. The U.S. Supreme Court granted review.

ISSUE: May a State impose term limits on its congressional delegation?

HOLDING AND DECISION: (Stevens, J.) No. States may not impose term limits on their congressional representatives. The qualifications to serve in Congress are delineated in Article I of the Constitution. What little legislative history exists demonstrates that the Framers intended that these be the sole qualifications for office. It was not intended that States be free to graft their own qualifications. Historically, States had no power over Congress at the beginning of the republic, as Congress had not previously existed. Finally, the law is not a valid exercise of a State's right to determine the manner of elections. Restricting ballot access is merely an attempt to impose term limits indirectly, and Arkansas cannot do indirectly that which is unconstitutional to do directly. Affirmed.

DISSENT: (Thomas, J.) It is ironic that the Court should say it defends the right of the people of Arkansas to choose whom they please to govern them, when over 60% of the voters in the State voted for the law the Court strikes down. I. Where the Constitution is silent on the question of the power to prescribe eligibility requirements for congressional candidates, it raises no bar to action by the States or its people. Contrary to the majority's suggestion, there does not need to be an affirmative grant of power in the Constitution to do this. Also, the federal government enjoys no authority beyond what the Constitution confers. Therefore, the remainder of the people's power is either delegated to the state government

or retained by the people. The majority, instead of finding this structure in the Tenth Amendment, announces an "enormous and untenable limitation" on the Tenth Amendment by finding that the state governments could not "reserve" any powers that they did not control at the time the Constitution was drafted. Such a restriction is erroneous because the Constitution derives its authority from the consent of the people, from whom all government powers stem. It therefore is incoherent to assert that the people could not reserve any powers that they had not previously controlled. The question in this case is whether Article I bars state action that it does not appear to forbid; it is not whether the States enjoyed such power before the Constitution was framed. The answer is on the face of the Tenth Amendment: unless the federal Constitution affirmatively prohibits an action by the States or the people, it raises no bar to such action. The majority is also wrong to suggest that it would be inconsistent with national sovereignty for the States or people to have reserved powers over the selection of members of Congress, because the direct link envisaged by the Framers was between the Representatives from each state and the people of that State, not between the people of a State and Representatives from all States. This is supported by the Constitution's treatment of presidential elections, where the States have no reserved power to set qualifications for the office of President, but do have the power to set qualifications for their presidential electors who are on the electoral college. Finally, the Times, Places, and Manner Clause of Article I affirmatively imposes a duty on the States, and also grants to Congress an exclusive power. However, a constitutional provision that imposes affirmative duties on the States is hardly inconsistent with the notion of reserved powers. II. A. Given that the people of a State have "reserved" powers over the selection of their representatives, the people enjoy such power unless something in the Constitution deprives them of such power. The majority sees the Qualifications Clauses as prohibiting the people from establishing eligibility requirements for their representatives. However, the Qualifications Clauses merely establish minimum qualifications, but do not bar the people from establishing additional eligibility requirements. Although the Qualifications Clauses do prevent the individual States from abolishing all eligibility requirements for Congress, nothing in them prevents the people from one State from adding eligibility requirements for their representatives. The rights of people from another State are not violated thereby, as long as all candidates meet the minimum requirements.

Continued on next page.

Additionally, there is no uniformity requirement in the Qualifications Clauses. II. B. The majority infers from the Framers' "democratic principles" that the Qualifications Clauses must have been understood to preclude the people and the state legislatures from prescribing additional qualifications for congressional representatives. However, the logical conclusion from the evidence of the Framers' intent on this point—the Constitution does not impose a broad set of disqualifications for congressional office, and Congress itself cannot add to the few disqualifications that are in the Constitution—is that the Framers did not want the people to be constrained by too many qualifications imposed on the national level. The fact that the Framers did not give Congress the power to enact qualifications does not imply that they wanted to deny this power to the people at the state level. II. C. More specific historical evidence also does not support the majority's view that the Framers did not intend to permit supplementation of the Qualifications Clauses. Instead, the historical evidence, as in the Federalist No. 52, shows merely that the Framers did not intend Congress to be able to enact qualifications laws. State practice immediately after ratification of the Constitution shows that it was not understood that the Qualifications Clauses were exclusive: five States supplemented the constitutional disqualifications in their very first election laws. III. The majority's holding not only negates term limits, but other qualifications that are in effect, e.g., those related to mental competency, conviction for certain crimes, etc. Although the majority invalidates § 3 of Amendment 73 because it sees that provision as prescribing unadulterated term limits, the statute only provides that if certain incumbents win reelection, they must do so by write-in votes. Whereas it is true that very few write-in candidates have won elections, it is also true that when a write-in candidate is well known and well funded, it is quite possible for him or her to win an election. The majority also emphasizes that the intent of the provision is to disqualify congressional incumbents from further service, but that ignores, at the summary judgment stage, arguments that in fact the purpose of the statute is to level the playing field on which challengers compete with incumbents. This is because federal law confers numerous advantages on incumbents (e.g., free postage, taxpayer-supported staffs, and other in-kind benefits), as well as imposing spending and contribution limits on congressional campaigns that can prevent challengers from spending enough to get the name recognition that incumbents already have. Also, more senior incumbents have a much better chance of being reelected, arguably because the seniority system within Congress permits these incumbents to distribute benefits to their constituents in proportion to the length of their tenure. Finally, laws that allegedly have the purpose and effect of handicapping a particular class of candidates are traditionally reviewed under the First and Fourteenth Amendments, not the Qualifications Clauses; term limits have tended to survive

such review without difficulty. The Qualifications Clauses should not be read to do any more than what they say.

▶ ANALYSIS

The clearest antecedent to this case is *Powell v. McCormack*, 395 U.S. 486 (1977). In that case, Congress refused to seat the controversial Adam Clayton Powell, a radical elected by an inner-city district in New York. The Supreme Court, ruling in Powell's favor, held that Congress could not refuse to seat a lawfully elected individual who met the qualifications of Article I.

■═■

Due Process

Quick Reference Rules of Law

Slaughter-House Cases (Butchers' Benev. Ass'n v. Crescent City Live-Stock Landing and Slaughter-House Co.)

Butchers (P) v. State (D)

83 U.S. (16 Wall.) 36, 21 L.Ed. 394 (1873).

NATURE OF CASE: Appeal of state enforcement of a monopoly.

FACT SUMMARY: Louisiana created a 25-year slaughterhouse monopoly to which several butchers (P) who were not included objected.

RULE OF LAW

The Fourteenth Amendment protects the privileges and immunities of national, not state, citizenship, and neither the Equal Protection, Due Process, nor Privileges and Immunities Clauses of that amendment may be used to interfere with state control of the privileges and immunities of state citizenship.

FACTS: A Louisiana law of 1869 granted a monopoly to one Slaughter-House Company for the three largest parishes in that state. Butchers' (P), who was not included in the monopoly, challenged the law creating it on the grounds that it violated the Thirteenth Amendment ban on involuntary servitude and the Fourteenth Amendment protections of the privileges and immunities of national citizenship and equal protection and due process of law. From a judgment sustaining the law, the butchers (P) appealed.

ISSUE: Does the Fourteenth Amendment Privileges and Immunities Clause make all privileges and immunities of citizenship federal rights subject to federal enforcement?

HOLDING AND DECISION: (Miller, J.) No. The Fourteenth Amendment protects the privileges and immunities of national, not state, citizenship, and neither the Equal Protection, Due Process, nor Privileges and Immunities Clauses of that amend-ment may be used to interfere with state control of the privileges and immunities of state citizenship. The underlying purpose of all three of the post-Civil War amendments was to eliminate the remnants of African slavery, not to effect any fundamental change in the relations of the government. The Fourteenth Amendment expressly was adopted to assure only that states would not "abridge the privileges and immunities of citizens of the United States" (i.e., Negro citizens in their pursuit of national rights such as the right to protection on the high seas). Similarly, the Equal Protection and Due Process Clauses of that amendment were drawn to protect former slaves from state denial of federal rights. No interpretation of this amendment (or the Thirteenth, which is an even clearer case) may be used to prevent the State of Louisiana from exercising its police power here (to promote public health in slaughterhouses) to define particular privileges and immunities of its citizens. Affirmed.

DISSENT: (Field, J.) Justice Field views the Fourteenth Amendment as protection for all citizens of the fundamental rights of free government from abridgment by the states. Among such rights clearly is the right to an equal opportunity to pursue employment.

DISSENT: (Bradley, J.) Justice Bradley views the Fourteenth Amendment as a ban upon state deprivation of life, liberty, or property without due process of law. He views the purpose of its passage as preventing future insubordination to government by law which fostered the Civil War.

ANALYSIS

The effect of this decision was to essentially render the Fourteenth Amendment Privileges and Immunities Clause ineffectual as a means of protecting individual rights from state abridgment. In addition, it ruled out the possibility that the Bill of Rights could be enforced upon the states as privileges and immunities of national citizenship. Subsequently, of course, the Court adopted the position of Justice Bradley and began selectively incorporating parts of those amendments into the Fourteenth Amendment Due Process Clause. In addition, the Equal Protection Clause has been used extensively to prohibit state action which is discriminatory in any irrational way (i.e., the rational basis test). Note, finally, that even the Thirteenth Amendment, summarily treated above, has been expanded to bar private discriminatory action which can be identified as a badge of slavery.

Quicknotes

DUE PROCESS CLAUSE Clauses found in the Fifth and Fourteenth Amendments to the United States Constitution providing that no person shall be deprived of "life, liberty, or property, without due process of law."

EQUAL PROTECTION A constitutional guarantee that no person shall be denied the same protection of the laws enjoyed by other persons in like circumstances.

MONOPOLY A privilege or right conferred upon an individual or entity granting it the exclusive power to manufacture, sell and distribute a particular service or commodity;

Continued on next page.

a market condition in which one or a few companies control the sale of a product or service thereby restraining competition in respect to that article or service.

PRIVILEGES AND IMMUNITIES CLAUSE OF 14TH AMENDMENT
A provision in the Constitution that accords the advantages of citizenship equally to the citizens of each state; out-of-state citizens must therefore be given the same privileges as a state's own citizens.

■══◾

Lochner v. New York

Employer (D) v. State (P)

198 U.S. 45 (1905).

NATURE OF CASE: Appeal from conviction for violation of a labor law.

FACT SUMMARY: A state labor law prohibited employment in bakeries for more than 60 hours a week or more than 10 hours a day. Lochner (D) permitted an employee in his bakery to work over 60 hours in one week.

🏛 RULE OF LAW
To be a fair, reasonable, and appropriate use of a state's police power, an act must have a direct relation, as a means to an end, to an appropriate and legitimate state objective.

FACTS: Lochner (D) was fined for violating a state labor law. The law prohibited employment in bakeries for more than 60 hours a week or more than 10 hours a day. Lochner (D) permitted an employee to work in his bakery for more than 60 hours in one week.

ISSUE: Is a state law regulating the hours bakery employees may work a valid exercise of state police power?

HOLDING AND DECISION: (Peckham, J.) No. The general right to make a contract in relation to one's business is part of the liberty of the individual protected by the Fourteenth Amendment. The right to purchase or sell labor is part of the liberty protected by this amendment. However, the states do possess certain police powers relating to the safety, health, morals, and general welfare of the public. If the contract is one which the state in the exercise of its police power has the right to prohibit, the Fourteenth Amendment will not prevent the state's prohibition. When, as here, the state acts to limit the right to labor or the right to contract, it is necessary to determine whether the rights of the state or the individual shall prevail. The Fourteenth Amendment limits the state's exercise of its police power, otherwise the state would have unbounded power once it stated that legislation was to conserve the health, morals, or safety of its people. It is not sufficient to assert that the act relates to public health. Rather, it must have a more direct relation, as a means to an end, to an appropriate state goal, before an act can interfere with an individual's right to contract in relation to his labor. In this case, there is no reasonable foundation for holding the act to be necessary to the health of the public or of bakery officials. Statutes such as this one are merely meddlesome interferences with the rights of the individual. They are invalid unless there is some fair ground to say that there is material danger to the public health or to the employees' health if the labor hours are not curtailed. It cannot be said that the production of healthy bread depends upon the hours that the employees work. Nor is the trade of a baker an unhealthy one to the degree which would authorize the legislature to interfere with the rights to labor and of free contract. Lochner's (D) conviction is reversed.

DISSENT: (Harlan, J.) Whether or not this be wise legislation is not a question for this Court. It is impossible to say that there is not substantial or real regulation between the statute and the state's legitimate goals. This decision brings under the Court's supervision matters which supposedly belonged exclusively to state legislatures.

DISSENT: (Holmes, J.) The word liberty in the Fourteenth Amendment should not invalidate a statute unless it can be said that a reasonable person would say that the statute infringes fundamental principles of our people and our law. A reasonable person might think this statute valid. Citizens' liberty is regulated by many state laws which have been held to be valid, i.e., the Sunday laws, the lottery laws, laws requiring vaccination.

▶ ANALYSIS

From the *Lochner* decision in 1905 to the 1930s, the Court invalidated a considerable number of laws on substantive due process grounds, such as laws fixing minimum wages, maximum hours, prices and law regulating business activities. The modern Court claims to have rejected the *Lochner* doctrine. It has withdrawn careful scrutiny in most economic areas but has maintained and increased intervention with respect to a variety of noneconomic liberties. However, not only economic regulations were struck down under *Lochner*. That doctrine formed the basis for absorbing rights such as those in the First Amendment into the Fourteenth Amendment concept of liberty. *Lochner* also helped justify on behalf of other noneconomic rights such as the right to teach in a foreign language (*Meyer v. State of Nebraska*, 262 U.S. 390 [1923]). *Meyer* was to be relied upon in the birth control decision, *Griswold v. Connecticut*, 381 U.S. 479 (1965).

▬▬▬

Quicknotes

FOURTEENTH AMENDMENT - 42 U.S.C. § 1983 Defamation by state officials in connection with a discharge implies a violation of a liberty interest protected by the due process requirements of the U.S. Constitution.

POLICE POWER The power of a government to impose restrictions on the rights of private persons, as long as

Continued on next page.

those restrictions are reasonably related to the promotion and protection of public health, safety, morals and the general welfare.

SUBSTANTIVE DUE PROCESS A constitutional safeguard limiting the power of the state, irrespective of how fair its procedures may be; substantive limits placed on the power of the state.

■━■

Nebbia v. New York

Grocer (D) v. State (P)

291 U.S. 502 (1934).

NATURE OF CASE: Appeal from conviction for violation of an order of the Milk Board.

FACT SUMMARY: The State Milk Board fixed nine cents as the price to be charged for a quart of milk. Nebbia (D) sold two quarts of milk and a loaf of bread for eighteen cents.

🏛 RULE OF LAW
Upon proper occasion and by appropriate measures, a state may regulate a business in any of its aspects, including fixing prices.

FACTS: In 1933, the New York Legislature established a Milk Control Board. The board was given the power to fix minimum and maximum retail prices to be charged by stores to consumers. The board fixed the price of a quart of milk at nine cents. Nebbia (D), a grocery store proprietor, charged eighteen cents for two quarts of milk and a five-cent loaf of bread. The law establishing the board was based on a legislative finding that, "Milk is an essential item of diet. Failure of producers to receive a reasonable return threatens a relaxation of vigilance against contamination. The production of milk is a paramount industry of the state, and largely affects the health and prosperity of its people."

ISSUE: Does the federal Constitution prohibit a state from fixing selling prices?

HOLDING AND DECISION: (Roberts, J.) No. The general rule is that both the use of property and the making of contracts shall be free from government interference. However, neither property rights nor contract rights are absolute. Equally fundamental with the private interest is the public's right to regulate it in the common interest. The Fifth and Fourteenth Amendments do not prohibit governmental regulation for the public welfare. They merely guarantee that regulation shall be consistent with due process. The guarantee of due process demands only that the law shall not be unreasonable, arbitrary, or capricious, and that the means selected shall have a real and substantial relation to the object sought to be attained. If an industry is subject to regulation in the public interest, its prices may be regulated. An industry which is "affected with a public industry" is one which is subject to police powers. A state is free to adopt whatever economic policy may be reasonably deemed to promote the public welfare. The courts are without authority to override such policies. If the laws passed have a rational relation to a legitimate purpose and are neither arbitrary nor discriminatory, the requirements of due process are satisfied. Price control may fulfill these requirements as well as any other type of regulation. The New York law creating the Milk Board and giving it power to fix prices does not conflict with the due process guarantees and is constitutionally valid. Nebbia's (D) conviction is affirmed.

SEPARATE OPINION: (McReynolds, J.) The court below says that it is not judging the wisdom of the legislature in enacting the challenged statute. However, this Court must be responsive to the wisdom of the enactment, and, therefore, the lower court's judgment should be reversed.

▶ ANALYSIS

The early attitude of the Court had been that the states could regulate selling prices only for industries affecting the public interest. Regulation of prices and rates charged by public utilities, dairies, grain elevators, etc., were upheld, but regulation of the prices of theatre tickets or ice were not. *Nebbia* held that price control regulation was to be treated the same as other police powers and a rational relation to a legitimate goal was all that was necessary. The dissent, representing the Court's earlier position, does not want to treat the legislation with the deference exercised by the majority. In its judgment, the method adopted by New York does not rationally relate to its goal. *Nebbia* represents the modern position of the Court, which is to presume the propriety of the legislation.

■■■

Quicknotes

DUE PROCESS CLAUSE Clauses found in the Fifth and Fourteenth Amendments to the United States Constitution providing that no person shall be deprived of "life, liberty, or property, without due process of law."

POLICE POWERS The power of a state or local government to regulate private conduct for the health, safety and welfare of the general public.

■■■

Board of Regents v. Roth

University (D) v. Instructor (P)

408 U.S. 564 (1972).

NATURE OF CASE: Appeal from summary judgment order of right to hearing.

FACT SUMMARY: Roth (P), a nontenured Wisconsin State University instructor, was not rehired after a year of teaching after making certain anti-University statements and alleged that he was deprived of a property right in his job and a liberty interest to make the statements.

🏛 RULE OF LAW
An employee of a state-operated facility has no property interest in future employment guaranteed by the Constitution beyond those granted in his employment contract.

FACTS: Roth (P) was a nontenured instructor at Wisconsin State University. After a year of teaching, Roth (P) was not rehired. His contract of employment with the University secured him no rights to employment after its expiration at the time of Roth's (P) termination. Roth (P) brought this action against the University Board (D) alleging insufficient notice and hearing and a deprivation of a property right in his job along with a deprivation of a liberty interest to make statements against the University, which he alleged led to his dismissal. The district court granted Roth's (P) motion for summary judgment against the Board (D) and the court of appeals affirmed. The Supreme Court granted certiorari.

ISSUE: Has an employee of a state-operated facility a property interest in future employment guaranteed by the Constitution beyond those granted in his employment contract?

HOLDING AND DECISION: (Stewart, J.) No. Not all interests are protected by the Fourteenth Amendment so as to require procedural due process in the form of a prior hearing before the interest is lost. Roth (P) was hired by his contract for one year and no more, and he is not deprived of a right because he was not offered another contract. Any property right he may have had was completely set forth in his contract, and no liberty right deprivation has been shown. An employee of a state-operated facility has no property interest in future employment guaranteed by the Constitution beyond those granted in his employment contract. Under these circumstances, no hearing or notice beyond what was given was required. Reversed and remanded.

DISSENT: (Marshall, J.) Every citizen who applies for a government job is entitled to it unless the government can establish some reason for denying it. This is the "property" right protected by the Fourteenth Amendment.

The liberty to work is similarly secured by that amendment. In order to take away these rights the government must say why they have done so.

▶ ANALYSIS

The broad protection of the Fourteenth Amendment in this area envisioned by Justice Powell finds little support in the cases that followed except where the deprivation or refusal to rehire forecloses a wide range of employment opportunities for the employee. If the foreclosure encompasses both the public and private sectors, a fair hearing will be required.

Quicknotes

FOURTEENTH AMENDMENT - 42 U.S.C. § 1983 Defamation by state officials in connection with a discharge implies a violation of a liberty interest protected by the due process requirements of the U.S. Constitution.

NOTICE Communication of information to a person by an authorized person or an otherwise proper source.

PROCEDURAL DUE PROCESS The constitutional mandate that if the state or federal government acts so as to deny a citizen of a life, liberty or property interest the individual is first entitled to notice and the right to be heard.

Perry v. Sindermann

College (D) v. Teacher (P)

408 U.S. 593 (1972).

NATURE OF CASE: Appeal from reversal of denial of right to notice and hearing.

FACT SUMMARY: Sindermann (P), a state college teacher, was terminated, allegedly because of insubordination, without notice and hearing.

🏛 RULE OF LAW
A person's interest in a benefit is a property interest if there are explicit understandings supporting a claim of entitlements.

FACTS: Sindermann (P) was a teacher in the Texas State College system from 1959 to 1969. He was employed by the college under a series of one-year contracts. The college had no formal teacher system, but specified in the faculty guide that the teacher should "feel he has a permanent tenure so long as his teaching services are satisfactory." During the 1968-1969 academic year, Sindermann (P) became involved in several political disputes with the college, and in May 1969, the Board of Regents voted not to renew his contract and allowed him no opportunity for a hearing to challenge the basis of the nonrenewal. Sindermann (P) filed suit, alleging that he had a right to a hearing before termination. The court of appeals reversed an order of summary judgment for the college and ordered the case remanded.

ISSUE: Is a person's interest in a benefit a property interest if there are explicit understandings supporting a claim of entitlement?

HOLDING AND DECISION: (Stewart, J.) Yes. The government may not deny a benefit to a person because of his exercise of constitutionally protected freedoms of speech or association. Here, the mere showing that Sindermann (P) was not rehired in one particular job, without more, did not amount to a showing of a loss of liberty. However, property interest subject to procedural due process protection is not limited by a few rigid, technical forms. Property denotes a broad range of interests that are secured by existing rules or understandings. A person's interest in a benefit is a "property" interest for due process purposes if there are such rules or mutually explicit understandings that support his claim of entitlement to the benefit and that he may invoke a hearing. Sindermann (P) must be given an opportunity to prove the legitimacy of his claim of an entitlement in light of the policies and practices of the State College. Affirmed.

▶ ANALYSIS

The Supreme Court engages in a two-step analysis in procedural due process cases. The first issue is whether something can be termed life, liberty, or property. If so, the government must offer the guarantees of procedural due process before depriving the person of it. The second issue then becomes what type of process and when is that process due.

■■■■

Quicknotes

NOTICE Communication of information to a person by an authorized person or an otherwise proper source.

PROCEDURAL DUE PROCESS The constitutional mandate that if the state or federal government acts so as to deny a citizen of a life, liberty or property interest the individual is first entitled to notice and the right to be heard.

■■■■

Goldberg v. Kelly

State (D) v. Residents (P)

397 U.S. 254 (1970).

NATURE OF CASE: Appeal from order requiring hearing prior to termination of welfare benefits.

FACT SUMMARY: Kelly (P) and other residents of New York City who had been receiving aid pursuant to a state welfare scheme, brought this action alleging that benefits had been terminated without prior notice and hearing.

> 🏛 **RULE OF LAW**
> A state which terminates public assistance payments to a recipient without affording him the opportunity for an evidentiary hearing prior to termination denies the recipient procedural due process.

FACTS: Kelly (P) and other residents of New York City who had been receiving aid pursuant to a state welfare scheme, brought this action alleging that welfare benefits had been or would be terminated, under New York law, without prior notice and hearing in violation of the Due Process Clause. The state contended that its post-termination notice and hearing procedure was constitutionally sufficient. Under the procedure a caseworker with doubts about a recipient's continued eligibility would first discuss the matter with the recipient, and then recommend termination of benefits if the recipient was still considered ineligible. Notification of termination was then sent in writing to the recipient together with information about the availability of a post-termination hearing. If the recipient prevailed he would be paid all funds erroneously held. The district court held that only a pre-termination evidentiary hearing would satisfy the Due Process Clause. Goldberg (D), as Commissioner of Social Services, appealed.

ISSUE: Does a state which terminates public assistance payments to a recipient without affording him the opportunity for an evidentiary hearing prior to termination deny the recipient procedural due process?

HOLDING AND DECISION: (Brennan, J.) Yes. A state which terminates public assistance payments to a recipient without affording him the opportunity for an evidentiary hearing prior to termination denies the recipient procedural due process. The extent to which procedural due process must be afforded the recipient is influenced by the extent to which he may be condemned to suffer grievous loss, and depends upon whether the recipient's interest in avoiding that loss outweighs the governmental interest in summary adjudication. It is true, of course, that some governmental benefits may be administratively terminated without affording the recipient a pre-termination evidentiary hearing. However, when welfare is discontinued so is the means to obtain essential food, clothing, housing, and medical care. Termination of aid pending resolution of a controversy over eligibility may deprive an eligible recipient of the very means by which he lives. Moreover, important governmental interests are promoted by affording recipients a pre-termination evidentiary hearing. Public assistance promotes the general welfare by allowing the poor to have the same opportunity to participate in the community as others in a superior economic position. Affirmed.

DISSENT: (Black, J.) The Fourteenth Amendment is given too broad a construction. The amendment came into being primarily to protect Negroes from discrimination. The Court, however relies upon the Fourteenth Amendment and in effect says that failure of government to pay a promised charitable installment to an individual deprives that individual of his own property. It strains credulity to say that a government's promise of charity is property belonging to a welfare recipient under the Due Process Clause.

▶ **ANALYSIS**

The Court points out in *Goldberg* that the pre-termination hearing need not take the form of a judicial or quasi-judicial trial. It must be born in mind that the statutory fair hearing will provide the recipient with a full administrative review. Accordingly, the pre-termination hearing has one function only: to produce an initial determination of the validity of the welfare department's grounds for discontinuance of payments in order to protect a recipient against an erroneous termination of benefits.

■■■

Quicknotes

DUE PROCESS CLAUSE Clauses found in the Fifth and Fourteenth Amendments to the United States Constitution providing that no person shall be deprived of "life, liberty, or property, without due process of law."

NOTICE Communication of information to a person by an authorized person or an otherwise proper source.

PROCEDURAL DUE PROCESS The constitutional mandate that if the state or federal government acts so as to deny a citizen of a life, liberty or property interest the individual is first entitled to notice and the right to be heard.

■■■

Mathews v. Eldridge

Government agency (D) v. Benefits recipient (P)

424 U.S. 319 (1976).

NATURE OF CASE: Appeal from order of evidentiary hearing.

FACT SUMMARY: Eldridge's (P) benefits under the federal disability insurance benefits program were terminated after a state agency found that his disability had ceased to exist.

> ## 🏛 RULE OF LAW
> An evidentiary hearing is not required prior to the termination of disability benefits.

FACTS: Eldridge (P), who had been receiving disability insurance benefits under the Social Security Act since 1968, received a questionnaire from the state agency charged with monitoring his medical condition in 1972. After considering Eldridge's (P) reply that he was still disabled as well as the reports of physicians and a psychiatric consultant, the agency informed Eldridge (P) by letter that it had made a tentative decision to terminate his disability payments and gave Eldridge (P) a reasonable time to reply. After Eldridge (P) replied, disputing the agency's findings, the state agency made a final determination against Eldridge (P), which was accepted by the Social Security Agency. Although Eldridge (P) had the right to seek reconsideration of the decision within six months, he instead filed suit challenging the constitutional validity of the administrative procedures used to assess the presence of a continued disability. The court of appeals held that Eldridge (P) had to be afforded an evidentiary hearing prior to termination of disability payments, and Mathews (D), on behalf of the Social Security Agency, appealed.

ISSUE: Is an evidentiary hearing required prior to the termination of disability benefits?

HOLDING AND DECISION: (Powell, J.) No. An evidentiary hearing is not required prior to the termination of disability benefits. The determination of what due process requires in the way of specific procedures requires consideration of three distinct factors: (1) the private interest that will be affected by the official action; (2) the risk of an erroneous deprivation of such interest through the procedures used and the probable value, if any, of additional or substitute procedural safeguards; and (3) the government's interest, including the function involved and the fiscal and administrative burdens that the additional or substitute procedural requirement would entail. Here, while the deprivation from termination of disability benefits may be significant, the recipient may have access to other forms of private or government assistance. Second, because the decision whether to discontinue disability benefits will usually turn upon routine and unbiased medical reports, there is little risk of an erroneous deprivation. Third, the government's and the public's interest in conserving scarce fiscal and administrative resources is a significant factor. Thus, the present administrative procedures fully comport with due process. Reversed.

DISSENT: (Brennan, J.) The very legislative determination to provide disability benefits, without any prerequisite determination of need in fact, presumes a need by the recipient which should not be denigrated.

▶ ANALYSIS

In *Sniadich v. Family Finance Corp.*, 395 U.S. 337 (1969), the Court invalidated a Wisconsin statutory garnishment procedure which gave no notice or opportunity to be heard before the in rem seizure of Sniadich's wages. The Court noted that because prejudgment garnishment may impose tremendous hardship on the wage earner and give the creditor enormous leverage, the general rule is that there must be notice and a prior hearing before garnishment.

Quicknotes

NOTICE Communication of information to a person by an authorized person or an otherwise proper source.

PROCEDURAL DUE PROCESS The constitutional mandate that if the state or federal government acts so as to deny a citizen of a life, liberty or property interest the individual is first entitled to notice and the right to be heard.

Cleveland Board of Education v. Loudermill

Board of Education (D) v. Employees (P)

470 U.S. 532 (1985).

NATURE OF CASE: Appeal from the dismissal of an action for deprivation of due process.

FACT SUMMARY: Loudermill (P) and Donnelly (P), in separate cases, contended their dismissals without a hearing denied them due process.

🏛 RULE OF LAW

A state statute creating a property right is not the final word on what process is due prior to the valid deprivation of that right.

FACTS: In separate cases, Loudermill (P) and Donnelly (P) were terminated from state employment under statutes which provided for the exclusive method of removal. These statutes did not provide for either pre- or post-termination hearings. They sued contending they had been denied property without due process. The state governmental entities defended contending the property right in continued employment was created by statute. Thus it could be validly taken away by the same statute without any further due process inquiry. The trial court dismissed Loudermill's (P) claim for failure to state a cause of action. Donnelly's (P) claim was granted, and both were appealed. The court of appeals held that each had been denied due process. The U.S. Supreme Court granted certiorari.

ISSUE: Is a state statute which creates a property right the final word on what process is due prior to the deprivation of that right?

HOLDING AND DECISION: (White, J.) No. A state statute creating a property right is not the final word on what process is due prior to the deprivation of that right. Property rights are created by state law. However the concept of due process is one of constitutional dimensions. Merely because a property right is created does not take the analysis out of constitutional scrutiny. As a result, even though the statutory procedures were followed in these cases, both individuals were denied post-termination hearings. Thus they were denied property without due process. Affirmed and remanded.

CONCURRENCE: (Marshall, J.) Due process requires a pretermination hearing.

CONCURRENCE AND DISSENT: (Brennan, J.) The record was insufficient to determine whether there was unconstitutional delay in resolving these cases.

DISSENT: (Rehnquist, J.) A state can create and take away a property right.

▶ ANALYSIS

A prerequisite to the use of a due process analysis is the existence of a property right. A property right in continued employment has been recognized since *Arnet v. Kennedy*, 416. U.S. 134 (1974). Once a property right is recognized it must be determined that the deprivation resulted from some governmental action. Private deprivation does not trigger any constitutional protection.

Quicknotes

DUE PROCESS CLAUSE Clauses found in the Fifth and Fourteenth Amendments to the United States Constitution providing that no person shall be deprived of "life, liberty, or property, without due process of law."

PROPERTY RIGHT Any kind of right to specific property, be it personal or real property, tangible or intangible.

Nixon v. Administrator of General Services

President (P) v. Administrator (D)

433 U.S. 425 (1977).

NATURE OF CASE: Appeal from judgment upholding constitutionality of federal legislation.

FACT SUMMARY: Former President Richard Nixon (P) contended that the Presidential Recordings and Materials Preservation Act constituted an unconstitutional bill of attainder.

RULE OF LAW
A law which imposes undesired consequences on an individual is not necessarily a bill of attainder.

FACTS: Former President Richard Nixon (P) objected to the constitutionality of the Presidential Recordings and Materials Preservation Act, which directed the Administrator of the General Services Administration (D) to take custody of his papers and other materials, including tapes, to promulgate regulations to govern eventual public access to some of the materials, and to screen the materials, all pursuant to various statutory guidelines. Nixon (P) argued that the Act was an unconstitutional bill of attainder because it was a law that legislatively determined guilt and inflicted punishment upon an identifiable individual without provision of the protections of a judicial trial. The district court found in favor of the administrator (D). Nixon (P) appealed.

ISSUE: Is a law which imposes undesired consequences on an individual necessarily a bill of attainder?

HOLDING AND DECISION: (Brennan, J.) No. The fact that the Act refers to Nixon (P) by name does not automatically offend the bill of attainder clause. Although at the time of the Act's passage only Nixon's (P) materials demanded immediate attention, the Act established a special commission to study and recommend appropriate legislation regarding the preservation of the records of future Presidents and all other federal officials. Further, Nixon (P) had executed a private agreement providing that his tape recordings would be destroyed if he were to die. Congress had a legitimate interest in insuring that these recordings would be available for use as evidence in future criminal trials in the Watergate affair. The Act provides for an award of just compensation for the taking of Nixon's (P) records, supporting the view that no punishment is being inflicted on Nixon (P). The Act is not a punitive bill of attainder. Affirmed.

CONCURRENCE: (Stevens, J.) Nixon (P) constituted a legitimate class of one because he resigned his office under unique circumstances and accepted a pardon for any offenses committed while in office. By so doing, he placed himself in a different class from all other Presidents.

ANALYSIS

The Court, in the landmark case of *U.S. v. Lovett*, 328 U.S. 303 (1946), gave a broad reading to the bill of attainder clause. "Legislative acts, no matter what their form, that apply either to named individuals or to easily ascertainable members of a group in such a way as to inflict punishment on them without a judicial trial are bills of attainder prohibited by the Constitution." The Court in the present case rejected the argument that punishment was being inflicted on Nixon (P) without a judicial trial.

Quicknotes

BILL OF ATTAINDER Legislative acts that apply to named individuals or members of a group in such a way as to inflict punishment on them without a judicial trial.

TAKING A governmental action that substantially deprives an owner of the use and enjoyment of his or her property, requiring compensation.

Home Building & Loan Association v. Blaisdell

Mortgagee (P) v. Mortgagor (D)

290 U.S. 398 (1934).

NATURE OF CASE: Appeal to determine the constitutionality of a state statute.

FACT SUMMARY: In 1933, Minnesota passed the Mortgage Moratorium Law, which provided for a delay in the final foreclosure of mortgages.

RULE OF LAW

The Contract Clause of the United States Constitution provides that no state shall pass any law impairing the obligations of contracts; but, even if such obligations will be impaired, a state may exercise its eminent domain power and/or its power to protect the public's health, safety, and welfare.

FACTS: In 1933, Minnesota passed the Mortgage Moratorium Law, to remain in effect during the emergency created by the Depression. This law provided that the period for redemption from foreclosure sales could be extended for a specified time (i.e., foreclosure of mortgages could be delayed) if the mortgagor obtained an order requiring him to pay a reasonable value of the income of the property or its fair rental value to the mortgagee. After passage of this law, the Blaisdells (D) secured an order delaying the final foreclosure of their mortgage on the condition that they pay the property's reasonable rental value to the Home Building & Loan Ass'n (P), the mortgagee. Thereupon, Home Building (P) brought an action against the Blaisdells (D) to complete foreclosure. After the Minnesota Supreme Court held for the Blaisdells (D) on the basis that the Mortgage Moratorium Law was constitutional, Home Building (P) appealed.

ISSUE: Does the Contract Clause of the Constitution "absolutely" bar a state from passing any law which will impair the obligations of contracts?

HOLDING AND DECISION: (Hughes, C.J.) No. The Contract Clause of the United States Constitution provides that no state shall pass any law impairing the obligations of contracts; but, even if such obligations will be impaired, a state may exercise its eminent domain power and/or its power to protect the public's health, safety, and welfare. These are "essential attributes of sovereign power," and, as such, must be retained by the states. Of course, though, they must be exercised reasonably (i.e., only those means appropriate to accomplish them can be used). Here, the Mortgage Moratorium Law is reasonably necessary under the circumstances to protect the public's welfare. Therefore, even though it impairs the obligations of contracts (i.e., by

delaying mortgagee's rights under mortgage agreements), it is valid. Affirmed.

ANALYSIS

This case illustrates the central limitation placed upon the Contract Clause of the Constitution. There are, however, other limitations. For example, the clause applies only to state legislation (i.e., only a legislature can "pass" a law). As such, a state court can overrule a prior decision even though such a reversal may affect contracts. Note, also, that the Contract Clause does not apply to the federal government. However, the concept of due process in the Fifth Amendment has been interpreted in a manner which provides basically the same protection against the federal government.

Quicknotes

CONTRACT CLAUSE Article 1, section 10 of the Constitution prohibiting states from passing any "law impairing the Obligation of Contracts."

EMINENT DOMAIN The governmental power to take private property for public use so long as just compensation is paid therefore.

FORECLOSURE An action to recover the amount due on a mortgage of real property where the owner has failed to pay their debt, terminating the owner's interest in the property which must then be sold to satisfy the debt.

MORTGAGE An interest in land created by a written instrument providing security for the payment of a debt or the performance of a duty.

REDEMPTION The repurchase of a security by the issuing corporation according to the terms specified in the security agreement specifying the procedure for the repurchase.

Allied Structural Steel Co. v. Spannaus

Steel company (P) v. State (D)

438 U.S. 234 (1978).

NATURE OF CASE: Appeal from dismissal of action to enjoin labor contract modification.

FACT SUMMARY: After Allied Structural Steel Co. (P) had for some years operated under a pension plan granting benefits to employees over 65 by calculating the time served with Allied (P), the State of Minnesota enacted a law requiring benefits to be provided for all employees who had worked for 10 years or more with a company, and required Allied (P) to contribute to a fund for that purpose.

RULE OF LAW
A state's interference with the contractual rights of private individuals not enacted in response to a broad, generalized social or economic emergency is invalid under the Contract Clause of the Constitution.

FACTS: Allied Structural Steel Co. (P) was a steel-producing concern located primarily in Illinois but maintaining some works in Minnesota, where it employed some 30 persons. For some years, Allied (P) had maintained a pension program for its employees providing benefits to those reaching the age of 65 and making payments calculated by the time spent in Allied's (P) employ. In 1974, the State of Minnesota enacted a law which required that benefits be provided to employees by the employer after 10 years of service. Alleging that this law unconstitutionally impaired its contract with the employees, Allied (P) filed suit in federal district court seeking an injunction from its application to Allied (P), and seeking to avoid making payment to a fund for the payment of employees not covered by the Allied (P) plan but within the ambit of the new law as required by Minnesota. The district court found no deprivation or impairment of any contract right, and Allied (P) appealed.

ISSUE: Is the interference of a state with the contractual rights of private individuals not enacted in response to a broad, generalized, economic or social emergency valid under the Contract Clause of the Constitution?

HOLDING AND DECISION: (Stewart, J.) No. The Contract Clause receded into comparative desuetude with the adoption of the Fourteenth Amendment, however it is not a dead letter and remains part of the Constitution. The first inquiry under a Contract Clause analysis is whether a state law has operated as a substantial impairment of a contractual relationship. Here, this has happened. Allied (P) reasonably relied heavily upon the rights set forth in its employment contracts and conducted its business and finances accordingly. The Minnesota law

retroactively modified these rights and expectations, changing the company's obligations. Not all such modifications are unconstitutional, however, and the question of constitutionality turns on the reasons for the state law's effect. The law, to constitutionally modify existing contract rights, must be an attempt to deal with a broad, generalized social or economic emergency situation. A state statute interfering with the contractual rights of private individuals not enacted in response to a broad, generalized, social or economic emergency is invalid under the Contract Clause of the Constitution. No such situation existed in this case which could be regarded as an emergency for purpose of the Contract Clause. Reversed.

DISSENT: (Brennan, J.) The law complained of in this case does not relieve any obligations existing pursuant to the contract of employment in question. It simply adds certain duties to the employer, Allied (P). The Contract Clause does not protect all contract-based expectations. It was directed at state legislative interference with the ability of creditors to obtain full payment provided by pre-Constitution contracts. It was therefore applicable only to laws which relieved a party of an obligation. The creation of new duties, as happened here, was not within the clause's protection and the Contract Clause thus has no application in this case.

ANALYSIS

The ability to collect, under the attempted modification, before meeting the contract requirements, is the "relief of an obligation" existing under the contract. Even under Justice Brennan's restrictive view, an "impairment" for Contract Clause purposes can be seen.

■═■

Quicknotes

CONTRACT CLAUSE Article 1, section 10 of the Constitution prohibiting states from passing any "law impairing the Obligation of Contracts."

FOURTEENTH AMENDMENT - 42 U.S.C. § 1983 Defamation by state officials in connection with a discharge implies a violation of a liberty interest protected by the due process requirements of the U.S. Constitution.

■═■

United States v. Causby

Federal government (D) v. Landowner (P)

328 U.S. 256 (1946).

NATURE OF CASE: Action for damages for the taking of property for public use.

FACT SUMMARY: The United States (D) was flying its airplanes over Causby's (P) land destroying its use as a chicken farm.

🏛 RULE OF LAW
Flights over private land that are so low and frequent as to be a direct and immediate interference with the enjoyment and use of the land constitute a taking of the land that must be compensated for.

FACTS: Causby (P) owned a small chicken farm near an airport. The glide path to one of the runways passed directly over his property and the planes using this runway were only 63 feet above his barn and 67 feet above his house. His egg production dropped off and about 150 of his chickens died from running into the walls from fright when the planes passed over. Causby (P) claimed that he and his family had been deprived of their sleep and had become nervous and frightened because there had been several accidents near the airport. Causby (P) asserted that there has been a taking of his property without just compensation because of the army and navy aircraft flights over his property. The court of claims held that the United States (D) had taken an easement over the property and therefore owed Causby (P) $2000.

ISSUE: Do flights over private land that are so low and frequent as to be a direct and immediate interference with the enjoyment and use of the land constitute a taking of the land that must be compensated for?

HOLDING AND DECISION: (Douglas, J.) Yes. The common law view that ownership of land includes all the airspace above the land has no place in the modern world. The air is a public highway and unless there is an actual interference with the property itself, no action will lie when aircraft flies through the airspace above the property. However the property owner is entitled to exclusive control of the immediate reaches of the airspace above his property. It isn't necessary that the land owner fill that airspace with buildings as long as he can show a need for that airspace. In this case the flight of the military aircraft over the property interfered with Causby's (P) full enjoyment of his property and limited his exploitation of it. Because the flights had caused a diminution in the value of the property, it was clear that a servitude had been imposed upon the land. The judgment of the court of claims was reversed however and the case was remanded back to the court of claims to determine whether the easement was permanent or temporary and to determine if the original award was sufficient. Reversed.

DISSENT: (Black, J.) The Court should not have decided this case on constitutional grounds because this will limit Congress in attempting to regulate air travel and to meet the changing conditions of air travel. While damages may have been appropriate in this case, there was not a taking in the constitutional sense.

▶ ANALYSIS

This is the leading case in this area of the law. It should be noted that an actual taking isn't necessary as long as there has been substantial damage to the property. In cases dealing with commercial aircraft, the Supreme Court has held that the county which owned the airport, rather than the federal government which regulates air travel, was liable for any taking of private property because of the noise of the aircraft.

■■■

Quicknotes

SERVITUDE A charge or burden resting upon one estate for the benefit or advantage of another.

TAKING A governmental action that substantially deprives an owner of the use and enjoyment of his or her property, requiring compensation.

■■■

Village of Belle Terre v. Boraas

Municipality (D) v. Resident (P)

416 U.S. 1 (1974).

NATURE OF CASE: Due process challenge to a zoning ordinance.

FACT SUMMARY: The Village of Belle Terre (D) had a zoning ordinance restricting land use to one-family dwellings and excluding Boraas (P) and five friends from renting a house in the Village.

> ### 🏛 RULE OF LAW
> Economic and social legislation does not violate the Equal Protection Clause if the law is "reasonable, not arbitrary" and bears "a rational relationship to a permissible state objective."

FACTS: The Village of Belle Terre (D) limited its land use to one-family dwellings. The purpose of this law was to provide a quiet neighborhood with few vehicles where families can raise their children. Boraas (P) was one of six tenants in a rented house. The Village of Belle Terre (D) served the owner of the house and the occupants with an order to remedy violations of the above law. Boraas (P) brought suit for an injunction declaring the ordinance unconstitutional. The court of appeals held the ordinance unconstitutional. The ordinance was challenged as violating Boraas' (P) right to association and right to privacy. The Village of Belle Terre (D) contended that the ordinance was reasonable and bore a rational relationship to the public welfare.

ISSUE: Must economic and social legislation meet a higher test than being reasonable and bearing a rational relationship to a permissible state objective?

HOLDING AND DECISION: (Douglas, J.) No. In economic and social legislation legislatures have historically drawn lines. These lines are respected against the charge of violation of the Equal Protection Clause if the law is "reasonable, not arbitrary" and bears "a rational relationship to a permissible state objective." This law is not aimed at transients, it involves no procedural disparity inflicted on some but not on others, and it involves no "fundamental" right guaranteed by the Constitution. The police power of the local government extends to laying out zones where family values, youth values, and the blessings of quiet seclusion and clean air make the area a sanctuary for people. Therefore, the law in question is constitutional. Judgment for the Village of Belle Terre (D).

DISSENT: (Marshall, J.) Zoning is a complex and important governmental function. Deference should be given governmental judgments concerning proper land-use allocation, but the ordinance in this case burdens Boraas' (P) First Amendment freedom of association and the constitutionally guaranteed right to privacy. It is improper to discriminate on the basis of personal lifestyle.

▶ ANALYSIS

States have very broad powers in the area of economic regulation. Subject to specific constitutional limitations, when the legislature has spoken, the public interest has been declared in terms well-nigh conclusive. In such cases the legislature is the main guardian of public needs to be served by social legislation.

Quicknotes

EQUAL PROTECTION CLAUSE A constitutional guarantee that no person should be denied the same protection of the laws enjoyed by other persons in like circumstances.

ZONING Municipal statutory scheme diving an area into districts in order to regulate the use or building of structures within those districts.

State Action

Quick Reference Rules of Law

The Civil Rights Cases (United States v. Stanley/Ryan/Nichols/ Singleton; Robinson v. Memphis & Charleston Ry. Co.)

Excluded citizens (P) v. Institutions (D)

109 U.S. 3, 27 L.Ed. 835 (1883).

NATURE OF CASE: Review of criminal and civil prosecutions under the 1875 Civil Rights Act.

FACT SUMMARY: In the 1875 Civil Rights Act, Congress sought to prohibit private discrimination under the Fourteenth and Thirteenth Amendments.

RULE OF LAW
Civil rights guaranteed by the Constitution cannot be impaired by the wrongful acts of individuals unless such acts are sanctioned or authorized by the state.

FACTS: Congress in 1875 passed the federal Civil Rights Act prohibiting private citizens from excluding other citizens from inns, public transportation, and places of amusement based on race. The Act was passed under the authority of the Thirteenth and Fourteenth Amendments. In four criminal prosecutions and one civil lawsuit involving exclusion of persons of color from hotels, theaters, and railroads, those prosecuted challenged the constitutionality of the Act.

ISSUE: Can civil rights guaranteed by the Constitution be impaired by the wrongful acts of individuals if such acts are not sanctioned or authorized by the state?

HOLDING AND DECISION: (Bradley, J.) No. Civil rights guaranteed by the Constitution cannot be impaired by the wrongful acts of individuals unless such acts are sanctioned or authorized by the state. Accordingly, Congress may not prohibit private discrimination under the Thirteenth and Fourteenth Amendments. The Fourteenth Amendment provides that no state shall deprive a person of equal protection or due process. It does not, by its terms, purport to affect private citizens' actions. While Congress does have the power to enforce the Amendment through appropriate legislation, such legislation cannot go so far as to turn an Amendment that limits states' rights into one that affects private parties. The Thirteenth Amendment, by prohibiting slaveholding, does regulate private citizens. However, racial segregation is not a "badge of slavery" sufficient to bring the Thirteenth Amendment into operation. Consequently, Congress exceeded its authority under these amendments in its 1875 legislation. Reversed.

DISSENT: (Harlan, J.) To deny a citizen equal participation due to race is a vestige of slavery sufficient to invoke the Thirteenth Amendment.

ANALYSIS

The Court's narrow reading of § 1 of the Fourteenth Amendment stands to this day. Although subsequent decisions have chipped away at it to some extent, the rule remains that the Fourteenth Amendment only affects state action. The major civil rights legislation of the 1960s came about, not through the Fourteenth Amendment, but through the seemingly unlikely jurisdictional basis of the Commerce Clause of Article III.

Quicknotes

DUE PROCESS CLAUSE Clauses found in the Fifth and Fourteenth Amendments to the United States Constitution providing that no person shall be deprived of "life, liberty, or property, without due process of law."

EQUAL PROTECTION A constitutional guarantee that no person shall be denied the same protection of the laws enjoyed by other persons in life circumstances.

STATE ACTION Actions brought pursuant to the Fourteenth Amendment claiming that the government violated the plaintiff's civil rights.

THIRTEENTH AMENDMENT The constitutional provision which abolished slavery in the United States.

Marsh v. Alabama

Jehovah's witness (D) v. State (P)

326 U.S. 501 (1946).

NATURE OF CASE: Appeal from a criminal conviction.

FACT SUMMARY: Marsh (D) attempted to distribute religious literature in a company-owned town.

RULE OF LAW
When private property is the equivalent of a public "business block," it ceases to be strictly private, and First Amendment rights may not be arbitrarily curtailed.

FACTS: Chickasaw was a company-owned town in Alabama. Its business district was open to the public and public highways ran through it. The company prohibited all solicitation or distribution of literature without a permit. Marsh (D), a Jehovah's Witness, attempted to pass out religious literature on the sidewalks of the business district. Marsh (D) was arrested and convicted of a misdemeanor for remaining on private property after being asked to leave. Marsh (D) alleged that this violated her First and Fourteenth Amendment rights and the sidewalks in the business block were quasi-public.

ISSUE: Where private property has taken on the public character of a public business block, may First Amendment rights be arbitrarily curtailed?

HOLDING AND DECISION: (Black, J.) No. Certain property becomes quasi-public as it becomes opened to the general public. The greater the access to and encouragement of public use, the less arbitrary freedom is granted to the owner as to the use and condition of his property. Where the property becomes the equivalent of a public business block, we find that private ownership will not excuse arbitrary curtailment of First Amendment rights. The public's right to free access to information and Marsh's (D) right to practice her First Amendment rights cannot be arbitrarily interfered with by the company. It cannot allow the distribution of certain material and arbitrarily deny access to others. Those living in company towns have a right to receive free access to divergent views. When the company's right to the free use of its quasi-public property is balanced against these other rights, the company's rights must give way. Reversed and remanded.

CONCURRENCE: (Frankfurter, J.) A company-owned town has invested itself with such a quasi-public character that it may no longer be deemed private property. First Amendment rights are far superior to any retained private interests.

DISSENT: (Reed, J.) We permit company towns and there is no compelling reason to accommodate trespasses. Absent public dedication there is no reason to treat company towns any differently than other private property.

ANALYSIS

Marsh has subsequently been limited to cases involving company towns and public dedications. Private property rights are still deemed superior to First Amendment rights in other situations. The rationale in *Marsh* is basically that the inhabitants of the town or those interested in influencing them have no other means to reasonably do so since the company can restrict newspapers, etc. In other situations, many public areas are available for distribution to the citizens of a community without requiring private property owners to suffer unwanted intrusions.

Quicknotes

FIRST AMENDMENT Prohibits Congress from enacting any law respecting an establishment of religion, prohibiting the free exercise of religion, abridging freedom of speech or the press, the right of peaceful assembly and the right to petition for a redress of grievances.

FOURTEENTH AMENDMENT Declares that no state shall make or enforce any law which shall abridge the privileges and immunities of citizens of the United States.

TRESPASS Unlawful interference with, or damage to, the real or personal property of another.

Hudgens v. National Labor Relations Board

Shopping center operator (D) v. Labor board (P)

424 U.S. 507 (1976).

NATURE OF CASE: Action alleging unfair labor practice.

FACT SUMMARY: Hudgens (D), a shopping center operator, refused to permit AFL-CIO Local 315 pickets on his premises to protest its treatment by Butler Shoe.

🏛 RULE OF LAW
A large self-contained shopping center is not the functional equivalent of a municipality for First and Fourteenth Amendment purposes.

FACTS: Hudgens (D) was the owner and operator of the North DeKalb Shopping Center in which was located a Butler Shoe Store. When Butler Shoe Co. employees, members of AFL-CIO Local 315, attempted to go onto the center's premises to picket Butler, Hudgens (D) threatened to have them arrested for criminal trespass unless they left. The Local subsequently filed this National Labor Relations Board (NLRB) (P) grievance charging, inter alia, that Hudgens (D) had violated their First Amendment right to free expression, made applicable to him by the Fourteenth Amendment because (by *Amalgamated Food Employees Union v. Logan Valley Plaza*, 391 U.S. 308 [1968]) his shopping center was the functional equivalent of a municipality.

ISSUE: Is the First Amendment's guarantee of freedom of expression applicable to the owners of large shopping centers?

HOLDING AND DECISION: (Stewart, J.) No. A large self-contained shopping center is not the functional equivalent of a municipality for First and Fourteenth Amendment purposes; and, as such, these amendments do not extend any federal protections against a private corporation which abridges freedom of expression. The contrary holding of this Court in *Logan Valley* was based on an erroneous reading of *Marsh v. Alabama*, 326 U.S. 501 (1946). In that case, an actual company town was involved, not a mere shopping center. Indeed, though other members of the Court today disagree, the recent holding of this Court in *Lloyd Corp. v. Tanner*, 407 U.S. 551 (1972), effectively overruled *Logan Valley* when it stated that the right to speak about Vietnam was not protected in a shopping center. The fact that Local 315 here was expressing itself about a business in the shopping center is immaterial. Whatever relief Local 315 may recover must come from some specific provision of the National Labor Relations Act. Vacated and remanded.

DISSENT: (Marshall, J.) *Logan Valley* and *Lloyd* are not only reconcilable but compel awarding relief here. The First Amendment applies whenever the shopping center owner "controls all places essential for the effective undertaking of some speech related activities—namely, those related to the activities of the center." It is the quality of this control which can make a shopping center the functional equivalent of a municipality.

▶ ANALYSIS

This case limits the concept of "state action" to activity engaged in by state agencies and agents (which company towns are on a de facto basis). Note also that the Court here expressed the idea that the extent of First Amendment protection depends upon the subject matter of the expression. Their very position, of course, has been used in the past, in more liberal decisions, to extend freedom of speech by prohibiting censorship (*Police Dept. of Chicago v. Mosley*, 408 U.S. 92 [1972]). *Hudgens* is the first case which has employed it to permit private censorship.

■=■

Quicknotes

FIRST AMENDMENT Prohibits Congress from enacting any law respecting an establishment of religion, prohibiting the free exercise of religion, abridging freedom of speech or the press, the right of peaceful assembly and the right to petition for a redress of grievances.

FOURTEENTH AMENDMENT – 42 U.S.C. § 1983 Defamation by state officials in connection with a discharge implies a violation of a liberty interest protected by the due process requirements of the U.S. Constitution.

TRESPASS Unlawful interference with, or damage to, the real or personal property of another.

■=■

Terry v. Adams

Parties not identified.

345 U.S. 461 (1953).

NATURE OF CASE: Racial discrimination suit.

FACT SUMMARY: The Jaybird Party, a Texas county political organization, excluded Negroes from its primaries on racial grounds.

🏛 RULE OF LAW
A state may not permit racial discrimination in private voting that is later ratified by public voting.

FACTS: The Jaybird Party, a Texas county political organization, was organized in 1889. Its membership was limited solely to white people. The Jaybirds would regularly hold a primary election before the general municipal primary election. While there was no legal compulsion on successful Jaybird candidates to enter Democratic primaries, they nearly always did so, and with few exceptions since 1889 had run and won without opposition in the Democratic primaries and the general elections that followed. The district court held that the combined Jaybird-Democratic general election machinery deprived Negroes (P) of their right to vote on account of their race and color, but the court of appeals reversed. Plaintiffs appealed.

ISSUE: May a state permit racial discrimination in private voting that is later ratified by public voting?

HOLDING AND DECISION: (Black, J.) No. It is apparent that Jaybird activities follow a plan purposefully designed to exclude Negroes from voting and at the same time to escape the Fifteenth Amendment's command that the right of citizens to vote shall neither be denied or abridged on account of race. The only election that has counted in the Texas county for more than 50 years has been that held by the Jaybirds from which Negroes were excluded. For a state to permit such a duplication of its election process is to permit a flagrant abuse of those processes to defeat the purposes of the Fifteenth Amendment. Reversed and remanded.

CONCURRENCE: (Frankfurter, J.) The vital requirement for state action is state responsibility—that somewhere, somehow, to some extent, there be an infusion of conduct by officials, panoplied with state power, into any scheme by which colored citizens are denied voting rights merely because they are colored.

CONCURRENCE: (Clark, J.) Apparently, the Jaybird Democratic Association operates as an auxiliary of the local Democratic Party organization. It selects its nominees and uses its machinery to destroy the weight and effect of ballots cast by blacks in Fort Bend County.

DISSENT: (Minton, J.) Apparently so far the Jaybirds have succeeded in convincing the voters of the county in most instances that their supported candidates should win. This seems to differ very little from situations common in many other places far north of the Mason-Dixon line, such as areas where a candidate must obtain the approval of a religious group.

▶ *ANALYSIS*

The holding in the present case stems from a line of decisions first enunciated in *Nixon v. Herdon*, 273 U.S. 536 (1927). In that case the Supreme Court held invalid a Texas law which expressly excluded blacks from voting in the state Democratic primary election.

■==■

Quicknotes

FIFTEENTH AMENDMENT States that the right of citizens of the United States to vote shall not be denied on account of race, color, or previous condition of servitude.

STATE ACTION Actions brought pursuant to the Fourteenth Amendment claiming that the government violated the plaintiff's civil rights.

■==■

Shelley v. Kraemer

Black family (D) v. Neighbor (P)

334 U.S. 1 (1948).

NATURE OF CASE: Appeal from enforcement of racially restrictive private covenants.

FACT SUMMARY: The Shelleys (D), a Negro family, purchased land adjacent to Kraemer (P), and Kraemer (P) brought suit to restrain Shelley (D) from taking possession due to a racially restrictive covenant in the earlier deeds to both parcels and others in the area.

RULE OF LAW

A state's enforcement of racially restrictive private agreements by court order constitutes "state action" that violates the Fourteenth Amendment.

FACTS: Kraemer (P) was the owner of a parcel of residential property where he resided and the Shelleys (D), a Negro family, purchased the adjacent parcel. At the time of the purchase, a restrictive covenant, which related to the Shelleys (D), Kraemer (P), and other properties, restricted any sale to Negroes. Shelley (D) had no actual knowledge of the restriction at the time of purchase. Kraemer (P) sued to enjoin Shelley (D) from taking possession and to restore title in the grantor. The trial court denied the relief on the ground that restrictive agreement was not finalized, but the Supreme Court of Missouri reversed and held that since the restrictions were private, enforcing them was not "state action" violative of the Fourteenth Amendment. Kraemer (P) appealed.

ISSUE: Does a state's enforcement of a racially restrictive private agreement by court order constitute a "state action" that violates the Fourteenth Amendment?

HOLDING AND DECISION: (Vinson, C.J.) Yes. The restrictions by agreement denying the right of occupancy of real property to persons on the basis of race or color could not stand under the Fourteenth Amendment if imposed by statute or local ordinance. But the decision of this Court in the *Civil Rights Cases* shows that merely private conduct, however discriminatory or wrongful, is not barred by the Fourteenth Amendment. Therefore, the restrictive agreements in this case do not violate the Fourteenth Amendment by themselves. However, the enforcement of these agreements by judicial action constitutes "state action." A state may not act to discriminate against persons on the basis of race or color. A state's enforcement of racially restrictive private agreements by court order constitutes "state action" that violates the Fourteenth Amendment by denying equal protection of the laws. Reversed.

▶ ANALYSIS

While this case did not hold the making of private racist agreements illegal, it denied access to the courts to

anyone seeking to enforce them. However, all racially based private discriminations are not denied judicial enforcement. For example, a private landowner may use trespass laws to prevent members of a racial minority from entering his property because such enforcement does not amount to the state's encouragement to others to discriminate.

Quicknotes

EQUAL PROTECTION A constitutional guarantee that no person shall be denied the same protection of the laws enjoyed by other persons in like circumstances.

FOURTEENTH AMENDMENT Declares that no state shall make or enforce any law which shall abridge the privileges and immunities of citizens of the United States.

RESTRICTIVE COVENANT A promise contained in a deed to limit the uses to which the property will be made.

STATE ACTION Actions brought pursuant to the Fourteenth Amendment claiming that the government violated the plaintiff's civil rights.

Evans v. Newton

Parties not identified.

382 U.S. 296 (1966).

NATURE OF CASE: Petition for writ of certiorari.

FACT SUMMARY: Suit against municipal trustees of an integrated city park, seeking appointment of private trustees to enforce the segregation provision of the will which established the park. Negro citizens intervened, requesting an order refusing the appointment as violative of federal law. The Georgia court accepted the resignation of the city as trustee and appointed private trustees.

RULE OF LAW
Where the tradition of state control has become firmly established, the mere substitution of trustees does not transfer a park from the public to the private sector.

FACTS: A will devised to the City of Macon, Georgia, a tract of land to be used as "a park and pleasure ground" for white people only. The city kept the park segregated for some years, but in time let Negroes use it, stating that the park was a public facility which it could not constitutionally manage and maintain on a segregated basis. Members of the Board of Managers of the park sued the City asking that the City be removed as trustee and that the court appoint new trustees. Several Negro citizens intervened, alleging that the prospective racial limitation was contrary to federal law, and asked the court to refuse to appoint private trustees. The Georgia court accepted the resignation of the City and appointed private trustees. On appeal, by the Negro intervenors, the Supreme Court of Georgia affirmed, holding that the testator could bequeath his property to a limited class, and that the appointment of new trustees to save the trust purpose was consistent with the court's equitable power to supervise charitable trusts.

ISSUE: Does the substitution of trustees transfer a park from the public to the private sector?

HOLDING AND DECISION: (Douglas, J.) No. Where the tradition of state control has become firmly established, the mere substitution of trustees does not transfer a park from the public to the private sector. This conclusion is supported by the nature of the service rendered the community by a park. While golf clubs, social centers, luncheon clubs, and other similar organizations in the private sector are sometimes racially oriented, a park is more like a fire department or police department that traditionally serves the community. Mass recreation through the use of parks is plainly in the public domain. State courts that aid private parties to perform that public function on a segregated basis implicate the state in conduct proscribed by the Fourteenth Amendment. The predominant character and purpose of this park is municipal. The service rendered even by a private park of this character is municipal in nature. The momentum it acquired as a public facility is certainly not dissipated ipso facto by the appointment of "private" trustees. The public character of this park requires that it be treated as a public institution subject to the command of the Fourteenth Amendment, regardless of who now has title under state law. Reversed.

CONCURRENCE: (White, J.) Racial conditions in the trust may not be given effect by the new trustee since it is incurably tainted by discriminatory legislation allowing such restraints/conditions, e.g., allows a limitation of "for the use of whites only." Because the statute allows for such discrimination, the state has failed to act in a neutral manner.

ANALYSIS

The majority opinion stresses the predominantly public character of the park and the tradition of state control as the basis for invoking the Fourteenth Amendment. The facts here are very similar to the *Girard* trust case. However, in this instance, the property was devised directly to the City of Macon, a political subdivision of the State of Georgia. The state is both owner and manager of the property (excepting reversion rights). More importantly, the court's analysis probes beyond legal property labels and discloses the fundamental public character of the park. The park by definition renders a "community service." This term, "community service," is subsequently developed by the court as one of the legal incidents in tests for state action. In keeping with this focus on the actual use and character of the park, the Court, per Justice Douglas, disallows the Georgia court's implicit attempt to use state property law to circumvent the federal constitution. However, this case must be read in light of the final resolution of the park controversy. In *Evans v. Abney*, 396 U.S. 425 (1970), the Court, by Justice Black (one of the dissenters in Newton), upheld the Georgia supreme court ruling that the trust purpose had failed, and that the park reverted to the heirs. Black took the Georgia court's ruling at face value, limiting Newton to the continued operation of the park. As long as the park ceased to exist, state law governed. Any resulting harshness is solely attributed to the state court's intention to carry out the terms of the will. Hence, this case must be read as a limited extension of the concept of state action.

Continued on next page.

Quicknotes

CHARITABLE TRUST A trust that is established for the benefit of a class of persons or for the public in general.

FOURTEENTH AMENDMENT Declares that no state shall make or enforce any law which shall abridge the privileges and immunities of citizens of the United States.

TRUSTEE A person who is entrusted to keep or administer something.

Evans v. Abney

Parties not identified.

396 U.S. 435 (1970).

NATURE OF CASE: Appeal from judgment of reversion under a testamentary trust.

FACT SUMMARY: The Supreme Court of Georgia ruled that a will failed because its racially restrictive covenants were not enforceable.

RULE OF LAW
A state court may invalidate a will when its unconstitutional provisions cannot be enforced.

FACTS: As a result of the Supreme Court's decision in *Evans v. Newton*, 382 U.S. 296 (1966), the Supreme Court of Georgia ruled that Senator Bacon's intention in his will to establish a park named Baconsfield for whites only had become impossible to fulfill, and that accordingly the trust had failed and the parkland and other trust property had reverted by operation of Georgia law to the heirs of the Senator. Evans (P) had argued that the action of the Georgia court violated the Constitution because it imposed a drastic "penalty," the "forfeiture" of the park, merely because of the city's compliance with the constitutional mandate expressed in *Evans v. Newton*, 382 U.S. 296 (1966).

ISSUE: May a state court invalidate a will when its unconstitutional provisions cannot be enforced?

HOLDING AND DECISION: (Black, J.) Yes. The action of the Georgia Supreme Court declaring the Baconsfield trust terminated presents no violation of constitutionally protected rights, and any harshness that may have resulted from the state court's decision can be attributed solely to its intention to effectuate as nearly as possible the explicit terms of Senator Bacon's will. The construction of wills is essentially a state-law question, and the Georgia court had no alternative under its relevant trust laws, which are neutral with regard to race, but to end the Baconsfield trust and return the property to the Senator's heirs. The effect of the Georgia decision eliminated all discrimination against Negroes in the park by eliminating the park itself, and the termination of the park was a loss shared equally by the white and Negro citizens of Macon since both races would have enjoyed a constitutional right of equal access to the park's facilities had it continued. Affirmed.

DISSENT: (Douglas, J.) Putting the property in the hands of the heirs will not necessarily achieve the racial segregation that Bacon desired.

DISSENT: (Brennan, J.) This is a case of a state court's enforcement of a racial restriction to prevent willing parties from dealing with one another. The decision of the Georgia courts thus constitutes state action denying equal protection.

ANALYSIS

This case follows the decision of the Court in *Evans v. Newton, (supra)*. In that case, the City of Macon refused to enforce racially restrictive policies in a park which was established by the will of United States Senator Augustus O. Bacon. In the prior case, the Court held that "mass recreation through the use of parks is plainly in the public domain, and state courts which aid private parties to perform that public function on a segregated basis implicate the state in conduct proscribed by the Fourteenth Amendment."

Quicknotes

RESTRICTIVE COVENANT A promise contained in a deed to limit the uses to which the property will be made.

REVERSION An interest retained by a grantor of property in the land transferred, which is created when the owner conveys less of an interest than he or she owns and which returns to the grantor upon the termination of the conveyed estate.

TESTAMENTARY TRUST A trust created by will and only effective after the grantor's death, since the assets that comprise the corpus of the trust are assumed to vest at that time.

Burton v. Wilmington Parking Authority

Black plaintiff (P) v. Municipal authority (D)

365 U.S. 715 (1961).

NATURE OF CASE: Action for declaratory and injunctive relief.

FACT SUMMARY: The City (D) leased space to a coffee shop which discriminated against Negroes.

RULE OF LAW

Discrimination by a business located in and considered a part of a state/city-owned facility is deemed state action violative of the Fourteenth Amendment.

FACTS: To secure additional revenue for a public parking facility, the Wilmington Parking Authority (D) entered into a long-term lease with various private parties to operate commercial facilities in the structure. One of the tenants, Eagle Coffee Shoppe (D), refused to serve Negroes. No restrictions were contained in the lease and the practice was not prohibited under state law. Burton (P), a Negro, brought an action for declaratory and injunctive relief against the Parking Authority (D), alleging state action in violation of the Fourteenth Amendment. The state supreme court found that only 15% of the facility was financed with public funds; the restaurant was separated from the facility and its only actual connection was the payment of rent. It therefore found insufficient state action/involvement in the private discrimination.

ISSUE: Does discrimination by a private party leasing facilities from the state constitute state action?

HOLDING AND DECISION: (Clark, J.) Yes. Where a private facility is intimately tied to a public one, the private discrimination will be deemed state action since the state appears to condone it and lends its authority in support of the private discrimination. The rental of private space in the facility was an integral part of its construction. A restaurant in such a facility was deemed an integral part of it. Merely because the lease did not prohibit discrimination, Eagle Coffee Shoppe (D) could not act in such areas with impunity. Because of the financial interdependency and the location of the restaurant it cannot be deemed to be wholly private action. Each case must be decided on its merits, no formula may be developed. Reversed and remanded.

CONCURRENCE: (Stewart, J.) Under Delaware law, a restaurant may refuse service to anyone it wishes. This amounts to state-authorized discrimination and the statute itself is unconstitutional.

DISSENT: (Harlan, J.) The Court's opinion leaves out what it is in the record that satisfies the requirement of state action.

ANALYSIS

Subsequent cases indicate the critical requirement for finding state action is the lease of state facilities for exclusively private uses. Montgomery, Alabama, leased public recreation facilities to private groups practicing racial discrimination. The Court found that this constituted state action. The grant of nonexclusive permits to such groups has not yet been deemed state action. The granting of a liquor license to a business or group practicing discrimination has not been deemed state action. *Moose Lodge No. 107 v. Irvis,* 407 U.S. 163 (1972).

Quicknotes

FOURTEENTH AMENDMENT Declares that no state shall make or enforce any law which shall abridge the privileges and immunities of citizens of the United States.

STATE ACTION Actions brought pursuant to the Fourteenth Amendment claiming that the government violated the plaintiff's civil rights.

Moose Lodge No. 107 v. Irvis

Private club (D) v. Black guest (P)

407 U.S. 163 (1972).

NATURE OF CASE: Constitutional challenge against racial discrimination in a private club.

FACT SUMMARY: The Moose Lodge (D) refused to serve liquor to the Negro guest of a member solely on the basis of his race.

🏛 **RULE OF LAW**
Merely granting a liquor license to a private club which engages in discriminatory practices is not sufficient state action to invoke the Fourteenth Amendment.

FACTS: Irvis (P), a Negro, was invited to the Moose Lodge (D) by a member. The Lodge (D) refused to serve liquor to Irvis (P) solely because he was a Negro. Irvis (P) brought an action in federal district court alleging that the state was authorizing and furthering discrimination. Irvis (P) requested the court to enjoin the Lodge's (D) discriminatory practices. Irvis' (P) claim of state action under the Fourteenth Amendment was based solely upon the granting of a liquor license to the Lodge (D). The district court found state action present based on the state's total control over the granting of licenses, its use of its police powers to regulate the Lodge's (D) physical facilities, and its licensing requirements, including the submission of a list of names and addresses of all members.

ISSUE: Is the issuance of a liquor license alone sufficient state action to invoke the Fourteenth Amendment?

HOLDING AND DECISION: (Rehnquist, J.) No. For state action to be found it must be shown that the state, through an exercise of its power and authority, fostered discrimination. Merely granting a permit enabling a private club to serve liquor to its members and their guests is essentially neutral conduct. It cannot be said that such conduct either fosters or encourages discriminatory practices. It also cannot be said that the state is lending either its prestige or support to a discriminatory group. Merely regulating the physical aspects of the club or granting a liquor license is not sufficient state action to invoke the prohibitions of the Fourteenth Amendment. The case might be decided contra if the rules and bylaws of the club required racial discrimination. Here they do not. The decision of the district court is reversed and the case remanded.

DISSENT: (Douglas, J.) Where the state grants a limited resource (e.g., small quota of liquor licenses as here) to a racially discriminatory private group, it is lending its prestige to the group and is fostering and encouraging discrimination.

DISSENT: (Brennan, J.) Merely granting the license was sufficient involvement. By granting the permit and regulating the operation the state became entangled in the business.

▶ **ANALYSIS**

Granting a lease in a public facility has been held to be sufficient governmental involvement to invoke the Fourteenth Amendment. *Burton v. Wilmington Parking Authority*, 365 U.S. 715 (1961). Another example of state action is where a private discriminatory facility contracts with the police to hire deputies to enforce the discriminatory practices. *Griffin v. Maryland*, 378 U.S. 130 (1964).

■—■

Quicknotes

FOURTEENTH AMENDMENT Declares that no state shall make or enforce any law which shall abridge the privileges and immunities of citizens of the United States.

POLICE POWERS The power of a state or local government to regulate private conduct for the health, safety and welfare of the general public.

■—■

Jackson v. Metropolitan Edison Co.

Customer (P) v. Utility (D)

419 U.S. 345 (1974).

NATURE OF CASE: Action seeking to restore continuous electrical service.

FACT SUMMARY: When Metropolitan Edison Co. (D), a utility empowered to bring electrical service pursuant to a certificate from the State of Pennsylvania, terminated Jackson's (P) electrical service for an alleged nonpayment of bills, Jackson (P) brought suit in federal district court alleging that the termination was a deprivation of property by "state action."

🏛 RULE OF LAW
A public utility's business conduct does not constitute "state action" for Fourteenth Amendment purposes despite the licensing of it by a state and the public service nature of its monopolistic business.

FACTS: Jackson (P) was a customer of Metropolitan Edison Co. (D), obtaining electrical service from it. Metropolitan (D) was a public utility operating under a Pennsylvania certificate of convenience and holding a monopoly on electrical service in its area. After Jackson (P) allegedly failed to pay certain bills, Metropolitan (D) cut her service. Jackson (P) brought this suit claiming entitlement to reasonably continuous service under state law. She alleged that the deprivation of it by Metropolitan (D) constituted "state action" violative of the Fourteenth Amendment because Metropolitan (D) was licensed by the state to do business and was a public service monopoly.

ISSUE: Does a public utility's business conduct constitute "state action" for Fourteenth Amendment purposes due to the licensing of it by a state and the public service nature of its monopolistic business?

HOLDING AND DECISION: (Rehnquist, J.) No. The fact that a business is a monopoly is not determinative of its actions constituting "state action," assuming that Metropolitan (D) is a monopoly. Metropolitan (D) performs an essential public service required by state law (providing electrical service), but this does not necessarily saddle the utility with a "public function." A "public function" is being carried out when powers traditionally associated with sovereignty are exercised. Electrical service is not one of those powers. Jackson (P) urged that because the service is one "affected with a public interest," it is "state action," but so many businesses and persons provide goods and services that are similarly essential and so "affected," that this, by itself, is not enough. Issuance by a state to a business of an operating license does not by itself transmute the actions of the business into "state action" when the state has no other involvement, i.e., does not

order the business to take any action, with the regular affairs of the business. This remains the case even when the business has a public service nature and is a state-sanctioned monopoly.

DISSENT: (Marshall, J.) When different constitutional violations are claimed, different standards should apply to "state action" analysis. The Court's decision today would seemingly uphold a policy of Metropolitan (D) of refusing service to minorities, welfare recipients or any other group, yet the Court would not hold that the state's involvement with the company was too remote to require nondiscrimination.

▶ ANALYSIS

"State action" will be found when powers traditionally associated with sovereignty are exercised, according to the Court, but which powers are so associated and which are not is a question not answered in full at this time. The power to provide utility service is not traditionally a power associated with sovereignty.

■=■

Quicknotes

FOURTEENTH AMENDMENT Declares that no state shall make or enforce any law which shall abridge the privileges and immunities of citizens of the United States.

MONOPOLY A privilege or right conferred upon an individual or entity granting it the exclusive power to manufacture, sell and distribute a particular service or commodity; a market condition in which one or a few companies control the sale of a product or service thereby restraining competition in respect to that article or service.

PUBLIC UTILITY A private business that provides a service to the public which is of need.

STATE SOVEREIGNTY The absolute power of self-government possessed by a state.

■=■

Reitman v. Mulkey

Landlord (D) v. Perspective tenants (P)

387 U.S. 369 (1967).

NATURE OF CASE: Action for injunctive relief and damages under §§ 51 and 52 of the California Civil Code.

FACT SUMMARY: Reitman (D) refused to rent the Mulkeys (P) an apartment on account of their race.

🏛 RULE OF LAW
If the ultimate effect of a state constitution or statute is to encourage racial discrimination, it violates the Equal Protection Clause of the Fourteenth Amendment and is unconstitutional.

FACTS: In a statewide ballot in 1964, the voters of California initiated a measure known as Proposition 14 which prevented the state from denying or limiting the right of any person to sell, lease, or rent his property to such persons as he, in his absolute discretion, chooses. Prior to the passing of this proposition, the Mulkeys (P) attempted to rent an apartment from Reitman (D), who refused to rent solely on the grounds of the Mulkeys' (P) race. As a result, the Mulkeys (P) sued under §§ 51 and 52 of the California Civil Code which provided that all persons are free and equal and are entitled to full and equal accommodations, advantages, facilities, privileges, or services in all business establishments of every kind whatsoever. They sought both injunctive relief and damages. Reitman (D) moved for summary judgment on the ground that §§ 51 and 52 had been rendered null and void by Proposition 14, which had been passed after the filing of the complaint. The trial court granted the motion and the case was appealed to the California Supreme Court, which held that Proposition 14, which had become Article 1, § 26 of the California Constitution, was invalid as it denied the equal protection of the laws guaranteed by the Fourteenth Amendment. Reitman (D) claimed that Proposition 14 did not violate the Equal Protection Clause, because it merely put the state in a neutral position by not allowing the state to interfere with the right of an individual to sell or rent his land to whom he pleased and because the state wasn't encouraging racial discrimination simply because it was not restricting it.

ISSUE: Does the abandonment of a positive nondiscrimination policy by a state in favor of a neutral stance, which would allow discrimination to occur in the sale and rental of private housing, constitute state action within the meaning of the Fourteenth Amendment?

HOLDING AND DECISION: (White, J.) Yes. The Court gave great deference to the reasoning and conclusion of the California Supreme Court when that court invalidated Proposition 14. While the states are not required to affirmatively forbid racial discrimination, they cannot foster it. Prior to the passage of Proposition 14 as a state constitutional amendment, the state had several statutes forbidding racial discrimination in the sale or rental of private housing units. As Justice Stewart pointed out in his concurring opinion in *Burton v. Wilmington Parking Authority*, 365 U.S. 715 (1961), the state may not authorize discrimination. By abandoning its open housing statutes in favor of a supposed position of neutrality, the state has encouraged private discrimination. If California's position had always been neutral and Proposition 14 was merely a codification of that position, no issue would be presented. But the California Supreme Court determined that the effect of Proposition 14 was to place the state in the position of sanctioning and encouraging private discrimination. While this Court undertakes no definite definition of that which would always constitute state action, there is no reason why it should reject the conclusions of the California court. Affirmed.

CONCURRENCE: (Douglas, J.) Because zoning is a state and municipal function, leaving that function to private parties who are licensed by the government and who racially discriminate by effectively zoning cities into white and black belts, enables the private parties to perform a governmental function in a way the state itself may not.

DISSENT: (Harlan, J.) This case presents no violation of the Fourteenth Amendment since Proposition 14 merely put the state in a neutral position in the area of private discrimination affecting the sale or rental of private residential property. The majority opinion was solely based on a conclusion of law and did not attempt to find any facts which pointed out that Proposition 14 actually did involve state discriminatory actions. For there to be state action sufficient to bring the Fourteenth Amendment into operation, there must be some affirmative and purposeful state action which actively fosters discrimination. There is no such action in this case.

▶ ANALYSIS

This case has been criticized because of the reasoning behind the Court's decision. Many writers felt that Proposition 14 was properly adopted and was within the power of the voters to adopt. Regardless of the views of the critics, the Court expanded the state action concept by this decision. The state cannot make lawful that which it has previously held to be discriminatory and unlawful. It was clear in this case that state action was involved,

Continued on next page.

but this case does little to indicate the scope of involvement necessary by the state to make private actions state actions.

■━━■

Quicknotes

EQUAL PROTECTION CLAUSE A constitutional guarantee that no person should be denied the same protection of the laws enjoyed by other persons in like circumstances.

■━━■

Washington v. Seattle School District No. 1

State (D) v. School district (P)

458 U.S. 457 (1982).

NATURE OF CASE: Appeal from decision invalidating antibusing initiative.

FACT SUMMARY: The District (P) challenged the constitutionality of a state initiative designed to terminate the use of mandatory busing for purposes of racial integration.

🏛 RULE OF LAW
A state may not allocate governmental power by explicitly using the racial nature of a decision to determine the decision-making process.

FACTS: In March 1978, in order to reduce the problem of racially imbalanced schools created by segregated housing patterns, the Seattle School Board (P) enacted the "Seattle Plan," which made extensive use of mandatory busing and other forms of mandatory student reassignments to achieve racial integration. An organization called Citizens for Voluntary Integration Committee, which opposed the Seattle Plan, drafted a statewide initiative designed to terminate the use of mandatory busing for purposes of racial integration. The initiative, known as Initiative 350, in essence required that students attend local schools and envisioned busing for racial purposes only pursuant to court order adjudicating constitutional issues relating to the public schools. After suit was brought challenging the constitutionality of the initiative, the district court held Initiative 350 unconstitutional, because it could not ascertain whether racial motivation was a factor in its passage. After the Ninth Circuit Court of Appeals affirmed, the State (D) appealed.

ISSUE: May a state not allocate governmental power by explicitly using the racial nature of a decision to determine the decision-making process?

HOLDING AND DECISION: (Blackmun, J.) Yes. Laws structuring political institutions or allocating political power according to neutral principles, such as the executive veto, or the typically burdensome requirements for amending state constitutions, are not subject to equal protection attack, although they may make it more difficult for minorities to achieve favorable legislation. However, the state may not allocate governmental power non-neutrally by explicitly using the racial nature of a decision to determine the decision-making process. Here, Initiative 350 must fall because it does not attempt to allocate governmental power on the basis of any general principle. Instead, it uses the racial nature of an issue to define the governmental decision-making structure, and thus imposes substantial and unique burdens on racial minorities. Initiative 350 removes the

authority to address a racial problem, and only a racial problem, from the existing decision-making body, in such a way as to burden minority interests. Those favoring the elimination of de facto school segregation must now seek relief from the state legislature, or from the statewide electorate. Yet authority over all other student assignment decisions, as well as over most other areas of educational policy, remains vested in the local school board. Affirmed.

DISSENT: (Powell, J.) The State of Washington (D), the governmental body ultimately responsible for the provision of public education, has determined that certain mandatory busing programs are detrimental to the education of its children. The Fourteenth Amendment leaves the states free to decide matters of concern to the state at the state, rather than local, level of government. A neighborhood school policy and a decision not to assign students on the basis of their race does not offend the Fourteenth Amendment.

▶ ANALYSIS

As the majority decision noted, its main concern was not whether the state had the authority to intervene in the affairs of local school boards, but was rather whether the state had exercised that authority in a manner consistent with the Equal Protection Clause. The Court's central objection to the events giving rise to this litigation was not the repeal of the Seattle Plan itself, but was the state's race-conscious restructuring of its decision-making process.

■═■

Quicknotes

EQUAL PROTECTION CLAUSE A constitutional guarantee that no person should be denied the same protection of the laws enjoyed by other persons in like circumstances.

FOURTEENTH AMENDMENT Declares that no state shall make or enforce any law which shall abridge the privileges and immunities of citizens of the United States.

INITIATIVE The power of the people to propose bills and laws, and to enact or reject them at the polls, independent of legislative assembly.

■═■

Crawford v. Board of Education

Parties not identified.

458 U.S. 527 (1982).

NATURE OF CASE: Appeal from decision upholding constitutionality of antibusing initiative.

FACT SUMMARY: Crawford (P) contended that California's Proposition I was unconstitutional because it employed an explicit racial classification and imposed a race-specific burden on minorities seeking to vindicate state created rights.

RULE OF LAW

No burden exists upon the states to impose stricter requirements relating to race than the Fourteenth Amendment mandates.

FACTS: In 1976, the California Supreme Court ruled that under the California Constitution "state school boards . . . bear a constitutional obligation to take reasonable steps to alleviate segregation in the public schools, whether the segregation be de facto or de jure in origin." In November 1979, the voters of the State of California ratified Proposition I, an amendment to the due process and equal protection clauses of the state constitution. Proposition I conformed the power of the state courts to order busing to that exercised by the federal courts under the Fourteenth Amendment. Crawford (P) and other plaintiffs challenged the constitutionality of the initiative, arguing that Proposition I employed an explicit racial classification and imposed a race-specific burden on minorities seeking to vindicate state created rights. By limiting the power of state courts to enforce the state created right to desegregated schools, Crawford (P) contended, Proposition I created a dual court system that discriminated on the basis of race. After the California Court of Appeals upheld the constitutionality of the act, Crawford (P) brought this appeal.

ISSUE: Does a burden exist upon the states to impose stricter requirements relating to race than the Fourteenth Amendment mandates?

HOLDING AND DECISION: (Powell, J.) No. No burden exists upon the states to impose stricter requirements relating to race than the Fourteenth Amendment mandates. Proposition I seeks only to embrace the requirements of the federal Constitution with respect to mandatory school assignments and transportation. Proposition I does not embody a racial classification, and neither says nor implies that persons are to be treated differently on account of their race. It simply forbids state courts from ordering pupil school assignment or transportation in the absence of a Fourteenth Amendment violation. Having gone beyond the requirements of the federal Constitution, the state was free to return in part to the standard prevailing generally throughout the United States. Affirmed.

CONCURRENCE: (Blackmun, J.) While the California electorate may have made it more difficult to achieve desegregation when it enacted Proposition I, it did so not by working a structural change in the political process so much as by simply repealing the right to invoke a judicial busing remedy.

DISSENT: (Marshall, J.) How can a fundamental redefintion of the governmental decision-making structure with respect to the same racial issue be unconstitutional when the state seeks to remove the authority from local school boards, yet constitutional when the state attempts to achieve the same result by limiting the power of its courts?

ANALYSIS

As the majority decision noted in upholding the constitutionality of the initiative, Proposition I only limited the state courts when enforcing the state constitution. The Court therefore surmised that the initiative would not preclude state court enforcement of state statutes requiring busing for desegregation or for any other purpose.

Quicknotes

INITIATIVE The power of the people to propose bills and laws, and to enact or reject them at the polls, independent of legislative assembly.

FOURTEENTH AMENDMENT Declares that no state shall make or enforce any law which shall abridge the privileges and immunities of citizens of the United States.

Flagg Brothers, Inc. v. Brooks

Storage company (D) v. Tenants (P)

436 U.S. 149 (1978).

NATURE OF CASE: Appeal from finding of "state action."

FACT SUMMARY: Flagg Brothers, Inc. (D) took possession of Brooks' (P) furniture and stored it after Brooks (P) was evicted from her residence, and Brooks (P) filed this suit to enjoin sale of the furniture by Flagg (D) to satisfy the storage bill pursuant to a New York statute permitting such sale.

🏛 RULE OF LAW
A private entity that sells goods stored by it to satisfy unpaid storage costs pursuant to a state statute does not engage in "state action" for Fourteenth Amendment purposes.

FACTS: Brooks (P) and Jones (P), who later joined in this suit, were evicted from their apartments, and the city marshall arranged for the storage of their possessions by Flagg Brothers, Inc. (D). Brooks (P) gave permission for the storage though she found the price too high. After disputes on price, Flagg (D) informed Brooks (P) by letter that her furniture would be sold within 10 days unless payment was made. She filed this class action and was joined by Jones (P) alleging that the conduct of Flagg (D) constituted state action depriving her of property, being done under color of the New York statute permitting such sale and being attributable to that state. The district court dismissed the case for failure to state a claim but the court of appeals reversed. The Supreme Court granted certiorari.

ISSUE: Does a private entity that sells goods stored by it to satisfy unpaid storage costs pursuant to a state statute engage in "state action" for Fourteenth Amendment purposes?

HOLDING AND DECISION: (Rehnquist, J.) No. While as a factual matter any person with sufficient physical power may deprive a person of his property, only a state or a person whose action may be fairly treated as that of the state may deprive him of any interest encompassed by the Fourteenth Amendment. In this case the challenged conduct occurred after the city marshall was no longer involved with the matter. Flagg (D) acted under state law, and the question is whether this is sufficient to make the conduct "state action." Brooks (P) argued that the resolution of private disputes is a function of the state "traditionally exclusively reserved to the states," but while this function is usually performed by the state, it is not exclusively reserved to it. Private resolution is permitted by the statute and was permitted in some areas before it. Moreover, resolution of this dispute under the questioned statute was not the only resolution possible because state law provided remedies here not invoked. Brooks (P) could

have sought a waiver in the agreement as to sale of the goods, and Jones (P) could have sought to replevy her goods under state law. The State of New York has not compelled any action, but has merely announced when it will not interfere with private action, as occurs when a statute of limitation bars suit. Therefore, a private entity selling goods stored by it to satisfy unpaid storage costs pursuant to a state statute does not engage in "state action" for Fourteenth Amendment purposes. Reversed.

DISSENT: (Stevens, J.) Under the majority's decision, a warehouseman's proposed sale pursuant to a state statute for nonpayment is purely private action because the state does not compel the sale, but merely permits it, and because the power to do so is not exclusively delegated to the state. Under this approach, private citizens can be empowered by the state to use self-help in many situations without federal challenge, including retention of excess proceeds of sale, entry of homes to recover goods, or acquisition of a weaker person's goods by a stronger one, simply because the state permits rather than "compels" such conduct.

▶ ANALYSIS

It is unclear how much involvement of the state is necessary to amount to "state action." The cases show a trend toward allowing a great deal to pass as private conduct where the state is undeniably involved, but in cases of discrimination official encouragement has been found to constitute "state action," such as where city officials made statements which encouraged property owners to invoke trespass laws in a manner discriminatory toward sit-in demonstrators (which invocation would be legal in the absence of state encouragement). *Lombard v. Louisiana*, 373 U.S. 267 (1963).

■═■

Quicknotes

FOURTEENTH AMENDMENT Declares that no state shall make or enforce any law which shall abridge the privileges and immunities of citizens of the United States.

REPLEVIN An action to recover personal property wrongfully taken.

STATE ACTION Actions brought pursuant to the Fourteenth Amendment claiming that the government violated the plaintiff's civil rights.

WAIVER The intentional or voluntary forfeiture of a recognized right.

■═■

Equal Protection

Quick Reference Rules of Law

Railway Express Agency, Inc. v. New York

Trucking company (D) v. City (P)

336 U.S. 106 (1949).

NATURE OF CASE: Appeal from conviction for violation of a state advertising statute.

FACT SUMMARY: New York (P) had a regulation which prohibited advertising on vehicles, but allowed advertising on business vehicles so long as the vehicles were engaged in their owner's usual work and are not used mainly for advertising.

🏛 RULE OF LAW
The Equal Protection Clause does not require that a statute eradicate all evils of the same type or none at all.

FACTS: A New York City (P) regulation prohibited advertising on vehicles. The statute did not prohibit, however, advertising on business vehicles so long as the vehicles were engaged in their owner's usual work and were not used merely or mainly for advertising. Railway Express Agency, Inc. (D) was engaged in a nationwide express business. It operated 1,900 trucks in New York City (P). It sold space on the exterior of its trucks for advertising. Such advertising is generally unconnected with its business.

ISSUE: Does a regulation, which prohibits general advertisements on vehicles while allowing advertisement of products sold by vehicle owners, violate equal protection?

HOLDING AND DECISION: (Douglas, J.) No. The court of special sessions concluded that advertising on vehicles using the streets of New York City (P) constituted a distraction to vehicle drivers and pedestrians, therefore affecting the public's safety in the use of the streets. The local authorities may well have concluded that those who advertise their own products on their trucks do not present the same traffic problem in view of the nature and extent of their advertising. The Court cannot say that such a judgment is not an allowable one. The classification has relation to the purpose for which it is made and does not contain the kind of discrimination against which the Equal Protection Clause protects. The fact that New York City (P) does not eliminate all distractions from its streets is immaterial. It is no requirement of equal protection that all evils of the same genus be eradicated or none at all. Conviction affirmed.

CONCURRENCE: (Jackson, J.) Laws must not discriminate between people except upon some reasonable differentiation fairly related to the object of regulation. There is a real difference between doing in self-interest and doing for hire, so that it is one thing to tolerate an action done in self-interest and another thing to permit the same action to be done for hire.

▶ ANALYSIS

Traditionally, the Equal Protection Clause supported only minimal judicial intervention. During the late sixties, however, it became the favorite and most far-reaching tool for judicial protection of fundamental rights not specified in the Constitution. For many years, the impact of the Equal Protection Clause was a very limited one. During the decades of extensive court intervention with state economic legislation, substantive due process, not equal protection, provided the cutting edge to determine a statute's constitutionality. Also, as the concurring opinion points out, equal protection demanded only a "reasonable differentiation fairly related to the object of regulation." As demonstrated by this case, the rational classification requirement could be satisfied fairly easily, as the courts were extremely deferential to legislative judgment and easily convinced that the means used might relate rationally to a plausible end.

Quicknotes

EQUAL PROTECTION CLAUSE A constitutional guarantee that no person should be denied the same protection of the laws enjoyed by other persons in like circumstances.

FUNDAMENTAL RIGHT A liberty that is either expressly or impliedly provided for in the United States Constitution, the deprivation or burdening of which is subject to a heightened standard of review.

SUBSTANTIVE DUE PROCESS A constitutional safeguard limiting the power of the state, irrespective of how fair its procedures may be; substantive limits placed on the power of the state.

Strauder v. West Virginia

Black man (D) v. State (D)

100 U.S. (10 Otto) 303, 25 L.Ed. 664 (1879).

NATURE OF CASE: Appeal from murder conviction.

FACT SUMMARY: Strauder (D), a colored man, was convicted of murder by a jury from which blacks were excluded.

RULE OF LAW
A state may not prevent persons from serving on juries because of their race or color.

FACTS: Strauder (D), a colored man, was indicted for murder in the Circuit Court of Ohio County, West Virginia, on October 20, 1874, and after a trial was convicted of the charge. The judgment was affirmed by the state supreme court. On appeal, Strauder (D) argued that at the trial he was denied rights to which he was entitled under the Constitution and laws of the United States "[because under state law blacks were ineligible to serve on the grand or petit jury.]"

ISSUE: May a state prevent people from serving on juries because of their race or color?

HOLDING AND DECISION: (Strong, J.) No. The Fourteenth Amendment is one of a series of constitutional provisions having a common purpose: namely, securing to a race recently emancipated, a race that through many generations had been held in slavery, all the civil rights that the superior race enjoy. The Fourteenth Amendment declares that the law in the states shall be the same for persons of color as for the white; that all persons, whether colored or white, shall stand equal before the laws of the states, and, in regard to the colored race, for whose protection the amendment was primarily designed, that no discrimination shall be made against them by law because of their color. The words of the amendment, it is true, are prohibitory, but they contain a necessary implication of a positive right to exemption from unfriendly legislation which implies inferiority in civil society. Here, the West Virginia statute respecting juries is clearly discriminatory. The very fact that colored people are singled out and expressly denied by a statute all right to participate in the administration of the law, as jurors, because of their color, though they are citizens and may be in other respects fully qualified, is practically a brand upon them, and a stimulant to that race prejudice which is an impediment to securing to individuals of the race that equal justice which the law aims to secure to all others. Reversed and remanded.

ANALYSIS

This case, one of the earliest decisions interpreting the Fourteenth Amendment, discusses two themes which later became significant in determining whether a group constituted a suspect classification, and whether the legislation in question violates constitutional prohibitions. First is whether the class, as in the case of blacks, is one that has historically been the victim of societal discrimination. A second issue is whether the legislation in question tends to stigmatize that class in the eyes of society.

Quicknotes

FOURTEENTH AMENDMENT Declares that no state shall make or enforce any law which shall abridge the privileges and immunities of citizens of the United States.

MURDER Unlawful killing of another person either with deliberation and premeditation or by conduct demonstrating a reckless disregard for human life.

SUSPECT CLASSIFICATION A class of persons that have historically been subject to discriminatory treatment; statutes drawing a distinction between persons based on a suspect classification, i.e., race, nationality or alienage, are subject to a strict scrutiny standard of review.

Yick Wo v. Hopkins

Laundry operator (D) v. City (P)

118 U.S. 356, 30 L.Ed. 220 (1886).

NATURE OF CASE: Appeal from conviction of violating a city health and safety ordinance.

FACT SUMMARY: Only Chinese aliens were prosecuted under an ordinance requiring laundries to be constructed out of brick.

🏛 RULE OF LAW
A valid law unevenly and discriminatorily administered violates the Equal Protection Clause of the Constitution.

FACTS: A San Francisco ordinance made it unlawful to operate a laundry without consent of the board of supervisors unless the laundry was constructed of either stone or brick. Under the ordinance, the supervisors denied permission to Chinese aliens but granted it to whites. Yick Wo (D) was arrested for violating the ordinance. He appealed his conviction on the basis that the law was being administered in a discriminatory fashion.

ISSUE: Can a valid law be declared unconstitutional because it is being arbitrarily and discriminatorily applied?

HOLDING AND DECISION: (Matthews, J.) Yes. When, as here, it can be objectively demonstrated that a law is being discriminatorily applied, a court may declare the law unconstitutional. We can decide this case without ever reaching the question of the ordinance's validity (which is seriously in question). Even if valid, the San Francisco Supervisors (P) have applied it in a highly discriminatory and systematic fashion to exclude those of Chinese origin from practicing the laundry business. Such discriminatory treatment violates both the spirit and letter of the Equal Protection Clause and Yick Wo's (D) conviction must be discharged. Reversed and remanded.

▶ *ANALYSIS*

Other examples in this area include the systematic exclusion of blacks from jury panels through the use of the prosecutor's preemptory challenge power or by excluding them from jury rolls. Also, in *Mayor of Philadelphia v. Educational Equality League*, 415 U.S. 605 (1974), the Mayor was charged with discrimination in his appointment of a selection committee for school board members. However, in this case, the proof of discrimination was insufficient to establish a prima facie case and the charges were dismissed. The Court held that mere statistical data concerning population mixtures was insufficient to prove discrimination as a matter of law.

Quicknotes

EQUAL PROTECTION CLAUSE A constitutional guarantee that no person should be denied the same protection of the laws enjoyed by other persons in like circumstances.

PEREMPTORY CHALLENGE The exclusion by a party to a lawsuit of a prospective juror without the need to specify a particular reason.

■=■

Plessy v. Ferguson

Railroad passenger (D) v. State (P)

163 U.S. 537, 41 L.Ed. 256 (1896).

NATURE OF CASE: Appeal from criminal prosecution for violating a state railway accommodation segregation law.

FACT SUMMARY: Plessy (D) was arrested for trying to sit in a railroad car which was designated "for whites only."

🏛 RULE OF LAW
Segregation of the races is reasonable if based upon the established custom, usage, and traditions of the people in the state.

FACTS: Plessy (D), who was seven-eighths Caucasian and whose skin color was white, was denied a seat in an all-white railroad car. When he resisted he was arrested for violating a state law which provided for segregated "separate but equal" railroad accommodations. Plessy (D) appealed the conviction on the basis that separation of the races stigmatized persons of color and stamped them with the badge of inferiority. He claimed that segregation violated the Thirteenth and Fourteenth Amendments. The trial court found Plessy (D) guilty on the basis that the law was a reasonable exercise of the state's police powers based upon custom, usage, and tradition in the state.

ISSUE: May the state segregate the races in "separate but equal" facilities or accommodations?

HOLDING AND DECISION: (Brown, J.) Yes. This is a valid exercise of the state's police power. Where this has been the established custom, usage, or tradition in the state, it may continue to require such segregation as is reasonable to preserve order and the public peace. Such decisions have been continuously upheld. This is not a badge of "slavery" under the Thirteenth Amendment and it violates no provision of the Fourteenth Amendment. The enforced separation of the races is not a badge of servitude or inferiority regardless of how Plessy (D) and other persons of the colored race deem to treat it. The conviction is sustained.

DISSENT: (Harlan, J.) The Constitution is colorblind. All citizens are equal before the law. Regrettably, the Court has concluded that a state may regulate the enjoyment by citizens of their equal rights solely upon the basis of race.

▶ ANALYSIS

Plessy is of importance only for its historical perspective. Later cases borrowed the "separate but equal" phraseology and turned it around 180 degrees. In *Brown v. Board of* *Education,* 347 U.S. 483 (1954), the Court, 58 years after *Plessy,* held that separate could never be considered equal. It thus expressly overruled *Plessy.*

■━■

Quicknotes

FIFTH AMENDMENT CLAUSE The constitutional mandate requiring the courts to protect and enforce individuals' rights and liberties consistent with prevailing principles of fairness and justice and prohibiting the federal and state governments from such activities that deprive its citizens of a life, liberty or property interest.

FOURTEENTH AMENDMENT Declares that no state shall make or enforce any law which shall abridge the privileges and immunities of citizens of the United States.

POLICE POWERS The power of a state or local government to regulate private conduct for the health, safety and welfare of the general public.

SEPARATE BUT EQUAL DOCTRINE Doctrine pursuant to the holding in *Plessy v. Ferguson* that "separate but equal" facilities for persons of different races does not violate equal protection.

THIRTEENTH AMENDMENT The constitutional provision which abolished slavery in the United States.

■━■

Brown v. Board of Education

Minors (P) v. School board (D)

347 U.S. 483 (1954).

NATURE OF CASE: Negro minors sought the Court's aid in obtaining admission to the public schools of their community on a nonsegregated basis.

FACT SUMMARY: Negro children were denied admission to public schools attended by white children.

🏛 RULE OF LAW
The "separate but equal" doctrine has no application in the field of education and the segregation of children in public schools based solely on their race violates the Equal Protection Clause.

FACTS: Negro children had been denied admission to public schools attended by white children under laws requiring or permitting segregation according to race. It was found that the black children's schools and the white children's schools had been or were being equalized with respect to buildings, curricula, qualifications, and salaries of teachers.

ISSUE: Does segregation of children in public schools solely on the basis of race, even though the physical facilities are equal, deprive the children of the minority group of equal protection of the law?

HOLDING AND DECISION: (Warren, C.J.) Yes. First of all, intangible as well as tangible factors may be considered. Hence, the fact that the facilities and other tangible factors in the schools have been equalized is not controlling. Segregation of white and colored children in public schools has a detrimental effect on the colored children because the policy of separating the races is usually interpreted as denoting the inferiority of the Negro children. A sense of inferiority affects a child's motivation to learn. Segregation tends to deprive Negro children of some of the benefits they would receive in an integrated school. Any language in *Plessy v. Ferguson*, 163 U.S. 537 (1896), contrary to this is rejected. The "separate but equal" doctrine has no place in the field of education. Separate facilities are inherently unequal. Such facilities deprive the plaintiffs and other similarly situated of their right to equal protection of the laws guaranteed by the Fourteenth Amendment.

▶ ANALYSIS

In *Plessy v. Ferguson* the Court sustained a Louisiana statute requiring "equal, but separate accommodations" for black and white railway passengers. The separate but equal doctrine was born and under it a long line of statutes providing separate but equal facilities were upheld. Justice Harlan was the only dissenter in *Plessy*. He stated, "The arbitrary separation of citizens, on the basis of race, while they are on a public highway . . . cannot be justified upon any legal grounds. The thin disguise of equal accommodations for passengers in railway cars will not mislead anyone, nor atone for the wrong done this day." After the 1954 decision in *Brown v. Board of Education*, 347 U.S. 483 (1954), the Court found segregation unconstitutional in other public facilities as well. Despite the emphasis on the school context in *Brown*, the later cases resulted in per curiam orders simply citing *Brown*. Facilities that were desegregated included beaches, buses, golf courses, and parks.

Quicknotes

EQUAL PROTECTION CLAUSE A constitutional guarantee that no person should be denied the same protection of the laws enjoyed by other persons in like circumstances.

SEPARATE BUT EQUAL DOCTRINE Doctrine pursuant to the holding in *Plessy v. Ferguson* that "separate but equal" facilities for persons of different races does not violate equal protection.

Bolling v. Sharpe

Parties not identified.

347 U.S. 497 (1954).

NATURE OF CASE: Constitutional challenge to school segregation in the District of Columbia (D).

FACT SUMMARY: The District of Columbia's (D) school segregation policy was challenged by Negro students (P).

🏛 RULE OF LAW
Separate school facilities are so fundamentally unfair and discriminatory as to violate the Due Process Clause of the Fifth Amendment.

FACTS: Negro students (P) challenged the validity of the District of Columbia's (D) practice of segregating schools by race. The District (D) argued that separate but equal facilities have long been recognized in the District (D) and have been allowed by the courts. The students (P) contended that this was a badge of servitude and inferiority.

ISSUE: Is the enforced separation of the races so fundamentally unfair so as to violate the Fifth Amendment Due Process Clause?

HOLDING AND DECISION: (Warren, C.J.) Yes. There is no Equal Protection Clause in the federal Constitution and the Fourteenth Amendment is only applicable to the states. However, where discrimination is so fundamentally unfair as to offend the American ideal of fairness and justice then it violates the Due Process Clause of the Fifth Amendment. Racial classifications are fundamentally suspect and must be scrutinized with care. Where racial classifications conflict with the individual's right to freedom, they can only be justified by the most compelling governmental interests. Segregation in the schools is not related to any proper governmental objective. Such an unreasonable classification constitutes an arbitrary deprivation of individual liberty and violates the Due Process Clause. In view of our decision in *Brown v. Board of Education*, 347 U.S. 483 (1954), we hold that the federal government has the same duty to desegregate as do the states.

▶ ANALYSIS

The decisions in *Brown* and *Bolling* were applied to many other previously segregated areas. Examples include segregated transportation, entertainment, restaurants, public restrooms, etc. Where state action, as such, was not present, Congress sought to regulate private discrimination under its Commerce Clause powers.

Quicknotes

COMMERCE CLAUSE Article 1, section 8, clause 3 of the United States Constitution, granting Congress the power to regulate commerce with foreign countries and between the states.

DUE PROCESS CLAUSE Clauses found in the Fifth and Fourteenth Amendments to the United States Constitution providing that no person shall be deprived of "life, liberty, or property, without due process of law."

EQUAL PROTECTION CLAUSE A constitutional guarantee that no person should be denied the same protection of the laws enjoyed by other persons in like circumstances.

FIFTH AMENDMENT Provides that no person shall be compelled to serve as a witness against himself, or be subject to trial for the same offense twice, or be deprived of life, liberty, or property without due process of law.

SUSPECT CLASSIFICATION A class of persons that have historically been subject to discriminatory treatment; statutes drawing a distinction between persons based on a suspect classification, i.e., race, nationality or alienage, are subject to a strict scrutiny standard of review.

Brown v. Board of Education

Minors (P) v. School board (D)

349 U.S. 294 (1955).

NATURE OF CASE: Decision to determine the manner in which relief from segregation in public schools is to be accorded.

FACT SUMMARY: In May 1954, the Court decided that racial discrimination in public education is unconstitutional. It requested further arguments on the question of relief.

🏛 RULE OF LAW
The cases are remanded to the lower courts to enter orders consistent with equitable principles of flexibility and requiring the defendant to make a prompt and reasonable start toward full racial integration in public schools.

FACTS: These cases were decided in May 1954. The opinions declared that racial discrimination in public education is unconstitutional. They are incorporated here. Because the cases arose under various local conditions and their disposition will involve a variety of local problems, the Court requested additional arguments on the question of relief. All provisions of federal, state, and local laws which permit segregation in public schools must be modified.

ISSUE: Shall relief in the public school racial desegregation cases be accorded by remanding the cases to the lower courts to enter orders requiring integration?

HOLDING AND DECISION: (Warren, C.J.) Yes. School authorities have the primary responsibility for assessing and solving the problem of achieving racial integration in the public schools. It will be for courts to consider whether the school authorities' actions are good faith implementation of the governing constitutional principles. Because of their proximity to local conditions and the possible need for further hearings, the courts which originally heard these cases can best perform this judicial appraisal. In doing so, the courts will be guided by the equitable principles of practical flexibility in shaping remedies and the facility for adjusting and reconciling public and private needs. The courts will require that the defendants make a prompt and reasonable start toward full racial integration in the public schools. Once such a start is made, the courts may determine that additional time is required to carry out the May 1954 ruling. However, the burden rests upon the defendant to determine that such time is necessary and consistent with good faith compliance with the Constitution. The courts may consider problems related to administration, the facilities, school transportation systems, and revision of school districts and local laws.

They will also consider the adequacy of any plans proposed by the defendants and will retain jurisdiction during the transition period. The cases are remanded to the lower courts to enter orders consistent with this opinion as necessary to insure that the parties to these cases are admitted to public schools on a racially nondiscriminatory basis with all deliberate speed. Judgments reversed, except in the Delaware case which is affirmed, and all cases remanded.

▶ ANALYSIS

After its promulgation of general guidelines in *Brown II* in 1955, the Court maintained silence about implementation for several years. Enforcement of the desegregation requirement was left largely to lower court litigation. In 1958, the Court broke its silence in *Cooper v. Aaron*, 358 U.S. 1, where it reaffirmed the Brown principles in the face of official resistance in Little Rock, Arkansas. It was not until the early 1960s, however, that the Court began to consider the details of desegregation plans. During the late 1960s, Court rulings on implementation came with greater frequency, specificity, and urgency. Finally, in *Alexander v. Holmes County Board of Education*, 369 U.S. 19 (1969), the Court called for an immediate end to dual school systems.

■═■

Quicknotes

DESEGRATION A judicial order prohibiting a person's race to be used as a basis for disqualification in attending the school of his or her choice, or to work at a place of his or her choice.

STRICT SCRUTINY Method by which courts determine the constitutionality of a law, when a law affects a fundamental right. Under the test, the legislature must have a compelling interest to enact the law and measures prescribed by the law must be the least restrictive means possible to accomplish its goal.

SUSPECT CLASSIFICATION A class of persons that have historically been subject to discriminatory treatment; statutes drawing a distinction between persons based on a suspect classification, i.e., race, nationality or alienage, are subject to a strict scrutiny standard of review.

■═■

Keyes v. School District No. 1

Petitioners (P) v. School district (D)

413 U.S. 189 (1973).

NATURE OF CASE: Appeal from refusal to order desegregation.

FACT SUMMARY: Keyes (P) filed suit seeking desegregation of all segregated schools in the School District (D), but the court ordered only the desegregation of the small segment directly affected by the conduct of the District (D).

⚖ RULE OF LAW

Where school authorities practice purposeful de jure segregation by race in a significant part of a school system, a de jure showing of segregation in each segment of the system is not required for a court order to desegregate the entire system.

FACTS: By gerrymandering the student attendance zones of Denver, Colorado, along with using "optional zones" and mobile classrooms, the School District (D) engaged in intentional segregation by race of the Park Hill segment of the school system. This was a predominantly white area which represented a small part of the system. Keyes (P) filed this suit for an order to desegregate the Park Hill schools and further to desegregate all Denver schools in the system. The district court held that the order should issue as to the Park Hill schools, but that a de jure showing of segregation, such as the one as to Park Hill, was required as to each and every other area which Keyes (P) sought to have included in the order. The court of appeals affirmed and the U.S. Supreme Court granted certiorari.

ISSUE: Where school authorities practice purposeful de jure segregation by race in a significant part of a school system, is a de jure showing of segregation in each segment of the system required for a court order to desegregate the entire system?

HOLDING AND DECISION: (Brennan, J.) No. It has never been the law that each and every school encompassed by the statute is subject to a court order to desegregate. But here there was no statute, although there was a dual system. The racially inspired actions of the District (D) had an impact beyond the schools that were subject to those actions. A finding of segregation in one segment of the system is probative of such a conclusion as to the others. Furthermore, in this case, there was a purpose to segregate, not just a segregating result. Where school authorities practice purposeful segregation by race in a significant part of a school system, a de jure showing of segregation in each segment of the system is not required for a court order to desegregate the entire system. Reversed.

CONCURRENCE: (Douglas, J.) For purposes of the Fourteenth Amendment Equal Protection Clause there is no difference between de facto and de jure segregation. The school board is a state agency and its actions comprise "state action" when it performs its functions.

CONCURRENCE IN PART: (Powell, J.) Segregation in schools is a nationwide problem that has gone untreated in many cities outside of the South. However, the distinction between de facto and de jure segregation does not aid in the analysis of this case. Under this approach, a petitioner must delineate between segregative acts and segregative intents. I would hold simply that where segregated schools exist, a prima facie case has been established which imposes upon school authorities a nationally applicable burden to demonstrate that they are operating an integrated school system.

DISSENT: (Rehnquist, J.) In the absence of a statute requiring segregation, some factual inquiry must be required in order to establish the existence of such segregation. Here, the Court has decided that if a single attendance zone is gerrymandered, the school district is guilty of operating a "dual" school system. Such a result can only be described as the product of judicial fiat.

▶ ANALYSIS

The impact of the retention of the de facto-de jure distinction in desegregation cases is that where some purposeful action of de jure segregation on the part of the government (through the school district) cannot be shown, the Fourteenth Amendment Equal Protection Clause is powerless to remedy segregation that concededly exists as a matter of fact (de facto segregation). However, once de jure segregation is found in part of a school system, intent need not be shown as to the other part of that system.

■=■

Quicknotes

DE FACTO SEGREGATION Segregation that is not caused by explicit policy of any state or public institution but rather by social, economic, and other, nonlegislative practices.

DE JURE SEGREGATION Segregation that is mandated or intended by governmental or school authorities.

EQUAL PROTECTION CLAUSE A constitutional guarantee that no person should be denied the same protection of the laws enjoyed by other persons in like circumstances.

Continued on next page.

GERRYMANDERING To create a civil decision of an unusual shape for an improper purpose such as redistricting a state with unnatural boundaries, isolating members of a particular political party, so that a maximum number of the elected representatives will be of that political party.

■▬■

Washington v. Davis

State (D) v. Employment applicants (P)

426 U.S. 229 (1976).

NATURE OF CASE: Appeal from reversal of order sustaining validity of employment qualification test.

FACT SUMMARY: Washington (D) administered a written test of verbal skill, vocabulary, and reading comprehension to applicants for jobs on the Police Department, and since four times as many blacks failed the test than whites, Davis (P) brought suit alleging the invalidity of the test due to its discriminatory impact.

🏛 RULE OF LAW
The administration of a race-neutral test on relevant criteria to employment applicants does not violate the Equal Protection Clause where the test results in the elimination of a disproportionate number of racial minorities as opposed to whites.

FACTS: Applicants for jobs as police officers with the District of Columbia Metropolitan Police Department were required by Washington (D) to take a qualifying test which was developed by the Civil Service Commission for use throughout the federal employment system, known as "Test 21." Four times as many black applicants failed this test as white applicants. Davis (P) brought this suit alleging that the disproportionate effect on racial minorities of the test rendered it a denial of equal protection, despite the facts that there was no proof of discriminatory intent, the test was race-neutral, and the test tested verbal skills, vocabulary, and reading comprehension, all of which are relevant to the performance of a police officer's duties. The district court upheld the test due to the absence of proof of intent, but the court of appeals reversed, holding that the discriminatory impact alone was sufficient to show the constitutional violation alleged. The U.S. Supreme Court granted certiorari.

ISSUE: Does the administration of a race-neutral test on relevant criteria to employment applicants violate the Equal Protection Clause where the test results in the elimination of a disproportionate number of racial minorities as opposed to whites?

HOLDING AND DECISION: (White, J.) No. The central purpose of the Equal Protection Clause of the Fourteenth Amendment is the prevention of official conduct which discriminates on the basis of race. It has never been held that a law or other official action is unconstitutional solely because it has a racially disproportionate impact. The school desegregation cases have held that a racially discriminatory purpose must be behind law if it is to be found invidiously discriminatory. The Constitution does not prevent the government from seeking to upgrade the communicative skills of its employees by employing a test of those skills that is racially neutral. The administration of a race-neutral test on relevant criteria to employment applicants does not violate the Equal Protection Clause where the tests result in the elimination of a disproportionate number of racial minorities. Some discriminatory intent or purpose must be shown. Reversed.

CONCURRENCE: (Stevens, J.) The line between discriminatory purpose and discriminatory impact is not nearly as bright, and perhaps not quite as critical, as the reader of the Court's opinion might assume. However, Test 21 survives the challenge of Davis (P) because it serves a neutral and legitimate purpose and is used on all applicants for the job in question, in addition to many others. The evidence of discrimination in this case is therefore insufficient.

▶ ANALYSIS

It is possible to conceive of a test that is race-neutral on its face, but which nonetheless is part of a plan—or purpose—to discriminate. If such a showing is made, the neutrality on the face of the test will not save it, as "de jure" discrimination will be found if the evidence shows the plan, purpose, or intent. It is only held here that discriminatory effect standing alone is insufficient to invoke the Equal Protection Clause.

■■■

Quicknotes

DE JURE DISCRIMINATION Discrimination that is intended or mandated by governmental or school authorities.

EQUAL PROTECTION CLAUSE A constitutional guarantee that no person should be denied the same protection of the laws enjoyed by other persons in like circumstances.

■■■

Village of Arlington Heights v. Metropolitan Housing Development Corp.

Municipality (D) v. Construction company (P)

429 U.S. 252 (1977).

NATURE OF CASE: Appeal from reversal of denial of rezoning application.

FACT SUMMARY: The Metropolitan Housing Development Corp. (MHDC) (P) sought to build townhouses for low income people in the Village of Arlington Heights (Village) (D).

RULE OF LAW
Official action will not be held unconstitutional solely because it results in a racially disproportionate impact.

FACTS: In 1971, Metropolitan Housing Development Corp. (MHDC) (P) applied to the Village of Arlington Heights (Village) (D) for the rezoning of a 15-acre parcel from single-family to multi-family classification. Using federal financial assistance, MHDC (P) planned to build 190 clustered townhouse units for low and moderate income tenants. After the Village Planning Commission considered the proposal at three public meetings, the rezoning request was denied. MHDC (P) brought suit in federal court, alleging that the denial was racially discriminatory, and that it violated the Fourteenth Amendment. The court of appeals ruled that the denial of the proposal had racially discriminatory effects and could be tolerated only if it served compelling interests. The court concluded that the denial violated the Equal Protection Clause of the Fourteenth Amendment, and the Village (D) appealed.

ISSUE: Is official action unconstitutional solely because it results in a racially disproportionate impact?

HOLDING AND DECISION: (Powell, J.) No. Official action will not be held unconstitutional solely because it results in a racially disproportionate impact. Determining whether an invidious discriminatory purpose was a motivating factor demands a sensitive inquiry into such circumstantial and direct evidence of intent as may be available. The impact of the official action is an important starting point. The specific sequence of events leading up to the challenged decision also may shed some light on the decision-maker's purposes. Departures from the normal procedural sequence also might afford evidence that improper purposes are playing a role. The legislative or administrative history may also be highly relevant. Here, the impact of the Village's (D) decision does arguably bear more heavily on racial minorities. But there is little about the sequence of events leading up to the decision that would spark suspicion. The Village (D) is undeniably committed to single family homes as its dominant residential

land use. The rezoning request progressed according to the usual procedures. The statements by the Planning Commission and Village Board members, as reflected in the official minutes, focused almost exclusively on the zoning aspects of the MHDC (P) petition, and the zoning factors on which they relied are not novel criteria in the Village's (D) rezoning decisions. Reversed.

ANALYSIS

In this case, the Court also held that proof that the decision by the Village (D) was motivated in part by a racially discriminatory purpose would not necessarily have required invalidation of the challenged decision. However, if that finding had been made, the burden of proof would have shifted to the Village (D) to establish that the same decision would have resulted even had the impermissible purpose not been considered.

Quicknotes

EQUAL PROTECTION CLAUSE A constitutional guarantee that no person should be denied the same protection of the laws enjoyed by other persons in like circumstances.

ZONING Municipal statutory scheme diving an area into districts in order to regulate the use or building of structures within those districts.

Regents of the University of California v. Bakke

University (D) v. Applicant (P)

438 U.S. 265 (1978).

NATURE OF CASE: Action under state and federal Equal Protection Clauses.

FACT SUMMARY: Bakke (P) challenged the constitutionality of the University of California, Davis's (UC) (D) minority admissions policy to its medical school.

RULE OF LAW

The Equal Protection Clause's guarantees are equally applicable to both minorities and the white majority, and preference of one group over another solely because of race is facially invalid.

FACTS: University of California, Davis (UC) (D) had a minorities admissions quota requiring that at least 16 out of every 100 students admitted to its medical school were from certain specified minority groups. Bakke (P), a Caucasian, alleged that his applications for admission were denied in 1973 and 1974 while less qualified minority applicants were accepted. Bakke (P) brought an action under Title VI of the C.R.A. of 1964 and the state and federal Equal Protection Clauses. The racial classifications were subjected to strict scrutiny. While the state goal of increasing professionals among minorities was deemed a compelling state interest, the California Supreme Court found that there were less intrusive methods available. The court held that the Equal Protection Clause of the Fourteenth Amendment prohibited rejection of better qualified applicants in favor of less qualified applicants on the basis of race. Bakke (P) was ordered admitted to the medical school since UC (D) could not meet its burden of proof that he would not have been admitted if the special minority admissions program had not been in effect.

ISSUE: Does the Equal Protection Clause prohibit even benign discrimination?

HOLDING AND DECISION: (Powell, J.) Yes. The Equal Protection Clause prohibits discrimination regardless of race. It protects both minorities and the white majority. Benign discrimination to aid minorities at the expense of the white majority is facially invalid where race is the sole criterion or justification. Where race is the basis of a classification, strict judicial scrutiny is required. In order to justify the use of a suspect classification, it must be established that the state's purpose is both constitutionally permissible and substantial and that the classification is necessary to the accomplishment of its purpose or a safeguarding of its interests. Since the classification herein denies white applicants the right to compete for 100 seats while it grants minorities the opportunity to compete for the full number of seats based solely on their race, the

classification is inherently suspect. The state justifications, i.e., remedial efforts to correct general societal discrimination, ethnic parity, aid to underserved communities, etc., are not sufficient to justify its use of racially based admissions. The use of racial quotas to achieve a proper racial mix/balance is facially invalid. UC (D) has no history of racial discrimination, so our rulings in cases involving remedial programs are not applicable. Innocent third parties should not be penalized for general societal discrimination. Neither the University's (D) special admissions program nor any of the requirements under it are related to supplying medical aid to underserviced areas. Hence, the admissions program may not be justified on this basis. While ethnic diversity is a proper goal, it is not substantial enough alone to justify the admissions policy, and other less intrusive methods are available if that is the University's (D) goal. As the only criterion, race is an improper basis for achieving such diversity. We find that the use of an explicit racial classification upon which admissions are based is a violation of the Equal Protection Clause of the Fourteenth Amendment. A properly devised admissions policy may consider race as one of the elements in its selection of students and the injunction against ever considering race must be reversed as overbroad. Affirmed in part and reversed in part.

CONCURRENCE AND DISSENT: (Brennan, J.) Government may only take race into account where it does not demean or insult any racial group and is to remedy past acts of discrimination. We agree that Title VI, as found by the majority, goes no further than the Fourteenth Amendment in prohibiting racial discrimination. Only impermissible use of racial standards violates Title VI. Because of the significant risk that ostensibly benign racial classifications may be misused, an articulated and important purpose must be established. However, while we should strictly scrutinize all racially based classifications for impermissible discriminatory effects, we should be more lenient in finding a substantial and important governmental purpose where the discrimination is "benign." Some preferential treatment may be afforded those minorities which have a history of being socially disadvantaged to redress past societal discrimination. UC's (D) policy of aiding previously disadvantaged minorities is justified. There is no stigmatization of races associated with the UC's (D) admissions policy. Its purpose is to bring the races together and the "quota" is based on population percentages. Since race was the reason for the original disadvantaged position, it is reasonable to use race as a grounds for remedying this situation. Each applicant is judged on his individual abilities and only when less than 16

Continued on next page.

minority applicants have been admitted on this basis does the quota system become applicable.

SEPARATE OPINION: (Marshall, J.) UC's (D) admissions program does not violate the constitution. The Fourteenth Amendment was adopted to protect racial minorities and should not be a bar to aiding such minorities to overcome the effects of past discrimination.

SEPARATE OPINION: (Blackmun, J.) The judiciary is poorly equipped to consider the validity of academic admission policies. I feel it should be left to them, but I find it encouraging that the majority finds race a proper consideration.

CONCURRENCE IN PART: (Stevens, J.) The settled practice of this Court is to avoid decisions on constitutional grounds if a statutory ground exists. Title VI (The Civil Rights Act of 1964, § 601) stands for the proposition that no person may be excluded from participation in a federally funded program on the ground of race, color or national origin.

▶ ANALYSIS

Bakke lacks focus based on the diversity of opinions expressed by the Justices. Racial quotas conceivably could be validly included in admissions programs if the university sets it up properly, i.e., race is only one of the criteria referred to in the program and admissions are on a case-by-case basis. Informal benign discrimination can easily be justified on the basis of achieving a homogenous student body. Therefore, *Bakke* should have a very limited effect on those who wish to aid minorities.

■■■■

Quicknotes

BENIGN DISCRIMINATION Government action which favors particular minorities and which is subject to a strict scrutiny standard.

EQUAL PROTECTION CLAUSE A constitutional guarantee that no person should be denied the same protection of the laws enjoyed by other persons in like circumstances.

QUOTA A goal or limited number.

STRICT SCRUTINY Method by which courts determine the constitutionality of a law, when a law affects a fundamental right. Under the test, the legislature must have a compelling interest to enact the law and measures prescribed by the law must be the least restrictive means possible to accomplish its goal.

SUSPECT CLASSIFICATION A class of persons that have historically been subject to discriminatory treatment; statutes drawing a distinction between persons based on a suspect classification, i.e., race, nationality or alienage, are subject to a strict scrutiny standard of review.

■■■■

Gratz v. Bollinger

College applicants (P) v. University (D)

539 U.S. 244 (2003).

NATURE OF CASE: Challenge of university's undergraduate affirmative action policies.

FACT SUMMARY: Gratz (P) and other "qualified" white students denied admission as undergraduates to the University of Michigan (D), sued the latter, arguing the admission policy of automatically distributing one-fifth of the points needed to guarantee admission to every single "underrepresented minority" solely because of race, constituted prohibited racial discrimination.

> 🏛 **RULE OF LAW**
> A university admissions policy that automatically distributes one-fifth of the points needed to guarantee admission to every single "underrepresented minority" solely because of race is not narrowly tailored to achieve the interest in educational diversity so as to avoid violation of the Equal Protection Clause of the Fourteenth Amendment.

FACTS: Gratz (P) and other white students who were denied admission as undergraduates to the University of Michigan (D), although they were deemed "qualified" by the college admissions committee, brought suit against the university (D), arguing that its applicant selection method violated the Equal Protection Clause of the Fourteenth Amendment on the grounds that the university (D) automatically distributes one-fifth of the points needed to guarantee admission to every single "underrepresented minority" solely because of race.

ISSUE: Is a university admissions policy that automatically distributes one-fifth of the points needed to guarantee admission to every single "underrepresented minority" solely because of race, narrowly tailored to achieve the interest in educational diversity so as to avoid violation of the Equal Protection Clause of the Fourteenth Amendment?

HOLDING AND DECISION: (Rehnquist, C.J.) No. A university admissions policy that automatically distributes one-fifth of the points needed to guarantee admission to every single "underrepresented minority" solely because of race, is not narrowly tailored to achieve the interest in educational diversity so as to avoid violation of the Equal Protection Clause of the Fourteenth Amendment. This Court emphasizes the importance of considering each particular applicant as an individual, assessing all of the qualities that an individual possesses, and in turn, evaluating that individual's ability to contribute to the unique setting of higher education. In this regard, the Court does not contemplate that any single characteristic automatically ensures a specific and identifiable contribution to a university's

diversity. Here, the university's (D) admission policy does not provide such individualized consideration; to the contrary, it automatically distributes 20 points to "underrepresented minority" groups, the only consideration being whether the applicant is a member of one of these minority groups. Even if an applicant's extraordinary artistic talent rivaled that of Monet or Picasso, the applicant would receive, at most, five points under the university's (D) admissions system. Clearly, such a system does not offer applicants the individualized selection process. Nor, does the fact that the implementation of a program capable of providing individualized consideration might present administrative challenges render constitutional an otherwise problematic system. The admissions policy violates the Equal Protection Clause of the Fourteenth Amendment. Reversed and remanded.

CONCURRENCE: (O'Connor, J.) The selection index, by setting up automatic, predetermined point allocations for the soft variables, ensures that the diversity contributions of applicants cannot be individually assessed. This is in sharp contrast to the law school's admission plan that enables admissions officers to make nuanced judgments as to the contributions each applicant is likely to make.

CONCURRENCE: (Thomas, J.) A state's use of racial discrimination in higher education admissions is categorically prohibited by the Equal Protection Clause.

DISSENT: (Ginsburg, J.) The stain of generations of racial oppression is still visible in our society, and the determination to hasten its removal remains vital. Here, there has been no demonstration that the university (D) unduly constricts admissions opportunities for students who do not receive special consideration based on race.

▶ **ANALYSIS**

As made clear by the U.S. Supreme Court in its *Gratz*, and also *Grutter*, 539 U.S. 306 (2003), decisions, achieving diversity in higher education, whether it be at college level or graduate school, remains as a compelling state interest sufficient to justify some degree of racial preferences without violating the Equal Protection Clause of the Fourteenth Amendment.

▬═▮

Quicknotes

EQUAL PROTECTION CLAUSE A constitutional guarantee that no person should be denied the same protection of the laws enjoyed by other persons in like circumstances.

▬═▮

Grutter v. Bollinger

Law school applicant (P) v. Law school (D)

539 U.S. 306 (2003).

NATURE OF CASE: Appeal in racial discrimination case.

FACT SUMMARY: When Grutter (P), a white Michigan resident, was denied admission to the University of Michigan Law School (D), she sued the latter in federal district court, alleging racial discrimination against her in violation of the Equal Protection Clause on the basis of the law school's (D) express consideration of race as a factor in the admissions process.

🏛 RULE OF LAW
Student body diversity is a compelling state interest that can justify the use of race in university admissions.

FACTS: To attempt to achieve student body diversity, the University of Michigan Law School (D) admissions committee required admissions officials to evaluate each applicant based on all the information in the file, including a personal statement, letters of recommendation, a student's essay, GPA score, LSAT score, as well as so-called "soft variables." The admissions policy, furthermore, specifically stressed the law school's (D) longstanding commitment to racial and ethnic diversity. When Grutter (P), a white Michigan resident, applied for admission but was denied, she sued the law school (D) in federal district court, alleging racial discrimination against her in violation of the Equal Protection Clause. [The district court upheld Grutter's (P) claim. The court of appeals reversed, and Grutter (P) appealed.]

ISSUE: Is student body diversity a compelling state interest that can justify the use of race in university admissions?

HOLDING AND DECISION: (O'Connor, J.) Yes. Student body diversity is a compelling state interest that can justify the use of race in university admissions. Here, the law school's (D) admissions program bears the hallmarks of a narrowly tailored plan. Truly individualized consideration demands that race be used in a flexible, nonmechanical way. It follows from this mandate that universities cannot establish quotas for members of certain racial groups or put members of those groups on separate admissions tracks. Nor can universities insulate applicants who belong to certain racial or ethnic groups from the competition for admission. Universities can, however, as was done here, consider race or ethnicity more flexibly as a plus factor in the context of individualized consideration of each and every applicant. The law school's (D) goal of attaining a critical mass of underrepresented minority students does not transform its program into a quota. The

evidence indicated that the law school (D) engaged in a highly individualized, holistic review of each applicant's file, giving serious consideration to all the ways an applicant might contribute to a "diverse educational environment." Furthermore, evidence showed that the law school (D) gives substantial weight to diversity factors besides race by frequently accepting nonminority applicants with grades and test scores lower than underrepresented minority applicants. There was no law school (D) policy, either de facto or de jure, of automatic acceptance or rejection based on any single "soft" variable. Narrow tailoring does not require exhaustion of every conceivable race-neutral alternative. Nor does it require a university to choose between maintaining a reputation for excellence or fulfilling a commitment to provide educational opportunities to members of all racial groups. Affirmed.

CONCURRENCE: (Ginsburg, J.) From today's vantage point, one may hope, but not firmly forecast, that over the next generation's span, progress toward nondiscrimination and genuinely equal opportunity will make it safe to sunset affirmative action.

CONCURRENCE AND DISSENT: (Scalia, J.) Unlike a clear constitutional holding that racial preferences in state educational institutions are impermissible, or even a clear anticonstitutional holding, today's decision seems perversely designed to prolong the controversy and the litigation. The Constitution proscribes government discrimination on the basis of race, and state-provided education is no exception.

DISSENT: (Rehnquist, C.J.) Although the law school (D) claims it must take the steps it does to achieve "critical mass" of underrepresented minority students, its actual program bears no relation to this asserted goal. Stripped of its "critical mass" veil, the law school's (D) program is revealed as a naked effort to achieve racial balancing.

DISSENT: (Kennedy, J.) Refusal of the Court to apply strict scrutiny that is meaningful will lead to serious consequences. By deferring to the law school's (D) choice of minority admissions programs, courts will lose the talents and resources of the faculties and administrators in devising new and fairer ways to ensure individual consideration.

▶ ANALYSIS

As seen in *Grutter* and predecessor Supreme Court decisions, not every decision influenced by race is equally

Continued on next page.

objectionable, and "strict scrutiny" is designed to provide a framework for carefully examining the importance and the sincerity of the reasons advanced by the governmental decisionmaker for the use of race in any given context.

■━━■

Quicknotes

EQUAL PROTECTION CLAUSE A constitutional provision that each person be guaranteed the same protection of the laws enjoyed by other persons in like circumstances.

■━━■

Adarand Constructors, Inc. v. Pena

Subcontractor (P) v. Federal government (D)

515 U.S. 200 (1995).

NATURE OF CASE: Challenges to federal program of encouraging the awarding of federal contracts to minority-owned businesses.

FACT SUMMARY: A federal program giving preferences in federal contracting to minority-owned businesses was challenged as unconstitutional.

🏛 RULE OF LAW
Federal contracting set-asides for minorities are unconstitutional unless they are narrowly tailored to remedy demonstrable past discrimination.

FACTS: The U.S. Dept. of Transportation awarded a construction contract. The contractor solicited subcontracts. Adarand Constructors, Inc. (P) submitted the low bid, but because of federal incentives favoring minority contracts, Adarand (P) was rejected in favor of a minority-owned business. Adarand (P) brought an action, contending that the incentive program was a violation of equal protection. The Ninth Circuit rejected the challenge, and the U.S. Supreme Court granted review.

ISSUE: Are federal contracting set-asides for minorities unconstitutional if they are not narrowly tailored to remedy demonstrable past discrimination?

HOLDING AND DECISION: (O'Connor, J.) Yes. Federal contracting set-asides for minorities are unconstitutional unless they are narrowly tailored to remedy demonstrable past discrimination. There is no equal protection provision in the Fifth Amendment, such as is found in the Fourteenth. However, it is clear that the federal government's due process obligations under the Due Process Clause require it to treat similarly situated individuals in a similar fashion, much as states must do. While, there is some prior authority for the proposition that "benign" racial discrimination by Congress is subject to less rigorous scrutiny than traditional discrimination, these decision were in error. Racial classification of any sort is subject to the highest level of judicial review: the classification must be narrowly tailored to serve a compelling state interest. The eradication of racism in contracting is such an interest, but the means to achieve it must be carefully drawn. It is not sufficient that a general history of discrimination be shown. Rather, specific patterns of discrimination must be shown, as well as a remedy that was chosen to be narrowly tailored to address the problem. This was not done in the present case. Vacated and remanded.

CONCURRENCE IN PART: (Scalia, J.) Government can never "make up" for past discrimination by present discrimination. In our constitutional system, there can never be a debtor race or a creditor race. The Constitution protects persons, not races.

CONCURRENCE IN PART: (Thomas, J.) There is no racial paternalism exception to the principle of equal protection.

DISSENT: (Stevens, J.) Congress has greater leeway in remedying past discrimination than do the states.

DISSENT: (Souter, J.) This decision does not address Congress's power under § 5 of the Fourteenth Amendment.

▶ ANALYSIS

In 1989, the Court decided *Richmond v. J.A. Croson Co.*, 488 U.S. 469 (1989). In that case, the Court applied strict scrutiny to a municipal preference scheme. The Court left open the question of whether this would also be the case with respect to congressional action. This question was answered by the present opinion.

■■■

Quicknotes

BENIGN DISCRIMINATION Government action which favors particular minorities and which is subject to a strict scrutiny standard.

DUE PROCESS CLAUSE Clauses found in the Fifth and Fourteenth Amendments to the United States Constitution providing that no person shall be deprived of "life, liberty, or property, without due process of law."

STRICT SCRUTINY Method by which courts determine the constitutionality of a law, when a law affects a fundamental right. Under the test, the legislature must have a compelling interest to enact the law and measures prescribed by the law must be the least restrictive means possible to accomplish its goal.

■■■

Ambach v. Norwick

Parties not identified.

441 U.S. 68 (1979).

NATURE OF CASE: Review of refusal to hire aliens as elementary and secondary schoolteachers.

FACT SUMMARY: The State of New York refused to employ aliens, though eligible for citizenship and otherwise qualified, as elementary and secondary public school teachers.

🏛 RULE OF LAW
Teaching in a public school constitutes a governmental function from which a state may bar aliens without violating the Fourteenth Amendment.

FACTS: The State of New York maintained a policy of refusing employment as elementary and secondary public school teachers to aliens. Aliens were excluded even if they were eligible for citizenship but did not obtain it and even if they were otherwise qualified for teaching positions.

ISSUE: Does teaching in a public school constitute a governmental function from which a state may bar aliens without violating the Fourteenth Amendment?

HOLDING AND DECISION: (Powell, J.) Yes. Some state functions are so bound up with the operation of the state as a governmental entity as to permit the exclusion from those functions of all persons who have not become part of the process of self-government. The Court recently held that New York could exclude aliens from the ranks of its police force, because such a job cloaked with substantial discretionary powers can be appropriately restricted to citizens. Though alienage is a "suspect classification," the standard usually applicable to justify an exclusion of aliens is lessened when a governmental function is involved. In such a case, like this one, a showing of some rational relationship between the interest to be protected and the limiting classification is sufficient to justify the exclusion. Public education, like the police function, fulfills a fundamental obligation of the government, and is thus properly regarded as a governmental function. Teachers have an obligation to promote civic virtue and serve as an example to students, and the state has an interest in furthering these goals. Teaching in a public school, therefore, constitutes a governmental function from which a state may bar aliens without violating the Fourteenth Amendment. There is a rational relationship between the state's educational goals and the barring of aliens from teaching.

DISSENT: (Blackmun, J.) The statutes of New York imposing a requirement of citizenship for certain occupations hail from a time when fear of the foreigner was the order of the day. Classifications based on alienage are inherently "suspect and subject to close judicial scrutiny" under our previous decisions. Furthermore, the restriction is not logically related to all the objectives of New York as to its schools. It is absurd that a Frenchman may not teach French or an Englishwoman may not teach English grammar. It is nonsensical to hire a poor citizen teacher rather than an excellent resident alien teacher.

▶ *ANALYSIS*

Citizenship may not be a precondition to employment in any position in the competitive class of the civil service system, *Sugarman v. Dougall*, 413 U.S. 634 (1973); nor can citizenship be required for admission to the bar, *In re Griffiths* 413 U.S. 717 (1973). In a footnote to the majority opinion in Ambach, these cases are distinguished on the curious ground that the New York statute barring aliens from teaching excludes only those employees (public school teachers) "employed by and acting as agents of the state."

Quicknotes

ALIENAGE The condition of being an individual who is a citizen of a foreign country.

SUSPECT CLASSIFICATION A class of persons that have historically been subject to discriminatory treatment; statutes drawing a distinction between persons based on a suspect classification, i.e., race, nationality or alienage, are subject to a strict scrutiny standard of review.

Plyler v. Doe

Parties not identified.

457 U.S. 202 (1982).

NATURE OF CASE: Constitutional challenge to a state educational restriction statute.

FACT SUMMARY: A class action suit challenged a Texas law which prohibited the use of state funds to educate the children of undocumented aliens.

🏛 RULE OF LAW
Absent a showing that such a policy furthers a substantial state interest, a state may not deny a public education to the children of undocumented aliens.

FACTS: In a class action suit, a Texas statute (Tex. Educ. Code Ann. § 21.031 [1981]) was sought to be invalidated on the ground that it unconstitutionally denied equal protection to the children of undocumented aliens. The statute prohibited the use of state funds for the education of any children not legally admitted to the United States. Both the district court and the Fifth Circuit Court of Appeals held that § 21.031 violated the Equal Protection Clause of the Fourteenth Amendment. Texas (D) appealed, contending that the statute was not unduly discriminatory and was, in fact, justified for three reasons: (1) it was designed to protect the state from an influx of illegal immigrants; (2) it would relieve some of the special burdens which educating undocumented aliens imposes on the educational system; and (3) it would relieve the state of the burden of educating children who are less likely to remain in the state and contribute than other children.

ISSUE: May a state deny a public education to the children of undocumented aliens, absent a showing that such a policy is justified by a substantial state interest?

HOLDING AND DECISION: (Brennan, J.) No. To begin with, the proper standard of judicial scrutiny must be identified. As the people involved (undocumented aliens) are not members of a suspect class and as the right to an education, although clearly important, has not been held to constitute a fundamental constitutional right, the statute in question will be upheld if it is found to be rationally related to a substantial state interest. Upon examination, however, none of the three state interests advanced by Texas (D)—protection from an influx of illegal immigrants; relief from special burdens on the educational system; or relief from the burdens of educating children who will be more likely to leave the state—justify the statute in question. The legislative scheme found in § 21.031 cannot in any way be deemed as advancing the interests asserted by the state (even assuming that these interests are "substantial state interests"). Denying children who are not responsible for their status a public education will stigmatize them with the heavy burden of illiteracy for the rest of their lives. They will be unable to participate in our civic institutions. The cost to the nation over their lifespans will be greater than the cost of providing them an education now. As such, the statute must fall, as it is in violation of the Equal Protection Clause. Affirmed.

CONCURRENCE: (Powell, J.) The unique nature of this case must be emphasized. The State of Texas (D) has attempted to "visit the sins of the parents" on their innocent children, and has asserted no substantial state interest justifying its doing so. Such a policy cannot be constitutionally upheld.

DISSENT: (Burger, C.J.) The Court oversteps its bounds in striking down the Texas statute. Once it is conceded that neither a suspect class or fundamental right is involved, only a rational relationship to a legitimate state interest need be found to uphold the law. Despite the fact that it may not be the same course the members of the Court would take if they were legislating, it cannot be said that the Texas law is irrational. As such, it is a valid law.

▶ ANALYSIS

As mentioned in Justice Marshall's concurrence, the Court seems to be taking one step closer to the "sliding scale" approach of equal protection analysis which has long been advocated by certain legal theorists. Under this approach, a court would have greater flexibility then merely identifying the analysis required as being either "strict scrutiny" or "rational basis," and as such, could better tailor the legal analysis to the facts of the case and the interests involved.

▬═▬

Quicknotes

EQUAL PROTECTION CLAUSE A constitutional guarantee that no person should be denied the same protection of the laws enjoyed by other persons in like circumstances.

FUNDAMENTAL RIGHT A liberty that is either expressly or impliedly provided for in the United States Constitution, the deprivation or burdening of which is subject to a heightened standard of review.

SUSPECT CLASSIFICATION A class of persons that have historically been subject to discriminatory treatment; statutes drawing a distinction between persons based on a suspect classification, i.e., race, nationality or alienage, are subject to a strict scrutiny standard of review.

▬═▬

Mathews v. Diaz

Parties not identified.

426 U.S. 67 (1976).

NATURE OF CASE: Appeal from judgment striking down residency requirement.

FACT SUMMARY: Only aliens who were residents of the United States for five years or more and who were admitted for permanent residency were eligible for a federal medical insurance program, and the district court found the residency requirement unconstitutional.

🏛 **RULE OF LAW**
Statutory discrimination within the class of aliens by the federal government is not unconstitutional if it is reasonably related to a legitimate governmental interest in providing medical benefits to those residing within its jurisdiction the longest and admitted for permanent residency.

FACTS: Congress enacted a federal medical insurance program which permitted participation of aliens who had lived in the United States for five years or more and had been admitted for permanent residency. Plaintiffs filed this suit alleging that the aliens failing to meet these two requirements were denied the equal protection of the laws by their exclusion from the program. The district court found the residency requirement unconstitutional and held that the admission requirement could not be severed from the residency requirement. The U.S. Supreme Court granted certiorari.

ISSUE: Is statutory discrimination within the class of aliens by the federal government unconstitutional if it reasonably relates to a legitimate governmental interest in providing medical benefits to those aliens residing within its jurisdiction the longest and admitted for permanent residency?

HOLDING AND DECISION: (Stevens, J.) No. The federal government is responsible for regulating the relationship between aliens and the United States. While this Court has held that state governments cannot deny welfare benefits to aliens not meeting residency requirements, the federal government is not subject to that constitutional restriction. When the federal government discriminates within the class of aliens it is acting under the constitutional power to control immigration and naturalization; the states may not act on this power granted solely to the federal government. The reason for the residency requirement and admission requirement is to provide benefits to those most entitled to them, and the requirements are not irrational for this purpose. Statutory discrimination within the class of aliens by the federal government is not unconstitutional if reasonably related to a legitimate governmental interest in providing medical benefits to those residing within its jurisdiction the longest and admitted for permanent residency. The federal government need not treat all aliens alike in order to satisfy the Equal Protection Clause. Reversed.

▶ **ANALYSIS**

If the use of alienage classifications by the federal government is not at all related to a national foreign policy consideration, the use is subject to the same strict scrutiny that a state's use would be. The treatment of foreigners in this country is sufficiently related to foreign policy to allow the federal government to use an alienage classification.

▬▬▬

Quicknotes

ALIENAGE The condition of being an individual who is a citizen of a foreign country.

EQUAL PROTECTION CLAUSE A constitutional guarantee that no person should be denied the same protection of the laws enjoyed by other persons in like circumstances.

STRICT SCRUTINY Method by which courts determine the constitutionality of a law, when a law affects a fundamental right. Under the test, the legislature must have a compelling interest to enact the law and measures prescribed by the law must be the least restrictive means possible to accomplish its goal.

▬▬▬

Lalli v. Lalli

Illegitimate son (P) v. Father (D)

439 U.S. 259 (1978).

NATURE OF CASE: Appeal from judgment upholding New York paternity requirement.

FACT SUMMARY: Though Lalli (P) was acknowledged repeatedly by Mario Lalli (D) as his illegitimate son, both orally and in documents, Lalli (P) was not permitted to inherit from Mario Lalli (D) as entitled by state intestate succession laws because he failed to produce a statutorily required court order of filiation, declaring paternity in a proceeding instituted during pregnancy or within two years of the birth of the child.

RULE OF LAW
An illegitimate child otherwise entitled under state intestate succession laws to inherit is not denied equal protection if he is not permitted to inherit for failure to provide a particular form of proof of paternity.

FACTS: Robert Lalli (P) claimed to be the illegitimate son of Mario Lalli (D), who died in the State of New York intestate. Mario Lalli (D) was shown to have openly and repeatedly acknowledged Lalli (P), and his sister Maureen, as his illegitimate children. In addition to evidence of statements made by Mario Lalli (D), Lalli (P) produced a notarized document in which Mario Lalli (D) referred to Lalli (P) as his "son." Lalli (P) was entitled to inherit under New York's intestate succession laws along with Maureen, but both were barred by a New York statute requiring illegitimate children to produce a court order of filiation, declaring paternity in a proceeding instituted during pregnancy or within two years of the birth of the child. Lalli (P) filed this suit challenging the constitutionality of the law on equal protection grounds because it did not apply to legitimate children. The New York Court of Appeals found no constitutional violation, and Lalli (P) appealed to the U.S. Supreme Court.

ISSUE: Is an illegitimate child otherwise entitled to inherit under state intestate succession laws denied equal protection if he is not permitted to inherit for failure to provide a particular form of proof of paternity?

HOLDING AND DECISION: (Powell, J.) No. Classifications based on illegitimacy are invalid under the Fourteenth Amendment if they are not substantially related to permissible state interests. This Court previously held that the Equal Protection Clause prohibited a state from requiring that the parents of illegitimate children marry in order for the children to inherit. Applying the same standard, the New York statute does not violate the Equal Protection Clause. The requirement is not one of dictating conduct of someone other than the illegitimate claimant in this case, but rather it is an evidentiary requirement. The State of New York has a permissible goal of providing a just and orderly disposition of property at death. The evidentiary requirement is substantially related to this goal. An illegitimate child otherwise entitled to inherit under state intestate succession laws is not denied equal protection if he is not permitted to inherit for failure to provide a particular form of proof of paternity. Affirmed.

CONCURRENCE: (Blackmun, J.) The Court should overrule the Trimble case which struck down the statute requiring the marriage of the parents of illegitimate children in order for them to inherit. It was decided on its appealing facts and offers little constitutional guidance.

DISSENT: (Brennan, J.) We have held in *Trimble v. Gordon*, 430 U.S. 762 (1977), that an illegitimate child may inherit if otherwise entitled by producing a "formal acknowledgement of paternity." The New York statute here challenged is inconsistent with this command. The fear that unknown illegitimates might assert belated claims hardly justifies cutting off the rights of known illegitimates such as Robert Lalli (P).

ANALYSIS

Classifications based on illegitimacy must advance permissible governmental purposes and cannot be burdens placed on the illegitimate because of his status as such. This is short of the "compelling state interest" test, falling into the "middle-level scrutiny" category.

Quicknotes

EQUAL PROTECTION CLAUSE A constitutional guarantee that no person should be denied the same protection of the laws enjoyed by other persons in like circumstances.

INHERIT The receipt of property pursuant to law upon the death of a relative who has died intestate.

INTESTATE SUCCESSION The scheme pursuant to which property is distributed in the absence of a valid will or of a disposition of particular property.

Frontiero v. Richardson

Parties not identified.

411 U.S. 677 (1973).

NATURE OF CASE: Suit challenging the constitutionality of a statute.

FACT SUMMARY: A statute provides that servicemen's wives are automatically eligible for benefits as dependents, while servicewomen must demonstrate that their husbands are dependent on them before they are eligible for the benefits.

> **RULE OF LAW**
> By according differential treatment to male and female members of the uniformed services for the sole purpose of achieving administrative convenience, the statutes violate the Due Process Clause of the Fifth Amendment by being unconstitutionally discriminatory.

FACTS: A servicewoman's request for increased benefits for her dependent husband was denied because she failed to affirmatively demonstrate that her husband was dependent on her for over one-half of his support. The controlling statute provided that a serviceman may claim his wife as a dependent without regard to whether she is actually dependent on him. A servicewoman can claim her husband as a dependent only if she demonstrates that he is actually dependent on her for over one-half of his support.

ISSUE: Are statutes providing stricter requirements for service-women's husbands claiming dependency benefits than for servicemen's wives claiming such benefits unconstitutionally discriminatory?

HOLDING AND DECISION: (Brennan, J.) Yes. Classifications based upon sex, like those based upon race, alienage, or national origin are inherently suspect and must be subjected to strict scrutiny. The U.S. has had a long and unfortunate history of sex discrimination. During the nineteenth century, the position of women was in many ways similar to that of blacks before the Civil War. Neither could hold office, serve on juries, or bring suit, and although black men were given the right to vote in 1870, women did not gain suffrage until 50 years later. Women (like blacks) still face pervasive, although at times more subtle, discrimination in education, employment, and especially in politics. Sex, like race, is an immutable characteristic, determined solely by birth which bears no relation to ability to perform in society. Hence, statutory distinctions between the sexes often have the effect of invidiously regulating an entire class to an inferior legal status. Hence, a compelling state interest must be demonstrated if such distinctions are to be upheld. Here, it is argued that Congress might have reasonably concluded that it would be cheaper and easier to presume that wives were dependent on their husbands while presuming that husbands are not dependent on their wives. However, to withstand scrutiny, it must be shown that this practice is actually cheaper, which was not done here. In fact, there was evidence that many servicemen's wives are not dependent on their husbands for over one-half of their support. Insofar as the statute requires female members to prove their husband's dependency while not so requiring male members, it violates the Due Process Clause of the Fifth Amendment. Reversed.

CONCURRENCE: (Stewart, J.) The statute constitutes an unconstitutional discrimination and should be struck down.

CONCURRENCE: (Powell, J.) Another reason exists for the Court's not declaring sex to be a suspect classification. As the Equal Rights Amendment is before the states for ratification, it should be left to the people to make this decision. The Court should not interfere in this democratic process.

ANALYSIS

Despite the holding of the plurality opinion, the majority has consistently failed to adopt the view that sex classifications are inherently suspect. This has led to widely varying results when challenges to statutes on the basis of sex discrimination are brought before the Court. The Court has sustained an attack on the Social Security System, which provided survivor's benefits to a minor child and widow but not to a widower, because it discriminated against women wage earners by affording them less protection for their survivors. A Utah court's finding—that support payments ended at 18 for a daughter and 21 for a son—was struck down as discriminatory. But in a California case, the Court upheld a provision in the state's disability insurance program that excluded coverage for a woman undergoing a normal pregnancy. Also upheld was a Florida statute that provided property tax exemptions for widows but not for widowers. And a naval regulation allowing women officers a longer tenure before discharge due to lack of promotion was approved. The proposed Twenty-Seventh Amendment to the Constitution provides that "equality of rights under the law shall not be denied or abridged by the United States or by any state on account of sex."

Continued on next page.

Quicknotes

DUE PROCESS CLAUSE Clauses found in the Fifth and Fourteenth Amendments to the United States Constitution providing that no person shall be deprived of "life, liberty, or property, without due process of law."

STRICT SCRUTINY Method by which courts determine the constitutionality of a law, when a law affects a fundamental right. Under the test, the legislature must have a compelling interest to enact the law and measures prescribed by the law must be the least restrictive means possible to accomplish its goal.

SUSPECT CLASSIFICATION A class of persons that have historically been subject to discriminatory treatment; statutes drawing a distinction between persons based on a suspect classification, i.e., race, nationality or alienage, are subject to a strict scrutiny standard of review.

■═■

Craig v. Boren

18- to 20-year-old male (P) v. State (D)

429 U.S. 190 (1976).

NATURE OF CASE: Appeal from an action to have an Oklahoma statute declared unconstitutional.

FACT SUMMARY: Craig (P) appealed after a federal district court upheld two sections of an Oklahoma statute prohibiting the sale of "nonintoxicating" 3.2% beer to males under the age of 21 and to females under the age of 18 on the ground that such a gender-based differential did not constitute a denial to males 18 to 20 years of age equal protection of the laws.

RULE OF LAW

Laws which establish classifications by gender must serve important governmental objectives and must be substantially related to achievement of those objectives to be constitutionally in line with the Equal Protection Clause.

FACTS: Craig (P) brought suit to have two sections of an Oklahoma statute which prohibited the sale of "nonintoxicating" 3.2% beer to males under the age of 21 and to females under the age of 18 declared unconstitutional. Craig (P) contended that such a gender-based differential constituted a denial to males 18-20 years of age of the equal protection of the laws in violation of the Fourteenth Amendment. Boren (D), representing the State of Oklahoma, argued that this law was enacted as a traffic safety measure and that the protection of public health and safety was an important function of state and local governments. Boren (D) introduced statistical data demonstrating that 18- to 20-year-old male arrests for "driving under the influence" and "drunkenness" substantially exceeded female arrests for the same age period. The district court upheld the ordinance on the ground that it served the important governmental objective of traffic safety. Craig (P) appealed.

ISSUE: Are laws which establish classifications by gender constitutional if they do not serve important governmental objectives and are not substantially related to achievement of those objectives?

HOLDING AND DECISION: (Brennan, J.) No. It appears that the objective underlying the statute in controversy is the enhancement of traffic safety. Clearly, the protection of public health and safety represents an important function of state and local governments. However, the statistics presented by Boren (D) in this Court's view cannot support the conclusion that the gender-based distinction closely serves to achieve the objective. The most relevant of the statistical surveys presented as evidence by Boren (D) in support of the statute, arrests of 18- to 20-year-olds for alcohol-related driving offenses, establish 2% more males than females are arrested for that offense. Such a disparity can hardly form the basis for employment of a gender line as a classifying device. Certainly, if maleness is to serve as a proxy for drinking and driving, a correlation of 2% must be considered unduly tenuous. Indeed, prior cases have consistently rejected the use of sex as a decision-making factor. Therefore, since the gender-based differential does not serve an important governmental objective, the Oklahoma statute constitutes a denial of the equal protection of the laws to males aged 18-20 and is unconstitutional. The judgment of the district court is reversed.

CONCURRENCE: (Powell, J.) The state legislature, by the classification it has chosen, has not adopted through the enactment of the statute a means that bears a fair and substantial relation to the objective of traffic safety.

CONCURRENCE: (Stevens, J.) It is difficult to believe that the statute in question was actually intended to cope with the problem of traffic safety, since it has only a minimal effect on access to a not-very-intoxicating beverage and does not prohibit its consumption.

DISSENT: (Rehnquist, J.) The Court's disposition of this case is objectionable on two grounds. First, is its conclusion that men challenging a gender-based statute which treats them less favorably than women may invoke a more stringent standard of judicial review than pertains to most other types of classifications. Second, is the Court's enunciation of this standard, without citation to any source, as being that "classifications by gender must serve important governmental objectives and must be substantially related to achievement of those objectives." The Equal Protection Clause contains no such language, and none of our previous cases adopt that standard.

▶ ANALYSIS

Cases concerning whether males and females should be considered as reaching a majority age equally has met with some stiff opposition. In *Stanton v. Stanton*, 30 Utah 2d. 315, 517 p.2d. 1010, a Utah Justice observed: "Regardless of what a judge may think about equality, his thinking cannot change the facts of life. To judicially hold that males and females attain their maturity at the same age is to be blind to the biological facts of life."

Continued on next page.

Quicknotes

EQUAL PROTECTION CLAUSE A constitutional guarantee that no person should be denied the same protection of the laws enjoyed by other persons in like circumstances.

HEIGHTENED SCRUTINY A purposefully vague judicial description of all levels of scrutiny more exacting than minimal scrutiny.

■━━■

Personnel Administrator of Massachusetts v. Feeney

State (D) v. Job applicant (P)

442 U.S. 256 (1979).

NATURE OF CASE: Appeal from judgment striking down veterans' job preference.

FACT SUMMARY: Massachusetts (D) enacted a statute granting veterans a preference in civil service employment consideration over nonveterans, and Feeney (P) filed this suit alleging a violation of the Fourteenth Amendment Equal Protection Clause because the law operated to the advantage of males.

RULE OF LAW
A statute giving preference in civil service job consideration to a group comprised primarily of males does not violate the Equal Protection Clause without a showing of a purpose to discriminate on the basis of sex.

FACTS: Under a Massachusetts (D) statute, veterans were given preferential consideration for civil service positions over nonveterans similarly qualified. Since veterans are nearly all males, Feeney (P) filed this suit alleging that the preference violated the Equal Protection Clause because it operated to the advantage of males over females. The district court found that the statute violated the Constitution, and Massachusetts (D) appealed.

ISSUE: Does a statute giving a preference in civil service job consideration to a group comprised primarily of males violate the Equal Protection Clause absent a showing of a purpose to discriminate on the basis of sex?

HOLDING AND DECISION: (Stewart, J.) No. The preference has been justified as a measure designed to reward veterans for the sacrifice of military service. The fact that most veterans are males means that the preference operated to the disadvantage of females. The statute is gender-neutral on its face and the attack centers on the proposition that Massachusetts (D) intentionally incorporated discriminatory federal laws preventing all but a handful of women from becoming veterans. The impact of the statute is cited as the natural and foreseeable consequence of its enactment. While the decision-makers here can be said to have foreseen the discriminatory impact, more discriminatory intent is required than mere awareness of discriminatory consequences. Therefore a statute giving preference in civil service job consideration to a group comprised primarily of males does not violate the Equal Protection Clause without a showing of a purpose to discriminate on the basis of sex. Feeney (P) has failed to demonstrate such a purpose. Reversed and remanded.

DISSENT: (Marshall, J.) Less than 2% of the veterans in Massachusetts are women, and a preference to veterans is inexorably a preference for men. Gender-based discrimination is permissible only where it is substantially related to important governmental objectives. While the objectives cited here by Massachusetts (D) are legitimate, this is not sufficient where the relationship between the objectives and the means to achieve them is wanting as in this case.

▶ ANALYSIS

Sex-based classifications are not "suspect," but fall into the middle level of judicial scrutiny. This is characterized by the language of the majority opinion that such classifications must bear a close and substantial relationship to important governmental interests. This is somewhere in between the "compelling" governmental interest test and the minimal level of scrutiny.

Quicknotes

EQUAL PROTECTION CLAUSE A constitutional guarantee that no person should be denied the same protection of the laws enjoyed by other persons in like circumstances.

INTERMEDIATE SCRUTINY A standard of reviewing the propriety of classifications pertaining to gender or legitimacy, under the Equal Protection Clause of the United States Constitution, which requires a court to ascertain whether the classification furthers an important state interest and is substantially related to the attainment of that interest.

Mississippi University for Women v. Hogan

State university (D) v. Applicant (P)

458 U.S. 718 (1982).

NATURE OF CASE: Appeal from decision that an admissions program violated Equal Protection Clause.

FACT SUMMARY: The State (D) appealed from a decision finding that the admissions program of one of its nursing schools, which denied admission to males solely on the basis of their sex, violated the Equal Protection Clause of the Fourteenth Amendment.

🏛 RULE OF LAW
A state can evoke a compensatory purpose to justify an otherwise gender-based discriminatory classification only if members of the gender benefitted by the classification actually suffer a disadvantage related to the classification.

FACTS: The Mississippi University for Women (MUW) (D) was established in 1884, and from its inception has limited its enrollment to women. In 1971, the MUW (D) established a School of Nursing. Hogan (P), a male registered nurse living in the city where MUW (D) was located, applied to its School of Nursing. Although qualified in all other respects, he was denied admission solely because of his sex. Hogan (P) challenged the admissions policy of MUW (D) as discriminatory under the Equal Protection Clause of the Fourteenth Amendment. From a decision of the court of appeals finding the admissions program unconstitutional, the State (D), which had established MUW (D), appealed.

ISSUE: May a state evoke a compensatory purpose to justify an otherwise gender-based discriminatory classification only if the gender benefitted by the classification actually suffers a disadvantage related to the classification?

HOLDING AND DECISION: (O'Connor, J.) Yes. A state can evoke a compensatory purpose to justify an otherwise gender-based classification only if members of the gender benefitted by the classification actually suffer a disadvantage related to the classification. In order for gender-based discriminations to pass scrutiny under the Equal Protection Clause of the Fourteenth Amendment, the state's objective must first be determined to be important and legitimate. Secondly, it must be determined whether the requisite direct, substantial relationship between the objective and the means is present. The mere recitation of a compensatory purpose does not shield the discriminatory scheme from scrutiny, neither does the fact that the program in the present case discriminates against males instead of females. In the present case, MUW (D) has made no showing that the admissions policy, which was limited to women, was necessary to provide opportunities for women who had been deprived of such opportunities.

Instead, at the time, nearly all of the nursing degrees awarded were given to women. The State (D) failed to show that the purpose of the program's discriminatory admissions criteria, that it constitutes educational affirmative action, is the actual purpose underlying the classification. The State (D) has also failed to show that the classification is substantially and directly related to its proposed discriminatory classification. MUW's (D) program of excluding males from its nursing program in the present case serves to perpetuate the stereotype that nursing is exclusively a woman's job. Since the State (D) has fallen far short of the proper justification needed to justify the classification, it must be held that the policy of denying males the right to enroll in MUW's (D) nursing program violated the Equal Protection Clause of the Fourteenth Amendment. Title IX regulations do not help MUW (D) in the present case, since Congress has no power to restrict, abrogate, or dilute the guarantees given under the Fourteenth Amendment. Affirmed.

DISSENT: (Burger, C.J.) While generally agreeing with Justice Powell's dissent, this holding is limited to the context of a professional nursing school.

DISSENT: (Blackmun, J.) The Court's holding today places in jeopardy any state supported institution that confines its student body in any area to members of one sex, even if the state provides elsewhere for members of both sexes.

DISSENT: (Powell, J.) Hogan (P) is not severely disadvantaged in the present case, rather he is inconvenienced. The Fourteenth Amendment was not meant to apply to this kind of case, where it is arguable that there are benefits associated with single sex educational programs.

▶ ANALYSIS

It has been suggested that the Supreme Court's ruling, refusing to hold that sex is a suspect classification, may have been in part related to the pending passage of the Equal Rights Amendment. The Court may have adopted the intermediate standard of review currently used as a way of pacifying parties on both sides of the amendment until its passage. The failure of the Equal Rights Amendment to pass may bring about a new standard of review with respect to classifications made on the basis of sex.

■■■

Continued on next page.

Quicknotes

EQUAL PROTECTION CLAUSE A constitutional guarantee that no person should be denied the same protection of the laws enjoyed by other persons in like circumstances.

INTERMEDIATE SCRUTINY A standard of reviewing the propriety of classifications pertaining to gender or legitimacy, under the Equal Protection Clause of the United States Constitution, which requires a court to ascertain whether the classification furthers an important state interest and is substantially related to the attainment of that interest.

SUSPECT CLASSIFICATION A class of persons that have historically been subject to discriminatory treatment; statutes drawing a distinction between persons based on a suspect classification, i.e., race, nationality or alienage, are subject to a strict scrutiny standard of review.

Dandridge v. Williams

State (D) v. Welfare recipients (P)

397 U.S. 471 (1970).

NATURE OF CASE: Constitutional challenge to state welfare law.

FACT SUMMARY: Williams (P) and other welfare recipients challenged the maximum payment portions of Maryland's welfare programs.

🏛 RULE OF LAW
In fields of economic and social legislation not involving fundamental rights, a statute will survive an equal protection challenge if supported by legitimate state interests.

FACTS: Maryland's welfare program set a maximum benefit limit of $240 to $250 per month regardless of the size or need of individual applicants. A sliding scale was used with increases up to the maximum based on the number of members in the family unit, circumstances, and need. Various welfare recipients with large families (including Williams [P]) challenged the validity of the maximum benefit limit on equal protection grounds, alleging that it failed to realistically meet family needs and discriminated against them due to the size of their family. The State (D) argued that proportionately smaller payments for larger families encouraged family planning, finding jobs, and allocating resources efficiently between welfare and nonwelfare families. The district court found that while the State (D) had a legitimate rational interest/concern in maximum benefits the statute was overreaching in scope and cut too broadly on an indiscriminate basis over the entire AFDC program.

ISSUE: Will legitimate state interests survive equal protection challenges in economic and social legislative areas not involving fundamental rights?

HOLDING AND DECISION: (Stewart, J.) Yes. A different standard is applied to most statutes involving economic and social legislation. Since fundamental rights are not involved, the Court will invalidate such legislation only if no legitimate state interests/concerns are shown. The Court will not substitute its ideas for that of a legislature merely because it deems the statute unwise or sees better alternative methods. Courts are not super legislatures. The Act herein serves several legitimate state purposes, i.e., family-size planning and encouragement to find work. These are sufficient to find the Act constitutional regardless of whether we feel it is humane, proper, etc. These are policy decisions made by the legislature, not the courts. Reversed.

▶ ANALYSIS

The two-tiered standard of equal protection analysis began in *U.S. v. Caroline Products Co.*, 304 U.S. 144 (1938). The two polar extremes (fundamental rights and economic interests) are easily handled under the analysis. Cases in the middle are very difficult at times to classify. Cases involving the administration of public welfare have caused numerous conceptual problems with analysis.

Quicknotes

FUNDAMENTAL RIGHT A liberty that is either expressly or impliedly provided for in the United States Constitution, the deprivation or burdening of which is subject to a heightened standard of review.

RATIONAL BASIS TEST A test employed by the court to determine the validity of a statute in equal protection actions, whereby the court determines whether the challenged statute is rationally related to the achievement of a legitimate state interest.

San Antonio Independent School District v. Rodriguez

School district (D) v. Resident (P)

411 U.S. 1 (1973).

NATURE OF CASE: Appeal from finding of unconstitutionality of dual public school financing system.

FACT SUMMARY: Rodriguez (P), who resided in the Edgewood district of the San Antonio Independent School District (SAISD) (D) where the highest school tax was paid and $356 per year per student was allocated, filed this suit alleging denial of equal protection since the Alamo Heights district of SAISD (D) was taxed at a lower rate but produced enough revenue to permit the allocation of $594 per year per student there.

🏛 **RULE OF LAW**
The allocation of educational funds per year per pupil in a school district according to the amount produced by taxation in that district does not violate the equal protection rights of residents of other districts in the area paying a higher rate of tax that produces less revenue resulting in a lower per pupil allocation.

FACTS: The average assessed property value per student in the predominantly white Alamo Heights district was more than $49,000 while the corresponding value in the predominantly minority Edgewood district was $5,960. This resulted in the allocation of $594 per year per student in Alamo Heights and only $365 per year per student in Edgewood, despite the fact that Edgewood residents paid a higher rate of tax. The allocations were made in each district separately according to the amount of revenue produced in each. Edgewood produced less revenue from the school tax even though residents there paid a higher rate, and Rodriguez (P) along with other residents filed this suit on the ground that the dual system and financial disparity denied Edgewood residents equal protection of the laws. The district court found the system unconstitutional, and the U.S. Supreme Court granted certiorari.

ISSUE: Does the allocation of educational funds per year per student in a school district according to the amount produced by taxation in that district violate the equal protection rights of residents of other districts in an area paying a higher rate of tax that produces less revenue resulting in a lower per pupil allocation?

HOLDING AND DECISION: (Powell, J.) No. The Equal Protection Clause does not require absolute equality or precisely equal advantages. The class of persons represented by Rodriguez (P) is not a "suspect" class. The members of the class are unified only by the fact that they live in a district with less taxable wealth than other districts. It has not been shown that these persons are "poorer" than

others or that the admittedly dual system has a purpose of denying rights to the poor. Because the Edgewood residents pay more and receive less, Rodriguez (P) argued, and the district court agreed, that the Equal Protection Clause was violated by the unequal distribution of the education funds throughout the entire SAISD (D). Since nothing in the Constitution either explicitly or implicitly guarantees education as a "fundamental" right and since Rodriguez (P) does not represent a "suspect" class, the "compelling state interest" standard applied by the district court was inappropriate. Here the system employed was not so irrational as to be invidiously discriminatory. The allocation of educational funds per year per pupil in a school district according to the amount produced by taxation in that district does not violate the equal protection rights of residents of other districts in the area paying a higher rate of tax that produces less revenue and results in a lower per pupil allocation. Reversed.

DISSENT: (Marshall, J.) The majority of this Court today seeks to establish that cases under the Equal Protection Clause fall into two categories for review: strict scrutiny or mere rationality. A reading of the decisions of this Court shows that a spectrum of standards has been employed in equal protection cases. The only justification for the system here questioned is the local control of schools. But the system does not really advance that interest because voters are unable to choose to allocate more to education and are instead bound by the amount of taxable property in their districts, a factor over which they have no control.

▶ **ANALYSIS**

The majority found in this case that there was no fundamental right to education secured by the Constitution except that some educational opportunity for all persons is required. However, if a "suspect" class had been singled out for unequal treatment in the same way, an equal protection violation would have resulted.

■■■

Quicknotes

FUNDAMENTAL RIGHT A liberty that is either expressly or impliedly provided for in the United States Constitution, the deprivation or burdening of which is subject to a heightened standard of review.

STRICT SCRUTINY Method by which courts determine the constitutionality of a law, when a law affects a funda-

Continued on next page.

mental right. Under the test, the legislature must have a compelling interest to enact the law and measures prescribed by the law must be the least restrictive means possible to accomplish its goal.

SUSPECT CLASSIFICATION   A class of persons that have historically been subject to discriminatory treatment; statutes drawing a distinction between persons based on a suspect classification, i.e., race, nationality or alienage, are subject to a strict scrutiny standard of review.

■■■

Griffin v. Illinois

Indigent (D) v. State (P)

351 U.S. 12 (1956).

NATURE OF CASE: Constitutional challenge to state law.

FACT SUMMARY: Illinois (P) denied a free stenographic transcript to indigents for their initial appeal of criminal convictions.

🏛 RULE OF LAW
Once appellate rights are offered, discrimination on the basis of wealth violates equal protection.

FACTS: Illinois (P) granted a first appeal of a criminal conviction as a matter of right. To obtain a complete review of a conviction, a stenographic transcript was required. The convicted party was required to pay in advance for the transcript with the exception of indigents convicted of murder. Griffin (D), an indigent, was convicted of a crime other than murder and wished to appeal. Illinois (P) refused to supply a free transcript and Griffin (D) alleged that the statute allowed for the discrimination against those convicted solely based on wealth.

ISSUE: Once a state offers an appeal of right, can it require the prepayment of costs as a condition for allowing the appeal?

HOLDING AND DECISION: (Black, J.) No. The statute invidiously discriminates against the poor. The requirement of prepayment of fees has no rational bearing as to the guilt or innocence of the convicted party. Once an appeal is allowed of right, the state may not constitutionally discriminate as to its free exercise based on wealth. If an appeal cannot be properly prosecuted without a complete transcript, the State (P) may not deny the right merely because of wealth. This is a violation of the Equal Protection Clause of the Fourteenth Amendment. We do not say that a State (P) must furnish a complete stenographic transcript in every case, but it must provide acceptable substitutes covering the portion challenged in order to comply with equal protection. Vacated and remanded.

▶ ANALYSIS

Griffin was extended to require a transcript even when the charge was a misdemeanor and when only a fine was assessed. *Mayer v. City of Chicago*, 404 U.S. 189 (1971). In *Gardner v. California*, 393 U.S. 367 (1969), the Court held that the state must provide indigents with a transcript of a lower court habeas corpus proceeding for use in connection with a new petition to a higher court.

Quicknotes

EQUAL PROTECTION CLAUSE A constitutional guarantee that no person should be denied the same protection of the laws enjoyed by other persons in like circumstances.

FUNDAMENTAL RIGHT A liberty that is either expressly or impliedly provided for in the United States Constitution, the deprivation or burdening of which is subject to a heightened standard of review.

Douglas v. California

Indigent (D) v. State (P)

372 U.S. 353 (1963).

NATURE OF CASE: Appeal from criminal conviction.

FACT SUMMARY: After his conviction, Douglas (D) was denied appointed counsel for assistance in pursuing his right of first appeal. The denial came after the appellate court had reviewed the transcript of his trial and, pursuant to state law, had determined that counsel would not be of help to the defendant.

RULE OF LAW
An indigent is entitled to appointed counsel to prepare an appellate brief where the appeal pursued is granted as a matter of right to all defendants.

FACTS: Douglas (D) was convicted in a state proceeding and was sentenced. He served notice he wished to appeal his conviction and that he was in need of appointed counsel due to indigence. The first appeal after trial conviction is granted as a matter of right in California. However, Douglas (D) was denied the appointment of counsel to prosecute the appeal. The denial came after the appellate court had reviewed the transcript and determined that appointed counsel would not be of help to either Douglas (D) or the court. The decision was in line with a state rule providing for this procedure.

ISSUE: Is an indigent entitled to appointed counsel to assist in preparation of an appeal from a state criminal conviction where the appeal is granted to all defendants as a matter of right?

HOLDING AND DECISION: (Douglas, J.) Yes. In spite of California's otherwise forward-looking favorable treatment of indigents, the problem presented by this case is the same as that presented by *Griffin v. Illinois*, 351 U.S. 12 (1956), i.e., discrimination against the indigent. By the system employed, only a defendant affluent enough to retain counsel will obtain a full judicial review of his conviction. The indigent is entitled to no more than a review of the bare transcript by the appellate court. Not all appealable issues will appear on the face of a transcript. While the Fourteenth Amendment does not demand absolute equality, due process cannot be denied by "invidious discrimination." While the rich man can employ counsel to focus on appealable issues and to raise hidden objections to the conduct of the trial, the indigent is denied this same right. Our decision is not directed toward discretionary appeals, but toward appeals granted as a matter of right to all defendants. In such an instance, the indigent is entitled to appointed counsel. Vacated and remanded.

ANALYSIS

Some commentators have viewed the *Douglas* decision as a precursor to a requirement for appointed counsel whenever retained counsel is permitted. In fact, some lower courts (not a majority) have held that the difference between appeals of right and discretionary appeals is not a barrier to the right to appointive counsel. However, the weight of the commentaries appears to favor viewing the *Douglas* and *Griffin* decisions as interposing the right to counsel only where the lack of such counsel, in relation to retained counsel cases, works an inequality so significant as to amount to fundamental unfairness. On that basis, the right to counsel on a discretionary appeal is not found since such appeals rarely delve into new ground not covered in the first appeal and involve broad policy decisions fully developed in the first appeal.

Quicknotes

DUE PROCESS CLAUSE Clauses found in the Fifth and Fourteenth Amendments to the United States Constitution providing that no person shall be deprived of "life, liberty, or property, without due process of law."

RIGHT TO COUNSEL Right conferred by the Sixth Amendment that the accused shall be provided effective legal assistance in a criminal proceeding.

Reynolds v. Sims

Parties not identified.

377 U.S. 533 (1964).

NATURE OF CASE: Appeal from a judgment finding a state's apportionment plan and two proposed plans invalid.

FACT SUMMARY: The current Alabama (D) apportionment plan was deemed invalid since it had not been reapportioned in nearly 60 years.

RULE OF LAW

The Equal Protection Clause requires apportionment by actual population for both houses of a state bicameral legislature.

FACTS: The Alabama Constitution required that both houses of the state legislature be composed of representatives elected from districts based on apportioned population. The districts were to be reapportioned periodically. Suit was brought to invalidate the current apportionment plan, it being alleged that no reapportionment had been had in nearly 60 years. Utilizing the 1960 census, only 45% of the population elected a majority of representatives of the upper house and 25.7% elected a majority of members to the lower house. Population variance between districts electing the same number of representatives was as much as 41 to 1.

ISSUE: Does the Equal Protection Clause require that the seats in both houses of a bicameral state legislature be properly apportioned?

HOLDING AND DECISION: (Warren, C.J.) Yes. The Equal Protection Clause requires apportionment by population in elections for both houses of a bicameral state legislature. Suffrage is a fundamental right. Plans which dilute this right are subjected to strict scrutiny. Dilution impairs the right to suffrage. To the extent that a citizen's right to vote is debased, he is that much less a citizen. The federal Congress was not intended as a model for state government. Both houses of a bicameral legislature must be elected based on apportioned population. Districts must be divided as evenly as possible. Legitimate population deviations for a rational state purpose are acceptable, e.g., historic, economic, and group interests. Failure to adhere to strict population guidelines will be strictly scrutinized and major disparities are constitutionally suspect. So, too, the failure to reapportion at least once every ten years will leave the apportionment plan constitutionally suspect. Remedial techniques will be left to the district courts. In the event of an imminent election, the old plan may be allowed to stand since equitable relief cannot be effectuated in time to remedy past evils. The Alabama (D) plan is unconstitutional. Affirmed and remanded.

DISSENT: (Harlan, J.) The majority of the Court asserts that the right of a person to vote cannot be "diluted" by systems of apportionment which entitle them to vote for fewer legislators than other voters. This is not what the Equal Protection Clause was designed to prevent. The Court goes on to eliminate from consideration in establishing legislative districts nearly every possible factor relevant to this process. The Court exceeds its authority in so doing in order to satisfy justified impatience with the slow workings of the political process.

ANALYSIS

By 1968, 37 states had complied with the decision, considered by many to be one of the great achievements of the Warren Court. However, various studies of the effect of the decision on state policy and the responsiveness of state legislatures have been conflicting. One thing is clear, rural low population areas no longer dominate high density urban areas which were previously grossly underrepresented.

Quicknotes

BICAMERALISM The necessity of approval by a majority of both houses of Congress in ratifying legislation or approving other legislative action.

EQUAL PROTECTION CLAUSE A constitutional guarantee that no person should be denied the same protection of the laws enjoyed by other persons in like circumstances.

FUNDAMENTAL RIGHT A liberty that is either expressly or impliedly provided for in the United States Constitution, the deprivation or burdening of which is subject to a heightened standard of review.

REAPPORTIONMENT PLAN The alteration of a voting districts' boundaries or composition to reflect the population of that district.

STRICT SCRUTINY Method by which courts determine the constitutionality of a law, when a law affects a fundamental right. Under the test, the legislature must have a compelling interest to enact the law and measures prescribed by the law must be the least restrictive means possible to accomplish its goal.

Harper v. Virginia State Board of Elections

Residents (P) v. State (D)

383 U.S. 663 (1966).

NATURE OF CASE: Suits challenging the constitutionality of Virginia's poll tax.

FACT SUMMARY: Harper (P) and other Virginia residents brought this suit to have Virginia's (D) poll tax declared unconstitutional.

🏛 RULE OF LAW
The right to vote is a fundamental and basic right, and where such rights are asserted under the Equal Protection Clause, classifications that might restrain those rights must be closely scrutinized and carefully confined. Lines drawn on the basis of wealth or property, like those of race, are traditionally disfavored.

FACTS: Harper (P) and other Virginia residents brought these suits to have Virginia's (D) poll tax declared unconstitutional. The three-judge district court, feeling bound by the Court's decision in *Breedlove v. Suttles*, dismissed the complaint. Harper (P) appealed. The law at issue conditions the right to vote in state elections upon the payment of a poll tax.

ISSUE: Is a poll tax, the payment of which is a required prerequisite for voting, constitutional?

HOLDING AND DECISION: (Douglas, J.) No. A state violates the Equal Protection Clause whenever it makes the affluence of the voter or the payment of a fee an electoral standard. The right to vote is a basic and fundamental one, especially since it preserves other rights. Any alleged infringement on the right to vote must be carefully scrutinized. A state's interest, when it comes to voting, is limited to the power to fix qualifications. Wealth, like race or creed or color, is irrelevant to one's ability to participate intelligently in the electoral process. Further lines drawn on the basis of wealth or property, like those of race, are traditionally disfavored. The requirement of the payment of a fee as a condition of obtaining a ballot causes invidious discrimination. *Breedlove v. Suttles*, 302 U.S. 277 (1937), sanctioned this use of the poll tax, and to that extent it is overruled. Reversed.

DISSENT: (Black, J.) So long as a distinction drawn is not irrational, unreasonable or invidious, it must be upheld. There are certainly rational reasons for Virginia's poll tax, such as the state's desire to collect revenue and its belief that voters who pay poll tax will be interested in furthering the state's welfare. Hence, the tax must be upheld. If it is to be struck down, it should be done by the legislature, rather than the courts.

DISSENT: (Harlan, J.) The Equal Protection Clause does not impose upon this country an ideology of unrestrained equalitarianism.

▶ ANALYSIS

If, as the dissenters in *Harper* argue, the poll tax classification is not wholly "irrational," the case represents a greater intervention than the courts undertook under old equal protection. There is some question as to whether this greater scrutiny was because the "fundamental rights" of voting are affected or because "lines drawn on the basis of wealth" are traditionally disfavored. In *McDonald v. Board of Election Commissioners*, 394 U.S. 802 (1969), the Court sees wealth as an independent ground (apart from impact on fundamental rights) for strict scrutiny. There is a series of cases preceding and following *Harper* (among them *Reynolds v. Sims*, 397 U.S. 533 [1964]) that support the invoking of strict scrutiny when voting rights are affected.

■=■

Quicknotes

EQUAL PROTECTION CLAUSE A constitutional guarantee that no person should be denied the same protection of the laws enjoyed by other persons in like circumstances.

FUNDAMENTAL RIGHT A liberty that is either expressly or impliedly provided for in the United States Constitution, the deprivation or burdening of which is subject to a heightened standard of review.

POLL TAX A tax imposed upon each person within a certain class (e.g., all males of a certain age) irrespective of ownership of property, occupation, or ability to pay.

STRICT SCRUTINY Method by which courts determine the constitutionality of a law, when a law affects a fundamental right. Under the test, the legislature must have a compelling interest to enact the law and measures prescribed by the law must be the least restrictive means possible to accomplish its goal.

■=■

Hill v. Stone

State (D) v. Nonrenderers (P)

421 U.S. 289 (1975).

NATURE OF CASE: Appeal from invalidation of state voting procedures.

FACT SUMMARY: Stone (P) claimed that Texas dual box election procedures denied him equal protection of the laws.

🏛 RULE OF LAW
In an election of general interest, restrictions on the franchise other than residence, age, and citizenship must promote a compelling state interest in order to be valid.

FACTS: Texas provided for a dual box election procedure to be used in all the state's local bond elections. Under this procedure, all persons owning taxable property rendered or listed for taxation vote in one box, and all other registered voters cast their ballots in a separate box. The result in both boxes were tabulated, and the bond issue was deemed to have passed only if it is approved by a majority vote both in the renderer's box, and in the aggregate of both boxes. On April 11, 1972, the City of Fort Worth conducted a tax bond election, using the dual box system to authorize the sale of bonds to improve the city transportation system, and to build a city library. After the library bonds were defeated in the renderers' box, Stone (P) and other nonrenderers filed suit, alleging that the laws violated the Equal Protection Clause. The district court held that the state laws were invalid.

ISSUE: In an election of general interest, must restrictions on the franchise other than residence, age, and citizenship promote a compelling state interest in order to be valid?

HOLDING AND DECISION: (Marshall, J.) Yes. In an election of general interest, restrictions on the franchise other than residence, age, and citizenship must promote a compelling state interest in order to survive constitutional attack. A general obligation bond issue, even where the debt service will be paid entirely out of property taxes as in Fort Worth, is a matter of general interest. The Texas scheme creates a classification based on rendering, and it in effect disenfranchises those who have not rendered their property for taxation in the year of the bond election. The rendering requirement seems unlikely to have any significant impact on the asserted state policy of encouraging each person to render all of his property, because the individual may vote if he renders any property at all, no matter how trivial. Affirmed.

▶ ANALYSIS

In *Kramer v. Union Free School District No. 15*, 395 U.S. 621 (1969), the Court invalidated a New York statute that limited eligibility to vote in local school board elections to persons who owned or leased taxable real property in the school district, or who had children enrolled in the public schools. The Court held that the fact that the school district was supported by a property tax did not mean that only those subject to direct assessment felt the effects of the tax burden.

■■■■

Quicknotes

EQUAL PROTECTION CLAUSE A constitutional guarantee that no person should be denied the same protection of the laws enjoyed by other persons in like circumstances.

FUNDAMENTAL RIGHT A liberty that is either expressly or impliedly provided for in the United States Constitution, the deprivation or burdening of which is subject to a heightened standard of review.

■■■■

Illinois State Board of Elections v. Socialist Workers Party

State (D) v. Political party (P)

440 U.S. 173 (1979).

NATURE OF CASE: Appeal in action to invalidate Illinois Election Code.

FACT SUMMARY: The Socialist Workers Party (P) challenged the constitutionality of portions of the Illinois Election Code dealing with qualification of new political parties.

🏛 RULE OF LAW
Restrictions on access to the ballot must be justified by a compelling state interest.

FACTS: Under the Illinois Election Code, new political parties and independent candidates must obtain the signatures of 25,000 qualified voters in order to appear on the ballot in statewide elections. However, the minimum number of signatures required in elections for offices of political subdivisions is five percent of the number of persons who voted at the previous election for offices of the particular subdivision. In 1977, an independent candidate of a new political party in Chicago, a city with approximately 718,937 voters eligible to sign nominating petitions for the mayoral election, had to secure over 10,000 more signatures on nominating petitions than an independent candidate or new party in state elections, which had a pool of approximately 4.5 million eligible voters from which to obtain signatures. The Socialist Workers Party (P) charged that this discrepancy violated the Equal Protection Clause of the Fourteenth Amendment.

ISSUE: Must restrictions on access to the ballot be justified by a compelling state interest?

HOLDING AND DECISION: (Marshall, J.) Yes. Restrictions on access to the ballot burden two fundamental rights: (1) the freedom to associate as a political party, and (2) the right to vote. When such vital individual rights are at stake, a state must establish that its classification is necessary to serve a compelling interest. Properly drawn statutes that require a preliminary showing of a significant modicum of support before a candidate or party may appear on the ballot have been upheld. However, even when pursuing a legitimate interest, the state must adopt the least drastic means to achieve their ends. Here, the signature requirements for independent candidates and new political parties seeking offices in Chicago are plainly not the least restrictive means of protecting the state's objectives. Therefore, those portions of the Illinois Election Code must be held to be unconstitutional.

CONCURRENCE: (Blackmun, J.) I must record my unrelieved discomfort with what seems to be a continuing tendency to use as tests such easy phrases as compelling state interest and least restrictive means.

▶ ANALYSIS

The Court has invalidated filing fee requirements as a prerequisite to ballot access as applied to independents in at least two cases. The underlying reasoning is that filing fees do not test the genuineness of a candidate, since a wealthy but frivolous candidate can write the filing check, but a serious but impoverished candidate may be prevented from running. See, *Bullock v. Carter*, 405 U.S. 134 (1972), and *Lubin v. Panish*, 415 U.S. 709 (1974).

■══■

Quicknotes

EQUAL PROTECTION CLAUSE A constitutional guarantee that no person should be denied the same protection of the laws enjoyed by other persons in like circumstances.

FREEDOM OF ASSOCIATION The right to peaceably assemble.

FUNDAMENTAL RIGHT A liberty that is either expressly or impliedly provided for in the United States Constitution, the deprivation or burdening of which is subject to a heightened standard of review.

■══■

Bush v. Gore

Candidate (D) v. Candidate (P)

531 U.S. 98 (2000).

NATURE OF CASE: Suit seeking stay of state supreme court order.

FACT SUMMARY: Bush (D) sought a stay of the Florida Supreme Court's order permitting a manual recount of ballots in the 2000 presidential election.

🏛 RULE OF LAW
Having once granted the right to vote on equal terms, the state may not, by later arbitrary and disparate treatment, value one person's vote over that of another.

FACTS: After a machine count and recount of ballots in the 2000 Florida presidential election, Gore (P) trailed Bush (D) by less than 1,000 votes. Gore (P) sought further recounts in certain Florida counties. The U.S. Supreme Court vacated a decision of the Florida Supreme Court extending the deadline for the completion of recounts. The Florida Supreme Court ordered a manual recount of all "undervotes"—those ballots on which the machine did not record any presidential choice. Bush (D) sought a stay of the Florida Supreme Court ruling. The U.S. Supreme Court stayed the Florida Supreme Court's order three days before the statutory deadline for the completion of proceedings bearing on the final certification of the state's electors.

ISSUE: Having once granted the right to vote on equal terms, may the state, by later arbitrary and disparate treatment, value one person's vote over that of another?

HOLDING AND DECISION: (Per curiam) No. Having once granted the right to vote on equal terms, the state may not, by later arbitrary and disparate treatment, value one person's vote over that of another. The right to vote is protected both in its allocation as well as its exercise. The recount mechanism implemented here does not satisfy the minimum requirement for non-arbitrary treatment of voters necessary to secure the fundamental right. The standards for accepting or rejecting contested ballots vary not only from county to county but within the county from team to team of recounters. Because any recount seeking to meet the December 12 date will be unconstitutional without substantial additional work, the decision of the Florida Supreme Court ordering the recount to proceed is reversed and remanded.

CONCURRENCE: (Rehnquist, C.J.) There are grounds for reversal in addition to those in the per curiam opinion. I. Where the election of the President is involved, and the Constitution imposes a duty on a branch of state government, the text of the state's election law, and not just its interpretation by the state courts, takes on independent significance. Therefore, 3 U.S.C. § 5 informs the application of the Constitution's mandate in Art. II, § 1, cl. 2 that the state legislature shall appoint electors to the electoral college in a manner of its choosing to the state's electoral scheme. Section 5 provides that the state's selection of electors will be conclusive if the selection is accomplished pursuant to laws enacted prior to the election and is complete six days prior to the meeting of the electoral college. To respect the legislature's powers, postelection state-court actions must not be allowed to frustrate the legislative desire to attain the "safe harbor" provided by § 5, and, to determine whether a state court has infringed upon the legislature's Article II authority, the Court must examine the state's election law. II. Here, the Florida court's interpretation of "legal vote" and, therefore, its decision to order a contest-period recount, plainly departed from the legislative scheme. The election code does not require the counting of improperly marked ballots, and for the court to reject this established practice, prescribed by the Secretary of State, was also a departure from the legislative scheme. III. The Florida Supreme Court's order jeopardizes the "legislative wish" to take advantage of the safe harbor provided by 3 U.S.C. § 5. The state court ordered a massive recount four days before the last date for a final determination that will satisfy § 5. However, no one claims that the ballots the court seeks to have recounted were not previously tabulated. Those ballots were initially read by voting machines at the time of the election, and then reread pursuant to the state's automatic recount provision. There is also no claim of fraud.

DISSENT: (Stevens, J.) While the use of differing sub-standards for determining voter intent in different counties employing similar voting systems may raise serious concerns, those concerns are alleviated by the fact that a single impartial magistrate will ultimately adjudicate all objections arising from the recount process.

DISSENT: (Souter, J.) The case should be remanded to the Florida courts with instructions to establish uniform standards in any further recounting.

DISSENT: (Ginsburg, J.) The recount may have yielded a result less fair or precise than the certification that proceeded that recount.

DISSENT: (Breyer, J.) In a system that allows counties to use different types of voting systems, voters arrive at the polls with an unequal chance that their votes will be counted.

▶ *ANALYSIS*

The Court here does not challenge the Florida Supreme Court's authority to resolve election disputes or to define a legal vote or order a manual recount. The Court rejects the standard employed, which was the "intent of the voter,"

Continued on next page.

and the absence of specific standards to ensure its equal application.

■━━■

Quicknotes

DUE PROCESS CLAUSE Clauses found in the Fifth and Fourteenth Amendments to the United States Constitution providing that no person shall be deprived of "life, liberty, or property, without due process of law."

EQUAL PROTECTION A constitutional guarantee that no person shall be denied the same protection of the laws enjoyed by other persons in like circumstances.

■━━■

Shapiro v. Thompson

Parties not identified.

394 U.S 618 (1969).

NATURE OF CASE: Appeal from decisions holding residency requirements for welfare applicants unconstitutional.

FACT SUMMARY: Statutory provisions denied welfare assistance to residents who have not resided within their jurisdiction for at least one year.

🏛 RULE OF LAW
Any classification that serves to penalize the exercise of a constitutional right is unconstitutional unless it is shown to be necessary to promote a compelling governmental interest, rather than merely shown to be rationally related to a legitimate purpose.

FACTS: A three-judge district court held unconstitutional certain state and District of Columbia statutory provisions. The provisions deny welfare assistance to residents of the state or district who have not resided within their jurisdictions for at least one year immediately preceding their applications for such assistance.

ISSUE: Does a statutory prohibition of welfare benefits to residents of less than a year create a classification denying them equal protection of the laws?

HOLDING AND DECISION: (Brennan, J.) Yes. The states justify the waiting period requirement as a protective device to preserve the fiscal integrity of their public assistance programs, by discouraging needy families from entering their jurisdictions. However, this act of inhibiting migration by needy persons into the state is constitutionally impermissible, since the right to travel from state to state is protected by the Constitution from laws or regulations that would unreasonably burden such movement. If a law has no other purpose than to chill the assertion of a constitutional right by penalizing those who choose to exercise them, it is patently unconstitutional. Further, the statutes create two classes of persons, different only in that one class has been in the area for one year. A state has a valid interest in preserving the fiscal integrity of its programs. But it cannot accomplish this purpose by invidious discrimination between classes of its citizens. The saving of welfare costs cannot be an independent ground for invidious classification. The states also assert that the waiting period serves certain administrative goals. They contend that a mere showing of a rational relationship and these permissible state goals will justify the classification. This is not true. As stated above, the right to travel is a constitutional right. Any classification that serves to penalize the exercise of a constitutional right is unconstitutional unless it is shown to be necessary to promote a compelling governmental interest. All of the administrative arguments advanced are either unfounded, irrational, or may be accomplished by a less drastic means. The district court's judgment is affirmed.

DISSENT: (Warren, C.J.) This case is not based merely on the state residency requirements which were enacted by the states solely on their own authority. Congress has authorized this type of requirement for the District of Columbia, so the real question is whether Congress may authorize this type of legislation under the commerce power. Since numerous other restrictions on interstate commerce have been sanctioned by this court, the insubstantial restriction imposed here is certainly justified by the rational justification advanced for it.

DISSENT: (Harlan, J.) The "compelling interest" doctrine constitutes an increasingly significant exception to the rule that a statute does not deny equal protection if it is rationally related to a legitimate governmental objective.

▶ ANALYSIS

Many agreed with Harlan's dissent that the Court was simply resurrecting the judicial intervention of substantive due process under the guise of a new stricter equal protection test. One commentator warned, "Looming down the path is the spectre of economic due process, of judges riding to the rescue of Oklahoma's opticians or the Railway Express Agency." Supporters of the new doctrine answered that it was limited to minorities that seem permanently voiceless and invisible and whom the power structure in the political process tends to ignore. Subsequent decisions have shown the Court to be willing to expand the number of suspect classifications to include national origin and sex as well as race.

■■■

Quicknotes

COMMERCE POWER The power delegated to Congress by the Constitution to regulate interstate commerce.

RIGHT TO TRAVEL Constitutional guarantee affording the privileges and benefits of one state to citizens of another residing therein for the statutory period.

SUBSTANTIVE DUE PROCESS A constitutional safeguard limiting the power of the state, irrespective of how fair its procedures may be; substantive limits placed on the power of the state.

Continued on next page.

SUSPECT CLASSIFICATION A class of persons that have historically been subject to discriminatory treatment; statutes drawing a distinction between persons based on a suspect classification, i.e., race, nationality or alienage, are subject to a strict scrutiny standard of review.

■══■

Zobel v. Williams

Residents (P) v. State (D)

457 U.S. 55 (1982).

NATURE OF CASE: Appeal from decision upholding state statutory income distribution plan.

FACT SUMMARY: The Zobels (P) challenged an Alaska scheme which distributed surplus income to its citizens depending on the length of residency.

🏛 RULE OF LAW
A state may not base the amount of surplus income to be distributed to its citizens on the length of time the citizen has resided in the state.

FACTS: In an effort to distribute the windfall the state of Alaska (D) received when large deposits of oil were discovered within its borders, the State (D) devised a scheme where its residents were to receive a dividend for each year of residency since Alaska (D) became a state in 1959. Under the plan, the longer a citizen was a resident of the State (D), the higher the amount he or she would receive. The plan was challenged by the Zobels (P), who had moved to Alaska (D) in 1978. They claimed it violated their right to equal protection, and their right to migrate to Alaska (D) and thereafter enjoy the full rights of Alaska citizenship without discrimination. The Supreme Court of Alaska upheld the statutory scheme, contending that it rationally served the legitimate state interest of recognizing certain undefined contributions made by state citizens during their years of residency. The Zobels (P) appealed.

ISSUE: May a state distribute surplus income to its citizens on a sliding scale based on the length of each citizen's residency?

HOLDING AND DECISION: (Burger, C.J.) No. The purpose advanced by Alaska (D) for the distribution scheme, i.e., that it recognizes certain undefined "contributions of various kinds, both tangible and intangible, which residents have made during their years of residency," is not a legitimate state purpose. This is because to find otherwise would be to find that a state can discriminate among its citizens solely on the ground of their length of residency. Such a finding would open the door to sliding tuition fees, variations in taxes, and even limited access to public facilities—all based ostensibly on a citizen's length of residency. This would be clearly impermissible. Accordingly, it must be held that a state may not, consistently with the notion of equal protection of the laws, base the amount of surplus income to be distributed to its citizens on the length of time the citizen has resided in the state. Reversed and remanded.

CONCURRENCE: (Brennan, J.) The constitutional flaws inherent in the Alaska (D) scheme are even more widespread than the majority points out. In effect, objections to the scheme could be based on the Constitutional "right to travel," and the Commerce Clause, in addition to equal protection.

CONCURRENCE: (O'Connor, J.) The Court arrived at the correct decision, but erred in the grounds for its decision. The right violated by the statutory scheme was clearly the constitutional right to travel. Furthermore, such a right is "fundamental" requiring the strictest of scrutiny in judicial analysis.

DISSENT: (Rehnquist, J.) There is nothing wrong with Alaska's (D) scheme to distribute its new-found wealth among its citizens. The Court has long held that state economic regulations are presumptively valid and will be deemed to violate the Fourteenth Amendment only in the rarest of instances. It is clear that the plan herein presented is not one of those instances.

▶ ANALYSIS

In addition to the stated purpose of rewarding citizens for their undefined "contributions" to the state, Alaska (D) advanced two other reasons for its scheme—the creation of a financial incentive for individuals to establish and maintain residency in the state, and the encouragement of prudent management of the windfall income. The Court found these two purposes wholly nonexplanatory as to why the scheme would discriminate retroactively among its citizens. However, it suggested that these purposes might support a similar scheme which differentiated prospectively among a state's residents.

■═■

Quicknotes

COMMERCE CLAUSE Article 1, section 8, clause 3 of the United States Constitution, granting Congress the power to regulate commerce with foreign countries and between the states.

DIVIDEND The payment of earnings to a corporation's shareholders in proportion to the amount of shares held.

RIGHT TO TRAVEL Constitutional guarantee affording the privileges and benefits of one state to citizens of another residing therein for the statutory period.

STRICT SCRUTINY Method by which courts determine the constitutionality of a law, when a law affects a fundamental right.

SURPLUS The excess of assets over liabilities.

■═■

Haig v. Agee

Secretary of State (D) v. Ex-CIA officer (P)

453 U.S. 280 (1981).

NATURE OF CASE: Review of order of restoration of passport.

FACT SUMMARY: The President, through the Secretary of State, Haig (D), revoked the passport of Phillip Agee (P), an ex-CIA officer who had engaged in activities abroad regarded as damaging to the national security.

RULE OF LAW

The President and the Secretary of State may revoke a passport where the holder's activities are causing, or are likely to cause, damage to national security.

FACTS: Phillip Agee (P) was an officer of the CIA who retired and launched a campaign to "fight the . . . CIA wherever it is operating." Agee (P) had divulged the names of CIA personnel working under cover along with classified information resulting in episodes of violence in violation of an express contractual agreement not to do so. Haig (D), as Secretary of State, revoked Agee's (P) passport and Agee (P) brought this action. The district court ordered restoration of the passport and the court of appeals affirmed. The U.S. Supreme Court granted certiorari.

ISSUE: May the President and the Secretary of State revoke a passport where the holder's activities are causing, or are likely to cause, damage to the national security?

HOLDING AND DECISION: (Burger, C.J.) Yes. Ever since the adoption of the Passport Act in 1926 the single most important criterion in passport decisions was the likelihood of damage to national security. As a passport is virtually a "letter of introduction" for the holder granted by the government, it is subject to reasonable governmental regulation. The President and the Secretary of State may revoke a passport where the holder's activities are causing, or are likely to cause, damage to the national security. It is Agee's (P) activities, and not his speech, which is being limited by the passport revocation, so that the First Amendment argument also fails. Reversed and remanded.

CONCURRENCE: (Blackmun, J.) The Court has here cut back the holdings of some of our previous decisions, but does not say so. I join in the opinion believing this to have been done, even if done sub silentio.

DISSENT: (Brennan, J.) In order to find power for the Secretary of State to revoke passports, the Passport Act requires that a practice be sufficiently substantial and consistent to warrant the conclusion that Congress implied such power. The practice has not been so demonstrated

and is, in fact, dangerous due to the degree of subjectivity with which it might be applied.

▶ ANALYSIS

Agee's (P) conduct, though in a sense only speech, had a serious potential to subvert the activities of a governmental agency charged with the duty to aid in matters of national security. Agee's (P) belief that that agency acted to the detriment of that duty did not prevail over Haig's (D) contrary belief ultimately, and it is against this administrative subjectivity that Justice Brennan's dissent warns.

Quicknotes

FIRST AMENDMENT Prohibits Congress from enacting any law respecting an establishment of religion, prohibiting the free exercise of religion, abridging freedom of speech or the press, the right of peaceful assembly and the right to petition for a redress of grievances.

SUB SILENTIO Under silence; without mention.

Skinner v. Oklahoma ex rel. Williamson

Criminal (D) v. State (P)

316 U.S. 535 (1942).

NATURE OF CASE: Constitutional challenge to state law.

FACT SUMMARY: Skinner (D) was deemed to be an habitual criminal and was ordered sterilized under an Oklahoma (P) statute.

🏛 RULE OF LAW
A statute that arbitrarily excludes a class from its purview violates the Equal Protection Clause of the Fourteenth Amendment where fundamental rights are involved.

FACTS: Skinner (D) was convicted of crimes on three separate occasions. Under an Oklahoma (P) statute he could be declared an habitual criminal and could be ordered to be sterilized to prevent the passing on of criminal genetic traits. The statute applied to those convicted of two or more crimes amounting to felonies involving moral turpitude. The attorney general could maintain a suit to have the convicted party sterilized. A full trial would be held. The issue was confined to whether the party was an habitual criminal and whether he should be sterilized. Offenses arising out of violations of prohibitory laws, revenue acts, embezzlement, or political offenses were not within the purview of the Act. Skinner (D) was adjudged an habitual criminal and was ordered sterilized. Skinner (D) challenged the constitutionality of the statute.

ISSUE: May a state arbitrarily discriminate between like classes where fundamental rights are involved?

HOLDING AND DECISION: (Douglas, J.) No. We do not pass on the constitutionality of sterilization of habitual criminals or the state's procedure. We do find that the Oklahoma (P) statute is unconstitutional under the Equal Protection Clause of the Fourteenth Amendment. We are dealing herein with a fundamental right, i.e., the right to have children. Statutes dealing with such rights are closely scrutinized. While a state may treat classes unequally based on experience, it may not arbitrarily seek to add or exclude a particular group from treatment. There must be a rational basis for the distinction. The law treats the embezzler in the same manner as other criminals, e.g., those convicted of grand larceny. There is no viable difference between their offenses or gene traits. Failure to treat them equally under the sterilization statute cannot be supported and violates the Equal Protection Clause. The statute is unconstitutional on its face. Reversed.

CONCURRENCE: (Stone, C.J.) There is no scientific proof that criminal tendencies are inherited. The statute violates personal liberties secured by the Due Process Clause. The law sets up arbitrary standards that cannot be supported by evidence/fact.

▶ ANALYSIS

A law that condemns, without hearing, all of the individuals of a class to a harsh measure merely because some or many are deserving of such treatment, lacks the basic attributes of due process (*Morrison v. California*, 291 U.S. 82 [1934]). In *Skinner*, the Court expressly left the constitutional issue as to sterilization open even if the equal protection problem was solved. This is based on the Court's concern to decide all cases on the narrowest possible grounds.

■═■

Quicknotes

DUE PROCESS CLAUSE Clauses found in the Fifth and Fourteenth Amendments to the United States Constitution providing that no person shall be deprived of "life, liberty, or property, without due process of law."

EQUAL PROTECTION CLAUSE A constitutional guarantee that no person should be denied the same protection of the laws enjoyed by other persons in like circumstances.

FOURTEENTH AMENDMENT- 42 U.S.C. § 1983 Defamation by state officials in connection with a discharge implies a violation of a liberty interest protected by the due process requirements of the U.S. Constitution.

FUNDAMENTAL RIGHT A liberty that is either expressly or impliedly provided for in the United States Constitution, the deprivation or burdening of which is subject to a heightened standard of review.

■═■

Griswold v. Connecticut

Doctor (D) v. State (P)

381 U.S. 479 (1965).

NATURE OF CASE: Appeal from conviction for violating state laws prohibiting the counselling of married persons to take contraceptives.

FACT SUMMARY: Doctor (D) and layman (D) were prosecuted for advising married persons on the means of preventing conception.

🏛 RULE OF LAW
The right to mental privacy, although not explicitly stated in the Bill of Rights, is a penumbra, formed by certain other explicit guarantees. As such, it is protected against state regulation that sweeps unnecessarily broad.

FACTS: Griswold (D), the Executive Director of the Planned Parenthood League of Connecticut, and Dr. Buxton (D) were convicted under a Connecticut law which made counselling of married persons to take contraceptives a criminal offense.

ISSUE: Is the right to privacy in the marital relationship protected by the Constitution despite the absence of specific language recognizing it?

HOLDING AND DECISION: (Douglas, J.) Yes. The various guarantees that create penumbras, or zones, of privacy include the First Amendment's right of association, the Third Amendment's prohibition against the peacetime quartering of soldiers, the Fourth Amendment's prohibition against unreasonable searches and seizures, the Fifth Amendment's self-incrimination clause, and the Ninth Amendment's reservation to the people of unenumerated rights. The Connecticut law by forbidding the use of contraceptives, rather than regulating their manner or sale, seeks to achieve its goals by means having a maximum destructive impact upon that relationship. Reversed.

CONCURRENCE: (Goldberg, J.) The Ninth Amendment, while not constituting an independent source of rights, suggests that the list of rights in the first eight amendments is not exhaustive. This right is a "fundamental" one that cannot be infringed on the state's slender justification in protecting marital fidelity.

CONCURRENCE: (Harlan, J.) The Court, instead of focusing on "specific provisions" of the Bill of Rights, should have instead relied on the Due Process Clause in finding this law violative of basic values "implicit in the concept of ordered liberty."

CONCURRENCE: (White, J.) The Due Process Clause should be the test in determining whether such laws are reasonably necessary for the effectuation of a legitimate and substantial state interest and are not arbitrary or capricious in application. Here, the causal connection between married persons engaging in extramarital sex and contraceptives, is too tenuous.

DISSENT: (Black, J.) While the law is offensive, neither the Ninth Amendment nor the Due Process Clause invalidates it. Both lead the Court into imposing its own notions as to what are wise or unwise laws. What constitutes "fundamental" values this court is incapable of determining. Keeping the Constitution "in tune with the times" is accomplished only through the amendment process. Similarly, the Due Process Clause is too imprecise and lends itself to subjective interpretation.

DISSENT: (Stewart, J.) The Due Process Clause is not the "guide" because there was no claim here that the statute is unconstitutionally vague, or that the defendants were denied any of the elements of procedural due process at their trial. The Ninth Amendment simply restricts the federal government to a government of express and limited powers. Finally, the Constitution is silent on the "right to privacy."

▶ ANALYSIS

Although the theory of "substantive due process" has declined as a means to review state economic regulation—at least since 1937—the Court, as here, has freely applied strict scrutiny of state laws affecting social areas.

■═■

Quicknotes

DUE PROCESS CLAUSE Clauses found in the Fifth and Fourteenth Amendments to the United States Constitution providing that no person shall be deprived of "life, liberty, or property, without due process of law."

PENUMBRA A doctrine whereby authority of the federal government is implied pursuant to the Necessary and Proper Clause; one implied power may be inferred from the conferring of another implied power.

PROCEDURAL DUE PROCESS The constitutional mandate that if the state or federal government acts so as to deny a citizen of a life, liberty or property interest the individual is first entitled to notice and the right to be heard.

RIGHT TO PRIVACY The violation of an individual's right to be protected against unwarranted interference in his personal affairs, falling into one of four categories:

Continued on next page.

(1) appropriating the individual's likeness or name for commercial benefit; (2) intrusion into the individual's seclusion; (3) public disclosure of private facts regarding the individual; and (4) disclosure of facts placing the individual in a false light.

STRICT SCRUTINY Method by which courts determine the constitutionality of a law, when a law affects a fundamental right. Under the test, the legislature must have a compelling interest to enact the law and measures prescribed by the law must be the least restrictive means possible to accomplish its goal.

SUBSTANTIVE DUE PROCESS A constitutional safeguard limiting the power of the state, irrespective of how fair its procedures may be; substantive limits placed on the power of the state.

Roe v. Wade

Pregnant woman (P) v. State (D)

410 U.S. 113 (1973).

NATURE OF CASE: Challenge to state laws making it a crime to procure an abortion except by medical advice to save the life of the mother.

FACT SUMMARY: Roe (P), a single woman, wished to have her pregnancy terminated by an abortion.

🏛 RULE OF LAW
The right of privacy found in the Fourteenth Amendment's concept of personal liberty and restrictions upon state action is broad enough to encompass a woman's decision whether or not to terminate her pregnancy.

FACTS: The Texas abortion laws challenged here were typical of those adopted by most states. The challengers were Roe (P), a single pregnant woman, a childless couple with the wife not pregnant (J and M Doe), and a licensed physician with two criminal charges pending (Halford). Only Roe (P) was found to be entitled to maintain the action. Although her 1970 pregnancy had been terminated, her case was not found moot since pregnancy "truly could be capable of repetition, yet evading review."

ISSUE: Does the constitutional right of privacy include a woman's right to choose to terminate her pregnancy?

HOLDING AND DECISION: (Blackmun, J.) Yes. While the Constitution does not explicitly mention any right of privacy, such a right has been recognized. This right of privacy, whether founded in the Fourteenth Amendment's concept of personal liberty and restrictions upon state action, as this Court feels it is, or in the Ninth Amendment's reservation of rights to the people, is broad enough to encompass a woman's decision to terminate her pregnancy. A statute regulating a fundamental right, such as the right to privacy, may be justified only by a compelling state interest and such statutes must be narrowly drawn. Here, Texas (D) argues that the fetus is a person within the meaning of the Fourteenth Amendment whose right to life is guaranteed by that amendment. However, there are no decisions indicating such a definition for "fetus." The unborn have never been recognized in the law as persons in the whole sense. Texas (D) may not, by adopting one theory of life, override the rights of the pregnant woman that are at stake. However, neither are the woman's rights to privacy absolute. The state does have a legitimate interest in preserving the health of the pregnant woman and in protecting the potentiality of life. Each of these interests grows in substantiality as the woman approaches term, and at a point, each becomes compelling. During the first trimester, mortality in abortion is less than mortality in childbirth. After that point, in promoting its interest in the mother's health, the state may regulate the abortion procedure in ways related to maternal health (i.e., licensing of physicians, facilities, etc.). Prior to viability, the physician, in consultation with the pregnant woman, is free to decide that a pregnancy should be terminated without interference by the state. Subsequent to viability, the state, in promoting its interest in the potentiality of life, may regulate, and even proscribe abortion, except where necessary to save the mother's life. Because the Texas (D) statute makes no distinction between abortions performed in early pregnancy and those performed later, it sweeps too broadly and is, therefore, invalid.

CONCURRENCE: (Burger, C.J.) The dissenting Justices discount the reality that most physicians observe the standards of their profession in making sound medical judgments. The majority clearly indicates that the Constitution does not require abortions on demand.

DISSENT: (Rehnquist, J.) The right of privacy is not involved in this case. The right involved here is the right to be free from searches and seizures under the Fourth Amendment. Perhaps the privacy right claimed here is a form of liberty protected by the Fourteenth Amendment. Such a liberty can be deprived so long as it is not a deprivation without due process of law. Due process is afforded where the state action or statute has a rational relation to a valid state objective. The transplanting of the compelling state interest test by the majority of the Court is inappropriate.

DISSENT: (White, J.) The Court today fashioned a new Constitutional right for pregnant mothers to be able to have an abortion at her request if she is able to find a medical adviser willing to undertake the procedure.

▶ ANALYSIS

Doe v. Bolton, 410 U.S. 179 (1973) was the companion case to *Roe v. Wade*. The Georgia laws attacked in Doe were more modern than the Texas laws. They allowed a physician to perform an abortion when the mother's life was in danger, if the fetus would likely be born with birth defects, or if the pregnancy had resulted from rape. The Court held that a physician could consider all attendant circumstances in deciding whether an abortion should be performed. No longer could only the three situations specified be considered. The Court also struck down the requirements of prior approval for an abortion by the hospital staff committee and of confirmation by two

Continued on next page.

physicians. They concluded that the attending physician's judgment was sufficient. Lastly, the Court struck down the requirement that the woman be a Georgia resident.

■══■

Quicknotes

MOOTNESS Judgment on the particular issue would not resolve the controversy.

RIGHT TO PRIVACY The violation of an individual's right to be protected against unwarranted interference in his personal affairs, falling into one of four categories: (1) appropriating the individual's likeness or name for commercial benefit; (2) intrusion into the individual's seclusion; (3) public disclosure of private facts regarding the individual; and (4) disclosure of facts placing the individual in a false light.

■══■

Planned Parenthood of Southeastern Pennsylvania v. Casey

Clinic (P) v. State (D)

505 U.S. 833 (1992).

NATURE OF CASE: Appeal from denial of injunction against enforcement of a state abortion statute.

FACT SUMMARY: Planned Parenthood (P) sought declaratory and injunctive relief from enforcement of Pennsylvania's statute regulating abortion, contending that its many restrictions were unconstitutional under the Supreme Court's decision in Roe v. Wade, 410 U.S. 113 (1973).

🏛 RULE OF LAW
Only where state regulation imposes an undue burden on a woman's ability to terminate a pregnancy does the power of the state reach into the heart of the liberty protected by the Due Process Clause.

FACTS: Planned Parenthood (P) sought to enjoin Casey (D), the Governor of Pennsylvania, from enforcing Pennsylvania's Abortion Control Act of 1982, arguing that it was unconstitutional under *Roe v. Wade* (*supra*). This Act's provisions included, in relevant part, a requirement that a woman seeking an abortion give her informed consent prior to the abortion procedure; that she be provided with certain information at least 24 hours before the abortion was performed (§ 3205); that a parent provide informed consent to a minor's abortion—subject to a judicial bypass if deemed necessary (§ 3206); that a wife inform her husband of an impending abortion (§ 3209); and that the facilities providing abortions file a report (§§ 3207, 3214). The court of appeals reversed the district court's ruling in part and upheld all the provisions except for the husband notification requirement.

ISSUE: Does the power of the state reach into the heart of the liberty protected by the Due Process Clause only where state regulation imposes an undue burden on a woman's ability to terminate a pregnancy?

HOLDING AND DECISION: (O'Connor, J.) Yes. Only where state regulation imposes an undue burden on a woman's ability to terminate a pregnancy does the power of the state reach into the heart of the liberty protected by the Due Process Clause. A finding of an undue burden is a shorthand for the conclusion that a state regulation has the purpose or effect of placing a substantial obstacle in the path of a woman seeking an abortion of a nonviable fetus. The constitutional protection of the woman's decision to terminate her pregnancy derives from the Due Process Clause of the Fourteenth Amendment, which declares that no state shall deprive any person of life, liberty, or property without due process of law. It is well settled now that the Constitution places limits on a state's right to interfere with a person's most basic decisions about family and parenthood, as well as bodily integrity. But the state may require doctors to inform a woman seeking an abortion of the availability of information relating to the consequences to the fetus, and the 24-hour waiting period is a reasonable measure to implement the state's interest in protecting the life of the unborn and does not amount to an undue burden. Regulations designed to foster the health of a woman seeking an abortion are valid if they do not constitute an undue burden. A state may require a minor seeking an abortion to obtain parental or guardian consent, provided that there is an adequate judicial bypass procedure and the recordkeeping and reporting requirements do not impose a substantial obstacle to a woman's choice. However, because there are millions of women in this country who are the victims of regular physical and psychological abuse at the hands of their husbands, the requirement that married women seeking abortions notify their husbands will operate as a substantial obstacle to a woman's choice to undergo an abortion. It is an undue burden and therefore invalid. Furthermore, under the doctrine of stare decisis, the central holding of *Roe v. Wade* (*supra*), is affirmed. A decision to overrule *Roe*'s central holding under the existing circumstances would address error, if error there was, at the cost of both profound and unnecessary damage to the Court's legitimacy and to the nation's commitment to the rule of law. However, the trimester framework established by *Roe* to govern abortion regulations is too rigid a prohibition on all previability regulations aimed at the protection of fetal life, since this framework, which employed a strict scrutiny test, misconceives the nature of the pregnant woman's interest and, in practice, undervalues the state's interest in potential life. Alternatively, the undue burden framework adopted here more reasonably reconciles the ostensibly conflicting interests of the state and pregnant woman. On the record as it appears in this case, the undue burden standard is not offended by the provisions in the Pennsylvania Abortion Control Act, except for the husband notification requirement. Remanded.

CONCURRENCE AND DISSENT: (Stevens, J.) The undue burden test should have been applied to strike down the provision concerning the 24-hour waiting period prior to a woman's decision to have an abortion. There is no evidence that the mandated delay benefits women or that it is necessary to enable the physician to convey any relevant information to the patient.

Continued on next page.

CONCURRENCE AND DISSENT: (Blackmun, J.) The Constitution and decisions of this Court require that a state's abortion restrictions be subjected to the strictest of judicial scrutiny. Application of the strict scrutiny standard results in the invalidation of all the challenged provisions. As this Court has invalidated virtually identical provisions in prior cases, stare decisis requires that they be struck down again.

CONCURRENCE AND DISSENT: (Rehnquist, C.J.) *Roe* was wrongly decided, and it should be overruled consistent with this Court's traditional approach to stare decisis in constitutional cases. The approach of the plurality in *Webster v. Reproductive Health Services*, 492 U.S. 490 (1989), should be adopted and used to uphold the challenged provisions in their entirety.

CONCURRENCE AND DISSENT: (Scalia, J.) A state's choice between two positions on which reasonable people can disagree is constitutional even when it intrudes upon a "liberty" in the absolute sense.

fundamental right. Under the test, the legislature must have a compelling interest to enact the law and measures prescribed by the law must be the least restrictive means possible to accomplish its goal.

■━■

ANALYSIS

This is only the second time in the modern Supreme Court jurisprudence that an opinion has been jointly authored. J. Kennedy's portion of the opinion addresses the importance of public acceptance of and faith in the Court's work by opening with the statement: "Liberty finds no refuge in a jurisprudence of doubt." J. O'Connor expounds on the essential nature of a woman's right to an abortion, while J. Souter discusses the stare decisis analysis, concluding that there is no reason to reverse the precedent. He warned that only the most convincing justification under accepted standards of precedent could suffice to demonstrate that a later decision overruling the earlier was anything but a surrender to political pressure. So to overrule under fire in the absence of the most compelling reason to reexamine a watershed decision would subvert the Court's legitimacy beyond any serious question. It appears that the instant case marks the first time the Court has downgraded a fundamental right to a protected liberty and by so doing removed from the usual strict scrutiny standard of review.

■━■

Quicknotes

DUE PROCESS CLAUSE Clauses found in the Fifth and Fourteenth Amendments to the United States Constitution providing that no person shall be deprived of "life, liberty, or property, without due process of law."

STARE DECISIS Doctrine whereby courts follow legal precedent unless there is good cause for departure.

STRICT SCRUTINY Method by which courts determine the constitutionality of a law, when a law affects a

Bowers v. Hardwick

State (D) v. Homosexual (P)

478 U.S. 186 (1986).

NATURE OF CASE: Appeal from decision finding state sodomy statute unconstitutional.

FACT SUMMARY: Bowers (D) and other state officials appealed from a court of appeals decision finding the Georgia sodomy statute unconstitutional in that it violated Hardwick's (P) fundamental rights, since it applied to consensual, homosexual sodomy.

🏛 RULE OF LAW
The Constitution does not grant a fundamental right to engage in consensual homosexual sodomy.

FACTS: Hardwick (P), a gay man, was charged with violating a state law criminalizing sodomy. After a preliminary hearing, the district attorney decided not to present the matter to the grand jury unless further evidence developed. Hardwick (P) brought suit, challenging the constitutionality of the statute in that it criminalized consensual sodomy. He claimed the law as administered by the state placed him in imminent danger of arrest and was unconstitutional on a number of grounds. The district court dismissed the claim for failing to state a claim, relying heavily on the Supreme Court decision in *Doe v. Commonwealth's Attorney for the City of Richmond*, 425 U.S. 901 (1976), which summarily affirmed a case involving a similar Virginia sodomy statute. The court of appeals reversed, finding that the statute violated Hardwick's (P) fundamental rights because the homosexual activity was a private and intimate association beyond the reach of state regulation. From this decision, Bowers (D) and other state officials appealed.

ISSUE: Does the Constitution grant a fundamental right to engage in consensual homosexual sodomy?

HOLDING AND DECISION: (White, J.) No. The Constitution does not grant a fundamental right to engage in consensual homosexual sodomy. None of the fundamental rights announced in previous cases bears any resemblance to the claimed constitutional right to engage in sodomy asserted in the present case. Fundamental liberties identified by this Court and deserving of heightened judicial scrutiny have either been liberties implicit in the concept of ordered liberty or liberties deeply rooted in this nation's history and traditions. Neither of these formulations would extend the liberty sought in the present case. Great restraint should be used when expanding the contours of constitutional due process. The fact that the conduct in question occurred in the privacy of the home does not necessarily shield it from regulation, as can be seen in statutes punishing a number of other victimless and/or sex crimes. The conduct at issue is not a fundamental right, and the State has provided a rational basis for the statute. Reversed.

CONCURRENCE: (Burger, C.J.) This is a question not of personal preference but of the legislative authority of the State, and nothing in the Constitution forbids the state statute at issue.

CONCURRENCE: (Powell, J.) Hardwick (P) may be protected under the Eighth Amendment, but he has not been tried, sentenced, or convicted, and has not raised any Eighth Amendment issues.

DISSENT: (Blackmun, J.) The State in the present case is legislating particular forms of private, consensual sexual conduct. The Court's obsession with homosexual activity is difficult to justify, since the statute's language encompasses nonhomosexual conduct. The Court fails to comprehend the magnitude of the liberty interest at stake in this case.

DISSENT: (Stevens, J.) The essential liberty to choose how to conduct private sexual conduct surely encompasses the right to engage in nonreproductive, sexual conduct that others may find offensive or immoral. The State cannot justify the selective application of the statute in question, given the conceded unconstitutionality of the statute as applied to nonhomosexual conduct. Hardwick (P) at this state of the litigation has stated a constitutional claim sufficient to withstand a motion to dismiss.

▶ ANALYSIS

Also plaintiffs in the original action were a "Doe" couple, who had alleged that they wished to engage in the proscribed activity and were chilled and deterred by the existence of the statute and Hardwick's (P) arrest. The district court dismissed their claim for lack of standing, as the selective enforcement of the law left them in no immediate danger, and this judgment was upheld by the court of appeals. The "Does" did not challenge this holding in the present case. The 2002-2003 Court held that the constitutional right to privacy protects private consensual homosexual activity, *Lawrence v. Texas*, 123 S. Ct. 2472 (2003).

■==■

Quicknotes

DUE PROCESS CLAUSE Clauses found in the Fifth and Fourteenth Amendments to the United States Constitution providing that no person shall be deprived of "life, liberty, or property, without due process of law."

Continued on next page.

FUNDAMENTAL RIGHT   A liberty that is either expressly or impliedly provided for in the United States Constitution, the deprivation or burdening of which is subject to a heightened standard of review.

STANDING   Whether a party possesses the right to commence suit against another party by having a personal stake in the resolution of the controversy.

Romer v. Evans

Parties not identified.

517 U.S. 620 (1996).

NATURE OF CASE: Review of order striking down state constitutional amendment.

FACT SUMMARY: A Colorado law that preempted local ordinances prohibiting discrimination against homosexuals was challenged as unconstitutional.

🏛 RULE OF LAW
States may not enact laws prohibiting localities from proscribing discrimination against a class of persons.

FACTS: In 1992, a statewide initiative was adopted by Colorado voters. The law, known as Amendment 2, preempted local ordinances from prohibiting discrimination on the basis of sexual preference. The Colorado Supreme Court struck down the law as contrary to Equal Protection. The U.S. Supreme Court granted review.

ISSUE: May states enact laws prohibiting localities from proscribing discrimination against a class of persons?

HOLDING AND DECISION: (Kennedy, J.) No. States may not enact laws prohibiting localities from proscribing discrimination against a class of persons. Amendment 2 has the peculiar property of imposing a broad rules on a single named group, as it places a particular burden in terms of access to the political process. Groups not affected by this law have greater access to this process. This clearly implicates the Equal Protection Clause of the Fourteenth Amendment. Such a law must bear a rational relationship to a legitimate government purpose. Amendment 2 is a status-based law undertaken for its own sake without serving any legitimate interest. Therefore, it is unconstitutional. Affirmed.

DISSENT: (Scalia, J.) Amendment 2 is a modest attempt against assaults on basic morals by a politically powerful interest group. States must be free to disfavor conduct its citizens find reprehensible.

▶ ANALYSIS

Interestingly, the majority opinion here did not mention the last major case involving homosexuality, *Bowers v. Hardwick*, 478 U.S. 18 (1986). That case held it constitutional for a state to criminalize homosexual conduct. In *Lawrence v. Texas*, 123 S. Ct. 2472 (2003), the Court ruled that private consensual homosexual activity is protected by the constitutional right to privacy.

Quicknotes

EQUAL PROTECTION A constitutional guarantee that no person shall be denied the same protection of the laws enjoyed by other persons in like circumstances.

INITIATIVE The power of the people to propose bills and laws, and to enact or reject them at the polls, independent of legislative assembly.

Lawrence v. Texas

Sodomy convict (D) v. State (P)

539 U.S. 558 (2003).

NATURE OF CASE: Appeal from a criminal conviction.

FACT SUMMARY: When Lawrence (D) and his male partner, both adults, were prosecuted and convicted for consensual sodomy in their own private dwelling, they argued the unconstitutionality of the statute.

🏛 RULE OF LAW
Legislation that makes consensual sodomy between adults in their own dwelling criminal violates due process.

FACTS: Two Houston, Texas, police officers were dispatched to a private residence in response to a reported weapons disturbance. They entered an apartment where Lawrence (D) resided. The right of the police to enter was not an issue. The officers observed Lawrence (D) and another man engaging in sodomy. Both men were arrested, charged, and convicted before a justice of the peace of the statutory crime of "deviate sexual intercourse, namely anal sex, with a member of the same sex." Each defendant entered a plea of nolo contendere and was fined $200. Both men were adults at the time of the alleged offense. Their conduct was in private and consensual. Lawrence (D) and his partner appealed to the U.S. Supreme Court, arguing the Texas statute to be unconstitutional.

ISSUE: Does legislation that makes consensual sodomy between adults in their own dwelling criminal violate due process?

HOLDING AND DECISION: (Kennedy, J.) Yes. Legislation that makes consensual sodomy between adults in their own dwelling criminal violates due process. Liberty protects the person from unwarranted government intrusions into a dwelling or other private places. In our tradition the state is not omnipresent in the home. Furthermore, freedom extends beyond spatial bounds. Liberty presumes an "autonomy of self" that includes freedom of thought, belief, expression, "and certain intimate conduct." This case involves liberty of the person both in its spatial and more transcendent dimensions. The penalties and purposes of the Texas statute in the instant case have far-reaching consequences, touching upon the most private human conduct, sexual behavior, and in the most private of places, the home. The statute seeks to control a personal relationship that, whether or not entitled to formal recognition in the law, is within the liberty of persons to choose without being punished as criminals. This Court acknowledges that adults may choose to enter into private relationships in the confines of their own homes and their own private lives and still retain their dignity as free persons. When sexuality finds expression in intimate conduct with another person, the conduct can be but one element in a personal bond that is more enduring. The liberty protected by the Constitution allows homosexual persons the right to make this choice. Here, two adults who, with full and mutual consent from each other, engaged in sexual practices common to a homosexual lifestyle. They are entitled to respect in their private lives. The state cannot demean their existence or control their destiny by making their private sexual conduct a crime. Reversed and remanded.

CONCURRENCE: (O'Connor, J.) Rather than relying on the substantive component of the Fourteenth Amendment's Due Process Clause, as the Court does, I base my conclusion of unconstitutionality on the Fourteenth Amendment's Equal Protection Clause.

DISSENT: (Scalia, J.) Homosexual sodomy is not a right "deeply rooted in our Nation's history and tradition." Constitutional entitlements do not spring into existence because some states choose to lessen or eliminate sanctions on criminal behavior. Today's opinion is the product of a Court that has largely signed on to the so-called homosexual agenda.

DISSENT: (Thomas, J.) The instant Texas statute is "uncommonly silly" and should be repealed, nevertheless, no general constitutional right of privacy was violated in this situation.

▍ ANALYSIS

In *Lawrence*, the Supreme Court noted that of the 13 states with laws prohibiting sodomy, only 4 have enforced their legislation. In those states in which sodomy was still proscribed, whether for same-sex or heterosexual conduct, there was a pattern of nonenforcement with respect to consenting adults acting in private. Even Texas admitted in 1994 that as of that date it had not prosecuted anyone under those circumstances.

■=■

Quicknotes

DUE PROCESS The constitutional mandate requiring the courts to protect and enforce individuals' rights and liberties consistent with prevailing principles of fairness and justice and prohibiting the federal and state governments from such activities that deprive its citizens of life, liberty, or property interest.

■=■

Cruzan v. Director, Missouri Department of Health

Injured (P) v. State (D)

497 U.S. 261 (1990).

NATURE OF CASE: Appeal from reversal of order allowing cessation of death-delaying medical procedures.

FACT SUMMARY: After Nancy Beth Cruzan (P) suffered severe injuries in an automobile accident that left her in a persistent vegetative state, her parents sought the withdrawal of her nutrition and hydration.

🏛 RULE OF LAW
A guardian may seek to withdraw the nutrition and hydration of an individual diagnosed in a persistent vegetative state if there is clear and convincing evidence of the individual's previously expressed desire for such withdrawal.

FACTS: Cruzan (P) suffered irreversible brain damage in an automobile accident. She remained in a coma for three weeks. In order to ease feeding, surgeons implanted feeding and hydration tubes. Eventually, she fell into a persistent vegetative state. In such a state, Cruzan (P) exhibited motor reflexes but was oblivious to her environment. Cruzan's (P) parents sought a court order directing the withdrawal of their daughter's feeding and hydration equipment. At the trial, evidence was produced that Cruzan (P) had told a housemate that if sick or injured she would not wish to continue her life unless she could live at least halfway normally. The court found that a person in Cruzan's (P) condition had a fundamental right under the Missouri and federal constitutions to refuse or direct the withdrawal of death-delaying procedures. The Missouri Supreme Court reversed, holding that no person could assume the choice for an incompetent in the absence of formalities required by the Missouri living will statute or clear and convincing evidence of the individual's previously expressed intent for such withdrawal. The court found that Cruzan's (P) statements to her roommate were unreliable for the purpose of determining her intent. The U.S. Supreme Court granted certiorari.

ISSUE: May a guardian seek to withdraw the nutrition and hydration of an individual diagnosed in a persistent vegetative state if there is clear and convincing evidence of the individual's previously expressed desire for such withdrawal?

HOLDING AND DECISION: (Rehnquist, C.J.) Yes. A guardian may seek to withdraw the nutrition and hydration of an individual diagnosed in a persistent vegetative state if there is clear and convincing evidence of the individual's previously expressed desire for such withdrawal. The choice between life and death is a deeply personal decision of obvious and overwhelming finality. The Due Process Clause protects an interest in life as well as Cruzan's (P) interest in refusing life-sustaining treatment. Missouri (D) may permissibly advance its interest through the adoption of a clear and convincing standard of proof to govern such proceedings. Here, Cruzan (P) made statements to the effect that she would not want to live as a vegetable. The observations did not deal specially with withdrawal of medical treatment or of hydration and nutrition. Affirmed.

CONCURRENCE: (O'Connor, J.) Today, it is decided only that one state's practice does not violate the Constitution; the more challenging task of crafting appropriate procedures for safeguarding an incompetent's liberty interest is entrusted to the "laboratory" of the states.

CONCURRENCE: (Scalia, J.) It should be announced clearly and promptly that the federal courts have no business in this field. American law has always accorded the state the power to prevent, by force if necessary, suicide, including suicide by refusing to take the appropriate measures necessary to preserve one's life. The Court has no authority to inject itself into every field of human activity where irrationality and oppression may theoretically occur, and if it tries to do so, it will destroy itself.

DISSENT: (Brennan, J.) The only state interest asserted here is a general interest in the preservation of life. But the state has no legitimate interest in someone's life, completely abstracted from the interest of the person living that life, that could outweigh the person's choice to avoid medical treatment. Missouri (D) may constitutionally impose only those procedural requirements that serve to enhance the accuracy of Cruzan's (P) wishes or at least are consistent with an accurate determination. The determination needed in this context is whether the incompetent person would choose to live in a persistent vegetative state on life support or to avoid medical treatment.

DISSENT: (Stevens, J.) Missouri (D) insists, without regard to Cruzan's (P) own interests, upon equating her life with the biological persistence of her bodily functions. Missouri's (D) protection of life in a form abstracted from the living is not commonplace; it is aberrant.

▶ ANALYSIS

Constitutional scholars often assert that the Supreme Court acts arbitrarily and subjectively in enunciating new fundamental rights accorded due process protection. But this case shows the Court's continuing concern with

Continued on next page.

linking any such pronouncements to past precedent. Chief Justice Rehnquist, for example, cites *Jacobson v. Massachusetts*, 197 U.S. 11 (1905), as authority for the proposition that a competent person has a constitutionally protected liberty interest in refusing unwanted medical treatment; of course, he carefully notes that, as here, the *Jacobson* case balanced a legitimate state interest (i.e., freedom to decline vaccine). Similarly, in his dissent, Justice Brennan cites *Skinner v. Oklahoma ex rel. Williamson*, 316 U.S. 535 (1942), as support for his position that the fundamental right to be free of life support when terminally ill rises to a "basic civil right of man." The *Skinner* case invalidated a statute authorizing sterilization of certain felons. Certainly the justices are mindful that they are often engaged in no more than a contemporary playing out of Justice Chase's proclamation that natural law restricts and regulates government power, *Calder v. Bull*, 3 U.S. (3 Dall.) 386 (1798), but they usually trace a line of development, albeit often weakly, to earlier cases in which similar issues (involving less advanced technologies) were addressed.

Quicknotes

CLEAR AND CONVINCING EVIDENCE An evidentiary standard requiring a demonstration that the fact sought to be proven is reasonably certain.

DUE PROCESS CLAUSE Clauses found in the Fifth and Fourteenth Amendments to the United States Constitution providing that no person shall be deprived of "life, liberty, or property, without due process of law."

FUNDAMENTAL RIGHT A liberty that is either expressly or impliedly provided for in the United States Constitution, the deprivation or burdening of which is subject to a heightened standard of review.

NATURAL LAW A body of law that is said to arise from the nature of men.

Washington v. Glucksberg

State (D) v. Physician (P)

521 U.S. 702 (1997).

NATURE OF CASE: Review of judgment striking down state prohibition against assisted suicide.

FACT SUMMARY: Glucksberg (P), a Washington state physician, wished to assist his terminally ill patients to commit suicide.

🏛 RULE OF LAW
The "liberty" protections of the Due Process Clause of the Fourteenth Amendment do not include a right to commit suicide with another's assistance.

FACTS: Glucksberg (P), a Washington state doctor, along with others, wanted to assist his terminally ill, mentally competent patients in ending their lives. Washington state law prohibited causing or aiding a suicide. In January of 1994, Glucksberg (P) filed suit, asserting that Washington's (P) ban on assisted suicide violated the Fourteenth Amendment's protection of liberty interests. The district court ruled for Glucksberg (P), and the Ninth Circuit affirmed. Washington (D) appealed.

ISSUE: Do the "liberty" protections of the Due Process Clause of the Fourteenth Amendment include a right to commit suicide with another's assistance?

HOLDING AND DECISION: (Rehnquist, C.J.) No. The "liberty" protections of the Due Process Clause of the Fourteenth Amendment do not include a right to commit suicide with another's assistance. Therefore, Washington's (D) prohibition against assisting a suicide does not violate the Fourteenth Amendment. Here, unlike seeking an abortion or terminating lifesaving medical assistance, Washington's (D) state interests outweigh any personal issues of autonomy that Glucksberg (P) may assert. First, assisted suicide is not a deeply rooted tradition in American culture, and the Supreme Court has required careful descriptions of liberty interests that are protected by the Fourteenth Amendment. No such historical guideposts exist for assisted suicide. Furthermore, an individual's interest in personal autonomy is outweighed by Washington's (D) interest in preventing coercion of patients and discrimination against the terminally ill. This Court has been very cautious in expanding rights under the Fourteenth Amendment, requiring asserted rights to meet a threshold so that those same rights do not ultimately get manipulated in the political process. The asserted right of assisted suicide does not meet any threshold. Reversed.

▌ *ANALYSIS*

The right to assisted suicide is one of the hottest areas of litigation in today's world of constitutional law. In the past, the Due Process Clause has mostly been used to protect individuals in a criminal context. But ever since the 1960s, it has been asserted in personal liberty litigation as well.

■━■

Quicknotes

DUE PROCESS CLAUSE Clauses found in the Fifth and Fourteenth Amendments to the United States Constitution providing that no person shall be deprived of "life, liberty, or property, without due process of law."

LIBERTY INTEREST A right conferred by the Due Process Clauses of the state and federal constitutions.

■━■

Vacco v. Quill

Parties not identified.

521 U.S. 793 (1997).

NATURE OF CASE: Review of order striking down state ban on assisted suicide.

FACT SUMMARY: A New York state law prohibiting physician-assisted suicide was challenged as a violation of the Equal Protection Clause of the Fourteenth Amendment.

 RULE OF LAW
State law prohibiting physician-assisted suicide is not a violation of the Equal Protection Clause.

FACTS: The state of New York had a statute expressly prohibiting physician-assisted suicide, categorizing it as murder. This statute was challenged by a consortium of groups and persons who advocated the right of a patient to choose to have a physician administer life-ending treatment. The Second Circuit held that state law allowing a terminal patient to refuse lifesaving treatment, while at the same time denying a patient the right to choose physician-assisted suicide, was a violation of the Equal Protection Clause. The Supreme Court granted review.

ISSUE: Does state law prohibiting physician-assisted suicide violate the Equal Protection Clause?

HOLDING AND DECISION: (Rehnquist, C.J.) No. State law prohibiting physician-assisted suicide is not a violation of the Equal Protection Clause. The basic rule is that states must treat like cases alike, but may treat unlike cases accordingly. In this case, the court of appeals held that state law prohibiting physician-assisted suicide treated like cases unlike in that it treated persons on life support in one fashion and those terminally ill in another, in that the latter had the right to refuse treatment and thus perish, while the former did not have this option. This Court disagrees with this analysis in that it does not consider these two classes of individuals to be alike. It is one thing for a person to refuse lifesaving measures; it is quite another for a person to undergo affirmative measures to end his life. The former does not involve intentional killing, while the latter does. Even though the end result may be the same, it is entirely legitimate for a state to make a distinction based on intent since criminal law does this as a matter of course. The basic fact is that persons on life support and persons who do not need medical assistance to survive are factually and legally distinct classes of persons, and it is not a violation of equal protection principles to treat them in a disparate fashion. Therefore, the law at issue is not a violation of the Equal Protection Clause. Reversed.

CONCURRENCE: (O'Connor, J.) I agree there is no generalized right to "commit suicide." There is no need to reach the narrower question of whether a mentally competent person experiencing great suffering has a constitutionally cognizable right to die.

CONCURRENCE: (Stevens, J.) It is not necessarily true that in all cases there will be a significant difference between those on life support and those who are terminally ill but not on life support. The majority's distinctions may be inapplicable to particular terminally ill patients and their doctors.

CONCURRENCE: (Souter, J.) The distinction here is not arbitrary, but it is conceivable that in some cases in this area such a distinction may be.

CONCURRENCE: (Breyer, J.) The law does not prohibit doctors from providing patients with drugs sufficient to control pain despite the risk they will kill.

ANALYSIS

The present action was a companion case, decided the same day, to the better-known *Washington v. Glucksberg*, 521 U.S. 702 (1997). The latter case held that the Fourteenth Amendment's Due Process Clause encompassed a right to physician-assisted suicide. The present case, along with *Glucksberg*, has for the present closed the book on the "right to die" issue in a constitutional sense. As the matter is still one of some political controversy, however, it would not be surprising if the Court revisits the issue someday.

Quicknotes

DUE PROCESS CLAUSE Clauses found in the Fifth and Fourteenth Amendments to the United States Constitution providing that no person shall be deprived of "life, liberty, or property, without due process of law."

EQUAL PROTECTION CLAUSE A constitutional guarantee that no person should be denied the same protection of the laws enjoyed by other persons in like circumstances.

CHAPTER 9

Congressional Enforcement of Civil Rights

Quick Reference Rules of Law

Katzenbach v. Morgan

Parties not identified.

384 U.S. 641 (1966).

NATURE OF CASE: Challenge to constitutionality of federal statute.

FACT SUMMARY: As part of the Voting Rights Act, Congress inserted a provision that prohibited restrictions on the right to register to vote and the applicant's inability to read and write English where the applicant had at least a sixth-grade education in a Puerto Rican school where instruction was primarily in Spanish. New York had a statutory requirement of an ability to read and write English as a prerequisite to voter registration.

RULE OF LAW
A federal statute enacted pursuant to the enabling clause of the Fourteenth Amendment supersedes any state constitutional or statutory provision that is in conflict with the federal law.

FACTS: New York had a statute which required all persons seeking to register to vote be able to read and write the English language. In the Voting Rights Act of 1965, Congress inserted a provision which prohibited a requirement of ability to read and write English where the person seeking to vote had completed at least a sixth-grade education in Puerto Rico where the language of instruction was primarily Spanish. This suit was instituted by a group of registered voters in New York who challenged that provision of the federal statute insofar as it would prohibit enforcement of the New York requirement. At issue were the several hundred thousand Puerto Rican immigrants in New York who were prevented from voting by the New York statute, but who would be qualified under the federal law. The Attorney General of New York filed a brief in which he argued that the federal legislation would supersede the state law only if the state law were found to violate the provisions of the Fourteenth Amendment without reference to the federal statute. Also advanced was the argument that the federal statute violated the Equal Protection Clause of the Fourteenth Amendment, since it discriminated between non-English-speaking persons from Puerto Rico and non-English-speaking persons from other countries.

ISSUE: Does a federal statute enacted pursuant to the enabling clause of the Fourteenth Amendment supersede a conflicting state law by reason of the Supremacy Clause of the U.S. Constitution?

HOLDING AND DECISION: (Brennan, J.) Yes. There is no need to determine if the New York English literacy law is violative of the Fourteenth Amendment Equal Protection Clause in order to validate the federal

law respecting voter qualifications. If Congress were limited to restricting only those state laws that violated the amendment, there would be no need for the federal law, since the state law could be invalidated in the courts. Rather, the test must be whether the federal legislation is appropriate to enforcement of the Equal Protection Clause. Section 5 of the Fourteenth Amendment is to be read to grant the same powers as the Necessary and Proper Clause of Article I, § 8. Therefore, the federal statute must be examined to see if it is "plainly adapted to that end" and whether it is not prohibited by, but is consistent with, "the letter and spirit of the Constitution." It was well within congressional authority to say that the need to vote by the Puerto Rican community warranted intrusion upon any state interests served by the English literacy test. The federal law was "plainly adapted" to furthering the aims of the Fourteenth Amendment. There is a perceivable basis for Congress to determine that this legislation was a proper way to resolve an inequity resulting from Congress's evaluation that an invidious discrimination existed. As to the contention that the federal law itself violates the Equal Protection Clause, the law does not restrict anyone's voting rights, but rather extends the franchise to a previously ineligible group. This was a reform measure and, as this Court has previously held, Congress need not correct an entire evil with one law but may "take one step at a time, addressing itself" to that problem which seems most pressing. We hold, therefore, that the federal law was a proper exercise of the powers granted Congress by the Fourteenth Amendment and that the Supremacy Clause prevents enforcement of the New York statute insofar as it is inconsistent with the federal law. Reversed.

DISSENT: (Harlan, J.) The majority has confused the question of legislative enforcement power with the area of proper judicial review. The question here is whether the state law is so arbitrary or irrational as to violate the Equal Protection Clause. That is a judicial, not legislative, determination. The majority has validated a legislative determination by Congress that a state law is violative of the Constitution. There is no record of any evidence secured by Congress to support this determination. The judiciary is the ultimate arbiter of constitutionality, not Congress.

ANALYSIS

As has occurred before, there was a footnote to the decision which caused as much controversy as the decision itself. In this footnote, the Court stated that Congress could

Continued on next page.

enact legislation giving force to the Fourteenth Amendment that expanded the rights provided in the amendment, but could not dilute or restrict the amendment by legislation. In other words, Congress can make determinations of constitutionality so long as they expand rights but cannot make those determinations if they restrict rights. However, there is serious debate as to whether allowing Congress to take an independent role in interpreting the Constitution can be justified under any circumstances in view of *Marbury v. Madison*, 5 U.S. 137 (1803). Once loosed in this area, can any restraint be thereafter imposed? Congress has traditionally tried to stay within judicially circumscribed bounds of constitutionality. But if it has an "independent role" in this area, the restraints are removed. An example of this may be seen in the Omnibus Crime Control Act, wherein Congress made legislative inroads to judicially granted rights as expressed in the *Miranda* decision. The Court can always rule on these inroads, but is it not better that Congress not be encouraged to embark on them in the first instance?

■══■

Quicknotes

ENABLING CLAUSE OF 14th AMENDMENT A constitutional provision giving the power to implement and enforce the law.

EQUAL PROTECTION CLAUSE A constitutional guarantee that no person should be denied the same protection of the laws enjoyed by other persons in like circumstances.

FOURTEENTH AMENDMENT Declares that no state shall make or enforce any law which shall abridge the privileges and immunities of citizens of the United States.

NECESSARY AND PROPER CLAUSE Act I, § 8, of the Constitution, which enables Congress to make all laws that may be "necessary and proper" to execute its other, enumerated powers.

SUPREMACY CLAUSE Art. VI, Sec. 2, of the Constitution, which provides that federal action must prevail over inconsistent state action.

■══■

City of Boerne v. Flores

Municipality (D) v. Archbishop (P)

521 U.S. 507 (1997).

NATURE OF CASE: Review of judgment sustaining the constitutionality of the Religious Freedom Restoration Act of 1993.

FACT SUMMARY: A decision by zoning authorities in The City of Boerne (D) to deny a church (P) a building permit was challenged under the Religious Freedom Restoration Act.

RULE OF LAW
The Religious Freedom Restoration Act unconstitutionally exceeds Congress's enforcement power under the Due Process Clause of the Fourteenth Amendment.

FACTS: The Religious Freedom Restoration Act (RFRA) prohibited the government from substantially burdening a person's exercise of religion, even if the burden is the result of a generally applicable law, unless the government has a compelling interest and is using the least restrictive means. Flores (P) sought a building permit to expand his church, a historic landmark. The City of Boerne (D) denied the permit and Flores (P) sued, invoking the RFRA. The district court determined that the RFRA exceeded congressional power, but the Fifth Circuit reversed, holding the Act constitutional. Boerne (D) appealed.

ISSUE: Does the RFRA unconstitutionally exceed Congress's enforcement power under the Due Process Clause of the Fourteenth Amendment?

HOLDING AND DECISION: (Kennedy, J.) Yes. The RFRA unconstitutionally exceeds Congress's enforcement power under the Due Process Clause of the Fourteenth Amendment. Here, Congress, with the RFRA, attempts to replace, with the compelling interest test, this Court's decision in *Employment Div., Dept. of Human Resources of Ore. v. Smith*, 494 U.S. 872 (1990). Smith held that the compelling interest test is inappropriate in cases where general prohibitions are opposed by free exercise challenges. But the RFRA violates the long tradition of separation of powers established by the Constitution. The judiciary is to determine the constitutionality of laws, and the powers of the legislature are defined and limited. While Congress can enact remedial, preventive legislation that deters violations, the RFRA is not a preventive law. Instead, the RFRA redefines the scope of the Free Exercise Clause and nothing in our history extends to Congress the ability to take such action. The RFRA is so out of proportion to a supposed remedial or preventive object that it cannot be regarded as a response to unconstitutional behavior. Reversed.

ANALYSIS

The Religious Freedom Restoration Act was one of the four federal laws overturned by the Supreme Court during its 1997 term. Although the Court has endorsed judicial restraint in recent years, it has not hesitated to quash improper intrusions on its authority to set unconstitutional standards. The Court, however, chose not to revisit the religious freedom issue in its *Boerne* decision, leaving intact the ruling in *Smith* that inspired Congress to pass the RFRA. In Smith, the Court approved Oregon's use of its ban on peyote to prohibit the drug's use in Native American religious rituals. The RFRA was intended to guarantee religious observance a higher degree of statutory protection than the *Smith* Court thought necessary.

Quicknotes

COMPELLING INTEREST TEST A standard employed by the court under strict scrutiny review to determine the constitutionality of a statute, whereby the proponent of the statute must demonstrate that classifications drawn therein serve a compelling interest and are necessary for the furtherance of a state objective.

DUE PROCESS CLAUSE Clauses found in the Fifth and Fourteenth Amendments to the United States Constitution providing that no person shall be deprived of "life, liberty, or property, without due process of law."

FREE EXERCISE CLAUSE The guarantee of the First Amendment to the United States Constitution prohibiting Congress from enacting laws regarding the establishment of religion or prohibiting the free exercise thereof.

ZONING Municipal statutory scheme dividing an area into districts in order to regulate the use or building of structures within those districts.

Jones v. Alfred H. Mayer Co.

Black home buyer (P) v. Real estate company (D)

392 U.S. 409 (1968).

NATURE OF CASE: Action for injunctive and other relief to deal with refusal of property owners to sell to Negroes.

FACT SUMMARY: Jones (P) brought suit in federal district court against the Alfred H. Mayer Co. (D) alleging that Mayer (D) refused to sell a home to him for the sole reason that Jones (P) is a Negro.

> ### RULE OF LAW
> Congress, pursuant to the authority vested in it by the Thirteenth Amendment, which clothes "Congress with power to pass all laws necessary and proper for abolishing all badges and incidents of slavery," may validly bar all racial discrimination, private as well as public, in the sale or rental of property.

FACTS: Relying upon 42 U.S.C. § 1982 (all citizens have the same right to inherit, purchase, lease, hold and convey real and personal property as is enjoyed by white citizens), Jones (P) brought suit in federal district court against the Alfred H. Mayer Co. (D) alleging that Mayer (D) refused to sell a home to him for the sole reason that Jones (P) is a Negro.

ISSUES: (1) Does purely private discrimination, unaided by any action on the part of the state, violate § 1982 if its effect were to deny a citizen the right to rent or buy property solely because of his race or color? (2) Does Congress have the power under the Constitution to do what § 1982 purports to do?

HOLDING AND DECISION: (Stewart, J.) (1) Yes. Section 1982 is only a limited attempt to deal with discrimination in a select area of real estate transactions, even though, on its face, § 1982 appears to prohibit all discrimination against Negroes in the sale or rental of property. If § 1982, originally enacted as § 1 of the Civil Rights Act of 1866, had been intended to grant nothing more than an immunity from governmental interference, then much of § 2 of the 1866 Act, which provides for criminal penalties where a person has acted "under color" of any law would have been meaningless. The broad language of § 1982 was intentional. Congress, in 1866, had before it considerable evidence showing private mistreatment of Negroes. The focus of Congress, then, was on private groups (e.g., the Ku Klux Klan) operating outside the law. (2) Yes. At the very least, the Thirteenth Amendment includes the freedom to buy whatever a white man can buy, and the right to live wherever a white man can live.

DISSENT: (Harlan, J.) The term "right" in § 1982 operates only against state-sanctioned discrimination. There is a difference between depriving a man of a right and interfering with the enjoyment of that right in a particular case. The enforcement provisions of the 1866 Act talk about "law, statute, ordinance, regulation or custom." As for legislative history, residential racial segregation was the norm in 1866. The court has always held that the Fourteenth Amendment reaches only "state action."

ANALYSIS

In *Sullivan v. Little Hunting Park, Inc.*, 396 U.S. 229 (1969), the Court invalidated a refusal by a homeowner's association to permit a member to assign his recreation share to a Black. Once again, Harlan in dissent questioned whether the Court should expand a century-old statute to encompass today's real estate transactions. After these two cases, it is questionable whether the Court will place any limits on its reading of the Thirteenth Amendment when reviewing legislation aimed at private discrimination.

Quicknotes

FOURTEENTH AMENDMENT Declares that no state shall make or enforce any law which shall abridge the privileges and immunities of citizens of the United States.

THIRTEENTH AMENDMENT The constitutional provision which abolished slavery in the United States.

Runyon v. McCrary

Private school (D) v. Students (P)

427 U.S. 160 (1976).

NATURE OF CASE: Action under 42 U.S.C. § 1981.

FACT SUMMARY: Michael McCrary (P) and others were denied admission to certain private schools because of their race.

🏛 RULE OF LAW

The power given to Congress by the Thirteenth Amendment to legislate against the "badges and incidents" of slavery justifies the 42 U.S.C. § 1981 prohibition against racial discrimination in the making and enforcement of private contracts; and, § 1981, in turn, prohibits "private, commercially operated nonsectarian schools from denying admission to prospective students because they are Negroes."

FACTS: Michael McCrary (P) and Colin Gonzales are both Negro children residing in the Arlington, Virginia, area. Runyon (D) is the owner and operator of Bobbe's Private School in Arlington, an all white institution. In response to brochures mailed to them (addressed to "resident") by Runyon (D), the boys' parents made inquiries about sending their children there. Colin eventually made an application to Bobbe's (among others) but was turned down, his father was told, because the school was not integrated. McCrary's (P) parents called and asked if the school was integrated but were told it was not. Both now file this action for an injunction and damages under 42 U.S.C. § 1981. From judgment in their favor, Runyon (D) appeals.

ISSUE: Does the Civil Rights Act of 1866 (42 U.S.C. § 1981) prohibit private schools from denying admission on the basis of race?

HOLDING AND DECISION: (Stewart, J.) Yes. The power given to Congress by the Thirteenth Amendment to legislate against the "badges and incidents" of slavery justifies the 42 U.S.C. § 1981 prohibition against racial discrimination in the making and enforcement of private contracts; and, § 1981, in turn, prohibits " . . . private, commercially operated nonsectarian schools from denying admission to prospective students because they are Negroes." In *Jones v. Alfred H. Mayer Co.,* 392 U.S. 409 (1968), this Court resurrected the 1866 Civil Rights Act and extended it to purely private discrimination against Negroes. As such, the rights of McCrary (P) and Gonzales here must take precedence over the tangible rights of white parents of Bobbe's since (1) their freedom of association does not extend to Bobbe's the right to practice discrimination; (2) their (the white parents') right to bring up their children as they wish is not at all effected here since they

are free to inculcate any ideas they wish into their children's heads; and (3) their right of privacy has never been held to bar reasonable government regulation of education. Affirmed.

CONCURRENCE: (Powell, J.) This decision was compelled by *Jones* but it is important to note that it does not sanction wholesale investigation into the motives of every private contract made by people of different races.

CONCURRENCE: (Stevens, J.) Given the unfortunate (and, incorrectly decided) decision in *Jones,* this Court is constrained by the stare decisis interest in "stability and orderly development of the law, to affirm the decision below."

DISSENT: (White, J.) The Civil Rights Act of 1866, on its face, only granted to Negroes the "same right to make . . . contracts . . . as are enjoyed by white citizens." No one, including whites, has ever had the right to make a contract with an unwilling person, *Jones* should have been overruled.

▶ ANALYSIS

It is important to note that four members of the court in this case felt that *Jones v. Alfred H. Mayer Co.* had been improperly decided. As such, *Runyon* should be read as "drawing the line" on congressional power to enforce civil rights laws against private individuals. Specifically, it should be noted that the court appears to be unwilling to extend such power in cases of sex discrimination, religious discrimination, or even racial discrimination where no "contract" is involved (e.g., social clubs). Note, of course, that *Jones* dealt with § 1982 (property rights) not § 1981, but the fact that both are sections of the same act gave rise to application of stare decisis.

■—■

Quicknotes

CIVIL RIGHTS ACT Federal laws passed in order to protect constitutional rights and prohibiting discrimination.

RIGHT TO PRIVACY The violation of an individual's right to be protected against unwarranted interference in his personal affairs, falling into one of four categories: (1) appropriating the individual's likeness or name for commercial benefit; (2) intrusion into the individual's seclusion; (3) public disclosure of private facts regarding the individual; and (4) disclosure of facts placing the individual in a false light.

Continued on next page.

STARE DECISIS Doctrine whereby courts follow legal precedent unless there is good cause for departure.

THIRTEENTH AMENDMENT The constitutional provision which abolished slavery in the United States.

■▬■

South Carolina v. Katzenbach

State (P) v. Attorney General (D)

383 U.S. 301 (1966).

NATURE OF CASE: Constitutional challenge to Voting Rights Act of 1965.

FACT SUMMARY: South Carolina (P) and other states (P) challenged the validity of the Voting Rights Act of 1965.

RULE OF LAW
Congress may, under the Fifteenth Amendment, prescribe appropriate voter registration and election procedures.

FACTS: The Voting Rights Act of 1965 was enacted to eliminate various discriminatory devices used to disenfranchise blacks. States were prohibited from using literacy tests and similar devices for five years after a finding of discrimination. New devices had to be submitted to federal officials for review before they could be implemented. Federal election officials were to monitor state activities once past discrimination had been shown. These and other facets of the Act were challenged by South Carolina (P) and other states (P) which had been adjudged guilty of voting discrimination. It was argued that the Congress lacked the power to prescribe state election procedures, the Act violated the equality of states, utilized an invalid presumption, and involved the district courts in a situation where they had to issue advisory opinions.

ISSUE: May Congress prescribe rules and regulations concerning election procedures/voter's registration to the states?

HOLDING AND DECISION: (Warren, C.J.) Yes. The Fifteenth Amendment declares that neither the states nor the federal government shall deny or abridge the rights of citizens to vote on the basis of race, color or previous condition of servitude. This is a self-executing provision which automatically invalidates statutes which are discriminatory on their face or in practice. The Fifteenth Amendment also grants to Congress the power to enforce it by appropriate legislation. If the end is legitimate and the means are constitutional, congressional acts may prescribe rules which are binding on the states. The Act is applied to states which have, in the past, utilized discrimination to disenfranchise various segments of their citizens. Past activities provide a reasonable inference of future evils and Congress may particularly address legislation to these offending states. The use of devices to discriminate in the past is adequate grounds for banning their use. Monitoring of local activities by federal officials merely assures compliance. The use of new voter registration restrictions by the district court is a reasonable requirement and is not an advisory opinion but an attempt to make certain that future discrimination does not occur. Congress has the power to enact legislation to prevent those states previously guilty of discrimination from continuing such practices and the means chosen under the Act are reasonably calculated to achieve this end. The Act is constitutional. Dismissed.

CONCURRENCE AND DISSENT: (Black, J.) While the Act is constitutional, certain portions of it cannot survive a careful scrutiny. The provision preventing states from amending their constitutions or laws relating to voting rights without prior federal approval violates the case and controversy requirement for jurisdiction. Secondly, we have overstepped the bounds of federalism and states rights under this provision. Section 5 of the Act is clearly unconstitutional.

ANALYSIS

Section 5 has been interpreted by the Court to include within its purview attempts to change from district to at-large elections. *Allen v. State Board of Elections*, 393 U.S. 544 (1969). It also covered changes in boundary lines through annexation. *Perkins v. Matthews*, 400 U.S. 379 (1971). Section 5 has been read to reach any plan which dilutes the voting power of a state's citizens. *Reynolds v. Sims*, 377 U.S. 533 (1964).

Quicknotes

ADVISORY OPINION A decision rendered at the request of an interested party of how the court would rule should the particular issue arise.

CASE OR CONTROVERSY Constitutional requirement in order to invoke federal court jurisdiction that the matter present a justiciable issue.

FEDERALISM A scheme of government whereby the power to govern is divided between a central and localized governments.

FIFTEENTH AMENDMENT States that the right of citizens of the United States to vote shall not be denied on account of race, color, or previous condition of servitude.

Miller v. Johnson

Parties not identified.

515 U.S. 900 (1995).

NATURE OF CASE: Review of order striking down the configuration of congressional voting districts.

FACT SUMMARY: The configuration of a congressional district in Georgia was challenged on the basis that its primary purpose was to maximize black voting power.

▥ RULE OF LAW
States may not constitutionally create voting districts based primarily on racial considerations.

FACTS: Under pressure from the U.S. Department of Justice acting under Voting Rights Act authority, the Georgia Legislature created its eleventh congressional district. The district, which sprawled over twenty-six counties, was distinguished by a complete lack of geographical consistency. The main concern was clearly to create a black-majority district. Georgia's population at the time was 27% black. The configuration of the district was challenged as unconstitutional. The court of appeals agreed and struck down the district. The Supreme Court granted review.

ISSUE: May a state constitutionally create a voting district based primarily on racial considerations?

HOLDING AND DECISION: (Kennedy, J.) No. States may not constitutionally create voting districts based primarily on racial considerations. At the heart of the Equal Protection Clause is the command that citizens are to be treated as individuals, not as components of a race, class, or gender. Citizens may be segregated on such basis only with extraordinary justification. Any classification based on race will trigger strict scrutiny, and the classification will have to be narrowly tailored to serve a compelling interest. Merely lumping members of race into a single district is not a narrowly tailored solution to the problem of racial discrimination. Underlying such a course of action is the somewhat insulting assumption that members of a race think and vote alike, which is plainly untrue. Districting is to some extent an art and properly involves considerations of geography, politics, and incumbency. Race can also be a factor; however, it cannot be the primary factor. Here, race was the primary factor, so the Eleventh District is unconstitutional. Affirmed and remanded.

CONCURRENCE: (O'Connor, J.) Race may be a concern in redistricting, but not the paramount concern.

DISSENT: (Stevens, J.) The plaintiffs lack standing in this action since they are white voters in the Eleventh District. Any harm they would suffer could only come as a result of the assumption that the majority has rejected.

DISSENT: (Ginsburg, J.) Strict scrutiny should be applied when race is the sole factor in districting.

▶ ANALYSIS

Constitutionality aside, there is some disagreement as to whether racial gerrymandering really helps advance minority interests. The concentration of the "black vote" may increase the likelihood of the election of a black representative. However, political scientists have pointed out that this often creates "safe" districts for nonminority candidates in other districts.

■■■

Quicknotes

EQUAL PROTECTION CLAUSE A constitutional guarantee that no person should be denied the same protection of the laws enjoyed by other persons in like circumstances.

GERRYMANDERING To create a civil decision of an unusual shape for an improper purpose such as redistricting a state with unnatural boundaries, isolating members of a particular political party, so that a maximum number of the elected representatives will be of that political party.

STANDING Whether a party possesses the right to commence suit against another party by having a personal stake in the resolution of the controversy.

STRICT SCRUTINY Method by which courts determine the constitutionality of a law, when a law affects a fundamental right. Under the test, the legislature must have a compelling interest to enact the law and measures prescribed by the law must be the least restrictive means possible to accomplish its goal.

■■■

Freedom of Speech

Quick Reference Rules of Law

CHAPTER 10

Schenck v. United States

Activist (D) v. Federal government (P)

249 U.S. 47 (1919).

NATURE OF CASE: Appeal from conviction for conspiracy to violate the Espionage Act, conspiracy to use the mails for transmissions of nonmailable material, and unlawful use of the mails.

FACT SUMMARY: During a time of war, Schenck (D) mailed circulars to draftees which were calculated to cause insubordination in the armed services and to obstruct the U.S. recruiting and enlistment program in violation of military laws.

🏛 RULE OF LAW
The test to determine the constitutionality of a statute restricting free speech is whether, under the circumstances, the speech is of such a nature as to create a clear and present danger that it will bring about the substantive evils which Congress has a right to prevent.

FACTS: During a time of war, Schenck (D) mailed circulars to draftees. The circulars stated that the Conscription Act was unconstitutional and likened conscription to conviction. They intimated that conscription was a monstrous wrong against humanity in the interest of Wall Street's chosen few, and described nonconscription arguments as coming from cunning politicians and a mercenary capitalist press. They urged: "Do not submit to intimidation," but advised only peaceful actions such as a petition to repeal the Conscription Act. Schenck (D) does not deny that the jury could find that the circulars could have no purpose except to influence draftees to obstruct the carrying out of the draft.

ISSUE: Does the right to freedom of speech depend upon the circumstances in which the speech is spoken?

HOLDING AND DECISION: (Holmes, J.) Yes. The character of every act depends on the circumstance in which it is done. The most stringent protection of free speech would not protect a person's falsely shouting fire in a theatre and causing a panic. "The question in every case is whether the words are used in such circumstances and are of such a nature as to create a clear and present danger that they will bring about the substantive evils that Congress has a right to prevent. It is a question of proximity and degrees. During a war, things that could be said during peaceful times may be such a hindrance to the war effort that they will not be permitted." Schenck's (D) convictions are affirmed.

▶ ANALYSIS

The Court's first significant encounter with the problem of articulating the scope of constitutionally protected speech came in a series of cases involving agitation against the draft and war during World War I (*Schenck, Frohwerk, Debs*). *Schenck* announces the "clear and present danger" test, the test for determining the validity of legislation regulating speech. In *Schenck*, Justice Holmes rejected perfect immunity for speech. But he also rejected a far more restrictive, far more widely supported, alternative test: that "any tendency in speech to produce bad acts, no matter how remote, would suffice to validate a repressive statute."

■■■

Quicknotes

CONSCRIPTION Compulsory service in the military; the state of being drafted.

CONSPIRACY Concerted action by two or more persons to accomplish some unlawful purpose.

■■■

Abrams v. United States

Activists (D) v. Federal government (P)

250 U.S. 616 (1919).

NATURE OF CASE: Appeal from a criminal conspiracy conviction.

FACT SUMMARY: Abrams (D) and others passed out leaflets condemning U.S. efforts "to crush" the Russian revolution.

🏛 RULE OF LAW
Only speech that is intended to produce a "clear and present danger" may be punished.

FACTS: Abrams (D) and others passed out leaflets condemning U.S. (P) efforts "to crush" the Russian revolution. Abrams (D) was convicted of violating the Espionage Act in that he incited, provoked, and encouraged resistance to the U.S. (P) and curtailment of its war efforts. The U.S. Supreme Court affirmed.

ISSUE: [Issue not stated in casebook excerpt.]

HOLDING AND DECISION: [Holding and decision not stated in casebook excerpt.]

DISSENT: (Holmes, J.) To violate the Espionage Act there must be an intent to do the prohibited acts or accomplish the proscribed ends. The motive involved is crucial. Mere protest does not violate the Act. Only if it is in furtherance of a plan to accomplish purposes made illegal under the Act, are the actions illegal. The U.S. (P) may only punish "speech" that is intended to produce a "clear and present danger," not as herein, a harmless leaflet. Neither leaflet was intended to injure the U.S. war effort against Germany. The Constitution has totally altered the common law crime of seditious libel. Free speech guarantees cannot be abridged.

▶ ANALYSIS

Reaction to this case has been both mixed and vigorous. Professor Zechariah Chafee, Jr. (1885–1957) thought it ridiculous to impose a 20-year sentence on each of five obscure and isolated aliens operating under misguided ideals. Professor John Henry Wigmore (1863–1943) argued the opposite. He feared that if the five herein could be allowed to urge a general munitions strike, then anyone could do the same, "and a thousand disaffected undesirables, aliens and natives alike, were ready and waiting to do so."

■■■

Quicknotes

CLEAR AND PRESENT DANGER A threat that is proximate and impending.

SEDITIOUS LIBEL A communication written which is specifically intended to incite people to overthrow the government by force or otherwise violent means.

■■■

Gitlow v. New York

Publisher (D) v. State (P)

268 U.S. 652 (1925).

NATURE OF CASE: Appeal from conviction for criminal anarchy.

FACT SUMMARY: Gitlow (D) published a radical manifesto encouraging workers to strike and to use militant means to overthrow the government and was convicted therefore under a "criminal anarchy statute" enacted in New York (P).

🏛 RULE OF LAW
A state may prohibit speech likely to cause a danger of substantive evil.

FACTS: Gitlow (D) published a socialist manifesto encouraging workers to strike and urging revolutionary anarchy in order to overthrow the government. He was convicted under New York's (P) "criminal anarchy statute," which prohibited speech of specified character which the legislature found to be likely to cause a danger of substantive evil. The speech covered by the challenged statute included utterances advocating the overthrow of organized government by force, violence, and unlawful means. There was no evidence that any reader was so inspired. Gitlow (D) appealed his conviction.

ISSUE: May a state prohibit speech likely to cause a danger of substantive evil?

HOLDING AND DECISION: (Sanford, J.) Yes. This Court has previously held that the question in First Amendment cases is whether the words in question create a "clear and present" danger that they will bring about substantive evils. However this is a situation where the legislature of a state has made a determination that such a "clear and present danger" exists as to certain speech specifically characterized by the New York (P) statute, and Gitlow's (D) speech falls within this category. Where this legislative determination has been made, the fact that the speech resulting in conviction may not have presented a "clear and present" danger in the view of the judiciary is irrelevant. The only question is whether the statute is itself unconstitutional. New York's (P) statute is not. A state may prohibit speech likely to cause a danger of substantive evil. Affirmed.

DISSENT: (Holmes, J.) Free speech is a "liberty" protected by the Fourteenth Amendment and therefore the test to be applied as to convictions for speech is the one set forth in *Schenck v. United States*. That is whether there was a "clear and present danger" of substantive evil, and where, as here, there is great doubt that the publication could produce the evil, the publication is probably futile and too remote to produce the proscribed consequences.

▶ ANALYSIS

Mr. Justice Holmes set forth the "clear and present danger" test in *Schenck v. United States*, 249 U.S. 47 (1919). The test is supplanted here with what has been called the "bad tendency test," but modern decisions have returned the focus to the likelihood of incitement to action that is illegal and have not permitted state legislators to pronounce by fiat which words create such a likelihood.

Quicknotes

CLEAR AND PRESENT DANGER TEST Doctrine that restraints on freedom of speech are permissible if the speech incites persons to engage in unlawful conduct.

FIRST AMENDMENT Prohibits Congress from enacting any law respecting an establishment of religion, prohibiting the free exercise of religion, abridging freedom of speech or the press, the right of peaceful assembly and the right to petition for a redress of grievances.

Whitney v. California

Communist party member (D) v. State (P)

274 U.S. 357 (1927).

NATURE OF CASE: Appeal from conviction for violation of criminal syndicalism act.

FACT SUMMARY: Miss Whitney (D), organizer and member of the Communist Labor Party of California, was convicted of aiding in that organization's violation of the Criminal Syndicalism Act.

RULE OF LAW
In order to support a finding of clear and present danger it must be shown either that immediate serious violence was to be advocated, or that the past conduct furnished reason to believe that such advocacy was then contemplated.

FACTS: In 1919, Miss Whitney (D) attended a convention of the Socialist Party. When the convention split into factions, Miss Whitney (D) went with the radicals and helped form the Communist Labor Party (CLP). Later that year, Miss Whitney (D) attended another convention to organize a new California unit of CLP. There Miss Whitney (D) supported a resolution that endorsed political action and urged workers to vote for CLP member-candidates at all elections. This resolution was defeated and a more extreme program of action was adopted, over Miss Whitney's (D) protests. At trial, upon indictment for violation of the California Criminal Syndicalism Act which held it unlawful to organize a group that advocated unlawful acts of violence as a means of effecting change in industrial ownership and in political change, Miss Whitney (D) contended that she never intended the CLP to become a terrorist organization. Miss Whitney (D) further contended that since she had no intent to aid the CLP in a policy of violent political reform, her mere presence at the convention was not a crime. Miss Whitney (D) contends that the Act thus deprived her of her liberty without due process, and freedom of speech, assembly, and association.

ISSUE: In order to support a finding of clear and present danger, must it be shown either that immediate serious violence was to be advocated, or that the past conduct furnished reason to believe that such advocacy was then contemplated?

HOLDING AND DECISION: [Holding and decision not stated in casebook excerpt.]

CONCURRENCE: (Brandeis, J.) Yes. Miss Whitney (D) is here punished for a step in the preparation of incitement which only threatens the public remotely. The Syndicalism Act of California aims at punishing those who propose to preach, not put into action, criminal syndicalism. The right of freedom of speech, assembly and association, protected by the Due Process Clause of the Fourteenth Amendment and binding on the states, is restricted if they threaten political, moral, or economic injury to the state. However, such restriction does not exist unless speech would produce a clear and imminent danger of some substantive evil to the state. The Court has not yet fixed standards in determining when a danger shall be clear. But no danger flowing from speech can be deemed clear and present unless the threatened evil is so imminent that it may strike before opportunity for discussion on it. There must be, however, probability of serious injury to the state. As to review by this Court of an allegation of unconstitutionality of a criminal syndicalism act, whenever fundamental rights of free speech and assembly are alleged to have been invaded, the defendant must be allowed to present the issue of whether a clear and present danger was imminent by his actions. Here, mere advocacy of revolution by mass action at some future date was within the Fourteenth Amendment protection. But our power of review was lacking since there was evidence of a criminal conspiracy, and such precludes review by this Court of errors at a criminal trial absent a showing that constitutional rights were deprived.

ANALYSIS

The *Whitney* case is important for having added to the *Schenck* test of "clear and present danger" the further requirement that the danger must be "imminent." The Brandeis opinion in the *Whitney* case should be viewed as a dissenting opinion. His addition of "imminent" flies directly in the face of the majority opinion that punished "mere advocacy" of threatened action against the state. The "mere advocacy" test has not survived. Modernly, through the Smith Act that continues to punish criminal syndicalism, "mere advocacy" is not punishable. The urging of action for forcible overthrow is necessary before punishment will be imposed. Thus, the "urging of action" is the modern test of "clear and present imminent danger" espoused by Brandeis in *Whitney*.

Quicknotes

CLEAR AND PRESENT DANGER TEST Doctrine that restraints on freedom of speech are permissible if the speech incites persons to engage in unlawful conduct.

CRIMINAL SYNDICALISM The advocating of unlawful conduct to effect a change in ownership or control.

Brandenburg v. Ohio

Ku Klux Klan member (D) v. State (P)

395 U.S. 444 (1969).

NATURE OF CASE: Appeal from conviction for violation of the Ohio criminal syndicalism statute.

FACT SUMMARY: Brandenburg (D) was convicted under a state statute which proscribes advocacy of the duty, necessity, or propriety of crime, sabotage, violence, or unlawful methods of terrorism as a means of accomplishing reform.

RULE OF LAW
The constitutional guarantees of freedom of speech and freedom of press do not permit a state to forbid or proscribe advocacy of the use of force or of law violation except where such advocacy is directed to inciting or producing imminent lawless action and is likely to produce or incite such action.

FACTS: Brandenburg (D), a Ku Klux Klan leader, was convicted under Ohio's criminal syndicalism statute. The statute prohibits advocacy of the duty, necessity, or propriety of crime, sabotage, violence, or unlawful methods of terrorism as a means of accomplishing reform, and the assembling with any group formed to teach or advocate the doctrine of criminal syndicalism. The case against Brandenburg (D) rested on some films. One film showed 12 hooded figures, some carrying firearms, gathered around a wooden cross which they burned. Scattered words could be heard that were derogatory to Jews and Blacks. Brandenburg (D) made a speech and stated, "We are not a revengent group, but if our President, our Congress, and our Supreme Court, continues to suppress the White, Caucasian race, it's possible that there might have to be some revengence taken."

ISSUE: Does a statute which proscribes advocacy of the use of force without more violate the rights guaranteed by the First and Fourteenth Amendments?

HOLDING AND DECISION: (Per curiam) Yes. The constitutional guarantees of free speech and free press do not permit a state to forbid or proscribe advocacy of the use of force or of law violation except where such advocacy is directed to inciting or producing imminent lawless action and is likely to incite or produce such action. The mere abstract teaching of the moral propriety or even moral necessity for a resort to force and violence, is not the same as preparing a group for violent action and steering it to such action. A statute which fails to draw this distinction impermissibly intrudes upon the freedoms guaranteed by the First and Fourteenth Amendments. It sweeps within its condemnation speech which the Constitution has immunized from governmental control. The Ohio statute purports to punish mere advocacy and to forbid assembly with others merely to advocate the described type of action. Hence, it cannot be sustained. Brandenburg's (D) conviction is reversed.

CONCURRENCE: (Black, J.) The "clear and present danger" test should have no place in the interpretation of the First Amendment. I concur with the majority's opinion which does not indicate any agreement with that test.

ANALYSIS

This case demonstrates that imminency of danger is an essential requirement to the validity of any statute curbing freedom of speech. This requirement was reiterated in *Bond v. Floyd*, 385 U.S. 116 (1966), in which the court reversed a state legislature's resolution excluding Bond from membership. The exclusion was based on the ground that Bond could not take the oath to support the state and U.S. constitutions after his endorsement of a Student Nonviolent Coordinating Committee statement and his remarks criticizing the draft and the Vietnam war. The Court found no incitement to violation of law in Bond's remarks.

Quicknotes

CLEAR AND PRESENT DANGER TEST Doctrine that restraints on freedom of speech are permissible if the speech incites persons to engage in unlawful conduct.

CRIMINAL SYNDICALISM The advocating of unlawful conduct to effect a change in ownership or control.

Hess v. Indiana

Demonstrator (D) v. State (P)

414 U.S. 105 (1973).

NATURE OF CASE: Appeal from conviction for disorderly conduct.

FACT SUMMARY: Hess (D) was convicted of disorderly conduct after uttering an exhortation to "take" a street that police were clearing during a demonstration.

🏛 RULE OF LAW
A state may not punish the advocacy of illegal action at some indefinite future time.

FACTS: Hess (D) was convicted of disorderly conduct for advocating illegal acts at an anti-war demonstration on the campus of Indiana University. While the police were attempting to clear a street where demonstrators had blocked traffic, two witnesses testified that Hess (D) had said in a loud voice that "We'll take the fucking street later." The witnesses indicated that Hess (D) did not appear to be exhorting the crowd to go back into the street, that he was facing the crowd and not the street when he uttered the statement, that his statement did not appear to be addressed to any particular person or group, and that his tone, although loud, was no louder than that of the other people in the area. Hess (D) appealed a decision by the Indiana Supreme Court upholding his conviction.

ISSUE: May a state punish the advocacy of illegal action at some indefinite future time?

HOLDING AND DECISION: (Per curiam) No. The constitutional guarantees of free speech and free press do not permit a state to forbid or proscribe advocacy of the use of force or of law violation except where such advocacy is directed at inciting or producing imminent lawless action and is likely to incite or produce such action. Since the uncontroverted evidence showed that Hess' (D) statement was not directed to any person or group of persons, it cannot be said that he was advocating in the normal sense any action. And since there was no evidence or rational inference from the import of the language, that his words were intended to produce, and likely produce, imminent disorder, those words could not be punished by the State (P) on the ground that they had a tendency to lead to violence. Reversed.

DISSENT: (Rehnquist, J.) The simple explanation for the result in this case is that the majority has interpreted the evidence differently from the courts below. In so doing, the Court has exceeded the proper scope of review, which requires considering the evidence in the light most favorable to the State (P), and resolving credibility questions against Hess (D).

▶ ANALYSIS

This case follows the test established in *Brandenburg v. Ohio*, 395 U.S. 444 (1969), for determining when the advocacy of illegal conduct may be punished by the state. That case held that abstract advocacy of illegal conduct at some future time could not be prohibited by the state.

Quicknotes

FREEDOM OF SPEECH The right to express oneself without governmental restrictions on the content of that expression.

FREEDOM OF THE PRESS The right to publish and publicly disseminate one's views.

New York Times Co. v. United States

Publisher (D) v. Federal government (P)

403 U.S. 713 (1971).

NATURE OF CASE: Action by federal government to restrain newspaper publication.

FACT SUMMARY: Government (P) sought to enjoin, in the interests of "national security," the New York Times (D) and the Washington Post (D) from further publishing of portions of the "Pentagon Papers," a classified, "top secret" study.

🏛 RULE OF LAW

Any system of prior restraints on the freedom of the press bears a heavy presumption against its constitutional validity.

FACTS: During the Vietnam War, the New York Times (D) and the Washington Post (D) published portions of a study which the Government (P) had classified as "top secret." The classified study was entitled "History of U.S. Decision-Making Process on Vietnam Policy," and was popularly known as the "Pentagon Papers." The Government (P), maintaining that "national security" interests were threatened by further publication, sought prior restraints against the Times (D) and the Post (D).

ISSUE: Must the government sustain a heavy burden in showing justification for prior restraint?

HOLDING AND DECISION: (Per curiam) Yes. Any system of prior restraints of expression comes to the court bearing a heavy presumption against its constitutional validity. The Government (P) thus carries a heavy burden of showing justification for the enforcement of such a restraint. No restraining order or injunction will issue. Affirmed in part, reversed in part, and remanded.

CONCURRENCE: (Black, J.) The guarding of military and diplomatic secrets at the expense of informed representative government provides no real security for the Republic, and would wipe out the First Amendment.

CONCURRENCE: (Douglas, J.) There is no congressional enactment barring the kind of publication in this case. Secrecy in government is fundamentally anti-democratic, perpetuating bureaucratic errors.

CONCURRENCE: (Brennan, J.) The First Amendment tolerates absolutely no prior restraints of the press predicated upon surmise or conjecture that untoward consequences may result. The country is not at war, and the Government (P) has failed to show that continued publication here would cause war, a nuclear holocaust, or would directly and immediately imperil our troops. The Government (P) must clearly define the basis for enlisting judicial aid in suppression of the press.

CONCURRENCE: (Stewart, J.) I cannot say that disclosure of any of the "Pentagon Papers" will surely result in direct, immediate, and irreparable damage to our Nation or its people.

CONCURRENCE: (White, J.) The President, who is charged with conducting foreign policy and protecting the nation's security, is entitled to an injunction when he can convince a court that the information to be revealed threatens "grave and irreparable" injury to the public interest. The injunction should issue whether or not the material to be published is classified, whether or not publication would be lawful under relevant criminal statutes enacted by Congress, and regardless of the circumstances by which the newspaper came into possession of the information. That burden, however, has not been met in the present case.

CONCURRENCE: (Marshall, J.) Congress is empowered by the Constitution to make the laws, and there is no government by injunction in which the Executive and Judicial Branches can make law without regard for Congress. Congress has twice refused to enact legislation that would have made the conduct in this case illegal. It has refused to give the President the power to directly prohibit the publication of information relating to national defense in wartime that might be helpful to the enemy. The refusal of the district court to enjoin Mr. Ellsberg was therefore proper.

DISSENT: (Burger, C.J.) The newspaper could have anticipated the Government's (P) objections to the publication of secret material and given the Government (P) an opportunity to review the material and come to an agreement as to what parts could be published without danger. The New York Times (D), like taxi drivers and Justices, has a duty to report the discovery or possession of stolen property such as the Ellsberg papers. I would remand the case to the district court for trial and give this case priority over other business.

DISSENT: (Harlan, J.) The judiciary must satisfy itself that the subject matter of the dispute does lie within the proper compass of the President's foreign relations power. It may also properly insist that the determination that disclosure of the subject matter would irreparably impair the national security be made by the head of the Executive Department concerned (i.e., State or Defense) after actual personal consideration by that officer. However, since the very nature of executive decisions as to foreign policy is political, the judiciary should not go beyond these two inquiries to redetermine for itself the probable impact of

Continued on next page.

disclosure on the national security. Even if some additional review is permitted, some deference must be given to the decision of the Executive Branch, a coequal partner in government.

DISSENT: (Blackmun, J.) First Amendment absolutism has never commanded a majority of this court. What is needed here is a weighing, upon properly developed standards, of the broad right of the press to print and of the very narrow right of the government to prevent. The question is one of proximity and degree.

▶ ANALYSIS

In *Pittsburgh Press Co. v. Pittsburgh Comm'n on Human Relations*, 413 U.S. 376 (1973), the Court upheld an administrative order which forbade a newspaper from carrying sex-designated "help wanted" ads, except for exempt jobs. Justice Powell, in writing for the majority, commented, "The present order does not endanger arguably protected speech. Because the order is based on a continuing course of repetitive conduct, this is not a case in which the court is asked to speculate as to the effect of publication. Cf. *New York Times v. United States*, 403 U.S. 713 (1971). Moreover, the order is clear and sweeps no more broadly than necessary. And because no interim relief was granted, the order will not have gone into effect until it was finally determined that the actions of Pittsburgh Press were unprotected."

■═■

Quicknotes

FIRST AMENDMENT Prohibits Congress from enacting any law respecting an establishment of religion, prohibiting the free exercise of religion, abridging freedom of speech or the press, the right of peaceful assembly and the right to petition for a redress of grievances.

PRIOR RESTRAINT A restriction imposed on speech imposed prior to its communication.

■═■

Snepp v. United States

Ex-CIA agent (D) v. Federal government (P)

444 U.S. 507 (1980).

NATURE OF CASE: Appeal from denial of constructive trust in breach of contract case.

FACT SUMMARY: Snepp (D) published a book based on his experience as a CIA agent, despite his promise not to divulge classified information or to publish only information without prepublication clearance.

RULE OF LAW

If a government agent publishes unreviewed material in violation of his contractual and fiduciary obligation, a constructive trust will be imposed, requiring him to disgorge the benefits of his breach of duty.

FACTS: Snepp (D), a former CIA agent, published a book about CIA activities in South Vietnam. The book was based on his personal experiences and was not submitted to the Agency for prepublication review. However, Snepp (D) had executed an agreement, as an express condition of his employment with the CIA, not to publish any Agency-related material, whether during or after his employment, without prior Agency approval. Snepp (D) had further promised not to divulge any classified information without CIA authorization. The Government (P) sought an injunction prohibiting future breaches of Snepp's (D) contract, and a constructive trust on all Snepp's (D) profits from the published book. Finding that the agreement had been breached, the district court granted the requested relief. The court of appeals upheld the injunction but it refused to impose a constructive trust on the ground that Snepp (D) was only obligated to not divulge classified material, and the Government (P) conceded for the purposes of this action that the book contained no classified information. Snepp (D) filed for certiorari, and the Government (P) cross-petitioned from the denial of a constructive trust.

ISSUE: Will a constructive trust be imposed on a government agent who benefits from the breach of his contractual and fiduciary obligation to the government?

HOLDING AND DECISION: (Per curiam) Yes. The Government (P) has a compelling interest in protecting the secrecy of information important to national security and the confidentiality necessary for an effective foreign intelligence service. An agreement not to divulge any classified information or not to publish any material relating to the Agency without Agency review is a reasonable means for protecting this compelling interest. It does not deny the government agent the right to publish unclassified material, but merely requires government review in order to determine whether publication would disclose classified information. The breach of such an agreement is a breach of trust and requires a remedy conforming relief to the dimensions of the wrong. Thus, if a government agent publishes unreviewed material in violation of his contractual and fiduciary duty, a constructive trust will be imposed, requiring him to disgorge the benefits of his breach. Here, whether Snepp (D) violated his contractual and fiduciary obligation does not depend on whether his book actually disclosed classified material. Rather, his failure to submit the material for prepublication review was a breach of his obligation, which, both the district court and the court of appeals agreed, has irreparably harmed the Government (P). Reversed, in so far as the court of appeals refused to impose a constructive trust, and remanded.

DISSENT: (Stevens, J.) Because the agreement in question imposes a serious prior restraint on the employee's freedom of speech, there is a heavy burden on the censor to justify the remedy sought. Since Snepp's (D) book contained no classified material, the Government's (P) review would have resulted in authorization for publication, and Snepp's (D) profits are thus not the result of his breach. Therefore, the remedy of constructive trust is unjustified.

ANALYSIS

Prior restraints are strongly disfavored under the First Amendment, and come before the Court with a heavy presumption against their constitutional validity. A narrow exception to this general rule is the prior restraint that exists in the interest of national security. In *Snepp*, the Court observed in a footnote that Snepp (D) claimed his agreement was unenforceable as a prior restraint, but noted that the government had a substantial and compelling interest in keeping classified information that is important to national security.

■━■

Quicknotes

CONSTRUCTIVE TRUST A trust that arises by operation of law whereby the court imposes a trust upon property lawfully held by one party for the benefit of another, as a result of some wrongdoing by the party in possession so as to avoid unjust enrichment.

FIDUCIARY DUTY A legal obligation to act for the benefit of another, including subordinating one's personal interests to that of the other person.

PRIOR RESTRAINT A restriction imposed on speech imposed prior to its communication.

■━■

Walker v. City of Birmingham

Ministers (D) v. City (P)

388 U.S. 307 (1967).

NATURE OF CASE: Appeal from criminal contempt conviction.

FACT SUMMARY: Eight black ministers (D) ignored a court order enjoining them from parading or congregating without a permit.

🏛 RULE OF LAW
One who disobeys an injunction, without first seeking orderly judicial review of the order, will be found in contempt of court.

FACTS: After permit requests for demonstrations had been denied by an official of Birmingham, Alabama (P), eight black ministers (D), including the late Rev. Martin Luther King, Jr. (D), proceeded with their plans to conduct demonstrations on Easter weekend. The officials of Birmingham (P) filed a complaint requesting an order to enjoin the ministers (D) and others from encouraging or participating in demonstrations, street parades, or picketing. A temporary injunction was issued ex parte, enjoining the ministers (D) from conducting such activities without the permit required by a Birmingham (P) ordinance. After being served with the writ, the ministers (D) disobeyed it without first seeking judicial review, claiming that the order was unconsti-tutional. At a hearing to determine whether the ministers (D) should be held in contempt, the ministers (D) sought to attack the constitutionality of the injunction and the Birmingham (P) parade ordinance. The court, holding that the only issues were whether it had jurisdiction to order the injunction and whether the injunction had been knowingly violated, found against the ministers (D) on both issues. The Supreme Court of Alabama affirmed. Certiorari was granted.

ISSUE: Where one believes an injunction to be unconstitutional, may he freely disobey the injunction without first seeking its orderly judicial review?

HOLDING AND DECISION: (Stewart, J.) No. The breadth and vagueness of an ordinance or an injunction would undoubtedly subject it to substantial constitutional question. But the proper way to raise that question is to apply to the courts for an authoritative construction of the ordinance or for the modification or dissolution of the injunction. Thus, where the injunction is not transparently invalid and where the court had jurisdiction to issue the order, one who disobeys the injunction without first seeking its orderly judicial review will be held in contempt of court. Here, the parade ordinance was not transparently invalid, as state and local governments have a strong interest in regulating the use of their streets and other public places. Further, the court certainly had jurisdiction over the ministers (D) and over the subject matter of the dispute. Finally, the ministers (D) made no application to the court to construe the ordinance or to modify or dissolve the injunction, despite the two-day interim between the issuance of the injunction and the first demonstration. The ministers (D) were not constitutionally free to ignore the procedures of the law. Affirmed.

DISSENT: (Warren, C.J.) The ministers (D) are in essentially the same position as persons who violate a statute and then defend their violation on constitutional grounds. They stood ready to accept the penalty if their defense failed. No disrespect for the law is indicated.

DISSENT: (Douglas, J.) Just as an ordinance invalid on its face or patently unconstitutional as applied need not be honored, the unconstitutional injunction that enforces the ordinance need not be obeyed.

▶ ANALYSIS

In *Shuttlesworth v. Birmingham*, 394 U.S. 147 (1969), the Supreme Court reversed the conviction of civil rights demonstrators who had violated the same ordinance as was at issue in *Walker*. Obviously, though one is free to violate an unconstitutionally vague statute restricting free speech, one cannot freely violate the same words when written up as a court injunction. The rationale here is that an individual cannot flout the judicial machinery where reasonable review is available; this would be an intolerable attack on the court's authority. It is worth noting that several years after *Walker*, the Court held unconstitutional the obtaining of an ex parte order to restrain rallies, unless it is impossible to serve or notify the parties. *Carroll v. President and Commissioners of Princess Anne*, 393 U.S. 175 (1968).

Quicknotes

CONTEMPT OF COURT Conduct that is intended to obstruct the court's effective administration of justice or to otherwise disrespect its authority.

EX PARTE A proceeding commenced by one party without providing any opposing parties with notice or which is uncontested by an adverse party.

INJUNCTION A court order requiring a person to do or prohibiting that person from doing a specific act.

Shuttlesworth v. City of Birmingham

Parade participants (D) v. City (P)

394 U.S. 147 (1969).

NATURE OF CASE: Appeal from conviction of violating a statutory prohibition against marching in a parade without a permit.

FACT SUMMARY: A Birmingham ordinance made it a misdemeanor to participate in a parade, demonstration, or procession without a permit.

🏛 RULE OF LAW
In determining whether a "narrowing construction" of a statute will allow a conviction to "pass constitutional muster," it is relevant to determine whether the statute was applied within the ambits of the limiting construction.

FACTS: Fifty-two blacks (D) were convicted of parading without a permit. The ordinance under which they were convicted prescribed that a permit was required for all parades, processions, or demonstrations. The Council (P) had to issue the permit unless it determined that the activity would have an adverse effect on the welfare, decency, or morals of the community. On appeal the Alabama Supreme Court narrowed the construction of the ordinance to only exclude activities which would unduly inhibit the public's use of the streets or highways. It upheld the conviction on this basis. There was no showing that the ordinance had ever been applied in this manner and the marchers had not interfered with either the use of the streets or highways during the procession.

ISSUE: May a conviction under a statute be upheld by a limiting construction when there is no showing that it was ever applied in the manner outlined in the narrowing construction?

HOLDING AND DECISION: (Stewart, J.) No. The ordinance as originally enacted gave the Council (P) unfettered authority to issue or deny a permit. While a parade is not pure speech as such, it is a manner of expressing speech/ideas and is protected under the First and Fourteenth Amendments. Officials cannot be given unfettered freedom to grant or deny permits for this type of protected activity. They may only regulate time, place, and manner. While the narrowing construction given the ordinance by the Alabama Supreme Court would pass constitutional muster, there is no showing that the City Council (P) applied the ordinance in this manner four years earlier when Shuttlesworth (D) and the other marchers were convicted. In determining whether a narrowing construction will sustain a conviction under an overbroad statute, it is relevant to inquire into whether the statute was administered within the ambits of the narrowed construc-tion. Since there has been no such showing the conviction must be overturned. The facts clearly show that the Council (P) used its full authority under the ordinance to either grant or deny permits. Reversed.

▶ ANALYSIS

Where an injunction is obtained prohibiting a parade, the injunction must be challenged. Failure to do so will subject the marchers to criminal contempt citations if the parade is held anyway. *Walker v. Birmingham*, 388 U.S. 307 (1967). However, a strong dissent stated that the injunction could be violated if it were based on an overbroad or vague statute and inadequate time was available to challenge the injunction.

■■■■

Quicknotes

ORDINANCE Law or statute usually enacted by a municipal government.

OVERBROAD Refers to a statute that proscribes lawful as well as unlawful conduct.

VAGUENESS Doctrine that a statute that does not clearly or definitely inform an individual as to what conduct is unlawful is unconstitutional, in violation of the Due Process Clause.

■■■■

Secretary of State of Maryland v. Joseph H. Munson, Inc.

State (D) v. Fundraiser (P)

467 U.S. 947 (1984).

NATURE OF CASE: Appeal from the invalidation of a state statute.

FACT SUMMARY: Joseph H. Munson, Inc. (P) contended that a Maryland (D) statute which prohibited the solicitation of charitable contributions by an organization that did not use 75% of its receipts for charitable purposes violated freedom of speech.

RULE OF LAW

A percentage limitation on funds expended in solicitation for charitable purposes is a violation of freedom of speech.

FACTS: Joseph H. Munson, Inc. (P), a professional fund raising company, sued to declare the Maryland statute, which required organizations soliciting funds to spend at least 75% on charitable purposes, unconstitutional as a deprivation of freedom of speech. Maryland (D) defended, contending the statute's provision that the percentage limitation could be waived if the organization could demonstrate financial need to spend less than 75% on charitable purposes. The Maryland Court of Appeals held the statute unconstitutional, and Maryland (D) appealed.

ISSUE: Is a percentage limitation on funds expended in solicitation for charitable purposes a violation of freedom of speech?

HOLDING AND DECISION: (Blackmun, J.) Yes. A percentage limitation on funds expended in solicitation for charitable purposes is a violation of freedom of speech. Percentage limitations restrict the ways in which charities may engage in solicitation activity and, therefore, can be valid only if they serve a strong governmental interest. As there is no necessary connection between fraud and high solicitation costs, therefore, limitations cannot be justified as a prevention device for fraud. Also, the exception for financially needy organizations does not save the statute from unconstitutionality because high fundraising costs are attributable to policy decisions concerning the use of funds rather than the inability to raise funds. As a result, the statute was invalid. Affirmed.

DISSENT: (Rehnquist, J.) The statute at issue was a legitimate restriction aimed at protecting charitable organizations from professional fundraisers. It differed markedly from other percentage limitations previously held unconstitutional.

ANALYSIS

The Court in this case held the statute invalid on its face on the basis that it was overbroad in scope. It held there was no easily identifiable and constitutionally proscribable conduct prohibited by the statute. The potential application of the statute to violate freedom of speech rendered it unconstitutional.

Quicknotes

FRAUD A false representation of facts with the intent that another will rely on the misrepresentation to his detriment.

OVERBROAD Refers to a statute that proscribes lawful as well as unlawful conduct.

Perry Education Association v. Perry Local Educators' Association

Bargaining representative (D) v. Board of Education (P)

460 U.S. 37 (1983).

NATURE OF CASE: Appeal from a constitutional challenge to a preferential access system.

FACT SUMMARY: The collective bargaining agreement which the Board of Education signed with Perry Education Association (PEA) (D), the duly elected bargaining representative of the teachers in the school district provided that no other union, such as Perry Local Educators' Association (PLEA) (P), would have access to the interschool mail system and the teacher mail boxes.

🏛 RULE OF LAW
Implicit in the concept of a nonpublic forum is the right to make distinctions in access on the basis of subject matter and speaker identity that are reasonable in light of the purpose that the forum at issue serves.

FACTS: At one time, both the Perry Education Association (PEA) (D) and the Perry Local Educators' Association (PLEA) (P) had access to the Perry Township School District's interschool mail system and the teacher mailboxes. Subsequently, an election was held and PEA (D) was certified as the exclusive bargaining representative. The School Board permits a school district to provide access to communication facilities to the union selected as the exclusive representative of the bargaining unit and its individual members without having to provide equal access to rival unions. When the PEA (D) managed to negotiate a collective bargaining agreement providing that only it would have access to the interschool system and teacher mailboxes, the PLEA (P) filed suit charging that this denial of equal access violated the First and Fourteenth Amendments. Reversing the district court's decision for the PLEA (P), the Seventh Circuit found the preferential access system unconstitutional.

ISSUE: With regard to a nonpublic forum, does the Constitution permit the making of distinctions in access on the basis of subject matter and speaker identity, as long as such distinctions are reasonable in light of the purpose that the forum at issue serves?

HOLDING AND DECISION: (White, J.) Yes. The school mail facilities here at issue fall within the category of public property which is not by tradition or designation a forum for public communication. Different standards apply to these "nonpublic" forums. In addition to time, place, and manner regulations, the state may reserve the forum for its intended purposes, communicative or otherwise, as long as the regulation on speech is reasonable and not an effort to suppress expression merely because the public officials oppose the speaker's view. Implicit in the concept of a nonpublic forum is the right to make distinctions in access on the basis of subject matter and speaker identity that are reasonable in light of the purpose that the forum at issue serves. The fact that other organizations like the Girl Scouts or clubs that engage in activities of interest and educational relevance to students may, from time to time, have been granted permission to use the system could not open it up as a forum to organizations which, like PLEA (P), have different concerns. Nor would the fact that both rival unions once had equal access to the system at a time when there was no official single representative of the teachers constitute a public forum. Thus, all that is left is to see if the limited access rule passes the "reasonableness" test. It does. It insures labor peace within the schools, enables the PEA (D) to perform effectively its obligations as the exclusive representative of all the teachers, and leaves alternative channels open to other rival unions who wish to communicate with the teachers. Reversed.

DISSENT: (Brennan, J.) The exclusive access provision in the collective bargaining agreement amounts to viewpoint discrimination that infringes First Amendment rights and fails to advance any substantial state interest. First of all, the Court, in focusing on the public forum issue, disregards the First Amendment's central proscription against censorship in the form of viewpoint discrimination, in any forum, public or nonpublic. As to the state interests allegedly served by the exclusive access policy, such exclusive access is both "over-inclusive and underinclusive" as a means of serving the state's interest in the efficient discharge of the PEA's (D) legal duties to the teachers as their bargaining representative. It is over-inclusive in that it does not strictly limit the PEA's (D) use of the mail system to performance of its special legal duties and underinclusive in that the board permits outside organizations with no special duties to the teachers, or to the students, to use the system. Furthermore, while the board may have a legitimate interest in granting the PEA (D) access to the system, it has no legitimate interest in making that access exclusive by denying access to the PLEA (P). Any attempt to justify the exclusive access policy by the state's alleged interest in preserving labor peace must also fail. There is no evidence that granting access to the PLEA (P) would result in labor instability and no reason to assume that its messages would be any more likely to cause labor discord when received by the members of the majority union than the PEA's (D) messages would when received by the PLEA (P). Reversed.

▌ ANALYSIS

Whatever restrictions the First Amendment places on the government are placed on it only in its capacity as

Continued on next page.

regulator. The First Amendment is viewed as placing no constraints on the government as speaker, at least as far as the current state of law sees it. Thus, there is no need for the government to be concerned about any First Amendment problem in denying access to whatever channels of communication it seeks to employ in its capacity as speaker rather than regulator. There are commentators who have advanced the argument that the First Amendment should be construed to place some limits on government speech, at least when, because of its nature or extent, it is likely to distort the political process or the marketplace of law.

■════■

Quicknotes

COLLECTIVE BARGAINING Negotiations between an employer and employee that are mediated by a specified third party.

PUBLIC FORUM Public area so associated with freedom of speech so that restriction of access to it for that purpose is unconstitutional (e.g., sidewalks, streets, parks, etc.).

TIME, PLACE, AND MANNER RESTRICTION Refers to certain types of regulations on speech that are permissible since they only restrict the time, place, and manner in which the speech is to occur.

■════■

International Society for Krishna Consciousness, Inc. v. Lee

Religious organization (P) v. Public authority (D)

505 U.S. 672 (1992).

NATURE OF CASE: Appeal from partial reversal of award of injunction against charitable solicitation.

FACT SUMMARY: The International Society for Krishna Consciousness, Inc. (Krishna) (P) sought declaratory and injunctive relief after the Port Authority of New York and New Jersey (Port Authority) (D) adopted a regulation forbidding repetitive solicitation of money or distribution of literature within three airport terminals.

🏛 RULE OF LAW
An airport terminal operated by a public authority is not a public forum, and thus, a regulation prohibiting solicitation in the interior of an airport terminal does not violate the First Amendment.

FACTS: Because members of the International Society for Krishna Consciousness, Inc. (Krishna) (P) were distributing religious literature and soliciting funds at three airports under the control of the Port Authority of New York and New Jersey (Port Authority) (D), of which Lee (D) was the police superintendent, Port Authority (D) adopted a regulation forbidding the repetitive solicitation of money or distribution of literature within the terminals but permitted solicitation and distribution on the sidewalks outside the terminal buildings. Krishna (P) sought declaratory and injunctive relief, alleging that the regulation worked to deprive them of rights guaranteed under the First Amendment. The district court, concluding that the airport terminals were akin to public streets and thus public fora, granted Krishna's (P) motion for summary judgment. The court of appeals concluded that the terminals were not public fora and, applying a reasonableness standard, found that the ban on solicitation was reasonable but the ban on distribution was not.

ISSUE: Is an airport terminal operated by a public authority a public forum requiring allowing solicitation in the interior of an airport terminal?

HOLDING AND DECISION: (Rehnquist, C.J.) No. An airport terminal operated by a public authority is not a public forum, and thus, a regulation prohibiting solicitation in the interior of an airport terminal does not violate the First Amendment. A traditional public forum is property that has as a principal purpose the free exchange of ideas. The record shows that Port Authority (D) management considers the principal purpose of the terminals to be the facilitation of passenger air travel, not the promotion of expression. Thus, the challenged restriction need only satisfy the requirement of reasonableness. Under this standard, the prohibition on solicitation passes muster,

since solicitation may have a disruptive effect on business which may cause particularly costly delays in an airport terminal. In addition, face-to-face solicitation presents risks of duress that are an appropriate target of regulation. The justification for the rule should not be measured by the disorder that would result from granting an exemption solely to Krishna (P), for if it is given access, so too must other groups. Affirmed.

CONCURRENCE: (O'Connor, J.) The Port Authority (D) is operating a shopping mall as well as an airport. The reasonableness inquiry, therefore, is not whether the restrictions on speech are consistent with preserving the property for air travel but whether they are reasonably related to maintaining the multipurpose environment that the Port Authority (D) has deliberately created. Applying that standard, the ban on solicitation is reasonable, the ban on distribution is not.

CONCURRENCE: (Kennedy, J.) The airport corridors and shopping areas outside of the passenger security zones are public forums, and speech in those places is entitled to protection against all government regulation inconsistent with public forum principles. The Port Authority's (D) blanket prohibition on the distribution or sale of literature is invalid under the First and Fourteenth Amendments. However, the Port Authority's (D) rule disallowing in-person solicitation of money for immediate payment is a valid regulation of the time, place, and manner of protected speech in this forum or else is a valid regulation of the nonspeech element of expressive conduct.

CONCURRENCE AND DISSENT: (Souter, J.) Justice Kennedy's view of the rule that should determine what a public forum is and his conclusion that the public areas of the airports at issue here qualify as such are both correct. The Court's conclusion sustaining the total ban on solicitation of money for immediate payment is incorrect.

▌ *ANALYSIS*

A traditional public forum is a place, such as a street, park, or public monument, which historically has been so associated with expressive activities that it is generally presumed open to them. A public forum by designation is a nontraditional place or channel for expression transformed into a forum when the government intentionally opens it to expressive activities such as assembly or speech or for the discussion of certain subjects. The majority declares that airports do not have sufficient history to

Continued on next page.

qualify as traditional public fora and that the Port Authority (D) has not created a public forum by designation either.

■■■

Quicknotes

PUBLIC FORUM Public area so associated with freedom of speech so that restriction of access to it for that purpose is unconstitutional (e.g., sidewalks, streets, parks, etc.).

TIME, PLACE, AND MANNER RESTRICTION Refers to certain types of regulations on speech that are permissible since they only restrict the time, place, and manner in which the speech is to occur.

■■■

Rust v. Sullivan

Parties not identified.

500 U.S. 173 (1991).

NATURE OF CASE: Review of order dismissing challenge to federal regulation.

FACT SUMMARY: Federal regulations of the U.S. Department of Health and Human Services (HSS) prohibited clinics receiving federal funding from providing abortion counseling or referrals.

RULE OF LAW
The government may constitutionally prohibit clinics receiving federal funding from providing abortion counseling or referrals.

FACTS: Certain 1988 HSS regulations prohibited clinics receiving federal funding under Title X of the 1970 Public Health Service Act from providing counseling or referral services regarding abortions. The act provided federal funds for preventative family-planning services, but not for pregnancy or prenatal care, and expressly prohibited a Title X project from even referring a woman who asked for assistance to a clinic or doctor where she could receive information on abortion. This was challenged as a violation of free speech. The Supreme Court granted review.

ISSUE: May the government constitutionally prohibit clinics receiving federal funding from providing abortion counseling or referrals.

HOLDING AND DECISION: (Rehnquist, C.J.) Yes. The government may constitutionally prohibit clinics receiving federal funding from providing abortion counseling or referrals. The argument against the regulations appears to be that, by withholding funds from clinics promoting ideas with which it disagrees, Congress has impermissibly attempted to curb free speech. However, this is simply not so. Nothing in the First Amendment prohibits the government from making a value judgment favoring birth over abortion and allocating funds in a manner to promote childbirth. A refusal to fund is not tantamount to prohibition. The government has simply insisted that public funds be spent for the purposes for which they were authorized. The program does not provide for post-conception medical care of any kind. In the same vein, the government has not violated the free speech rights of the health care workers at affected clinics. They are free to do or say what they want at any time they are not involved with federal funding. In light of these considerations, the regulations are constitutional. Affirmed.

DISSENT: (Blackmun, J.) The court upholds a viewpoint-based suppression of speech simply because such suppression was accomplished by withholding funds. The

provisions intrude upon a wide range of communicative conduct, including the very words spoken to a woman by her physician. This clearly violates the First Amendment.

ANALYSIS

The Court's distinction between the right to be free from government interference with abortion rights and the right of the government to control funding related thereto is not new. In 1975 the Court decided *Maher v. Roe*, 432 U.S. 464 (1977). This decision held that, although the government could not prohibit abortions, it could withhold Medicare funding therefor.

Quicknotes

FIRST AMENDMENT Prohibits Congress from enacting any law respecting an establishment of religion, prohibiting the free exercise of religion, abridging freedom of speech or the press, the right of peaceful assembly and the right to petition for a redress of grievances.

VIEWPOINT DISCRIMINATION Impermissible restriction on speech by the state which discriminates on the basis of the viewpoint being espoused.

National Endowment for the Arts v. Finley

Foundation (D) v. Artists (P)

524 U.S. 569 (1998).

NATURE OF CASE: Appeal of decision finding that a statute is discriminatory and void for vagueness.

FACT SUMMARY: Congress added an amendment that required the National Endowment for the Arts (NEA) (D) to consider general standards of decency and respect for the diverse beliefs and values of the American public.

RULE OF LAW

Where a statute merely takes decency and respect into consideration, and it was aimed at reforming procedures rather than precluding speech, the legislation is not unconstitutional.

FACTS: Two provocative works of art sponsored by the National Endowment for the Arts (NEA) (D) generated formal complaints about misapplied funds and abuse of the public's trust. In response, Congress amended the bipartisan National Foundation on the Arts and Humanities Act with the Williams/Coleman Amendment. Under this amendment, which eventually became § 954(d)(1), the NEA (D) was required to judge the artistic merit of grant applications to take into consideration general standards of decency and respect for the diverse beliefs and values of the American public. Finley (P) and other artists argued that this provision violated the First Amendment.

ISSUE: Is 20 U.S.C. § 954(d)(1) unconstitutional?

HOLDING AND DECISION: (O'Connor, J.) No. Where a statute merely takes decency and respect into consideration, and it was aimed at reforming procedures rather than precluding speech, the legislation is not unconstitutional. Section 954(d)(1) does not preclude awards to projects that might be deemed "indecent" or "disrespectful," nor place conditions on grants, or even specify that those factors must be given any particular weight in reviewing an application. Given the different interpretations of the various criteria and the vague admonition to take decency and respect for diverse beliefs into consideration, this requirement seems unlikely to introduce any greater element of selectivity than other criteria, such as "artistic excellence." Section 954(d)(1) is also not unconstitutionally vague, since in the context of selective subsidies, it is not always feasible for Congress to legislate with clarity. In addition, here the government is acting as a patron rather than as a sovereign, thus the consequences of imprecision are not as constitutionally severe. Reversed and remanded.

CONCURRENCE: (Scalia, J.) The Court ignores the plain text of the Constitution that says that Congress shall make no law abridging the freedom of speech. Section 954 (d)(1) does not abridge the speech of those who disdain the beliefs and values of the American public, nor did it abridge indecent speech. These artists that want to create disrespectful and controversial art are as unconstrained now as they were before the enactment of the statute.

DISSENT: (Souter, J.) The decency and respect criteria forces viewpoint-based decisions in the disbursement of government subsidies. This sort of viewpoint discrimination by a public authority violates the First Amendment and there is no reason for exemption.

ANALYSIS

Although artists are still free to create offensive works on their own, without funding they may not be able to afford to do so. Therefore, Congress is restricting speech by pulling the purse strings. On the other hand, the NEA (D) should consider the possible popularity of proposed works since they would not want to fund a project that few people would ever appreciate.

Quicknotes

FIRST AMENDMENT Prohibits Congress from enacting any law respecting an establishment of religion, prohibiting the free exercise of religion, abridging freedom of speech or the press, the right of peaceful assembly and the right to petition for a redress of grievances.

VAGUENESS Doctrine that a statute that does not clearly or definitely inform an individual as to what conduct is unlawful is unconstitutional, in violation of the Due Process Clause.

VIEWPOINT DISCRIMINATION Impermissible restriction on speech by the state which discriminates on the basis of the viewpoint being espoused.

Madsen v. Women's Health Center, Inc.

Antiabortion protesters (D) v. Clinic (P)

512 U.S. 753 (1994).

NATURE OF CASE: Review of injunction prohibiting picketing activities.

FACT SUMMARY: A court enjoined various antiabortion protesters (D) from engaging in certain types of protest activity near an abortion clinic.

RULE OF LAW
An injunction against protest activity must be no more restrictive than is necessary to serve a significant government interest.

FACTS: Women's Health Center, Inc. (Center) (P) operated an abortion clinic in Melbourne, Florida. The clinic became the target of organized protest activity. The activity included impeding pedestrian and vehicular traffic, handing out leaflets, speech-making, and harassment of clinic employees. The Center (P) sought an injunction against the protesters (D). A trial court issued an injunction prohibiting the following: (1) coming within a 36-foot radius of clinic property; (2) interfering with patient and staff ingress and egress; (3) making excessive noise or carrying images observable to patients in the clinic; (4) coming within 300 feet of any patient; (5) coming within 300 feet of a residence of a staff member; (6) harassing a clinic patient or employee; and (7) inciting another to do a prohibited act. The injunction was affirmed in state court of appeals, but the U.S. Court of Appeals held it unconstitutional. The Supreme Court granted review.

ISSUE: Must an injunction against protest activity be no more restrictive than is necessary to serve a significant government interest?

HOLDING AND DECISION: (Rehnquist, C.J.) Yes. An injunction against protest activity must be no more restrictive than is necessary to serve a significant government interest. An injunction against protest activity does affect constitutionally protected activity, so heightened scrutiny is required. However, so long as such an injunction does not regulate the content of speech, strict scrutiny is not appropriate. The mere fact that an injunction applies only to individuals having a particular point of view does not render it content-based; any injunction will, to some extent, affect persons similarly situated. The intermediate level of scrutiny that would appear appropriate would be that the injunction be no more restrictive than is necessary to serve a significant government interest. Here, the governmental interest is allowing patients the opportunity to exercise their constitutional right to reproductive choice, a significant interest. The question then becomes whether the injunction's restrictions are necessary

to serve this interest. The 36-foot buffer zone in the public right-of-way would appear, based on the record, to be necessary to allow patients access to the clinic. Furthermore, the noise restrictions burden no more speech than necessary to protect the patients' well-being. The buffer zone as to private property, however, appears to have no impact upon patient access. The other elements of the injunction likewise either do not advance the government interest at stake here or are more restrictive than necessary. Therefore, they must be dissolved. Affirmed in part, reversed in part.

CONCURRENCE AND DISSENT: (Scalia, J.) The injunction in this case departs so far from the established course of our jurisprudence that in any context other than abortion it would be a candidate for summary reversal. Again, this Court's ill-advised foray into the abortion issue has caused a jurisprudential distortion.

CONCURRENCE AND DISSENT: (Stevens, J.) A lower standard of scrutiny should apply to an injunction than to legislation, because legislation impacts an entire community, whereas an injunction only applies to an individual or small group. A statute prohibiting demonstrations within 36 feet of an abortion clinic might be unconstitutional, whereas an injunction prohibiting the same conduct might be constitutional. Therefore, the Court should defer to the judgment of the lower court.

ANALYSIS

The usual standard of review for content-neutral regulations is that the regulation must be narrowly tailored to serve a significant government interest. Because the present case involved an injunction rather than a law or regulation, the Court felt a different standard to be necessary. The Court viewed the standard for injunctions to be somewhat more rigorous than that for statutes.

Quicknotes

CONTENT-NEUTRAL REGULATION Refers to statutes that regulate speech regardless of their content.

HEIGHTENED SCRUTINY A purposefully vague judicial description of all levels of scrutiny more exacting than minimal scrutiny.

INJUNCTION A court order requiring a person to do or prohibiting that person from doing a specific act.

STRICT SCRUTINY Method by which courts determine the

Continued on next page.

constitutionality of a law, when a law affects a fundamental right. Under the test, the legislature must have a compelling interest to enact the law and measures prescribed by the law must be the least restrictive means possible to accomplish its goal.

■══■

Cohen v. California

Draft protester (D) v. State (P)

403 U.S. 15 (1971).

NATURE OF CASE: Criminal prosecution for violation of disturbing the peace statute.

FACT SUMMARY: Cohen (D) wore a jacket with the words "Fuck the Draft" on it in a courthouse corridor and was arrested and convicted under a disturbing the peace statute.

🏛 RULE OF LAW
A state cannot bar the use of offensive words either because such words are inherently likely to cause a violent reaction or because the state wishes to eliminate such words to protect the public morality.

FACTS: Cohen (D) was arrested in a courthouse because he was wearing a jacket bearing the words, "Fuck the Draft." Cohen (D) did not engage in any act of violence or any other unlawful act. There was also no evidence that anyone who saw the jacket became violently aroused or even protested the jacket. Cohen (D) testified that he wore the jacket to inform people of his feelings against the Vietnam War and the draft. He was convicted under a statute prohibiting "maliciously and willfully disturbing the peace or quiet by offensive conduct." The state court held that "offensive conduct" meant conduct which had a tendency to provoke others to disturb the peace.

ISSUE: Can a state constitutionally prevent the use of certain words on the ground that the use of such words is offensive conduct?

HOLDING AND DECISION: (Harlan, J.) No. A state cannot constitutionally prohibit the use of offensive words. Here, Cohen (D) could not be punished for criticizing the draft, so the statute could be upheld, if at all, only as a regulation of the manner, not the substantive content, of his speech. Cohen's (D) speech does not come within any of the exceptions to the general rule that the form and content of speech cannot be regulated: (1) this is not a prohibition designed to protect courthouse decorum because the statute is not so limited; (2) this is not an obscenity case because Cohen's (D) words were not erotic; (3) this is not a case of fighting words which are punishable as inherently likely to provoke a violent reaction because here the words were not directed as a personal insult to any person; and (4) this is not a captive audience problem since a viewer could merely avert his eyes, there is no evidence of objection by those who saw the jacket, and the statute is not so limited. The state (P) tries to justify the conviction because the words are inherently likely to cause a violent reaction, but this argument cannot be upheld because these are not fighting words and there is no evidence that words that are merely offensive would cause such a response. Next the state (P) justifies the conviction on the ground that the state is guardian of the public morality. This argument is unacceptable because "offensive" is an unlimited concept and forbidding the use of such words would also cause the risk of suppressing the accompanying ideas. Therefore, there are no valid state interests which support the regulation of offensive words in public. Reversed.

▶ ANALYSIS

This case reasserts the *Chaplinsky v. New Hampshire*, 315 U.S. 568 (1942) holding that fighting words are not protected by the First Amendment. Fighting words, then, are only those words which are likely to cause an immediate breach of the peace by another person, and are not just offensive words. More importantly, this case holds that a state has no valid interest in preventing the use of offensive words when there is no competing privacy interest. Here, the public in general has no right to protection from hearing either offensive words or offensive ideas.

━■━

Quicknotes

FIGHTING WORDS Unprotected speech that inflicts injury by their very utterance and proves violence from the audience.

OBSCENITY Conduct tending to corrupt the public morals by its indecency or lewdness.

━■━

R.A.V. v. City of St. Paul

Cross burner (D) v. City (P)

505 U.S. 377 (1992).

NATURE OF CASE: Appeal from reversal of dismissal of "hate crime" prosecution.

FACT SUMMARY: When R.A.V. (D) was charged with allegedly burning a cross inside the fenced yard of a black family, the City of St. Paul (P) charged R.A.V. (D) under the Bias-Motivated Crime Ordinance.

RULE OF LAW

Where content discrimination in an ordinance is not reasonably necessary to achieve a city's compelling interests, the ordinance cannot survive First Amendment scrutiny.

FACTS: R.A.V. (D) and several other teenagers allegedly assembled a crudely made cross and burned it inside the fenced yard of a black family. This conduct could have been punished under any of a number of laws, but the City of St. Paul (P) chose to charge R.A.V. (D) under the Bias-Motivated Crime Ordinance, which made criminally punishable conduct known as "hate crimes." R.A.V. (D) moved to dismiss on the ground that the ordinance was substantially overbroad and impermissibly content-based and therefore facially invalid under the First Amendment. The trial court granted this motion, but the Minnesota Supreme Court reversed because the modifying phrase "arouses anger, alarm or resentment in others" limited the reach of the ordinance to conduct that amounted to "fighting words," and therefore the ordinance reached only expression "that the First Amendment does not protect." The court also concluded that the ordinance was not impermissibly content-based because it was a narrowly tailored means toward accomplishing the compelling governmental interest of protecting the community against bias-motivated threats to public safety and order.

ISSUE: Where content discrimination in an ordinance is not reasonably necessary to achieve a city's compelling interests, can the ordinance survive First Amendment scrutiny?

HOLDING AND DECISION: (Scalia, J.) No. Where content discrimination in an ordinance is not reasonably necessary to achieve a city's compelling interests, the ordinance cannot survive First Amendment scrutiny. Assuming that all of the expression reached by the ordinance is proscribable under the fighting words doctrine, the ordinance is nonetheless facially unconstitutional in that it prohibits otherwise permitted speech solely on the basis of the subjects the speech addresses. Some areas of speech can, consistent with the First Amendment, be regulated because of their constitutionally proscribable content,

namely, obscenity, defamation, and fighting words. Although the Minnesota Supreme Court construed the modifying phrase in the ordinance to reach only those symbols or displays that amount to fighting words, the remaining, unmodified terms make clear that the ordinance applies only to fighting words that insult, or provoke violence, on the basis of race, color, creed, religion, or gender. The First Amendment does not permit St. Paul (P) to impose special prohibitions on those speakers who express views on disfavored subjects. Burning a cross in someone's front yard is reprehensible, but St. Paul (P) has sufficient means at its disposal to prevent such behavior without adding the First Amendment to the fire. Reversed and remanded.

CONCURRENCE: (White, J.) The judgment of the Minnesota Supreme Court should be reversed. However, this case could easily be decided under First Amendment law by holding that the ordinance is fatally overbroad because it criminalizes not only unprotected expression but expression protected by the First Amendment. The Court's new "underbreadth" creation serves no desirable function.

CONCURRENCE: (Blackmun, J.) The result of the majority opinion is correct because this particular ordinance reaches beyond fighting words to speech protected by the First Amendment. However, by its decision today, the majority appears to relax the level of scrutiny applicable to content-based laws, thus weakening the traditional protections of speech.

CONCURRENCE: (Stevens, J.) The ordinance is unconstitutionally overbroad, but it is not an unconstitutional content-based regulation of speech. Content-based distinctions, far from being presumptively invalid, are an inevitable and indispensable aspect of a coherent understanding of the First Amendment. Thus, if the ordinance were not overbroad, it should be upheld.

ANALYSIS

The text of the St. Paul Bias-Motivated Crime Ordinance provides that: "Whoever places on public or private property a symbol, object, appellation, characterization or graffiti, including, but not limited to, a burning cross or Nazi swastika, which one knows or has reasonable grounds to know arouses anger, alarm or resentment in others on the basis of race, color, creed, religion or gender commits disorderly conduct and shall be guilty of a misdemeanor." The flaw in the wording of the ordinance was

Continued on next page.

that it required the person who committed the hateful act to discern the reaction of the victim to the perpetrator's conduct. It is likely that hate crime ordinances which are worded to punish conduct intended by the perpetrator to frighten, anger, etc., on the basis of race, religion, etc., would be upheld. Even if no hate crime ordinance could be upheld, the hateful conduct could still be punished under criminal trespass, arson, battery, homicide statutes, etc.

■■■

Quicknotes

CONTENT BASED Refers to statutes that regulate speech based on its content.

DEFAMATION An intentional false publication, communicated publicly in either oral or written form, subjecting a person to scorn, hatred or ridicule, or injuring him or her in relation to his or her occupation or business.

DISCRIMINATION Unequal treatment of a class of persons.

OVERBROAD Refers to a statute that proscribes lawful as well as unlawful conduct.

■■■

Wisconsin v. Mitchell

State (P) v. Batterer (D)

508 U.S. 476 (1993).

NATURE OF CASE: Appeal of sentence enhancement for conviction for aggravated battery.

FACT SUMMARY: Mitchell's (D) sentence for aggravated battery was increased because it was determined that he had selected his victim on the basis of race.

RULE OF LAW

States may provide for penalty-enhancement for bias-motivated crimes.

FACTS: A group of black men, including Mitchell (D), were discussing a scene from the movie "Mississippi Burning" in which a black boy is assaulted by a white man. Shortly thereafter, Mitchell (D) saw a white boy walking nearby and told his group that they should beat him. The group battered the boy severely. After Mitchell (D) was convicted of aggravated battery, the jury determined that Mitchell (D) had intentionally selected the boy because of his race, and the maximum sentence was increased from two years to seven years pursuant to Wisconsin (P) statute § 939.645. Mitchell (D) appealed the sentence enhancement, contending it violated the First Amendment. The Wisconsin Supreme Court overruled the penalty enhancement, holding that the statute punished offensive thought, which was unconstitutional under the First Amendment. Wisconsin (P) appealed, and the U.S. Supreme Court granted review.

ISSUE: May a state increase criminal penalties on the basis that the crime was motivated by race?

HOLDING AND DECISION: (Rehnquist, C.J.) Yes. States may provide for penalty enhancement for crimes motivated by race. Traditionally, judges have considered a wide range of factors in determining what sentence is appropriate for a convicted defendant. Motive is one of these important factors. However, a defendant's abstract beliefs may not be taken into consideration by a sentencing judge because the First Amendment protects individuals' beliefs and associations. Wisconsin's (P) sentence enhancement statute is not aimed at expressions of beliefs, but rather at conduct. A statute is only overbroad when free expression will be chilled because of the concern about enhanced sentences. The Wisconsin statute, however, is not aimed at expression, and it does not allow judges to take the defendant's abstract beliefs into account. The statute only singles out bias-inspired conduct to redress the perceived social harms of that conduct. Additionally, the chilling effect on free speech which Mitchell (D) asserts is far too speculative to support an overbreadth claim. Therefore, the Wisconsin (P) statute does not violate the First Amendment. Reversed.

ANALYSIS

The decision attempts to distinguish the decision in *R.A.V. v. St. Paul*, 505 U.S. 377 (1992), of the previous year by claiming that the St. Paul ordinance was directed at speech and the Wisconsin statute was not. In *R.A.V.*, the Court overruled the conviction of a boy who burned a cross on the lawn of a black family. St. Paul's invalidated "hate crime" ordinance is distinguishable on the following basis: it punished acts which would frighten or upset victims, rather than determining the intent of the perpetrator. The reaction of the victim is irrelevant; the intent with which the perpetrator chooses his victim is determinative. Thus, if the victim is selected on the basis of a classification prescribed by statute, the defendant can be so-charged and/or his sentence for the underlying crime, e.g., trespass or battery, can be enhanced.

Quicknotes

OVERBROAD Refers to a statute that proscribes lawful as well as unlawful conduct.

SENTENCE ENHANCEMENT The imposition of a more severe term of punishment as a result of a defendant's past criminal record or for other reasons warranting an increased sentence.

Virginia v. Black

State (P) v. Person convicted under cross burning statute (D)

538 U.S. 343 (2003).

NATURE OF CASE: Appeal from a criminal conviction.

FACT SUMMARY: When Black (D) was prosecuted and convicted under Virginia's (P) cross burning statute, he argued its unconstitutionality because of a provision treating any cross burning as prima facie evidence of intent to intimidate.

RULE OF LAW

A provision in a state's cross burning statute treating any cross burning as prima facie evidence of intent to intimidate is unconstitutional.

FACTS: Black (D) was prosecuted and convicted by a jury under Virginia's (P) cross burning statute, which bans cross burning with an intent to intimidate a person or group of persons. The statute contains a provision that any burning of a cross constitutes prima facie evidence of an intent to intimidate a person or group of persons. The Supreme Court of Virginia upheld the conviction, and Black (D) appealed to the U.S. Supreme Court on the grounds that the prima facie evidence provision was unconstitutional.

ISSUE: Is a provision in a state's cross burning statute treating any cross burning as prima facie evidence of intent to intimidate unconstitutional?

HOLDING AND DECISION: (O'Connor, J.) Yes. A provision in a state's cross burning statute treating any cross burning as prima facie evidence of intent to intimidate is unconstitutional. To this day, regardless of whether the message is a political one or whether the message is also meant to intimidate, the burning of a cross is a symbol of hate. While cross burning sometimes carries no intimidating message, at other times the intimidating message is the only message conveyed. This Court has long held that the government may regulate certain categories of expression consistent with the Constitution and that indeed intimidation in the constitutionally proscribable sense of the word is a type of true threat. The First Amendment, accordingly, permits Virginia (P) to outlaw cross burnings done with the intent to intimidate because burning a cross is a particularly virulent form of intimidation. Furthermore, instead of prohibiting all intimidating messages, Virginia (P) may choose to regulate this subset of intimidating messages in light of cross burnings long and pernicious history as a signal of impending violence. However, this particular cross burning statute is unconstitutionally overbroad due to its provision stating that any burning of a cross is prima facie evidence of an intent to intimidate a person or group of persons. The prima facie provision strips away the very reason why a state may ban cross burning with the intent to intimidate because this provision permits a jury to convict in every cross burning case in which defendants exercise their constitutional right not to put on a defense. It is apparent that the provision as so interpreted "would create an unacceptable risk of the suppression of ideas." Anger or hatred is not sufficient to ban all cross burnings in the absence of actual intimidation or threat. The First Amendment does not permit shortcuts. Affirmed. Remanded.

CONCURRENCE AND DISSENT: (Souter, J.) While agreeing that the statute makes a content-based distinction within the category of punishable intimidating or threatening expression, I disagree that any exception should save the statute from unconstitutionality. No content-based statute should survive without a high probability that no official suppression of ideas is being encouraged.

DISSENT: (Thomas, J.) The majority errs in imputing an expressive component to the activity in question. In our culture, cross burning has almost invariably meant lawlessness and understandably instills in its victims well-grounded fear of physical violence. Those who hate cannot terrorize and intimidate to make their point.

ANALYSIS

As articulated by the plurality in the *Black* decision, the prima facie evidence provision in the Virginia cross burning statute ignored all of the contextual factors which would be necessary in order for a court or jury to decide whether a particular cross burning was in fact intended to intimidate. On the other hand, some legal commentators express the viewpoint such as that conveyed in Justice Thomas's dissent, that a cross burning always and necessarily represents intimidation.

■=■

Quicknotes

FIRST AMENDMENT Prohibits Congress from enacting any law respecting an establishment of religion, prohibiting the free exercise of religion, abridging freedom of speech or the press, the right of peaceful assembly and the right to petition for a redress of grievances.

PRIMA FACIE EVIDENCE Evidence presented by a party that is sufficient, in the absence of contradictory evidence, to support the fact or issue for which it is offered.

■=■

Miami Herald Pub. Co. v. Tornillo

Publisher (D) v. Candidate (P)

418 U.S. 241 (1974).

NATURE OF CASE: "Right of reply" statute.

FACT SUMMARY: The Miami Herald Publishing Co. (D) appealed from a decision validating a statute which required newspapers to give political candidates equal space to reply to criticisms and attacks in the press.

🏛 RULE OF LAW
Newspapers cannot be compelled by statute to publish "replies" to editorial opinions with which certain persons (including the subject of the editorial) may disagree.

FACTS: The Miami Herald Publishing Co. (D) published editorials critical of Tornillo's (P) candidacy for the Florida House of Representatives. Tornillo (P) demanded that the Miami Herald Publishing Co. (D) print his verbatim replies. The Miami Herald Publishing Co. (D) declined to do this, and Tornillo (P) sued for declaratory and injunctive relief under a "right of reply" statute. The "right of reply" statute granted a political candidate a right to equal space to reply to criticism and attacks on his record by a newspaper. The circuit court found the statute unconstitutional as an infringement on the freedom of the press under the First and Fourteenth Amendments. On appeal, the Florida Supreme Court reversed, found the statute constitutional, and entered a judgment for Tornillo (P). The Miami Herald Publishing Co. (D) appealed.

ISSUE: Can newspapers be compelled by statute to publish "replies" to editorial opinions with which certain persons (including the subject of the editorial) may disagree?

HOLDING AND DECISION: (Burger, C.J.) No. Newspapers cannot be compelled by statute to publish "replies" to editorial opinions with which certain persons (including the subject of the editorial) may disagree. The statute is void on its face because it purports to regulate the content of a newspaper in violation of the First Amendment. The choice of material to go into a newspaper is an exercise of editorial control and judgment. It has yet to be demonstrated how governmental regulation of this editorial process can be exercised consistent with First Amendment guarantees of a free press. The judgment of the Supreme Court of Florida is reversed.

CONCURRENCE: (Brennan, J.) The Court's opinion does not express a view on the constitutionality of "retraction" statutes which afford plaintiffs able to prove defamatory falsehoods a statutory action to require publication of a retraction.

▶ ANALYSIS

The basic concept that the First Amendment prohibits the government from dictating to the press the contents of its news columns or the slant of its editorials was established in such landmark cases as *N.Y. Times v. Sullivan*, 376 U.S. 254 (1964) and *N.Y. Times Co. v. U.S.*, 403 U.S. 713 (1971). This statute would have resulted in self-censorship by the press in an effort to avoid printing political replies.

■══■

Quicknotes

DEFAMATION An intentional false publication, communicated publicly in either oral or written form, subjecting a person to scorn, hatred or ridicule, or injuring him or her in relation to his or her occupation or business.

FIRST AMENDMENT Prohibits Congress from enacting any law respecting an establishment of religion, prohibiting the free exercise of religion, abridging freedom of speech or the press, the right of peaceful assembly and the right to petition for a redress of grievances.

■══■

Federal Communications Commission v. League of Women Voters

Federal agency (D) v. Organization (P)

468 U.S. 364 (1984).

NATURE OF CASE: Appeal from judgment holding a ban on television editorializing unconstitutional.

FACT SUMMARY: The League of Women Voters (League) (P) contended that the Public Broadcasting Amendments Act of 1981, which prohibited public broadcasting stations from editorializing, was a violation of the First Amendment right to freedom of speech.

RULE OF LAW
Restrictions on broadcasters are constitutionally valid only if they are narrowly tailored to further a substantial interest.

FACTS: Congress enacted the Public Broadcasting Amendments, which required public broadcasters who received funding from the Corporation for Public Broadcasting to refrain from editorializing. The stated purposes of the Act were to protect such stations from being coerced into being vehicles for government propaganda, and to protect them from special interest groups. The League (P) sued, contending the statute violated freedom of speech, and the district court held it invalid. The Federal Communications Commission (D) appealed, contending the statute furthered a substantial interest. The Supreme Court granted certiorari.

ISSUE: Are broadcast restrictions valid only if they further a substantial interest?

HOLDING AND DECISION: (Brennan, J.) Yes. Restrictions on broadcasters are constitutionally valid only if they are narrowly tailored to further a substantial interest. In this case, the limitations placed on ownership of public broadcasting stations adequately protect stations from the evils sought to be eliminated by the Act. Further, the Act restricts speech based on content. Editorialization is the backbone of free speech protection. Therefore, because of the extent of the interference in relation to the lack of precision with which the scope of the statute was drafted, it was invalid. Affirmed.

DISSENT: (Rehnquist, J.) There is no viable way that government funding will not be spent to finance private editorializing on public broadcasting stations. Therefore, the statute was a valid exercise of governmental power.

DISSENT: (White, J.) Congress may condition the use of its funds on abstaining from political endorsements.

DISSENT: (Stevens, J.) Government funding necessarily chills anti-government statements and induces pro-government editorials. Therefore, the only viable way to prevent such slanted editorials is to ban all editorials.

ANALYSIS

In this case, the Court recognized and reiterated the fact that restrictions on broadcasters differ from those on other forms of media. Broadcasters are required to present opposing viewpoints while print media communicators are not. This and other regulations placed on broadcasters are to insure that the public is given adequate information in the face of finite numbers of channels available for use.

Quicknotes

FIRST AMENDMENT Prohibits Congress from enacting any law respecting an establishment of religion, prohibiting the free exercise of religion, abridging freedom of speech or the press, the right of peaceful assembly and the right to petition for a redress of grievances.

CONTENT-BASED Refers to statutes that regulate speech based on its content.

Branzburg v. Hayes

Newsmen (D) v. Government (P)

408 U.S. 665 (1972).

NATURE OF CASE: Appeal from contempt citations for failure to testify before state and federal grand juries.

FACT SUMMARY: Newsmen refused to testify before state and federal grand juries, claiming that their news sources were confidential.

RULE OF LAW
The First Amendment's freedom of press does not exempt a reporter from disclosing to a grand jury information that he has received in confidence.

FACTS: Branzburg (D), who had written articles for a newspaper about drug activities he had observed, refused to testify before a state grand jury regarding his information. Pappas (D), a television newsman, even though he wrote no story, refused to testify before a state grand jury on his experiences inside Black Panther headquarters. Caldwell (D), a reporter who had interviewed several Black Panther leaders, and written stories about the articles, refused to testify before a federal grand jury which was investigating violations of criminal statutes dealing with threats against the President and traveling interstate to incite a riot. Branzburg (D) and Pappas (D) were held in contempt.

ISSUE: Does the First Amendment protect a newsman from revealing his sources before a grand jury which has subpoenaed him to testify, even if the information is confidential?

HOLDING AND DECISION: (White, J.) No. The First Amendment does not invalidate every incidental burdening of the press that may result from the enforcement of civil or criminal statutes of general applicability. Newsmen cannot invoke a testimonial privilege not enjoyed by other citizens. The Constitution should not shield criminals who wish to remain anonymous from prosecution through disclosure. Forcing newsmen to testify will not impede the flow of news. The newsman may never be called. Many political groups will still turn to the re-porter because they are dependent on the media for exposure. Grand jury proceedings are secret and the police are experienced in protecting informants. More important, the public's interest in news flow does not override the public's interest in deterring crime. Here, the grand juries were not probing at will without relation to existing need; the information sought was necessary to the respective investigations. A grand jury is not restricted to seeking information from non-newsmen—it may choose the best method for its task. The contempt citations are affirmed.

CONCURRENCE: (Powell, J.) The newsman always has resort to the courts to quash subpoenas where his testimony bears only a remote and tenuous relationship to the subject of the investigation.

DISSENT: (Stewart, J.) The press should not be treated as an investigating tool of the government. Concrete evidence exists proving that fear of an unbridled subpoena power deters sources. The Court's inquiry should be (1) whether there is a rational connection between the government's and the deterrence of First Amendment activity, and (2) whether the effect would occur with some regularity. The government has the burden of showing (1) that the information sought is clearly relevant to a precisely defined subject of governmental inquiry; (2) it is reasonable to think the witness in question has that information; and (3) there is no other means of obtaining that information less destructive of First Amendment freedoms.

ANALYSIS

Guidelines promulgated by the Attorney General for federal officials to follow when subpoenaing members of the press to testify before grand juries or at criminal trials included the following test for information: whether there is "sufficient reason to believe that the information sought is essential to a successful investigation" and cannot be obtained from nonpress sources. However, in "emergencies and other unusual situations, subpoenas which do not conform to the guidelines may be issued."

Quicknotes

GRAND JURY A group summoned to investigate, inform, and accuse persons of crimes when sufficient evidence exists to do so.

SUBPOENA A mandate issued by court to compel a witness to appear at trial.

Zurcher v. Stanford Daily

State (D) v. Paper (P)

436 U.S. 547 (1978).

NATURE OF CASE: Appeal from affirmation of grant of declaratory relief.

FACT SUMMARY: The Stanford Daily (Stanford) (P) published pictures of an altercation between police and students, and the police, pursuant to a warrant, entered and searched Stanford's (P) offices for any photographs of the event, after which Stanford (P) filed this civil action.

🏛 RULE OF LAW
A search of a newspaper premises for evidence of a crime pursuant to a warrant issued by a neutral magistrate does not violate the newspaper's First Amendment right to freedom of speech.

FACTS: After a story appeared in the Stanford Daily (Stanford) (P) regarding a clash between demonstrators and police on campus, police sought any photographs of the event, some of which had been published by Stanford (P) with the news story. A warrant was issued by the municipal court authorizing the search of the offices of Stanford (P) and the police entered and searched the offices finding only the published photographs. Stanford (P) then filed this civil action and the district court granted certiorari.

ISSUE: Does a search of a newspaper's premises for evidence of a crime pursuant to a warrant issued by a neutral magistrate violate the newspaper's First Amendment right to freedom of speech?

HOLDING AND DECISION: (White, J.) No. The Fourth Amendment protects persons from unreasonable searches and seizures. It is required by that amendment that searches must be reasonable and that the magistrate issuing a warrant for the search must be neutral. These requirements have been held to apply with "scrupulous exactitude" to cases where the materials to be seized may be protected by the First Amendment. Stanford (P) urged that more is required in the case of newspapers because of the impairment of free speech and freedom of the press by the result of such searches in drying up confidential sources, deterring reporters from preserving their observations, and the like. However, there is no reason to believe that a neutral magistrate cannot guard against these dangers. The search of a newspaper's premises for evidence of a crime pursuant to a warrant issued by a neutral magistrate does not violate the newspaper's First Amendment right to freedom of speech. This Court declines to impose a constitutional barrier or to demand prior notice or hearing.

CONCURRENCE: (Powell, J.) There is no constitutional basis for reading a new and per se exception into the Fourth Amendment prohibiting searches in any case where a subpoena may be used instead. A magistrate must determine the reasonableness of the search in each case, and a warrant that is sufficient for the search of a home or automobile may not be sufficient for the search of a newspaper office. It is, however, for the magistrate to decide in each case.

DISSENT: (Stewart, J.) The possibility of disclosure of confidential sources of information is a serious burden on the freedom of the press by unannounced police searches of newspaper offices. This freedom must be protected in order to ensure that the press can fulfill its constitutionally designated function of informing the public. A search warrant permits police to ransack an office in search of material that a subpoena duces tecum would produce without needless exposure to unwarranted dangers.

▶ ANALYSIS

The Privacy Protection Act of 1980 has substantially undercut the effect of the *Zurcher* case. Where a person may be reasonably found to be holding materials with a purpose of disseminating the information contained therein by publication or broadcast, the material may not be seized or searched for with certain exceptions designed to prevent crime and/or protect national security.

Quicknotes

FOURTH AMENDMENT Provides that persons be secure as to their person and private belongings against unreasonable searches and seizures.

SUBPOENA DUCES TECUM A court mandate compelling the production of documents under a witness' control.

WARRANT An order issued by a court directing an officer to undertake a certain act (i.e., an arrest or search).

Nebraska Press Association v. Stuart

Publishers (P) v. State (D)

427 U.S. 539 (1976).

NATURE OF CASE: Appeal from order of prior restraint of publication.

FACT SUMMARY: After the district court ordered the Nebraska Press Association (Nebraska) (P) to refrain from publishing or broadcasting accounts of any confessions or admissions made by a criminal defendant accused of six murders, Nebraska (P) filed suit seeking to avoid the order as an unconstitutional prior restraint on the freedom of speech.

🏛 RULE OF LAW
A prior restraint of pretrial publication of accounts of a crime is violative of the First Amendment protection of free speech when used as a means of attempting to protect the criminal defendant's right to a fair trial.

FACTS: The district court handed down an order of prior restraint—or "gag order"—prohibiting the Nebraska Press Association (Nebraska) (P) from publishing or broadcasting accounts of confessions or admissions made by a criminal defendant on trial for six murders. The order was designed to protect the defendant's right to a fair trial. Nebraska (P) filed this suit seeking to resist the order on the ground that it constituted an unconstitutional prior restraint on speech protected by the First Amendment.

ISSUE: Is a prior restraint of pretrial publication of accounts of a crime violative of the First Amendment protection of free speech when used as a means of attempting to protect the criminal defendant's right to a fair trial?

HOLDING AND DECISION: (Burger, C.J.) Yes. There is no priority assigned to one constitutional amendment as opposed to another; that is to say the right of an accused is not subordinate to the right to publish in all circumstances. The approach for determining whether the order, as a means of protecting the Sixth Amendment right of the defendant to a fair trial, operated in violation of the First Amendment's protection of Nebraska's (P) freedom of speech and the press is as follows: the trial court should consider whether the gravity of the evil (here, the risk of an unfair trial), discounted by its improbability, justifies the invasion of free speech as is necessary to avoid the danger. The trial judge did not consider any alternative means of protecting the defendant, and it is probable that the order would not have protected the defendant from adverse sentiments because word of mouth in a small community can be even more dangerous than news publication. A prior restraint of pretrial publication of accounts of a crime is violative of the First Amendment protection of free speech when used as a means of attempting to protect the criminal defendant's right to a fair trial. Order vacated.

CONCURRENCE: (White, J.) I doubt whether orders such as entered in this case would ever be justified.

CONCURRENCE: (Brennan, J.) Resort to prior restraint on the press is a constitutionally impermissible method for enforcing the right to a fair trial.

▶ ANALYSIS

It is clear that there is a possibility of a case where the prior restraint of speech or publication is the only means of protecting a criminal defendant from being denied any kind of fair trial at any time or place, and that the First Amendment hurdles will be cleared. Since those hurdles are so high, however, the trend is for courts to direct restraining orders upon attorneys, police, witnesses and parties, which have thus far survived constitutional challenge.

■=■

Quicknotes

PRIOR RESTRAINT A restriction imposed on speech imposed prior to its communication.

SIXTH AMENDMENT Provides the right to a speedy trial by impartial jury, the right to be informed of the accusation, to confront witnesses, and to have the assistance of counsel in all criminal prosecutions.

■=■

Richmond Newspapers, Inc. v. Virginia

Newspapers (P) v. State (D)

448 U.S. 555 (1980).

NATURE OF CASE: Appeal of order denying news media access to courtroom to observe a trial.

FACT SUMMARY: Richmond Newspapers, Inc. (Richmond) (P) was denied access to the courtroom in which a trial was to be held of a criminal defendant who requested the closure on the ground that the media's attendance would impair his right to a fair trial.

🏛 RULE OF LAW
The public and the news media have a First Amendment right to attend criminal trials over the objection of criminal defendants that attendance will impair the fairness of the trial unless overriding threats to fairness are articulated in findings.

FACTS: A criminal defendant requested that his trial be closed to the news media so as to protect his right to a fair trial, which he alleged was threatened by their attendance. When the court ordered the closure and denied Richmond Newspapers, Inc. (Richmond) (P) access to the courtroom where the trial was to be held, Richmond (P) filed this suit seeking admission on the ground that the closure constituted a violation of Richmond's (P) First Amendment rights.

ISSUE: Have the public and the news media a First Amendment right to attend criminal trials over the objection of criminal defendants that attendance will impair the fairness of the trial absent overriding threats to fairness articulated in findings?

HOLDING AND DECISION: (Burger, C.J.) Yes. The public and the news media have an interest protected by the First Amendment in a right of access to courtrooms in order to gather information. Conversely, a criminal defendant has a right to a fair trial under the Sixth Amendment. However, that Amendment grants the defendant a public trial in furtherance of fairness, but not a private trial. While there may be cases when fairness of a trial can only be protected by a closed proceeding, there was no demonstration here that a less stringent measure would not guarantee a fair trial. There was no finding, in fact, that the closure was necessary at all. The public and the news media have a First Amendment right to attend criminal trials over the objection of criminal defendants that attendance will impair the fairness of the trial unless overriding threats to fairness are articulated in findings. Reversed.

CONCURRENCE: (Stevens, J.) Never before has this Court held that the acquisition of newsworthy information is protected by the First Amendment. Thus, an arbitrary interference with access to important information is an abridgement of the freedoms of speech and the press.

CONCURRENCE: (Blackmun, J.) It is gratifying to see the Court now looking to legal history to determine the fundamental public character of the criminal trial. It is also gratifying to see that the opinions in this case clarify the meaning and effect of the *Gannett* decision, which now appears to stand for the proposition that there is no Sixth Amendment right on the part of the public or the press to an open hearing on a motion to suppress. I continue to believe that *Gannett* is erroneous and that a right to a public trial exists in the Sixth Amendment.

▶ ANALYSIS

The presence of the media in the courtroom is becoming more and more widespread and new problems will crop up. The flaw in the closure order in this case was that there was no reason expressed why the presence of the public or the media would render the trial unfair. A judge has the power to prevent both the media and the public from turning the trial into a circus which unfairly deprives the defendant of his right to defend himself.

■■■

Quicknotes

FIRST AMENDMENT Prohibits Congress from enacting any law respecting an establishment of religion, prohibiting the free exercise of religion, abridging freedom of speech or the press, the right of peaceful assembly and the right to petition for a redress of grievances.

SIXTH AMENDMENT Provides the right to a speedy trial by impartial jury, the right to be informed of the accusation, to confront witnesses, and to have the assistance of counsel in all criminal prosecutions.

■■■

Chandler v. Florida

Police officers (D) v. State (P)

449 U.S. 560 (1981).

NATURE OF CASE: Review of criminal conviction at trial televised over objection of defense.

FACT SUMMARY: Chandler (D) and other Miami police officers were charged with conspiracy, burglary, and larceny and unsuccessfully moved to prevent electronic media coverage of the trial in which they were convicted.

🏛 RULE OF LAW
The televising of criminal trials over defense objection is not a denial of due process.

FACTS: Chandler (D) was a Miami police officer charged along with other officer-defendants with burglary, larceny, and conspiracy in the breaking into a restaurant. An amateur radio operator overheard and recorded conversations between the officers during the break-in. This attracted the attention of the electronic news media and the trial court permitted the televising of the trial. Chandler (D) objected and made several related motions, but the televising was allowed and Chandler (D) was found guilty. The conviction was affirmed on appeal, and the U.S. Supreme Court granted review.

ISSUE: Is the televising of criminal trials over defense objection a denial of due process?

HOLDING AND DECISION: (Burger, C.J.) No. An absolute ban on broadcast coverage of criminal trials cannot be justified simply because there is a danger that in some cases prejudice might result. The Florida statute permitting such broadcast places the trial judge under a positive obligation to protect the right of an accused to a fair trial. Our review in this case is restricted to whether there was a constitutional violation in this case under the Due Process Clause. No prejudice was demonstrated in this case and there was no evidence that any participant in litigation was affected by the presence of the cameras. The televising of criminal trials over defense objection is not a denial of due process. The state courts must, of course, be alert to any factors that may impair the fundamental rights of the accused. Affirmed.

▶ ANALYSIS

Rather than a hierarchy of rights establishing per se rules, due process analysis requires a balancing of the respective rights of the parties. Where one is not substantially endangered by another which provides a great benefit, the balance is easily struck. However, where the rights of the criminal defendant are weighed against those of the public to accurate dissemination of news, the process is more difficult.

Quicknotes

BURGLARY Unlawful entry of a building at night with the intent to commit a felony therein.

CONSPIRACY Concerted action by two or more persons to accomplish some unlawful purpose.

DUE PROCESS CLAUSE Clauses found in the Fifth and Fourteenth Amendments to the United States Constitution providing that no person shall be deprived of "life, liberty, or property, without due process of law."

LARCENY The illegal taking of another's property with the intent to deprive the owner thereof.

Central Hudson Gas & Electric Corp. v. Public Service Commission

Utility (P) v. Commission (D)

447 U.S. 557 (1980).

NATURE OF CASE: Review of order prohibiting utility advertising.

FACT SUMMARY: The Public Service Commission (Commission) (D) ordered Central Hudson Gas & Electric Corp. (Central) (P) to cease all advertising encouraging the use of electricity because of a national policy of conserving energy.

🏛 RULE OF LAW
An order prohibiting nonmisleading commercial speech concerning lawful activity violates the First Amendment when such order will not reasonably serve a substantial governmental interest.

FACTS: The Public Service Commission (Commission) (D) ordered Central Hudson Gas & Electric Corp. (Central) (P) to cease all advertising which might encourage the use of electricity pursuant to a national policy of conserving energy. Central (P), being a utility providing electrical and other energy, was effectively precluded from advertising. There was no showing that the complete prohibition was necessary to or likely to reduce energy consumption. Central (P) sought to avoid the order on the ground that it violated its right to free speech.

ISSUE: Does an order prohibiting nonmisleading commercial speech concerning lawful activity violate the First Amendment when such order will not reasonably serve a substantial governmental interest?

HOLDING AND DECISION: (Powell, J.) Yes. Where commercial speech is restricted in some challenged way, the constitutionality of the restriction must be analyzed as to whether the speech related to some lawful activity, whether it was misleading, and then whether the restriction serves a substantial governmental interest and reasonably advances the interest. An order prohibiting nonmisleading commercial speech concerning lawful activity violates the First Amendment when such order will not reasonably serve a substantial governmental interest. In this case the interest of reducing energy consumption is not furthered by the order in question which would forbid advertising encouraging use. A less extensive provision would better serve the goals in mind. The complete suppression of Central's (P) advertising was improper.

CONCURRENCE: (Blackmun, J.) The ban imposed here violated the First and Fourteenth Amendments. The Court's test for correctly so concluding, however, is inadequate. It is doubtful that the suppression of information concerning the availability and price of a legally offered product is ever a permissible way for a state to "dampen"

demand for the product. The Court would permit the ban if a more limited restriction would not be an effective deterrence to the consumer.

CONCURRENCE: (Stevens, J.) The Court too broadly defines commercial speech as that related solely to the economic interests of the speaker and audience. Even Shakespeare may have been motivated by the prospect of pecuniary reward. The other definition used by the Court is "speech proposing a commercial transaction." This definition should not be construed to include the entire range of communication embraced within the term "promotional advertising."

▶ ANALYSIS

Recent cases have abandoned the notion that commercial speech is not afforded First Amendment protection. It is not clear, however, what exactly is commercial speech. Some noncommercial message is included in every advertisement and some economic motive may exist for any given publication.

■■■

Quicknotes

FIRST AMENDMENT Prohibits Congress from enacting any law respecting an establishment of religion, prohibiting the free exercise of religion, abridging freedom of speech or the press, the right of peaceful assembly and the right to petition for a redress of grievances.

UTILITY A private business that provides a service to the public which is of need.

■■■

Posadas de Puerto Rico Associates v. Tourism Co. of Puerto Rico

Casino operator (P) v. Government (D)

478 U.S. 328 (1986).

NATURE OF CASE: Appeal from dismissal of First Amendment action.

FACT SUMMARY: Puerto Rico (D) enacted a statute banning casino advertising calculated to reach native Puerto Ricans.

⚖ RULE OF LAW
A statute banning the advertising of casino gambling to natives of a jurisdiction is constitutional.

FACTS: Puerto Rico (D) enacted a statute whereby advertising of gambling casinos was made illegal if calculated to reach native Puerto Ricans. Advertising to tourists was allowed. Posadas de Puerto Rico Associates (Posadas) (P), which ran a casino, was fined several times for advertising to the local population. Posadas (P) brought suit against Puerto Rico (D), claiming that the statute unconstitutionally abridged protected speech. The trial court found the statute valid, and the Puerto Rican Supreme Court refused to hear an appeal. The U.S. Supreme Court granted certiorari.

ISSUE: Is a statute banning the advertising of gambling casinos to natives of a jurisdiction constitutional?

HOLDING AND DECISION: (Rehnquist, J.) Yes. A statute banning the advertising of casino gambling to natives of a jurisdiction is constitutional. Purely commercial speech such as involved here enjoys a limited First Amendment freedom. If the activity involved is legal and not misleading, commercial speech may not be restricted unless the government's interests are substantial, the restrictions advance the government's interest, and the restrictions are no more extensive than necessary. Here, Puerto Rico (D) does have a substantial interest, that being to minimize the vices gambling can induce in the native population. The regulation here obviously does advance the intended end, as the purpose of the advertising would be to attract gambling patrons. Finally, since the ban on advertising only goes as far as local dissemination of information, the statute goes no farther than necessary. Affirmed.

DISSENT: (Brennan, J.) Commercial speech should be afforded the same constitutional protection as other forms of speech.

DISSENT: (Stevens, J.) The ban at issue discriminates against speech based on type of publication and intended audience, which should not be permitted.

▶ ANALYSIS

Part of the Court's analysis was that since casino gambling could be banned outright, partial restrictions upon it were permissible. This part of the decision did not appear central to the Court's analysis, but it could have wide ramifications. As most commercial activities could theoretically be banned by a state, the rule announced here could be applied to most commercial activity advertising.

■==■

Quicknotes

COMMERCIAL SPEECH Any speech that proposes a commercial transaction, or promotes products or services.

FIRST AMENDMENT Prohibits Congress from enacting any law respecting an establishment of religion, prohibiting the free exercise of religion, abridging freedom of speech or the press, the right of peaceful assembly and the right to petition for a redress of grievances.

■==■

Florida Bar v. Went For It, Inc.

State bar association (D) v. Referral service (P)

515 U.S. 618 (1995).

NATURE OF CASE: Review of order striking down state bar rule circumscribing attorney solicitation.

FACT SUMMARY: The Florida Bar (D) adopted a rule prohibiting attorney solicitation mailings to accident victims for the first 30 days following a victim's accident.

RULE OF LAW
States may prohibit attorneys from targeting recent accident victims for solicitation.

FACTS: The Florida Bar (D) adopted Rule 4–7.4(b)(1), which prohibited attorneys or their representatives from using the mails to solicit accident victims as clients for thirty days following a victim's accident. Went For It, Inc. (P), an attorney-owned referral service, challenged the rule as a violation of the First Amendment. The Eleventh Circuit struck down the rule.

ISSUE: May states prohibit attorneys from targeting recent accident victims for solicitation?

HOLDING AND DECISION: (O'Connor, J.) Yes. States may prohibit attorneys from targeting recent accident victims for solicitation. Truthful advertizing may be regulated if the government satisfies a three-pronged test: (1) a substantial interest must be advanced; (2) the restriction materially advances that interest; and (3) the regulation must be narrowly drawn. Here, the interest cited is the protection of recent accident or disaster victims, who may be emotionally unable to make informed decisions regarding solicitations. This is a substantial interest. With respect to the second factor, the Florida Bar (D) relied on a lengthy, thorough study demonstrating that the Florida public views direct-mail solicitations as violative of victims' privacy and a negative reflection upon the Bar and law in general. This satisfies the second prong. Finally, the rule is narrowly drawn. It only prohibits mailings for the first month, when victims are likely to be most unable to make informed decisions. For these reasons, the rule is constitutional. Reversed.

DISSENT: (Kennedy, J.) The rule at issue could result in claimants losing valuable investigative opportunities due to nonrepresentation.

ANALYSIS

State bars traditionally have looked askance at advertising by lawyers. Prior to 1977, most, if not all, states prohibited it entirely. In 1977, the Supreme Court held in *Bates v. State Bar of Arizona*, 433 U.S. 350 (1977), that attorney advertising had a First Amendment component.

New York Times Co. v. Sullivan

Publisher (D) v. Public official (P)

376 U.S. 254 (1964).

NATURE OF CASE: Appeal from an award of damages for defamation.

FACT SUMMARY: Sullivan (P) brought this action for defamation against the New York Times (Times) (D), alleging that the paper had published an advertisement in which false and defamatory statements were made about him.

> ## 🏛 RULE OF LAW
> A public official is prohibited from recovering damages for a defamatory falsehood relating to his official conduct unless he proves that the statement was made with actual malice.

FACTS: A full-page advertisement published by the New York Times (Times) (D) recited a number of grievances and protested claimed abuses on the part of the Alabama authorities, including police of the City of Montgomery, in suppressing the rights of Negroes. Sullivan (P), who was one of the elected Commissioners of Montgomery and whose duties included supervision of the Police Department, brought this civil libel proceeding against the Times (D). The falsity of some of the statements was uncontroverted. Ruling as a matter of law that the statements in question were libelous per se, the trial court judge instructed the jury that the Times (D) could be held liable if the jury found that they had published the advertisement and that the statements were about Sullivan (P). The court found that malice is to be presumed under these circumstances. The Alabama Supreme Court affirmed a judgment for Sullivan (P) in the amount of $500,000. The New York Times (D) appealed. Affirmed in part, reversed in part, and remanded.

ISSUE: Is a public official prohibited from recovering damages for a defamatory falsehood relating to his official conduct unless he proves that the statement was made with actual malice?

HOLDING AND DECISION: (Brennan, J.) Yes. The constitutional guarantees of the First and Fourteenth Amendments require a federal rule that prohibits a public official from recovering damages for a defamatory falsehood relating to his official conduct unless he proves that the statement was made with actual malice, that is, with knowledge that it was false or with reckless disregard of whether it was false or not. Such a privilege for criticism of official conduct is appropriately analogous to the protection accorded a public official when he is sued for libel by a private citizen. It would give public servants an unjustified preference over the public they serve, if critics of official conduct did not have a fair equivalent of the immunity granted to the officials themselves. First Amendment protections do not turn upon the truth, popularity, or social utility of ideas and beliefs which are involved. Rather, they are based upon the theory that erroneous statements are inevitable in free debate and must be protected if such freedom is to survive. Only where malice is involved do such protections cease. While Alabama law apparently requires proof of actual malice for an award of punitive damages, where general damages are concerned malice is presumed. Such a presumption is inconsistent with the federal rule. Reversed.

▶ ANALYSIS

Mr. Justice Black wrote a concurring opinion joined by Justices Douglas and Goldberg. In their view the majority opinion did not go far enough since it recognized that a public official could recover damages for a defamatory falsehood related to his official conduct if he proved that the statement was made with actual malice. In their opinion the Constitution accords persons an unconditional freedom to criticize official conduct. Nonetheless, there is no doubt that this case effectuated a significant change in the country's defamation law. It constitutionalized the applicable standard in cases where public officials are defamed and in doing so worked a radical change in the tort law of most jurisdictions.

■=■

Quicknotes

ACTUAL MALICE The issuance of a publication with knowledge of its falsity or with reckless disregard as to its truth.

DEFAMATORY Subjecting to hatred, ridicule or injuring one in his occupation or business.

LIBEL A false or malicious publication subjecting a person to scorn, hatred or ridicule, or injuring him or her in relation to his or her occupation or business.

PUBLIC FIGURE Any person who is generally known in the community.

PUNITIVE DAMAGES Damages exceeding the actual injury suffered for the purposes of punishment, deterrence and comfort to plaintiff.

■=■

Gertz v. Robert Welch, Inc.

Attorney (P) v. Publisher (D)

418 U.S. 323 (1974).

NATURE OF CASE: Action for defamation.

FACT SUMMARY: Gertz (P) sued Robert Welch, Inc. (D), a publisher of a John Birch Society newsletter, when Welch (D) published an article calling Gertz (P) a long-time Communist who helped frame a Chicago policeman's conviction for murder, all of which was untrue.

🏛 RULE OF LAW
In an action for defamation, a private individual must show the publisher to be at fault and may recover no more than actual damages when liability is not based on a showing of knowledge of falsity or reckless disregard for the truth.

FACTS: Robert Welch, Inc. (D) published The American Opinion, a monthly newsletter of the John Birch Society. An article appeared in that publication purporting to illustrate that the conviction of Nuccio, a Chicago policeman, for the murder of Nelson, a young man, was a Communist frameup led by Gertz (P). It was said further that Gertz (P) had a criminal record, was an official of the Marxist League, a Lenninist, and an officer of the National Lawyers Guild, which was falsely proscribed as a communist organization in the forefront of the attack on Chicago police during the 1968 Democratic Convention. The only element of truth was that 15 years earlier Gertz (P) had been a National Lawyers Guild officer. Actually, he was a reputable lawyer whose only connection with the Nuccio case was to represent the Nelson family in civil litigation against Nuccio. Gertz (P) attended the coroner's inquest into Nelson's death and filed an action for damages, but did not discuss the matter with the press or play any part in the criminal proceedings. At trial, the evidence showed that American Opinion's managing editor knew nothing of the defamatory content, but had relied on the reputation and accuracy of the author. The jury found the matter libelous per se and not privileged, and awarded a $50,000 judgment, but the judge applied the New York Times standard as pertaining to any discussion of a public issue without regard to the status of the person defamed. Judgment n.o.v. was entered for Robert Welch, Inc. (D). The court of appeals affirmed, and Gertz (P) appealed.

ISSUE: In an action for defamation, must a private individual show the publisher to be at fault and recover no more than actual damages when liability is not based on a showing of knowledge of falsity or reckless disregard for the truth?

HOLDING AND DECISION: (Powell, J.) Yes. In an action for defamation, a private individual must show the publisher to be at fault and may recover no more than actual damages when liability is not based on a showing of knowledge of falsity or reckless disregard for the truth. The *New York Times* [*New York Times Co. v. Sullivan*, 376 U.S. 254 (1964)] standard applies to public figures and public officials, but the state interest in compensating injury to reputation of private individuals requires that a different rule should apply to them. A public figure or official has greater access to the media to counteract false statements than private individuals normally enjoy. Being more vulnerable to injury, the private individual deserves greater protection and recovery. As long as the states do not impose liability without fault, the states themselves may define the appropriate standard of liability for a publisher of defamatory matter injurious to a private person. And the states may not permit the recovery of presumed or punitive damages, at least when liability is not based on a showing of knowledge of falsity or reckless disregard for the truth. Juries' largely uncontrolled discretion to award damages beyond the suffered loss inhibits the exercise of free speech. Also, the doctrine of presumed damages invites juries to punish unpopular opinion rather than compensate an injured party. The states have no interest in compensating petitioners with awards far in excess of actual injury. Here, Gertz (P) was not publicly involved. The public figure question should look to the nature and extent of an individual's participation in the controversy giving rise to the action. Reversed and remanded for new trial as the jury was allowed to impose liability without fault and presume damages without proof of damages.

▶ ANALYSIS

The majority advances the view that it is necessary to restrict victims of defamation who do not prove knowledge of falsity or reckless disregard for the truth to compensation for actual injury only. Actual injury is not limited to out-of-pocket loss. Actual harm includes impairment of reputation and standing in the community, personal humiliation, and mental anguish and suffering. While the court discusses that juries in the past were tempted to award excess damages, there was no proof that trial judges have failed to keep judgments within reasonable bounds.

■=■

Quicknotes

ACTUAL DAMAGES Measure of damages necessary to compensate victim for actual injuries suffered.

Continued on next page.

DEFAMATION An intentional false publication, communicated publicly in either oral or written form, subjecting a person to scorn, hatred or ridicule, or injuring him or her in relation to his or her occupation or business.

LIBEL PER SE A false or malicious publication that subjects a person to scorn, hatred or ridicule, or that injures him in relation to his occupation or business of such an extreme nature that the law will presume that the person has suffered such injury.

PUBLIC FIGURE Any person who is generally known in the community.

Dun & Bradstreet, Inc. v. Greenmoss Builders, Inc.

Publisher (D) v. Building company (P)

472 U.S. 749 (1985).

NATURE OF CASE: Appeal from an award of damages for defamation.

FACT SUMMARY: Dun and Bradstreet, Inc. (Dun) (D) contended Greenmoss Builders, Inc. (Greenmoss) (P) could not recover punitive damages for defamation even though the subject was not one of public concern.

🏛 RULE OF LAW
In defamation cases involving subjects that do not involve public concern, no actual malice need be shown to support an award of punitive damages.

FACTS: Dun and Bradstreet, Inc. (Dun) (D) circulated a false and defamatory credit report on Greenmoss Builders, Inc. (Greenmoss) (P) which injured the latter in its business relations. The report had been prepared negligently, and no action had been taken to verify the contents. Greenmoss (P) sued and received an award for compensatory and punitive damages. Dun (D) appealed, contending that even though the subject of the defamation was not one of public concern, the constitutional limits on recoverable damages based on a showing of actual malice applied to deny recovery. The Supreme Court granted certiorari.

ISSUE: Must actual malice be shown in cases where the defamatory statements do not involve a subject of public concern?

HOLDING AND DECISION: (Powell, J.) No. In defamation cases involving subjects that are not of public concern, actual malice need not be shown to support a recovery of damages. The requirement of actual malice relates to constitutional guarantees of free press. Public figures or events of public concern generate enough media exposure to allow both parties an opportunity to present their views publicly. However where a private entity is defamed in a matter which is not of concern to the general public, this opportunity to rebut the defamation does not exist. As a result, a less stringent standard must apply to allow recovery in this case. Affirmed.

CONCURRENCE: (Burger, C.J.) This holding should extend to matters of public concern as well.

CONCURRENCE: (White, J.) Common law remedies should be retained for private plaintiffs suing in defamation.

DISSENT: (Brennan, J.) Actual malice must be shown in this area of quasi-public speech.

▶ ANALYSIS

This case represents a refusal of the Court, in the plurality, to extend its holding in *New York Times v. Sullivan*, 376 U.S. 254 (1964), and *Gertz v. Robert Welch, Inc.*, 418 U.S. 323 (1974). In those cases the Court developed rules whereby public figures and issues of public concern were given constitutional requirements for recovery in defamation. More than mere negligence was required to be shown. Actual malice or a reckless disregard for the truth was made an element of the cause of action.

Quicknotes

ACTUAL MALICE The issuance of a publication with knowledge of its falsity or with reckless disregard as to its truth.

DEFAMATION An intentional false publication, communicated publicly in either oral or written form, subjecting a person to scorn, hatred or ridicule, or injuring him or her in relation to his or her occupation or business.

NEGLIGENCE Conduct falling below the standard of care that a reasonable person would demonstrate under similar conditions.

PUBLIC FIGURE Any person who is generally known in the community.

PUNITIVE DAMAGES Damages exceeding the actual injury suffered for the purposes of punishment, deterrence and comfort to plaintiff.

Cox Broadcasting Corp. v. Cohn

Broadcasting company (D) v. Father (P)

420 U.S. 469 (1975).

NATURE OF CASE: Appeal from conviction for invasion of privacy.

FACT SUMMARY: Cohn (P) sued the Cox Broadcasting Corp. (D) for invading his privacy by identifying his daughter as a rape victim.

⚖ RULE OF LAW
The First and Fourteenth Amendments prevent state sanctions for publication of truthful information contained in official court records that are open to public inspection.

FACTS: Cohn's (P) daughter was a murder and rape victim. The Georgia code prohibits the publication of the name or identity of a rape victim. At the trial a reporter for the Cox Broadcasting Corp. (D) obtained Cohn's (P) daughter's name by examining public records. The girl's name was broadcast during a news report concerning the crime and the trial. Cohn (P) sued the Cox Broadcasting Corp. (D) for violating the Georgia code which protects the privacy of rape victims. The trial court granted a judgment for Cohn (P). The Georgia Supreme Court affirmed for Cohn (P). The Cox Broadcasting Corp. (D) appealed.

ISSUE: May a state impose sanctions upon the publication of truthful information contained in official court records open to public inspection?

HOLDING AND DECISION: (White, J.) No. The First and Fourteenth Amendments prevent state sanctions for publication of truthful information contained in official court records open to public inspection. The right to privacy is not invaded by any publication made in a court of justice, and reports of any such proceedings which are open to public inspection may be published without invading a person's right to privacy. If there are privacy interests to be protected in judicial proceedings, the states must respond by means that avoid public documentation or other exposure of private information. Here the defendant simply published truthful information contained in official court records that were open to public inspection, it did not invade the plaintiff's privacy. Judgment is entered for Cox Broadcasting Corp. (D). Reversed.

▶ ANALYSIS

By declaring that persons have no reasonable expectation of privacy in information contained in public records, the Court in *Cox* materially constricted the constitutional right to privacy. Note that this rule runs contrary to the well established defamation rule that the scope of publication of any statement may increase liability. Note also that this rule runs the risk of motivating and justifying (especially on the facts of *Cox*) government secrecy "gag orders" etc. under the subterfuge of protecting citizens from press embarrassment. Note also that *Cox* appears, at least theoretically, to threaten the privacy cause of action based on unauthorized disclosure of privileged information—since disclosure here, though not subject to privilege, was illegal.

▪━▪

Quicknotes

GAG ORDER Court order mandating that the parties or reporters not discuss or publicize the case so that the defendant may receive a fair trial.

INVASION OF PRIVACY The violation of an individual's right to be protected against unwarranted interference in his personal affairs, falling into one of four categories: (1) appropriating the individual's likeness or name for commercial benefit; (2) intrusion into the individual's seclusion; (3) public disclosure of private facts regarding the individual; and (4) disclosure of facts placing the individual in a false light.

▪━▪

Zacchini v. Scripps-Howard Broadcasting Co.

Entertainer (P) v. Broadcaster (D)

433 U.S. 562 (1977).

NATURE OF CASE: Appeal from denial of damages for invasion of right of publicity.

FACT SUMMARY: Scripps-Howard Broadcasting Co. (D) filmed and broadcast the entire performance of Zacchini (P), a "human cannonball," without Zacchini's (P) consent.

🏛 RULE OF LAW

The First and Fourteenth Amendments do not require a state to extend to the press the privilege of broadcasting a performer's entire act without his consent.

FACTS: Zacchini (P), an entertainer, performed a "human cannonball" act in which he was shot from a cannon into a distant net. He performed this act regularly at a county fair in Ohio, during August and September 1972. On August 30, a reporter for Scripps-Howard Broadcasting Co. (D) attended the fair, but did not film the spectacle, as Zacchini (P) had asked him not to do so. Following instructions from the producer of the station's daily newscast, the reporter returned the next day and filmed Zacchini's (P) entire act. This film was broadcast in its entirety by Scripps-Howard Broadcasting Co. (D), and Zacchini (P) sued for damages. The trial court granted Scripps-Howard Broadcasting Co. (D) summary judgment, but the court of appeals reversed. The Ohio Supreme Court found that though Zacchini (P) had a right of publicity, the press must be given wide latitude as to how much of each story it presents, and thus Scripps-Howard Broadcasting Co. (D) was constitutionally free to broadcast Zacchini's (P) entire act. This appeal followed.

ISSUE: Does the constitution require a state to extend to the media the privilege of broadcasting a performer's entire act without his consent?

HOLDING AND DECISION: (White, J.) No. The Ohio Supreme Court relied heavily on *Time, Inc. v. Hill,* 385 U.S. 374 (1967), to reach its conclusion. But in *Time, Inc. v. Hill,* where the conduct of a private individual and his family was falsely described, the issue was one of privacy law. This stands in contrast to the interest protected by a right of publicity. In the latter case, it is the individual's commercial interest in his performance which is protected, in order to encourage his continued efforts to produce something of interest to the public. This is clearly akin to the considerations underlying patent and copyright laws; thus, the Constitution does not prevent a state from similarly requiring that a performer be compensated for the use of his material. In other words, the First and Four- teenth Amendments do not require a state to extend to the press the privilege of broadcasting a performer's entire act without his consent. Here, then, although Ohio may as a matter of its own law extend such a privilege to Scripps-Howard Broadcasting Co. (D) and other broadcasters, it is under no constitutional obligation to do so. Reversed.

DISSENT: (Powell, J.) If a station's routine news report may give rise to substantial liability, the result may be media self-censorship. The First Amendment should protect the station from a right of publicity action, as long as the film is used as a routine portion of a regular newscast and not as an instrument for private or commercial gain.

▶ ANALYSIS

Zacchini illustrates that interests in property and livelihood rest on a powerful constitutional base. But the more important point is the possibility of special constitutional protection for the press. In *First National Bank of Boston v. Bellotti,* 435 U.S. 765 (1978), Chief Justice Burger noted that the Court has not decided whether the First Amendment press clause confers upon the press any freedom from governmental regulation not accorded to others. Instead, most press claims have been analyzed in terms of the speech clause and the general principles of freedom of expression. As a result, the Court has frequently supported such claims to the extent that they reach no further than claims that could be made by the general public.

■=■

Quicknotes

FIRST AMENDMENT Prohibits Congress from enacting any law respecting an establishment of religion, prohibiting the free exercise of religion, abridging freedom of speech or the press, the right of peaceful assembly and the right to petition for a redress of grievances.

RIGHT OF PUBLICITY The right of a person to control the commercial exploitation of his name or likeness.

■=■

National Association for the Advancement of Colored People v. Alabama ex rel. Patterson

Organization (D) v. State (P)

357 U.S. 449 (1958).

NATURE OF CASE: Appeal from civil contempt conviction.

FACT SUMMARY: The National Association for the Advancement of Colored People (NAACP) (D) refused to comply with a court order requiring it to produce its membership lists.

🏛 RULE OF LAW
Where immunity from state inspection of membership lists is closely related to the members' right to pursue their lawful private interests, and where the state offers no controlling justification for the disclosure, the Fourteenth Amendment will grant immunity from inspection.

FACTS: In the course of an injunction proceeding brought in 1956 to halt the National Association for the Advancement of Colored People (NAACP) (D) activities in Alabama (P), on the ground that it had failed to comply with the requirement that foreign corporations qualify before doing business in the state, Alabama (P) moved for the production of the names and addresses of all the NAACP's (D) Alabama members and agents. The NAACP (D) failed to comply with a court order on the ground that it could not be constitutionally compelled to disclose its membership lists, and the trial court adjudged the NAACP (D) in contempt and fined it $100,000. The petition for certiorari from the Supreme Court of Alabama, which affirmed, was granted.

ISSUE: Can a state, consistently with the Due Process Clause of the Fourteenth Amendment, compel an association to reveal its membership lists where immunity from such disclosure is closely related to the members' right to pursue their lawful private interests, and the state offers no controlling justification for the disclosure?

HOLDING AND DECISION: (Harlan, J.) No. It may first be noted that an association has sufficient nexus with its members to allow it standing to assert the constitutional right of those members to be safe from compelled disclosure of their affiliation with the association. As to whether such a constitutional right exists, it is beyond question that the freedom to associate in order to advance beliefs is part of the "liberty" assured by the Fourteenth Amendment Due Process Clause, which embraces freedom of speech. Abridgement of this right to associate may result from various governmental actions, and one such action is compelled disclosure of affiliation. Disclosure may cause economic reprisal, physical coercion, and other hostilities,

forcing a choice between membership in the association and acceptance of such consequences. It is not determinative that these consequences would follow from private actions and not state action, since it is only after the exertion of state authority to compel disclosure that the private action would occur. Therefore, unless the state can demonstrate a sufficiently strong interest in the disclosure to justify the undesirable effects it may have the constitutional right of association must be protected; the Fourteenth Amendment will grant immunity from state inspection of membership lists where such immunity is closely related to the members' right to pursue lawful private interests, whether they are pursued privately or in association with others. Here, Alabama (P) does not show a controlling justification for the deterrent effects that disclosure is likely to generate; thus, the NAACP (D) may not be compelled to disclose its lists. Reversed.

▶ ANALYSIS

NAACP v. Alabama ex rel. Patterson and a related case, *Bates v. Little Rock*, 361 U.S. 516 (1960) (where the city sought similar disclosure as an adjunct to its taxing power), can be considered cases where the government's interest was less important than the abridgement of association rights that was likely to occur through disclosure, or they may be viewed as cases where the means utilized bore insufficient relationship to the purported state interest. In *Barenblatt v. U.S.*, 360 U.S. 109 (1959), on the other hand, the Court upheld the congressional committee's power to compel a witness to discuss his association with the Communist Party, as there is a close nexus between the Party and the violent overthrow of government. The Court found that any investigation of the preparation for overthrow included the right to identify a witness as a Party member and to question him about the Party.

■➡■

Quicknotes

CIVIL CONTEMPT CITATION One party's failure to comply with a court order requiring that party to undertake an action for the benefit of another party to the action.

DUE PROCESS CLAUSE Clauses found in the Fifth and Fourteenth Amendments to the United States Constitution providing that no person shall be deprived of "life, liberty, or property, without due process of law."

FOURTEENTH AMENDMENT Declares that no state shall

Continued on next page.

make or enforce any law which shall abridge the privileges and immunities of citizens of the United States.

RIGHT TO ASSOCIATE The right of individuals to peacefully assemble pursuant to the First Amendment to the United States Constitution.

■═■

Cole v. Richardson

State (D) v. Employee (P)

405 U.S. 676 (1972).

NATURE OF CASE: Appeal from a judgment that a loyalty oath was unconstitutional.

FACT SUMMARY: Richardson's (P) employment at a Massachusetts state hospital was terminated when she refused to take a loyalty oath by which the affiant would swear to uphold and defend the state and federal constitutions and to oppose the overthrow of the state or federal governments by unconstitutional means.

RULE OF LAW

Since there is no constitutionally protected right to overthrow a government by force, violence, or illegal or unconstitutional means, no constitutional right is infringed by an oath to abide by the constitutional system in the future.

FACTS: Richardson (P) refused to take the following loyalty oath: "I do solemnly swear (or affirm) that I will uphold and defend the Constitution of the United States of America and the Constitution of the Commonwealth of Massachusetts and that I will oppose the overthrow of the government of the United States of America or of this commonwealth by force, violence, or by any illegal or unconstitutional method." As a result of her refusal, Richardson's (P) employment at a Massachusetts state hospital was terminated. A three-judge federal district court sustained the "uphold and defend" clause, but found the "oppose" clause fatally vague and unspecific. Cole (D), for the commonwealth, appealed.

ISSUE: Is any constitutional right infringed by an oath to abide by the constitutional system in the future?

HOLDING AND DECISION: (Burger, C.J.) No. Since there is no constitutionally protected right to overthrow a government by force, violence, or illegal or unconstitutional means, no constitutional right is infringed by an oath to abide by the constitutional system in the future. The "oppose" clause does not expand the obligation of the "uphold and defend" clause; "it simply makes clear the application of the first clause to a particular issue." Neither is the oath void for vagueness. It is punishable only by perjury prosecution. As perjury requires intent, punishment without fair warning cannot occur. Reversed and remanded.

DISSENT: (Marshall, J.) The oath is vague in that the affiant does not know whether he swears to oppose overthrow by every means available or whether he merely accepts the responsibility of opposing illegal or unconstitutional overthrows.

▌*ANALYSIS*

Mr. C.J. Burger has positioned himself in favor of a narrowing of the overbreadth doctrine. The Court generally has assumed that a statute should be regarded in the same light as its most vague clause, without regard to any of its other language. He would rather see the words be given their common meaning and be considered as closely as possible in context. This view has not yet been taken by a majority.

Quicknotes

OVERBREADTH That quality or characteristic of a statute, regulation, or order which reaches beyond the problem it was meant to solve causing it to sweep within it activity it cannot legitimately reach.

PERJURY The making of false statements under oath.

VAGUENESS Doctrine that a statute that does not clearly or definitely inform an individual as to what conduct is unlawful is unconstitutional, in violation of the Due Process Clause.

Branti v. Finkel

Employer (D) v. Employees (P)

445 U.S. 507 (1980).

NATURE OF CASE: Action to determine the constitutionality of employment termination.

FACT SUMMARY: Finkel (P) and Tabakman (P), both Republicans and assistants to the county public defender, had their employment terminated when the new public defender, a Democrat named Branti (D), took office.

RULE OF LAW
Unless the government can show an overriding interest of vital importance demanding that an employee's beliefs coincide with those of the hiring authority, it cannot discharge an employee solely on the basis of his private beliefs.

FACTS: In Rockland County, the county legislature appoints the public defender, who in turn appoints nine assistants to serve him. In 1972, the county legislature appointed a Republican, Branti's (D) predecessor. By 1977, the Republican-dominated legislature had become Democrat-dominated, and Branti (D), a Democrat, was appointed to replace the incumbent. When Branti (D) took office, he discharged all or nearly all the Republican assistant public defenders, including Finkel (P) and Tabakman (P). The district court found that Finkel (P) and Tabakman (P) had their employment terminated solely because they were Republicans and therefore lacked the necessary Democratic sponsors. The court of appeals affirmed the entry of an injunction against the termination of the employment, and Branti (D) appealed.

ISSUE: Does the Constitution allow the discharge of an employee solely on the basis of his private beliefs, if the government cannot show an overriding interest of vital importance demanding that the employee's beliefs coincide with those of the hiring authority?

HOLDING AND DECISION: (Stevens, J.) No. In *Perry v. Sindermann*, 408 U.S. 593 (1972), the Court held that even if an employee has no contractual right to a government benefit, such as continued employment, and even if the government can deny him the benefit for any of several reasons, there are some reasons the government may not rely upon. The government cannot dismiss the employee for engaging in constitutionally protected speech or associations and thus constitute impermissible interference with constitutional rights. This First Amendment protection extends to discharge based on the employee's beliefs. Therefore, unless the government can show an overriding interest of vital importance, demanding that an employee's beliefs coincide with those of the hiring authority, the government cannot discharge him solely on the basis of his private beliefs. This rule was applied by the Court in *Elrod v. Burns*, 427 U.S. 397 (1976), where the discharge of noncivil service employees, based on their failure to support the Democratic party, was a violation of their constitutional rights. In *Elrod*, the Court recognized that party affiliation may be an acceptable requirement for some types of government employment; here, though, Branti (D) has failed to show that the job of assistant public defender falls into this category. An assistant public defender's primary task is to represent individual clients and not partisan political interests. Further, the information he obtains due to his position has no bearing on party concerns. Affirmed.

DISSENT: (Powell, J.) The Court largely ignores the fact that the benefits of political patronage serve substantial government interests and justify the selection of assistant public defenders on the basis of political beliefs. Regarding future cases, the standard framed by the Court is so vague that it is sure to create great uncertainty when applied to the selection and removal of key government personnel.

DISSENT: (Stewart, J.) Elrod v. Burns does not control here because that case concerned "nonconfidential" employees. Here, the relationship between the public defender and his assistants requires mutual trust and confidence.

ANALYSIS

Branti v. Finkel illustrates that the right to freely associate is important, but neither that right nor the right to participate in political activities is absolute. The Court has upheld the government's power to prohibit its employees from engaging in certain activities. Significantly, such prohibitions apply equally to all parties. They were adjudged to be necessary to the fair and efficient operation of government.

Quicknotes

CONTRACTUAL RIGHT A right or expectation that is created pursuant to a contract.

FIRST AMENDMENT Prohibits Congress from enacting any law respecting an establishment of religion, prohibiting the free exercise of religion, abridging freedom of speech or the press, the right of peaceful assembly and the right to petition for a redress of grievances.

Roberts v. United States Jaycees

State (D) v. Private organization (P)

468 U.S. 609 (1984).

NATURE OF CASE: Appeal from judgment requiring a professional organization to admit women as members.

FACT SUMMARY: The court of appeals held that the Minnesota Human Rights Act violated the United States Jaycees' (P) rights to free association guaranteed by the First and Fourteenth Amendments by requiring them to allow women to become members.

🏛 RULE OF LAW

The right to associate for expressive purposes may be limited by regulations adopted to serve compelling state interests, unrelated to the suppression of ideas, that cannot be achieved through means significantly less restrictive of associational freedoms.

FACTS: The United States Jaycees (P) sued for a declaratory judgment, contending the Minnesota Human Rights Act violated its right to freely associate by requiring it to allow women to become members. The Jaycees (P) contended their right to associate with whom they chose was protected expressive conduct under the First Amendment. The State (D) defended, contending the statute served the compelling state interest in ending sexual discrimination. The district court denied declaratory relief, upholding the constitutionality of the statute. The court of appeals reversed, and the State (D) appealed.

ISSUE: May the right to freely associate be limited by restrictions serving compelling state interests?

HOLDING AND DECISION: (Brennan, J.) Yes. The right to associate for expressive purposes may be limited by regulations adopted to serve compelling state interests, unrelated to the suppression of ideas, that cannot be achieved through means significantly less restrictive of associational freedoms. The restriction here does not regulate speech. It directly promotes the state's compelling interest in prohibiting and correcting injustices based on sexual discrimination. Further, no less restrictive means of achieving this end was shown to exist by the Jaycees (P). As a result, the statute was constitutional. Reversed.

CONCURRENCE: (O'Connor, J.) The association pursued by the Jaycees (P) was commercial in nature. Therefore, it was entitled to less constitutional protection than other types of expressive conduct such as political speech. Because the statute met the rational relationship test of minimum scrutiny, it was valid.

▶ ANALYSIS

There are two distinct senses in which the freedom of association has been protected by the Court. The first recognizes the freedom of association as a fundamental element of personal liberty. In another line of cases, the Court places the freedom to associate within the freedom of speech characterizing it as expressive conduct. The Court recognized in this case that these two characterizations may coincide.

■━■

Quicknotes

FIRST AMENDMENT Prohibits Congress from enacting any law respecting an establishment of religion, prohibiting the free exercise of religion, abridging freedom of speech or the press, the right of peaceful assembly and the right to petition for a redress of grievances.

RIGHT TO ASSOCIATE The right of individuals to peacefully assemble pursuant to the First Amendment to the United States Constitution.

■━■

Hurley v. Irish-American Gay, Lesbian and Bisexual Group of Boston

Parade sponsor (D) v. Permit applicants (P)

515 U.S. 557 (1995).

NATURE OF CASE: Review of order mandating parade permit.

FACT SUMMARY: The sponsors of a parade in Boston contended that a law compelling them to issue a permit to an organization they found repugnant violated the First Amendment.

🏛 RULE OF LAW
Private citizens organizing a parade may not be forced to include groups whose message they do not wish to convey.

FACTS: Since 1947, Boston's annual St. Patrick's Day parade had been organized by the South Boston Allied War Veterans Council (D). In 1983 the Irish-American Gay, Lesbian and Bisexual Group of Boston (Group) (P) applied for and was refused a permit. It filed suit. The trial court held that the parade was a public accommodation subject to Massachusetts's antidiscrimination laws and ordered the Group (P) admitted. The state supreme court affirmed. The U.S. Supreme Court granted review.

ISSUE: May private citizens organizing a parade be forced to include groups whose message they do not wish to convey?

HOLDING AND DECISION: (Souter, J.) No. Private citizens organizing a parade may not be forced to include groups whose message they do not wish to convey. A parade is a collection of marchers who make a collective point. A parade's dependence on watchers is so extreme that a parade without spectators and media coverage is arguably not a parade at all. Consequently, a parade is without question a form of expressive conduct protected by the First Amendment. Expression in the context of a parade is more than banners and speeches; the type of participants is also part of the overall message. Free speech in the demonstration/parade context necessarily involves the right on the part of the parade organizer to not include those whose inclusion would send a message the organizer does not wish said. Here, the Veterans Council (D) was of the opinion that inclusion of the Group (P) in its parade conveyed an unwanted message. It was therefore acting within its rights not to allow the Group (P) to march. Reversed and remanded.

▶ ANALYSIS

A conceptually similar case, which came out differently, was *Turner Broadcasting Systems, Inc. v. F.C.C.*, 512 U.S. 622 (1994). In that case, FCC regulations mandated that cable operators include certain types of programming. This was held constitutional.

■■■

Quicknotes

FIRST AMENDMENT Prohibits Congress from enacting any law respecting an establishment of religion, prohibiting the free exercise of religion, abridging freedom of speech or the press, the right of peaceful assembly and the right to petition for a redress of grievances.

PLACE OF PUBLIC ACCOMMODATION Refers to a business providing food, lodging or entertainment to customers that either has an effect on interstate commerce or is supported by state action and in which racial discrimination is prohibited pursuant to the Civil Rights Act of 1964.

■■■

Boy Scouts of America v. Dale

Nonprofit organization (D) v. Member (P)

530 U.S. 640 (2000).

NATURE OF CASE: Review of the constitutionally of a private organization's membership policies.

FACT SUMMARY: Dale's (P) membership in the Boy Scouts of America (D) was revoked when the Boy Scouts (D) learned that he is an avowed homosexual and gay rights activist.

🏛 RULE OF LAW
A group may constitutionally exclude an unwanted person if forced inclusion would infringe the group's freedom of expressive association by affecting in a significant way the group's ability to advocate public or private viewpoints.

FACTS: James Dale (P) is a former Eagle Scout whose adult membership in the Boy Scouts of Ameirca (D) was revoked when the Boy Scouts (D) learned that he is a homosexual and gay rights activist. The New Jersey Supreme Court held that the Boy Scouts (D) must admit Dale (P) and the Boy Scouts (D) appealed.

ISSUE: May a group constitutionally exclude an unwanted person if forced inclusion would infringe the group's freedom of expressive association by affecting in a significant way the group's ability to advocate public or private viewpoints?

HOLDING AND DECISION: (Rehnquist, C.J.) Yes. A group may constitutionally exclude an unwanted person if forced inclusion would infringe the group's freedom of expressive association by affecting in a significant way the group's ability to advocate public or private viewpoints. The New Jersey Supreme Court held that the state's public accommodations law requires that the Boy Scouts (D) admit Dale (P). Application of the law in this way, however, violates the Boy Scouts' (D) First Amendment right of expressive association. The statute prohibits in part discrimination on the basis of sexual orientation in places of public accommodation. The Supreme Court held that the Boy Scouts (D) was a place of public accommodation subject to the law, that the organization was not exempt from the law under any of its express exemptions, and that the Boy Scouts (D) violated the law by revoking Dale's (P) membership based on his homosexuality. The forced inclusion of an unwanted person in a group infringes the group's freedom of expressive association if that person's presence affects in a significant way the group's ability to advocate public or private viewpoints. However, the freedom of expression is not absolute. It may be overridden by regulations enacted to serve compelling state interests, unrelated to the suppression of ideas that cannot be achieved through means significantly less restrictive of associational freedoms. In determining whether a group is protected by the First Amendment's expressive associational right, it must first be determined whether the group engaged in "expressive association." Given that the Boy Scouts (D) engages in expressive activity, it must be determined whether the forced inclusion of Dale (P) as assistant scoutmaster would significantly affect the Boy Scouts' (D) ability to advocate public or private viewpoints. The Boy Scouts (D) asserts that homosexual conduct is inconsistent with the values instilled in the Scout Oath, "To keep myself physically strong, mentally awake, and morally straight." The Boy Scouts (D) asserts that it does not wish to promote homosexual conduct as a legitimate form of behavior. Thus we must determine whether Dale's (P) presence as an assistant scoutmaster would significantly burden this goal. The court must give deference both to an association's assertions regarding the nature of its expression as well as the association's view of what would impair its expression. Dale's (P) presence would force the organization to send a message that it accepts homosexual conduct as a legitimate form of behavior. Reversed.

DISSENT: (Stevens, J.) The law does not impose any serious burdens on the Boy Scouts' (D) "collective effort on behalf of its shared goals," nor does it force the Boy Scouts (D) to communicate any message that it does not wish to advocate. Thus it does not infringe any constitutional right of the Boy Scouts (D).

▶ ANALYSIS

Public accommodation laws, such as the one here, were initially promulgated in order to prevent discrimination in public places of accommodation. Such laws have gradually expanded to include many other forms of accommodation.

■=■

Quicknotes

FREEDOM OF ASSOCIATION The right to peaceably assemble.

PUBLIC ACCOMMODATION LAWS Laws passed pursuant to the Civil Rights Act of 1964 prohibiting discrimination in business establishments having an effect on interstate commerce.

■=■

Rumsfeld v. Forum for Academic and Institutional Rights, Inc.

U.S. Secretary of Defense (D) v. Association of law schools (P)

547 U.S. 47 (2006).

NATURE OF CASE: Suit challenging a federal statute's ability to condition federal educational funds on U.S. military recruiters having equal access to educational institutions.

FACT SUMMARY: Law schools restricted access to military recruiters because of the military's policy of excluding openly homosexual persons from military service.

🏛 RULE OF LAW
The Solomon Amendment does not infringe on the freedoms of speech and association of U.S. law schools by conditioning the receipt of federal educational funds on the law schools' grant of equal access to military recruiters.

FACTS: An association of U.S. law schools, the Forum for Academic and Institutional Rights, Inc. (FAIR) (P), protested the U.S. military's policy of excluding openly homosexual persons by restricting military recruiters' access to the schools' facilities and students. Congress responded by enacting the Solomon Amendment, 10 U.S.C. 983, which provided that an entire educational institution would lose federal funding if any part of the institution fails to provide access to military recruiters that is equal to the access enjoyed by all other recruiters. FAIR (P) sued, alleging that the Solomon Amendment violated the law schools' (P) rights to freedom of speech and association. The trial court ruled for the Government (D), but the court of appeals reversed. The Government (D) sought further review in the U.S. Supreme Court.

ISSUE: Does the Solomon Amendment infringe on the freedoms of speech and association of U.S. law schools by conditioning the receipt of federal educational funds on the law schools' grant of equal access to military recruiters?

HOLDING AND DECISION: (Roberts, C.J.) No. The Solomon Amendment does not infringe on the freedoms of speech and association of U.S. law schools by conditioning the receipt of federal educational funds on the law schools' grant of equal access to military recruiters. The Solomon Amendment requires the law schools (P) to permit military recruiters the same access to facilities and students that are granted to any other employers; if a law school (P) fails to permit such equal access, the entire institution will lose certain federal funds. Congress enacted the Solomon Amendment pursuant to the Constitution's Spending Clause, and not under Congress's military authority, but that choice does not affect the great judicial deference required for a statute that promotes military recruiting. The condition imposed on universities in this case clearly would satisfy the First

Amendment even if it the condition had been passed directly under Congress's military authority, and the condition, therefore, also satisfies the First Amendment if, as here, it was passed indirectly under the Spending Clause. The law schools (P) remain totally free to say whatever they please about military policies: the statute regulates conduct, not speech, toward the goal of ensuring equal access for military recruiters. This freedom exists even though the law schools (P) must provide notices to students about military recruiters, and even though the schools (P) must to some extent accommodate speech made by the military. These requirements are not tantamount to compelling the law schools (P) to express the military's message; unlike prior cases, the complaining party here does not have its own speech affected in any way by the speech that it must accommodate. Ultimately, a law school's (P) decision to permit access to a recruiter simply is not inherently expressive, as prior cases require. Moreover, the Solomon Amendment also fails to regulate conduct in violation of the First Amendment. The expressive purpose of a law school's (P) restriction on certain recruiters is not overwhelmingly apparent from the fact of the restriction itself, unlike, for example, the conduct involved in burning the American flag. Here, any understanding of a school's (P) expressive purpose arises solely from other speech by the law schools (P) that merely accompanies the regulated conduct. The Solomon Amendment also does not impose an improper incidental burden on speech because the statute promotes a substantial government interest that would not be achieved as effectively without the regulation. Finally, the Amendment also satisfies the freedom of association guaranteed by the First Amendment because the statute does not force law schools (P) to accept expressive members whom they do not want. Reversed.

▶ ANALYSIS

In this unanimous opinion, the Court holds that the Solomon Amendment does not violate FAIR's (P) First Amendment rights to freedom of speech and association. The great distance between the non-expressive speech compelled here and the strongly expressive speech compelled in, for example, *West Virginia Bd. of Educ. v. Barnette,* 319 U.S. 624 (1943), helped to fatally undermine the speech claims in this case. Similarly, the statute's failure to require FAIR (P) to admit military recruiters as expressive members of the law schools (P) greatly weakened FAIR's (P) freedom-of-association claim, too.

■━■

Quicknotes

FIRST AMENDMENT Prohibits Congress from enacting any law respecting an establishment of religion, prohibiting the free exercise of religion, abridging freedom of speech or the press, the right of peaceful assembly and the right to petition for a redress of grievances.

■━■

United States v. O'Brien

Federal government (P) v. Draft card burner (D)

391 U.S. 367 (1968).

NATURE OF CASE: Appeal from conviction for draft card burning.

FACT SUMMARY: O'Brien (D) was convicted of a violation of a federal statute after he publicly burned his draft card during a demonstration against the compulsory draft and the war in Vietnam.

🏛 RULE OF LAW
When both speech and nonspeech elements are combined in the same conduct, a sufficiently important governmental interest in regulating the nonspeech element can justify incidental limitations of First Amendment freedoms.

FACTS: During a public demonstration directed against the compulsory draft and the war in Vietnam, O'Brien (D) and several others burned their Selective Service Registration Certificates. His act was witnessed by several FBI agents who arrested him. The arrest was for violating a federal statute prohibiting the knowing destruction or knowing mutilation of a Selective Service Certificate. The act also prohibited any changes, alterations, or forgeries of the Certificates. O'Brien (D) was convicted and then appealed, contending a violation of his First Amendment right to free speech.

ISSUE: May the government incidentally limit First Amendment rights where it seeks to regulate the nonspeech aspect of conduct composed of both speech and nonspeech elements, where that regulation is supported by a vital governmental interest?

HOLDING AND DECISION: (Warren, C.J.) Yes. The Court considered two aspects of O'Brien's (D) appeal. First, that the statute was unconstitutional in its application to him, and secondly, that the statute was unconstitutional as enacted. Where conduct is composed of speech and nonspeech elements, the speaker can invoke his freedom of speech rights to defend against unwarranted governmental interference. What must be determined is whether the attempted regulation of the nonspeech element also impermissibly inhibits the speech aspect. An incidental restriction on speech can be justified where the government can show a substantial interest in furthering a constitutional power which is not directed at the suppression of speech. In order to facilitate the implementation of this power to raise and support armies, Congress has enacted a system for classifying individuals as to eligibility for military service. The Selective Service cards provide an efficient and reasonable method for identifying those persons previously deemed fit for military service should a national emergency

arise. The Court found the requirement that the card be in the possession of the holder to be a valid requirement. The Court also found an independent justification for both the possession requirement and the prohibition against mutilation or destruction. While admitting some overlap, the possession requirement was intended for a smooth functioning of the draft system while the prohibition against mutilation was a sabotage prevention measure. A person could destroy another's card while retaining his own intact. The statute was intended as a necessary and proper method to carry out a vital governmental interest. No reasonable alternative is apparent and the narrow construction of the statute indicates it was not intended to suppress communication. As to the contention the statute was unconstitutional on its face, the Court found congressional intent to be the smooth functioning of the draft system, not the suppression of antiwar sentiment. Affirmed.

▶ ANALYSIS

Many articles written about this decision have been critical of the Court's superficial analysis of the interests involved on both sides of this case. The commentators felt that O'Brien's (D) contention that the draft card was not a vital document was dismissed out of hand. They also felt there should have been a more probing analysis of the operation of the Selective Service System and an examination of the actual, not supposed, importance of the draft card in that system. The strongest criticism of this case has been that the Court justified the suppression of expression, not on the basis of a compelling interest, but on a bureaucratic system designed for convenience. There was no analysis of alternative systems. Finally, some observers saw in this decision a desire to counterbalance the long string of cases decided by the Warren Court upholding individual rights in the face of much stronger governmental interests.

Quicknotes

FIRST AMENDMENT Prohibits Congress from enacting any law respecting an establishment of religion, prohibiting the free exercise of religion, abridging freedom of speech or the press, the right of peaceful assembly and the right to petition for a redress of grievances.

SYMBOLIC SPEECH Communication of ideas through conduct.

Tinker v. Des Moines Independent Community School District

Students (P) v. School district (D)

393 U.S. 503 (1969).

NATURE OF CASE: Appeal from denial of an injunction.

FACT SUMMARY: The Tinkers (P), brother and sister, were high school students who sought to enjoin school officials from disciplining them for wearing black armbands in class in protest of the Vietnam conflict.

RULE OF LAW
The prohibition of a particular opinion without evidence that it is necessary to avoid material and substantial interference with school work or discipline is not constitutionally permissible.

FACTS: The Tinkers (P), brother and sister, were high school students who sought to enjoin school officials from disciplining them. They wore black armbands to school as a symbolic protest of their opposition to the continuing American participation in the Vietnam conflict. They refused to remove the armbands when asked to do so. In accordance with a ban on armbands adopted by the Des Moines Independent Community School District's (District's) (D) principals two days before the anticipated protest, the Tinkers (P) were suspended from school until they returned to school without the armbands. The lower federal courts upheld the District's (D) action on grounds that it was reasonable in order to prevent a disturbance which might result.

ISSUE: Is the prohibition of a particular opinion, without evidence that it is necessary to avoid material and substantial interference with school work or discipline, constitutionally permissible?

HOLDING AND DECISION: (Fortas, J.) No. The prohibition of a particular opinion without evidence that it is necessary to avoid material and substantial interference with school work or discipline is not constitutionally permissible. Under the circumstances here, the wearing of armbands "was entirely divorced from actually or potentially disruptive conduct by those participating in it." The symbolic action was closely akin to pure speech which receives great First Amendment protection. Students and teachers do not lose the right to free expression at the schoolhouse gate. There was no evidence of interference with the school's work or with the rights of other students. "Undifferentiated fear or apprehension of disturbance is not enough to overcome the right of freedom of expression." The state must show more than a mere desire to avoid the unpleasantness that accompanies an unpopular viewpoint. Reversed and remanded.

DISSENT: (Black, J.) The record showed that the armbands did divert students from their schoolwork. "It is a myth to say that any person has a constitutional right to say what he pleases, where he pleases, and when he pleases."

▶ ANALYSIS

The Second Circuit held that school officials violated a teacher's rights by firing him for wearing a black armband in class as a symbolic protest to American involvement in Vietnam. The court noted that the teacher's action did not disrupt the classroom, *James v. Board of Education of Central District No. 1*, 461 F.2d 566 (1972). The Supreme Court denied certiorari to a Tenth Circuit case which upheld the indefinite suspension of male Pawnee Indian students who wore their hair in long braids in violation of the school dress code which forbid hair from touching the ears or collar, *Rider v. Board of Education*, 414 U.S. 1088 (1974), Justices Douglas and Marshall dissenting.

Quicknotes

FIRST AMENDMENT Prohibits Congress from enacting any law respecting an establishment of religion, prohibiting the free exercise of religion, abridging freedom of speech or the press, the right of peaceful assembly and the right to petition for a redress of grievances.

Texas v. Johnson

State (P) v. Flag burner (D)

491 U.S. 397 (1989).

NATURE OF CASE: Review of order reversing conviction for desecration of a venerated object.

FACT SUMMARY: Johnson (D) was convicted for burning a U.S. flag as a form of political protest.

🏛 RULE OF LAW
Burning the U.S. flag as a form of political protest may not be subject to criminal penalty.

FACTS: During a political protest mounted in conjunction with the 1984 Republican National Convention, Johnson (D) burned a U.S. flag. The protest itself was essentially peaceful. Johnson (D) was convicted under a Texas statute prohibiting desecration of a venerated object. The Texas Court of Appeals reversed, holding such conviction contrary to the First Amendment. The Supreme Court accepted review.

ISSUE: May burning the U.S. flag as a form of political protest be subject to criminal penalty?

HOLDING AND DECISION: (Brennan, J.) No. Burning the U.S. flag as a form of political protest may not be subject to criminal penalty. While the First Amendment textually only protects speech, other forms of expressive conduct are also subject to First Amendment protection. While government may regulate expressive conduct, the regulations must be for reasons separate from the content of such conduct. Here, the State (P) offers two such rationales. The first is to prevent breaches of the peace. This rationale is insufficient for it does not automatically follow that conduct such as that engaged in by Johnson (D) leads to breaches of the peace. Indeed, in the demonstration in question, no violence erupted. The second rationale is the preservation of the flag as a symbol of national unity. While this is a laudable goal, it is a political issue which implicates quite clearly the First Amendment. Such regulation cannot be separated from the stifling of expression. Since Johnson's (D) actions were protected under the First Amendment, and Texas (P) has not presented a rationale for the law in question apart from stifling expression, the conviction was contrary to the First Amendment. Affirmed.

CONCURRENCE: (Kennedy, J.) It is poignant but fundamental that the flag protects those who hold it in contempt.

DISSENT: (Rehnquist, C.J.) The flag enjoys a unique position as a national symbol, and from this it derives a special class of deserved protection.

DISSENT: (Stevens, J.) What is prohibited here is not expression of an idea but rather the means of doing so. To prohibit this one form of expression would not remove a person's right to protest but would serve the important purpose of protecting our national symbol.

▶ ANALYSIS

This was one of the most controversial decisions of the Court over the last half-century. As soon as it was rendered, calls for a constitutional amendment to reverse the decision were made from many quarters. A statute was later enacted, but the amendment ran out of steam in Congress, which apparently had second thoughts about amending the Bill of Rights, an action totally without historical precedent.

Quicknotes

FIRST AMENDMENT Prohibits Congress from enacting any law respecting an establishment of religion, prohibiting the free exercise of religion, abridging freedom of speech or the press, the right of peaceful assembly and the right to petition for a redress of grievances.

United States v. Eichman

Federal government (P) v. Flag desecrator (D)

496 U.S. 310 (1990).

NATURE OF CASE: Review of dismissal of criminal prosecution.

FACT SUMMARY: Eichman (D) was prosecuted under the Federal Flag Protection Act of 1989, which he contended was unconstitutional.

🏛 RULE OF LAW
The government may not prohibit the desecration of the U.S. flag without violating the First Amendment.

FACTS: In 1989, Congress enacted the Flag Protection Act, which made it a federal offense to do various acts amounting to desecration of the U.S. flag. Eichman (D) violated the law and was prosecuted thereunder. The court of appeals held the law unconstitutional and the U.S. Supreme Court granted certiorari.

ISSUE: May the government prohibit flag desecration without violating the First Amendment?

HOLDING AND DECISION: (Brennan, J.) No. The government may not prohibit flag desecration without violating the First Amendment. The burning of the flag constitutes expressive conduct, and, as such, is protected under the First Amendment. Such conduct is not afforded protection if it constitutes obscenity or "fighting words." While burning the flag might provoke violence, its primary purpose is to communicate an idea, a protected activity. The Government's (P) assertion that it is necessary to preserve the integrity of the flag as a national symbol is unavailing; this makes the Act all the more an abridgement of expression, which is inconsistent with the First Amendment. Affirmed.

DISSENT: (Stevens, J.) The considerations identified in my dissent in *Texas v. Johnson*, 491 U.S. 397 (1989), support a prohibition on the desecration of the U.S. flag in this case.

▶ ANALYSIS

The 1989 Flag Protection Act was passed in response to the case, *Texas v. Johnson*, 491 U.S. 397 (1989). This case first elevated flag-burning to a constitutional right. The unpopularity of *Johnson* at first led to calls for a constitutional amendment. However, the consensus for such a course wasn't there, and the Act was a result. However, as any reading of *Johnson* would indicate, the Act was doomed to failure.

Quicknotes

FIGHTING WORDS Unprotected speech that inflicts injury by their very utterance and proves violence from the audience.

FIRST AMENDMENT Prohibits Congress from enacting any law respecting an establishment of religion, prohibiting the free exercise of religion, abridging freedom of speech or the press, the right of peaceful assembly and the right to petition for a redress of grievances.

OBSCENITY Conduct tending to corrupt the public morals by its indecency or lewdness.

■=■

Buckley v. Valeo

Senator (P) v. Federal government (D)

424 U.S. 1 (1976).

NATURE OF CASE: Declaratory judgment action.

FACT SUMMARY: Senator Buckley (P) challenged the constitutionality of the Federal Election Campaign Act.

🏛 RULE OF LAW
Limitations on campaign contributions are constitutional, but limitations on campaign expenditures are not.

FACTS: In order to curtail alleged corrupt political practices, Congress enacted the Federal Election Campaign Act of 1971. The Act provided for an intricate scheme regulating federal elections: (1) no more than $1,000 contributed by a person to any one candidate; (2) no more than $5,000 contributed by a committee to a candidate; (3) $1,000 limits on expenditures by the candidate, his family, and relatives for the candidate's campaign; (4) disclosures of all contributions of $10 or more by the candidate and all contributions of $1,000 or more by individuals; (5) federal financing of presidential elections; (6) a six-man Federal Election Commission to review all activities. Two members were to be chosen by the Speaker of the House, two by the President Pro Tem, and two by the President. Senator Buckley (P) and others sought a declaratory judgment that the acts limiting expenditures and contributions and requiring reporting violated the First Amendment. Buckley (P) also challenged the validity of the Commission on the ground that Congress would not usurp the Executive Branch's authority of appointment under § 2, Clause 2 of Article II of the Constitution.

ISSUE: Are limitations on campaign expenditure constitutional?

HOLDING AND DECISION: (Per curiam) No. Limitations on campaign expenditures violate the right of free speech and political expression guaranteed under the First Amendment. By restricting the amount of money a candidate may spend, the issues which can be covered and the depth of the coverage may be curtailed. Political candidates should be allowed to reach a large audience and to state their views on any number of topics. This right cannot be arbitrarily restricted. The limited expenditure rule is too broad and is not designed to serve a legitimate congressional end. The limitations on contributions is designed to limit the influence which individuals and groups may exert on candidates. It is a very slight intrusion on their First Amendment rights and is reasonably related to curbing political abuse and toward requiring candidates to seek wide and divergent financial support. These restrictions are justified on balance. The government has a compelling interest in its own protection and this justifies the limited burden on candidates and contributors to report contributions. The public financing of presidential elections is sustained since it involves no First Amendment issue. Finally, the Committee is unconstitutionally constituted. The Committee has significant executive functions. Under § 2, Clause 2, of Article II, Congress may not unilaterally usurp appointment powers from the Executive Branch. Committee members are clearly exercising executive functions and may be appointed only by the President.

CONCURRENCE AND DISSENT: (Burger, C. J.) The impropriety of subsidizing political dialogue from general revenues is as basic to our national tradition as the separation of church and state.

CONCURRENCE AND DISSENT: (White, J.) Since the expenditure limitations under the Act are neutral as to the content of speech, have no bearing on questions of expression, and are based on a rational purpose, i.e., elimination of campaign abuses, there is no First Amendment violation.

▶ ANALYSIS

In this case, the Court has identified one of the few "compelling government interests" which may be employed to justify congressional regulation of an area subject to strict judicial scrutiny. That interest is the interest in maintaining the integrity of the political process. Note, however, that even though the interest is held compelling, the Court does not automatically affirm its imposition. Note that the Court's decision left the Federal Election Campaign Act rift with loopholes. Perhaps the most exploited was that which permitted individuals to "expend" (i.e., separately from any candidate or his organization) large sums to endorse a vote for a particular candidate.

■━■

Quicknotes

FIRST AMENDMENT Prohibits Congress from enacting any law respecting an establishment of religion, prohibiting the free exercise of religion, abridging freedom of speech or the press, the right of peaceful assembly and the right to petition for a redress of grievances.

POLITICAL SPEECH Speech pertaining to the political process which is afforded the greatest amount of protection under the First Amendment.

STRICT SCRUTINY Method by which courts determine the constitutionality of a law, when a law affects a

Continued on next page.

fundamental right. Under the test, the legislature must have a compelling interest to enact the law and measures prescribed by the law must be the least restrictive means possible to accomplish its goal.

■■■

McConnell v. Federal Election Commission

Election contributor (P) v. Federal Commission (D)

540 U.S. 93 (2003).

NATURE OF CASE: [Procedural posture of case is not set forth in textbook excerpt.]

FACT SUMMARY: Several provisions of the Federal Election Campaign Act of 1971 (FECA), as amended, were attacked as abridging First Amendment rights.

🏛 RULE OF LAW
The Federal Election Campaign Act of 1971, as amended, does not abridge First Amendment rights.

FACTS: The Federal Election Campaign Act of 1971 (FECA), as amended, contains a wide variety of limits on political contributions, including limits on so-called soft money contributions. Suit was brought attacking the constitutionality of many of FECA's provisions on the grounds that they abridged First Amendment rights. [The procedural posture of the case is not set forth in the textbook excerpt.]

ISSUE: Does the Federal Election Campaign Act abridge First Amendment rights?

HOLDING AND DECISION: (Stevens, J.) No. The Federal Election Campaign Act does not abridge First Amendment rights. A contribution limit or restriction involving even "significant interference" with associational rights is valid if it is being "closely drawn" to match a "sufficiently important interest." This Court's treatment of contribution restrictions reflects more than the limited burdens they impose on First Amendment freedoms. It also reflects the importance of the interests that underlie contribution limits: interests in preventing both the actual corruption threatened by large financial contributions and the eroding of public confidence in the electoral process through the appearance of corruption. When this Court reviews a congressional decision to enact contribution limits, there is no place for a strong presumption against constitutionality of the sort often thought to accompany the words "strict scrutiny." The less rigorous standard of review which this Court has applied to contribution limits shows proper deference to Congress's ability to weigh competing constitutional interests in an area in which it enjoys particular expertise. It also provides Congress with sufficient room to anticipate and respond to concerns about circumvention of regulations designed to protect the integrity of the political process. Here, FECA's restrictions have only a "marginal impact" on the ability of contributors, candidates, office-holders, and parties to engage in effective political speech; the regulations simply limit the source and individual amount of donations.

Furthermore, the solicitation provisions leave open ample opportunities for soliciting federal funds on behalf of entities subject to FECA's source and amount restrictions. Restrictions on national party committees, for example, simply effect a return to schemes approved by this Court in earlier cases; the idea that large soft money contributions to a national party can corrupt is neither novel nor implausible. Both common sense and the ample record confirm the belief of Congress that they do. So too, FECA's amendments restricting corporations' and labor unions' funding of electioneering communications does not violate First Amendment free speech since the statute is not overbroad and the government has a compelling interest in eliminating corruption in use of such funds. [Rehnquist, C.J., delivered the portion of the Court's opinion holding invalid a section of the statute prohibiting individuals 17 years old or younger from making contributions to candidates and political parties, on the grounds that "Minors enjoy the protection of the First Amendment." Breyer, J., upheld requirements that broadcasters maintain records for political advertisements.] Affirmed in part and reversed in part.

CONCURRENCE AND DISSENT: (Scalia, J.) This is a sad day for freedom of speech. The plurality here smiles with favor "upon a law that cuts to the heart of what the First Amendment is meant to protect." The present legislation targets for prohibition certain categories of campaign speech that are particularly harmful to incumbents. This legislation is about preventing criticism of government.

▶ ANALYSIS

As made clear by the U.S. Supreme Court in *McConnell*, just as troubling to a functioning democracy as classic quid pro quo corruption is the danger that officeholders will decide issues not on the merits or the desires of their constituents, but according to the wishes of those who have made large financial contributions valued by the officeholder. Stating that the best means of prevention is to identify and to remove the temptation, the *McConnell* court accordingly rejected nearly all the First Amendment challenges to FECA.

◼◼◼

Quicknotes

FIRST AMENDMENT Prohibits Congress from enacting any law respecting an establishment of religion, prohibiting the free exercise of religion, abridging freedom of speech or the press, the right of peaceful assembly and the right to petition for a redress of grievances.

◼◼◼

Roth v. United States

Publishers (D) v. Federal government (P)

354 U.S. 476 (1957).

NATURE OF CASE: Appeal from criminal conviction under an obscenity statute.

FACT SUMMARY: Two defendants were convicted under obscenity statutes for selling obscene material. Roth (D) was convicted under a federal statute, Alberts under a state statute.

🏛 RULE OF LAW
Obscenity is not a constitutionally protected expression and if the material, taken as a whole, has a dominant theme that appeals to prurient interest as judged by contemporary community standards, then it may be proscribed.

FACTS: Roth (D) was a publisher and seller of books, magazines, and photographs. He was convicted under a federal statute for mailing obscene circulars and advertising and an obscene book. Alberts was convicted under a California statute which prohibited the keeping for sale of obscene and indecent books or the writing, composing, and publishing of an obscene advertisement therefor.

ISSUE: Is obscenity outside the protection of the First Amendment freedom of expression guarantees and is there a proper standard for defining prohibitable conduct?

HOLDING AND DECISION: (Brennan, J.) Yes. The apparently unconditional phrasing of the First Amendment has been held by this Court not to protect every utterance. However, all ideas leaving even the slightest degree of socially redeeming value are fully protected unless they encroach upon the limited areas of more important interests. Obscenity has been held to carry no socially redeeming value and is, therefore, outside the protection of the First Amendment. A properly drawn and enforced statute outlawing obscenity will withstand the test of constitutionality. The portrayal of sex is not obscenity per se, as is evidenced by the large range of classic presentations in art, literature, and scientific works. Any attempt to proscribe obscenity must clearly define that which is prohibited. A work must be judged in its entirety, not by selected portions since many valuable and socially important materials could thereby be suppressed. The test should be, whether to the average person, applying contemporary community standards, the dominant theme of the material, taken as a whole, appeals to prurient interest. The words of this standard are sufficiently clear to give notice as to what is, or is not, permissible conduct. Both defendants were convicted under statutes applying the stated standard and both convictions are affirmed.

CONCURRENCE: (Warren, C.J.) It is constitutionally permissible to punish individuals for the commercial exploitation of the morbid and shameful craving for materials with prurient effect.

CONCURRENCE AND DISSENT: (Harlan, J.) The majority opinion seems to assume that obscenity is a distinct classification of material which is readily recognizable. This recognition is left, ostensibly, to the trier of fact in the trial court. But where appellate review is undertaken, the appellate court itself must reexamine the material to determine if it is, in fact, obscene. This means that no generalized standard has been promulgated. This Court may be required to review each conviction on a case-by-case basis. The majority adopts the standard used in the Model Penal Code. Yet, the two statutes, one state, the other federal, set down different standards from the Code and from each other. The majority ignored this disparity in upholding the validity of the statutes and the convictions. Since the matter of sexual conduct is predominantly an area of state, not federal, concern, this Court should not strike down the determination by California in this area. I would confirm Albert's conviction. The *Roth* conviction is another matter. When the federal government attempts to impose a national standard restricting expression, a serious threat to freedom is presented. This decision sets too dangerous a precedent and I would reverse *Roth*'s conviction.

DISSENT: (Douglas, J.) The First Amendment is expressed in absolute terms and any law which purports to regulate material which can only produce thoughts is a clearly impermissible encroachment on these absolute guarantees. While the state and federal governments can regulate conduct, they should not be allowed to regulate the thoughts which precede the conduct.

▶ ANALYSIS

The purported standard of the *Roth* case soon became a thorn in the side of the Court. As Justice Harlan had predicted, the Court was reduced to a case-by-case review of obscenity convictions. In each case, the Court was forced to make a factual analysis of the material to determine if it was obscene. This despite the fact the same determination had already been made in every lower court. The one clarification of the *Roth* standard came in *Jacobellis v. Ohio* (378 U.S. 184) in 1964. In that case, a split Court stated the "community standard" was a national standard since a national constitution was being applied.

Continued on next page.

The other noteworthy concept to come from that case was from Justice Stewart. He stated that the Court was attempting to deal with "hard-core" pornography. While he admitted he could not define that term, he stated he knew it when he saw it and the motion picture involved in that case was not it.

■═■

Quicknotes

OBSCENITY Conduct tending to corrupt the public morals by its indecency or lewdness.

PRURIENT INTEREST Abnormal or obsessive interest in sex.

■═■

Miller v. California

Distributor (D) v. State (P)

413 U.S. 15 (1973).

NATURE OF CASE: Criminal prosecution for knowingly distributing obscene matter.

FACT SUMMARY: Miller (D) sent out advertising brochures for adult books to unwilling recipients.

🏛 RULE OF LAW

Material is obscene and not protected by the First Amendment if: (1) the average person, applying contemporary community standards, would find that the work, taken as a whole, appeals to the prurient interest; (2) the work depicts in a patently offensive way sexual conduct specifically defined by the applicable state law; and (3) the work, taken as a whole, lacks serious literary, artistic, political, or scientific value.

FACTS: Miller (D) conducted a mass mailing campaign to advertise the sale of adult books. The advertising brochures were themselves found obscene. These brochures were sent to unwilling recipients who had not requested the material. Miller (D) was convicted of violating a statute which forbade knowingly distributing obscene matter.

ISSUE: Is the *Memoirs* requirement that material must be " utterly without redeeming social value" to be considered obscene, a proper constitutional standard?

HOLDING AND DECISION: (Burger, C.J.) No. The proper standard for judging obscenity is (1) whether the average person, applying contemporary community standards, would find that the work, taken as a whole, appeals to the prurient interest; (2) whether the work depicts in a patently offensive way sexual conduct specifically defined by the applicable state law; and (3) whether the work, taken as a whole, lacks serious literary, artistic, political, or scientific value. If material meets this definition of obscenity, then the state can prohibit its distribution if the mode of distribution entails the risk of offending unwilling recipients or exposing the material to juveniles. The burden of proof of the *Memoirs* [*Memoirs v. Massachusetts*, 383 U.S. 413 (1966)] test, that the material be utterly without redeeming value, is virtually impossible for the prosecution to meet and must be abandoned. There is no fixed national standard of "prurient interest" or "patently offensive" and these first two parts of the test are questions of fact to be resolved by the jury by applying contemporary community standards. Vacated and remanded.

▶ ANALYSIS

The *Miller* test of obscenity is the most current test. If the three requirements are met, then the material in question is considered obscene and outside the protection of the First Amendment. *Miller* is a turnaround from *Memoirs* for many reasons: the *Memoirs* standard was too difficult to prove, the lower courts had no clearcut guidelines because *Memoirs* was a plurality opinion, the Court decided to use local community standards to allow greater jury power, and the Court was beginning to feel institutional pressures, since every obscenity question was a constitutional question. Therefore, *Miller* was an attempt by the Court to decentralize decision-making.

■■■

Quicknotes

OBSCENITY Conduct tending to corrupt the public morals by its indecency or lewdness.

PRURIENT INTEREST Abnormal or obsessive interest in sex.

■■■

Paris Adult Theatre I v. Slaton

Movie theatre (D) v. State (P)

413 U.S. 49 (1973).

NATURE OF CASE: Civil action by state to have films exhibited in theatres declared obscene and their exhibition enjoined.

FACT SUMMARY: Paris Adult Theatre (D) warned prospective customers that "adult" films were exhibited, and that no minors would be admitted. Nonetheless, Georgia (P), in a civil action, sought to enjoin Paris Adult Theatre (D) from showing the films.

🏛 RULE OF LAW
Obscene, pornographic films do not acquire constitutional immunity from state regulation simply because they are exhibited for consenting adults only.

FACTS: Georgia (P) filed civil complaints seeking to have two films exhibited in Paris Adult Theatre (D) declared obscene and their exhibition enjoined. The two films were soft-core sex films. While the entrances to the theatres were conventional, inoffensive, and without pictures, a sign proclaimed "Atlanta's Finest Mature Feature Films." On the door was a sign which read "Adult Theatre—You must be 21 and be able to prove it. If viewing the nude body offends you, Please Do Not Enter." The trial court dismissed the complaint, but the Georgia Supreme Court reversed. Paris Adult Theatre (D) appealed.

ISSUE: Is the display of obscene films in a commercial theatre, when surrounded by requisite notice to the public of their nature and by reasonable protection against exposure of these films to minors, constitutionally protected against state regulation?

HOLDING AND DECISION: (Burger, C.J.) No. States have a legitimate interest in regulating commerce in obscene material and in regulating exhibition of obscene material in places of public accommodation, including so-called "adult" theatres from which minors are excluded. The interest goes beyond the arguable connection between obscene material and crime or immoral behavior. A state also has a right to maintain a decent society. Granting a right to an individual to view obscene films in a public, albeit, discrete place, impinges on other privacies. Georgia may have reasonably concluded that commercial exhibitions of obscene material have a tendency to exert a corrupting and debasing impact leading to anti-social behavior. Vacated and remanded for reconsideration in light of *Miller v. California*, 413 U.S. 15 (1973).

DISSENT: (Brennan, J.) The Court's inability in these cases to define a standard which can be predictably applied to any given piece of material not only creates problems of fair notice, it chills protected speech. It also imposes stress on state and federal judicial machinery. No matter what decision is rendered by a lower court, the matter of whether a work is obscene is left unsettled until a final, independent determination by this Court. Obscenity has been defined by such indefinite concepts as "prurient interest," and "serious literary value." It depends on the experience, outlook, and idiosyncrasies of the person defining these concepts, and also upon nuances of presentation and the context of dissemination. The Court's approach permits works of some social value to be barred as obscene if the state concludes that they were not sufficiently "serious," as measured by some unspecified standard, to warrant constitutional protection. As for the present case, Georgia's interest in regulating morality by suppressing obscenity remains essentially unfocused and ill-defined. Efforts to suppress obscenity which are predicated on unprovable assumptions about human behavior, morality, sex, and religion cannot validate a statute that substantially undermines the guarantees of the First Amendment.

▶ ANALYSIS

In *Kaplan v. California*, 413 U.S. 115 (1973), the issue was "whether expression by words alone can be legally 'obscene' in the sense of being unprotected by the First Amendment." The Court, by a 5-5 majority, answered in the affirmative, noting that "(while) a book seems to have a different and preferred place in our hierarchy of values . . . this generalization, like so many, is qualified by the book's content."

■=▮

Quicknotes

OBSCENITY Conduct tending to corrupt the public morals by its indecency or lewdness.

PRURIENT INTEREST Abnormal or obsessive interest in sex.

■=▮

New York v. Ferber

State (P) v. Distributor (D)

458 U.S. 747 (1982).

NATURE OF CASE: Appeal from conviction under statute prohibiting persons from distributing child pornography.

FACT SUMMARY: Ferber (D) contended that a New York statute prohibiting persons from knowingly promoting sexual performances by children under the age of 16 by distributing material which depicts such performances was unconstitutional in that it encroached upon protected First Amendment interests.

RULE OF LAW
Child pornography does not constitute speech protected under the First Amendment.

FACTS: New York criminal code § 263.15 prohibits persons from knowingly promoting sexual performances by children under the age of 16 by distributing material which depicts such performances. A sexual performance is defined as any performance or part thereof which includes sexual conduct by a child less than 16 years of age. Criminal code § 263.10 bans only the knowing dissemination of obscene material. Ferber (D), the proprietor of a Manhattan bookstore specializing in sexually oriented products, was indicted on two counts of violating § 263.10 and two counts of violating § 263.15 after selling two films to an undercover police officer. The films were devoted almost exclusively to depicting young boys masturbating. After a jury trial, Ferber (D) was acquitted of the two counts of promoting an obscene sexual performance, but found guilty of two counts under § 263.15, which did not require proof that the films were obscene. After the New York Court of Appeals reversed the conviction, the State (P) brought this appeal.

ISSUE: Does child pornography constitute speech not protected under the First Amendment?

HOLDING AND DECISION: (White, J.) Yes. Child pornography does not constitute speech protected under the First Amendment. The states are entitled to great leeway in the regulation of pornographic depictions of children. A state's interest in safeguarding the physical and psychological well being of a minor is compelling. The use of children as subjects of pornographic materials is harmful to the physiological, emotional, and mental health of the child. The distribution of photographs and films depicting sexual activity by juveniles is intrinsically related to the sexual abuse of children in at least two ways. First, the materials produced are a permanent record of the children's participation and the harm to the child is exacerbated by their circulation. Second, the distribution network for child pornography must be closed if the production of material which requires the sexual exploitation of children is to be effectively controlled. The value of permitting live performances and photographic reproductions of children engaged in lewd sexual conduct is exceedingly modest, if not de minimis. Reversed and remanded.

CONCURRENCE: (O'Connor, J.) It is quite possible that New York's statute is overbroad because it bans depictions that do not actually threaten the harms identified by the Court. It is not necessary to address these possibilities further, however, because this potential overbreadth is not sufficiently substantial to warrant facial invalidation of New York's (P) statute.

CONCURRENCE: (Brennan, J.) The application of § 263.15 or any similar statute to depictions of children that in themselves do have serious literary, artistic, scientific, or medical value, would violate the First Amendment.

ANALYSIS

This decision separated the test for child pornography from the general standard for determining obscenity under the well-known *Miller* standard, *Miller v. California*, 413 U.S. 15 (1973). The *Miller* standard was adjusted in three respects. A trier of fact need not find that the material appeals to the prurient interest of the average person; it is not required that sexual conduct portrayed be done so in a patently offensive manner; and the material at issue need not be considered as a whole.

■═■

Quicknotes

FIRST AMENDMENT Prohibits Congress from enacting any law respecting an establishment of religion, prohibiting the free exercise of religion, abridging freedom of speech or the press, the right of peaceful assembly and the right to petition for a redress of grievances.

OBSCENITY Conduct tending to corrupt the public morals by its indecency or lewdness.

OVERBREADTH That quality or characteristic of a statute, regulation, or order which reaches beyond the problem it was meant to solve causing it to sweep within it activity it cannot legitimately reach.

PRURIENT INTEREST Abnormal or obsessive interest in sex.

■═■

Young v. American Mini Theatres, Inc.

City (D) v. Theatre owner (P)

427 U.S. 50 (1976).

NATURE OF CASE: Review of order enjoining zoning law enforcement.

FACT SUMMARY: After Detroit enacted a zoning ordinance prohibiting the operation of "adult" theatres within 1,000 feet of any two other "regulated use" establishments, which were those showing specified sexual acts and specified anatomical areas, American Mini Theatres, Inc. (American) (P), owner of two offending theatres, sought an injunction against enforcement of the ordinance on free speech grounds.

RULE OF LAW

A zoning ordinance may validly place reasonable limits on locations where establishments displaying sexual conduct or sexual organs may be operated within a municipality without offending the First Amendment.

FACTS: A Detroit ordinance set forth a zoning requirement that any "regulated use" establishment must be located at least 1,000 feet away from any two other such establishments. "Regulated use" establishments were those which showed sexual conduct specified by the ordinance or anatomical areas also specified in the ordinance. American Mini Theatres, Inc. (American) (P) owned two theatres which violated the ordinance by being within 1,000 feet of two other "regulated use" establishments, and American (P) sought to enjoin the municipality from enforcing the law against them on the ground that such enforcement constituted a violation of American's (P) First Amendment right to free speech. The U.S. Supreme Court granted certiorari to review the court of appeals grant of the injunction.

ISSUE: May a zoning ordinance validly place reasonable limits on locations where establishments displaying sexual conduct or sexual organs may be operated within a municipality without offending the First Amendment?

HOLDING AND DECISION: (Stevens, J.) Yes. American (P) urged that the ordinance in question failed to provide adequate procedures for waiver of the 1,000-foot requirement and thus the ordinance is too vague. American (P), however, falls within the law and is not entitled to a waiver under any construction of it. The interest of the government in exhibiting material on the borderline of pornography and artistic expression is less vital than that in disseminating political ideas, and the vagueness regarding the hypothetical applicability of the ordinance to the letter will not suffice to overturn it. The ordinance is furthermore not a prior restraint on protected expression. The 1,000-foot restriction does not prevent the operation of American's (P) theatres, but merely controls the locations of them. A zoning ordinance may validly place reasonable limits on locations where establishments displaying sexual conduct or organs may be operated within a municipality without offending the First Amendment. American (P) was not entitled to the injunction granted by the court of appeals. Reversed.

CONCURRENCE: (Powell, J.) This case is one of permissible land-use regulation and involves the First Amendment only incidentally. There is no restriction on the availability of adult movies. The ordinance is addressed only to the places at which this type of expression may be presented. This restriction does not interfere with content.

DISSENT: (Stewart, J.) The Court today permits a city to use a system of prior restraints and criminal sanctions to enforce a content-based restriction on the geographic location of theatres exhibiting sexually oriented films.

DISSENT: (Blackmun, J.) An exhibitor of motion pictures will not be able to tell if films he proposes to show fall within the class bringing on the ordinance's restriction if the sexual activities or anatomical areas shown are only a part of a given film's content. He must then determine if his neighbors within 1,000 feet of him are showing such films that bring them within the ambit of the law. This is thus not merely a "zoning" ordinance. We cannot approve suppression of films without a determination that they are "obscene" according to this Court's carefully delineated standards.

ANALYSIS

It seems that the Court is affording expressions of sexual content less First Amendment protection than other forms of expression even in the absence of a finding of obscenity. As a content-based discrimination, this ordinance was subject to the constitutional argument presented here, but bolstered by the municipality's zoning power, it was nevertheless upheld.

∎═∎

Quicknotes

FIRST AMENDMENT Prohibits Congress from enacting any law respecting an establishment of religion, prohibiting the free exercise of religion, abridging freedom of speech or the press, the right of peaceful assembly and the right to petition for a redress of grievances.

Continued on next page.

PRIOR RESTRAINT A restriction imposed on speech imposed prior to its communication.

ZONING ORDINANCE A statute that divides land into defined areas and which regulates the form and use of buildings and structures within those areas.

■══■

Reno v. American Civil Liberties Union

Attorney general (D) v. Union (P)

521 U.S. 844 (1997).

NATURE OF CASE: Review of judgment striking down provisions of the Communications Decency Act of 1996 (CDA).

FACT SUMMARY: The American Civil Liberties Union (ACLU) (P) challenged the constitutionality of provisions of the CDA that purported to protect minors from harmful transmissions over the Internet.

> ## 🏛 RULE OF LAW
> Content-based government regulations on speech are unconstitutional unless the government can demonstrate that it has a compelling interest for the regulation and that the regulation is the least restrictive means of achieving that interest.

FACTS: The CDA contained provisions designed to protect minors from "indecent" and "patently offensive" communication on the Internet. The "indecent transmission" provision prohibited the knowing transmission of obscene or indecent messages to any recipient under eighteen years of age. The "patently offensive display" provision prohibited the knowing sending or displaying of patently offensive messages to a person under eighteen years of age. The American Civil Liberties Union (ACLU) (P) filed an action alleging that the CDA abridged freedom of speech protected by the First Amendment. The district court found in its favor and enjoined the enforcement of the "indecent" communications provisions, but expressly preserved the government's right to investigate and prosecute the obscenity or child pornography activities prohibited by the provision. The court also issued an unqualified injunction against the enforcement of the "patently offensive displays" provision because it contained no separate reference to obscenity or child pornography.

ISSUE: Are content-based government regulations on speech unconstitutional unless the government can demonstrate that it has a compelling interest for the regulation and that the regulation is the least restrictive means of achieving that interest?

HOLDING AND DECISION: (Stevens, J.) Yes. Content-based government regulations on speech are unconstitutional unless the government can demonstrate that it has a compelling interest for the regulation and that the regulation is the least restrictive means of achieving that interest. Although the congressional goal of protecting children from harmful materials is a legitimate and important one, the CDA provisions at issue here are so broad and imprecise that they cannot be upheld. The Internet is a unique medium in that it provides a relatively unlimited, low-cost capacity for communication of all kinds including traditional print and news services, audio, video, still images, and interactive real-time dialogue. It unquestionably deserves the highest level of First Amendment protection. The breadth of the CDA's coverage is wholly unprecedented and would undoubtedly impact adult as well as minor access to such materials. It does not limit its restrictions to commercial speech or entities, but encompasses anyone posting messages on a computer, regardless of time of day, website, or any other factor. The district court heard evidence that in the near future a reasonably effective and less restrictive method by which parents can prevent their children from accessing sexually explicit material will become widely available. The current provisions cannot stand as they are more likely to interfere with the free exchange of ideas than to encourage it. Affirmed.

CONCURRENCE AND DISSENT: (O'Connor, J.) The CDA is little more than an attempt by Congress to create "adult zones" on the Internet. Such zoning laws are valid if: (1) they do not unduly restrict adult access to materials, and (2) the materials are such that minors have no right to read or view. The CDA "display" provision and some applications of the "indecency transmission" provision fail to adhere to the first of these requirements, and should therefore be invalidated only to those extents.

▌ ANALYSIS

Issues surrounding speech, pornography, and access to the Internet will undoubtedly be revisited often in the next several years. The issues are extremely complex because the technology is so novel, and are further complicated by the fact that the Internet extends worldwide. The Court was appropriately cautious in striking down the provisions and leaving the issue in the hands of parents until further developments evolve.

■═■

Quicknotes

FIRST AMENDMENT Prohibits Congress from enacting any law respecting an establishment of religion, prohibiting the free exercise of religion, abridging freedom of speech or the press, the right of peaceful assembly and the right to petition for a redress of grievances.

OBSCENITY Conduct tending to corrupt the public morals by its indecency or lewdness.

Continued on next page.

ZONING Municipal statutory scheme dividing an area into districts in order to regulate the use or building of structures within those districts.

Barnes v. Glen Theatre, Inc.

State (P) v. Theatre (D)

501 U.S. 560 (1991).

NATURE OF CASE: Review of order invalidating state prohibition against nude dancing.

FACT SUMMARY: Glen Theatre, Inc. (D) contended that state prohibition against nude dancing violated the First Amendment.

🏛 RULE OF LAW
State prohibitions against nude dancing do not violate the First Amendment.

FACTS: Glen Theatre, Inc. (D) operated a nightclub which featured nude dancing. Authorities in South Bend, Indiana brought a criminal action against it under a state statute prohibiting nude dancing. Glen Theatre, Inc. (D) contended that the ordinance violated the First Amendment. A state court held the statute unconstitutional, and the U.S. Supreme Court granted review.

ISSUE: Do state prohibitions against nude dancing violate the First Amendment?

HOLDING AND DECISION: (Rehnquist, C.J.) No. State prohibitions against nude dancing do not violate the First Amendment. There is authority for the proposition that nude dancing is expressive conduct protected by the First Amendment. However, that is not the end of the inquiry. "Time, place, and manner" restrictions that incidentally affect expressive conduct are valid. Here, the prohibitions in question are part of a general statutory prohibition against public nudity and indecency. That a state may regulate against public indecency is beyond question. The interest served by such regulation is unrelated to restricting free expression. Further, the actual restriction on whatever message is conveyed by nude dancing is minor, as almost-nude dancing is permitted. In view of these considerations, the prohibition against nude dancing does not violate the First Amendment. Reversed.

CONCURRENCE: (Scalia, J.) Laws regulating conduct and not aimed at expression do not implicate the First Amendment.

CONCURRENCE: (Souter, J.) The state's substantial interest in combating the secondary effects of adult establishments legitimizes the statute at issue here.

DISSENT: (White, J.) The law at issue here is not part of a general prohibition against nudity but is directed against specific conduct.

▶ ANALYSIS

The opinion here is of a plurality; therefore, a reader must examine the various opinions to ascertain the case's pre-cedential value. It would seem that at least five justices would permit a prohibition against nude dancing if a state had a generalized prohibition against public nudity. Justices White, Marshall, Blackmun, and Stevens would appear to require that a prohibition against nude dancing actually be in the same statute that created a generalized prohibition.

■═■

Quicknotes

FIRST AMENDMENT Prohibits Congress from enacting any law respecting an establishment of religion, prohibiting the free exercise of religion, abridging freedom of speech or the press, the right of peaceful assembly and the right to petition for a redress of grievances.

TIME, PLACE, AND MANNER RESTRICTION Refers to certain types of regulations on speech that are permissible since they only restrict the time, place, and manner in which the speech is to occur.

■═■

Freedman v. Maryland

Movie theatre (D) v. State (P)

380 U.S. 51 (1965).

NATURE OF CASE: Appeal from conviction of violating motion picture censorship law.

FACT SUMMARY: Maryland (P) had a prior approval censorship statute before a motion picture could be licensed for exhibition. Freedman (D) exhibited a motion picture without previously submitting the picture for review and licensing.

🏛 **RULE OF LAW**
While prior restraint is not unconstitutional under all circumstances, a noncriminal process requiring prior submission of a film to a censor will avoid constitutional infirmity only if that process provides procedural safeguards designed to obviate the dangers of a censorship process.

FACTS: A Maryland statute required that before a film could be licensed for exhibition, it must be submitted to a state Board of Censors and receive the Board's approval. If the Board does not grant its approval, no license would be issued for the film. An exhibitor wishing to challenge the Board's ruling must go to court and bear the burden of showing the Board's decision was unwarranted. There is no statutory time limit for Board action, nor for judicial review in the event of an appeal. In order to test the constitutionality of this statute, Freedman (D) exhibited a film without having previously submitted it for Board review. It was conceded that had the film been submitted it would have received approval from the Board. Freedman (D) was found guilty of violating the statute. The judgment was affirmed by the Maryland Court of Appeals, based on a prior case decided by this Court [*Times Film Corp. v. City of Chicago*, 365 U.S. 43 (1961)] upholding a prior submission statute in the City of Chicago.

ISSUE: May a statute requiring submission of a film to an administrative review board be adjudged constitutional when the Board may refuse to license a film without resort to the judicial process?

HOLDING AND DECISION: (Brennan, J.) No. The reliance of the Maryland courts on our decision in *Times Film Corp. v. City of Chicago*, 365 U.S. 43 (1961), was misplaced. The only issue ruled on in that case was whether prior restraint was necessarily unconstitutional under all circumstances. We determined that it was not. But what is critical is an examination of the circumstances surrounding the attempt at prior restraint. Any system of prior restraints of expression is tainted with a heavy presumption against its constitutional validity. And this Court has previously determined that motion pictures are a form of expression that fail within the protections of the First Amendment. Therefore, the burden must fall on the state to prove that the expression sought to be limited is outside those guarantees. To put into the hands of a censor the sole discretion of determining what is or is not to be permitted gives rise to an impermissible power to infringe on constitutional guarantees. This Court has determined that only the adversary proceedings of a judicial hearing can ensure the necessary sensitivity to freedom of expression required by the First Amendment. The Maryland (D) system fails to meet the requisite standards. The burden of proof falls on the exhibitor to show that the film is protected expression, not on the censor to show that it is not. Resort to judicial process can only occur by action of the exhibitor. If he is unwilling or unable to appeal the Board's decision, then his First Amendment rights have been determined by an administrative, not judicial, body. Since the business of a censor is to censor, there is always the danger that he will become too zealous in his work. Because of the nature of the motion picture exhibition business, undue delay or indeterminate periods of review may very well preclude a distributor from bothering to submit to the Maryland (P) process and simply choose not to show the picture at all. Maryland's (P) procedure fails to provide the adequate safeguards against undue inhibition of protected speech that we hold to be necessary to validate a system of prior restraint. Reversed.

CONCURRENCE: (Douglas, J.) Motion pictures are a protected form of expression and, as such, cannot be subjected to any form of censorship if the First Amendment is to be read to mean what it says.

▎ *ANALYSIS*

The *Times Film Corp. v. City of Chicago* case referred to in this decision involved a system similar to Maryland's. However, there was one important difference. The Chicago ordinance required prior submission to a board of censors for licensing purposes as in the Maryland scheme. But if the censors found the film to be objectionable, their recourse was to go to court to seek a restraint on the showing of the film. The Board itself could not prevent the showing. The Court's comment about the tendency of a censor to become overzealous was not just speculation. In every reported case the Maryland Court of Appeals reversed the Board's disapproval of a submitted film. It would appear that almost any attempt by a state or locality to limit by prior restraint the showing of certain films will be met with almost insurmountable obstacles of

Continued on next page.

constitutionality. The Court laid down certain guidelines to the drafting of legislation that might meet with their approval. But the guidelines laid down required speed of action and judicial review that would be difficult to manage. Further, the process must not place any onerous burden on the exhibitor that would deter him from showing protected films. It would appear that the best course to be followed by localities would be to attempt criminal prosecution after the fact of exhibition since this would not be met with the obvious distaste the Court holds for any type of prior restraint.

■■■

Quicknotes

JUDICIAL REVIEW The authority of the courts to review decisions, actions or omissions committed by another agency or branch of government.

PRIOR RESTRAINT A restriction imposed on speech prior to its communication.

■■■

Quick Reference Rules of Law

Walz v. Tax Commission of City of New York

Taxpayer (P) v. City (D)

397 U.S. 664 (1970).

NATURE OF CASE: Appeal from denial of injunction against a tax exemption.

FACT SUMMARY: Walz (P) sought to enjoin the New York City Tax Commission (Commission) (D) from granting property tax exemptions to religious organizations.

🏛 RULE OF LAW
A state law granting property tax exemptions to religious organizations does not violate the Establishment Clause as long as it neither advances nor inhibits religion and does not involve excessive government entanglement.

FACTS: Walz (P) sought to enjoin the New York City Tax Commission (Commission) (D) from granting property tax exemptions to religious organizations for religious properties used solely for religious worship, as authorized by the Commission (D) on the ground that this constituted a violation of the Establishment Clause. The New York courts sustained the constitutionality of the practice and Walz (P) appealed.

ISSUE: Does a state law granting property tax exemptions to religious organizations violate the Establishment Clause?

HOLDING AND DECISION: (Burger, C.J.) No. A state law granting property tax exemptions to religious organizations for religious properties used solely for religious worship does not violate the Establishment Clause as long as it neither inhibits nor advances religion and does not involve excessive government entanglement. In the present case, the legislative purpose of the tax exemption is neither the advancement nor the inhibition of religion; it is neither sponsorship nor hostility. New York, in common with the other states, has determined that certain entities that exist in a harmonious relationship to the community at large and that foster its moral improvement should not be inhibited in their activities by property taxation or the hazard of loss of those properties for nonpayment of taxes. This does not end the inquiry. It must also be shown that the end result of the tax exemption is not excessive government entanglement with religion. The test is inescapably one of degree. Either course, taxation of churches or exemption, occasions some degree of involvement with religion. Granting tax exemptions to churches necessarily operates to afford an indirect economic benefit and also gives rise to some. However, in the present case the involvement is not excessive. Affirmed.

DISSENT: (Douglas, J.) A tax exemption to a nonsectarian social welfare operation would be constitutionally permissible, but the First Amendment prohibits a state from providing worship under the Establishment Clause.

▶ ANALYSIS

All of the 50 states provide for tax exemption of places of worship, most of them doing so by constitutional guarantees. For so long as federal income taxes have had any potential impact on churches—over 75 years—religious organizations have been expressly exempt from the tax. Such treatment is an aid to churches no more and no less in principle than the real estate tax exemption granted by states. Few concepts are more deeply embedded in the fabric of national life, according to Chief Justice Burger.

■■■■

Quicknotes

ESTABLISHMENT CLAUSE The constitutional provision prohibiting the government from favoring any one religion over others, or engaging in religious activities or advocacy.

FIRST AMENDMENT Prohibits Congress from enacting any law respecting an establishment of religion, prohibiting the free exercise of religion, abridging freedom of speech or the press, the right of peaceful assembly and the right to petition for a redress of grievances.

■■■■

Zorach v. Clauson

Parties not identified.

343 U.S. 306 (1952).

NATURE OF CASE: Taxpayer's suit challenging the constitutionality of a state statute.

FACT SUMMARY: A religious released time program allows public schools to release students during the school day to attend religious classes.

RULE OF LAW
A religious released time program, which permits public school students to leave school to attend religious instruction and for which the schools do no more than accommodate their schedules, does not violate the First Amendment.

FACTS: A religious released time program permits public schools to release students during the school day so that they may leave the school grounds to attend religious instruction. Students which are not released remain in the classrooms. The religious groups report to the school from which children were released but did not attend the religious instruction there. No use of public funds or buildings is involved. The religious groups bear all of the program's costs.

ISSUE: Does a religious released time program, which releases public school children during the school day to attend religious instruction and for which the public schools do nothing more than accommodate their schedules, violate the First Amendment?

HOLDING AND DECISION: (Douglas, J.) No. The First Amendment does not say that in every and all respects there must be a separation of church and state. If it did, religion and state would be hostile to one another. Municipalities would not be allowed to render police or fire protection to religious institutions, and prayers in public meetings would have to be banned. This would not be in keeping with our heritage as a religious people. In *McCullum v. Board of Education*, 333 U.S. 203 (1948), a similar religious released time program was found to violate the First Amendment. However, there the public school classrooms were turned over to religious instructors. Here, the instruction occurs off school grounds, and the public schools do no more than accommodate their schedules to the program. No one is forced to attend. The program does not violate the First Amendment. Affirmed.

DISSENT: (Black, J.) New York is manipulating its compulsory education laws to help religious sects get students.

DISSENT: (Jackson, J.) First, the state compels students to yield a large part of their time for public secular education and, second, some of this time may be released to the students on the condition that they devote it to religious study. Simply shortening the school day would facilitate optional attendance at religious classes. It is objected that if the students are made free, they will not attend religious classes. Hence, they must be deprived of their freedom and allowed to choose between attending religious instruction or remaining at school, which serves as a temporary jail for the child who will not attend religious instruction.

ANALYSIS

One of the few establishment cases that did not involve schools was *McGowan v. Maryland*, 366 U.S. 420 (1961), wherein the Court rejected claims that Sunday closing laws violated the First Amendment. The Court stated, "The present purpose and effect of most of them is to provide a uniform day of rest for all citizens; the fact that this day is Sunday, a day of particular significance for the dominant Christian sects, does not bar the state from achieving its secular goals." *Epperson v. Arkansas*, 393 U.S. 97 (1968), which gained national notoriety in the *Scopes* trial, is one of the best known establishment controversies. There the Court held that a state law forbidding the teaching of evolution in public schools violated the First Amendment. "The overriding fact is that Arkansas law selects from the body of knowledge a particular segment which it proscribes for the sole reason that it is deemed to conflict with a particular religious doctrine." This was not religious neutrality.

Quicknotes

ESTABLISHMENT CLAUSE The constitutional provision prohibiting the government from favoring any one religion over others, or engaging in religious activities or advocacy.

FIRST AMENDMENT Prohibits Congress from enacting any law respecting an establishment of religion, prohibiting the free exercise of religion, abridging freedom of speech or the press, the right of peaceful assembly and the right to petition for a redress of grievances.

Committee for Public Educ. and Religious Liberty v. Regan

Committee (P) v. State (D)

444 U.S. 646 (1980).

NATURE OF CASE: Appeal from decision upholding reimbursement scheme.

FACT SUMMARY: The Committee for Public Education and Religious Liberty (Committee) (P) appealed a decision upholding a New York (State) (D) statute which reimbursed church-supported and secular nonpublic schools for performing various testing and reporting services mandated by state law against the Committee's (P) Establishment Clause challenge.

RULE OF LAW

A state statute that reimburses a church-supported school for state-mandated testing and reporting services is not violative of the Establishment Clause of the Constitution so long as the reimbursement has a primarily secular purpose and effect, and has no excessive entanglement with religion.

FACTS: In 1970, New York (State) (D) appropriated public funds to reimburse church-supported and private secular schools for certain services mandated by the State (D). Included among these services was the administration, grading, and reporting of tests and test results. Covered tests included both state-prepared and teacher-prepared tests. This enactment was struck down on Establishment Clause grounds because with respect to teacher-prepared tests, no provision was made to assure that these tests were free from religious instruction. A new statute was enacted in 1974, which allowed only for the reimbursement of costs associated with state-prepared tests, and provided a means by which the reimbursements would be audited, insuring that only the actual costs incurred in connection with providing for the state mandated services would be reimbursed. This statute was likewise invalidated by the district court, which held that substantial and to a religious-pervasive institution amounted to aid to the sectarian school enterprise as a whole, and thus amounted to the forbidden establishment of religion. This judgment was vacated in light of an intervening decision which held that state aid may be extended to a sectarian school's educational activities if it can be shown that there is a high degree of certainty that the aid will only have secular value of legitimate interest to the State (D). In light of the intervening case, the district court, on remand, upheld the statute as not violative of the Establishment Clause, and the Committee for Public Education and Religious Liberty (Committee) (P) appealed.

ISSUE: Is a state statute that reimburses a church-supported school for state-mandated testing and reporting services violative of the Establishment Clause of the

Constitution, if the reimbursement has a primarily secular purpose and effect, and has no excessive entanglement with religion?

HOLDING AND DECISION: (White, J.) No. A state statute that reimburses a church-supported school for state-mandated testing and reporting services is not violative of the Establishment Clause of the Constitution so long as the reimbursement has a primarily secular purpose and effect, and has no excessive entanglement with religion. The tests for which reimbursement is provided are state-prepared, which provides a substantial guarantee that the content of the tests will be free of religious influence, and none of the tests deal with religious subject matter. The tests are for the most part multiple choice, and the completed tests are submitted to the Department of Education for review. These safeguard against the risk of the tests being used for religious purposes through grading. The reporting services for which church-supported schools are reimbursed are ministerial in character and are lacking entirely in any ideological content or use. The reimbursement process involved here is straightforward and susceptible to routinization, and therefore there is no excessive entanglement with religion. Affirmed.

DISSENT: (Blackmun, J.) The line which is drawn in determining what aid may be permissible to a sectarian educational is necessarily not a straight one, but the line has been drawn in precedent nonetheless, and the majority departs significantly from this standard. The direct type of financial aid provided in the present case is significantly different from any aid previously authorized by this Court.

DISSENT: (Stevens, J.) The Court's position today opens the door for the reimbursement of many costs which might be financially expedient, but which would be violative of the Establishment Clause of the Constitution.

▶ ANALYSIS

The Court in the present case has retreated from an earlier stand which would have required it to hold as violative of the Establishment Clause any substantial financial aid to any school that was "pervasively sectarian." The present case addresses the effect to be prohibited by the Establishment Clause more specifically than in the past, but the sectarian nature of the school aided is still an important consideration in determining whether financial aid is appropriate.

Continued on next page.

Quicknotes

ESTABLISHMENT CLAUSE The constitutional provision prohibiting the government from favoring any one religion over others, or engaging in religious activities or advocacy.

∎══∎

Mueller v. Allen

Parties not identified.

463 U.S. 388 (1983).

NATURE OF CASE: Action challenging the constitutionality of a state tax deduction law.

FACT SUMMARY: Plaintiffs instituted suit challenging the constitutionality of a Minnesota law allowing taxpayers, in computing their state income tax, to deduct certain expenses incurred in providing for their children's education, whether or not the children attended public schools or private parochial schools.

RULE OF LAW

The three-prong test for determining if a program aiding parochial schools violates the Establishment Clause is as follows: (1) does it have a secular purpose?; (2) does it have "the primary effect of advancing the sectarian aims of the nonpublic schools"?; and (3) does it "excessively entangle" the state in religion?

FACTS: Minnesota passed a law allowing taxpayers, in figuring their state income tax, to deduct actual expenses incurred for the "tuition, textbooks, and transportation" of dependents attending elementary or secondary schools, whether or not they are nonsectarian or sectarian. A maximum $500 deduction for each dependent in grades K through six and $700 for each dependent in grades seven through twelve was permitted.Plaintiffs brought suit challenging the validity of the law under the Establishment Clause. The court of appeals held that the clause was not offended by this statute.

ISSUE: In order to decide if a program aiding parochial schools (directly or indirectly) violates the Establishment Clause, must the following three-part test be applied: (1) does it have a secular purpose?; (2) does it have "the primary effect of advancing the sectarian aims of the nonpublic schools"?; and (3) does it "excessively entangle" the state in religion?

HOLDING AND DECISION: (Rehnquist, J.) Yes. A three-part test was laid down in the Lemon case and is the means by which it can be ascertained whether a particular program that in some manner aids parochial schools (either directly or indirectly) violates the Establishment Clause. The first part inquires whether the program has a secular purpose. In this case, the answer is yes. The tax deduction attempts to give parents an incentive to educate their children and this serves the secular purpose of ensuring a well-educated citizenry. The second part of the test asks the related question of whether the program has "the primary effect of advancing the sectarian aims of the nonpublic schools." Here, the answer is no. The deduc-

tion is available to all parents, including those sending their children to public schools, and it channels whatever funds available to such schools only as a result of numerous, private choices of individual parents of school-age children. The third part of the test to which this program must be put inquires whether or not the program "excessively entangles" the state in religion. It does not. The only decision that might remotely involve state officials in state surveillance of religious type issues would be the decisions state officials have to make in determining whether particular textbooks qualify for the deduction. In making this decision, they must disallow deductions taken from "instructional materials used in the teaching of religious tenets, doctrines, or worship, the purpose of which is to inculcate such tenets, doctrines or worship." Making this type of decision does not differ substantially from making the types of decisions approved in early opinions of this Court. Thus, the program at issue here must be considered constitutional, as it has passed the three parts of the appropriate test. Affirmed.

DISSENT: (Marshall, J.) As this Court requoted in *Nyquist*, 413 U.S. 756 (1973), indirect assistance in the form of financial aid to parents for tuition payments is impermissible because it is not "subject to restrictions" which "guarantee the separation between secular and religious educational functions and . . . ensure that state financial aid supports only the former." The Minnesota statute at hand here is little more than a subsidy of tuition masquerading as a subsidy of general education expenses. While tax deductions are ostensibly available to parents sending their children to public schools, most such parents have no tuition payments to make and would be able to deduct only what they pay for such things as gym clothes, pencils, notebooks, etc. These deductible expenses are de minimis in comparison to tuition expenses paid by most parents sending their children to parochial schools. Thus, the parochial schools are the ones benefitted. In this case, the Court for the first time approves a program providing financial support for religious schools without any reason at all to assume that the support will be restricted to the secular functions of those schools and will not be used to support religious instruction. This result is flatly at odds with the fundamental principle that a state may provide no financial support whatsoever to promote religion.

▶ ANALYSIS

In the previously decided *Nyquist* case, on which the constitutional challenge to this tax deduction program relied

Continued on next page.

heavily, New York had passed a statute that gave the parents of children attending private schools thinly disguised "tax benefits" that actually amounted to tuition grants. This was found to violate the Establishment Clause. By simply providing in its tax deduction statute that all parents could take such tuition deductions, Minnesota kept its tax deduction scheme from being declared unconstitutional. Yet, it is really a change in form more than substance, for most public school parents do not have to pay tuition. So, giving them the opportunity to deduct tuition expenses is of little practical consequence and does little to change the effect of the program in providing indirect aid mostly to parochial schools.

■══■

Quicknotes

ESTABLISHMENT CLAUSE The constitutional provision prohibiting the government from favoring any one religion over others, or engaging in religious activities or advocacy.

■══■

Zelman v. Simmons-Harris

School superintendent (D) v. Taxpayers (P)

536 U.S. 639 (2002).

NATURE OF CASE: Appeal from affirmance of injunction against a school voucher program that can be used for parochial school education.

FACT SUMMARY: To address the dismal performance of the Cleveland public school system, Ohio enacted a school voucher program that enabled parents to choose to send their children to participating private schools. An overwhelming number of the private schools participating in the program had a religious affiliation, and Ohio taxpayers (P) challenged the voucher program as a violation of the Establishment Clause.

🏛 RULE OF LAW
A school voucher program that gives parents the choice to send their children to a private school does not violate the Establishment Clause where the overwhelming number of participating private schools is comprised of religiously affiliated parochial schools.

FACTS: Ohio's Pilot Project Scholarship Program gave educational choices to families in any Ohio school district that was under state control pursuant to a federal court order. The program provided tuition aid for certain students in the Cleveland City School District, the only covered district because of its dismal performance as compared to most other districts in the nation, to attend participating public or private schools of their parent's choosing and tutorial aid for students who chose to remain enrolled in public school. Both religious and nonreligious schools in the district could participate, as could public schools in adjacent school districts. Tuition aid was distributed to parents according to financial need, and where the aid was spent depended solely upon where parents chose to enroll their children. The number of tutorial assistance grants provided to students remaining in public school had to equal the number of tuition aid scholarships. In the 1999–2000 school year, 82% of the participating private schools had a religious affiliation, none of the adjacent public schools participated, and 96% of the students participating in the scholarship program were enrolled in religiously affiliated schools. Sixty percent of the students were from families at or below the poverty line. Cleveland schoolchildren also had the option of enrolling in community schools, which were funded under state law but run by their own school boards and received twice the per-student funding as participating private schools, or magnet schools (public schools emphasizing a particular subject area, teaching method, or service). Ohio taxpayers (P) sought to enjoin the program on the ground that it violated the Establishment Clause. The district court granted them

summary judgment, and the court of appeals affirmed. The Supreme Court granted review.

ISSUE: Does a school voucher program that gives parents the choice to send their children to a private school violate the Establishment Clause where the overwhelming number of participating private schools is comprised of religiously-affiliated parochial schools?

HOLDING AND DECISION: (Rehnquist, C.J.) No. A school voucher program that gives parents the choice to send their children to a private school does not violate the Establishment Clause where the overwhelming number of participating private schools is comprised of religiously affiliated parochial schools. Because the program here was undisputedly enacted for the valid secular purpose of providing educational assistance to poor children in a demonstrably failing public school system, the question is whether the program nonetheless has the forbidden effect of advancing or inhibiting religion. The Court's jurisprudence [see, e.g, *Mueller v. Allen*, 463 U.S. 388 (1983), and its progeny] makes clear that a government aid program is not readily subject to challenge under the Establishment Clause if it is neutral with respect to religion and provides assistance directly to a broad class of citizens who, in turn, direct government aid to religious schools wholly as a result of their own genuine and independent private choice. The Ohio program is one of true private choice, and is thus constitutional. It is neutral in all respects toward religion, and is part of Ohio's general and multifaceted undertaking to provide educational opportunities to children in a failed school district. It confers educational assistance directly to a broad class of individuals defined without reference to religion and permits participation of all district schools—religious or nonreligious—and adjacent public schools. The only preference in the program is for low-income families, who receive greater assistance and have priority for admission. Rather than creating financial incentives that skew it toward religious schools, the program creates financial disincentives: Private schools receive only half the government assistance given to community schools and one-third that given to magnet schools, and adjacent public schools would receive two to three times that given to private schools. Families, too, have a financial disincentive, for they have to copay a portion of private school tuition, but pay nothing at a community, magnet, or traditional public school. Thus, no reasonable observer would think that such a neutral private choice program carries with it the imprimatur of government endorsement. Even though 46 of the 56 private

Continued on next page.

schools participating in the program are religious schools, the Establishment Clause question whether Ohio is coercing parents into sending their children to religious schools must be answered by evaluating all options Ohio provides Cleveland schoolchildren, only one of which is to obtain a scholarship and then choose a religious school. Eighty-two percent of Cleveland's private schools are religious, as are 81% of Ohio's private schools. To attribute constitutional significance to the 82% figure would lead to the absurd result that a neutral school-choice program might be permissible in parts of Ohio where the percentage is lower, but not in Cleveland, where Ohio has deemed such programs most sorely needed. The taxpayers (P) additionally argue that constitutional significance should be attached to the fact that 96% of the scholarship recipients have enrolled in religious schools. However, a closer look at the 96% figure reveals that if over 1,900 Cleveland children enrolled in alternative community schools, 13,000 children enrolled in alternative magnet schools, and 1,400 children enrolled in traditional public schools with tutorial assistance are factored in, the percentage drops to 20%. In sum, the Ohio program is entirely neutral with respect to religion. It provides benefits directly to a wide spectrum of individuals, defined only by financial need and residence in a particular school district. It permits such individuals to exercise genuine choice among options public and private, secular and religious. The program is therefore a program of true private choice. Reversed.

CONCURRENCE: (O'Connor, J.) This case does not depart from precedent. It is different from prior indirect aid cases because a significant portion of the funds appropriated for the voucher program reaches religious schools without restriction on the use of these funds. The share of public resources that reach religious schools is not as significant as the taxpayers (P) suggest (82% of participating schools are religious; 96% of participating students are enrolled in religious schools) because the statistics on which these assertions are based do not take into account all of the reasonable educational choices that may be available to students in the district. When one considers the option to attend community schools, the percentage of students enrolled in religious schools falls to 62.1%. If magnet schools are included in the mix, this percentage falls to 16.5%. In addition, the state spent $1 million more on students in community schools than in religious schools although one-half as many students attended community schools than attended religious schools. Moreover, the amount spent on religious private schools ($8.2 million) was minor compared to the $114.8 million spent on students in magnet schools. Although $8.2 million is no small sum, it pales in comparison to the billions of dollars that federal, state, and local governments already provide religious institutions in the form of different tax breaks, public health programs, educational programs, and other social welfare programs. These funds, like the voucher program funds, typically are unaccompanied by restrictions on

subsequent use. The Court's decision does not mark a dramatic break with the Court's prior Establishment Clause jurisprudence. Here, the Court clarifies that the Establishment Clause requires that state aid going to religious organizations through the hands of beneficiaries must do so only at the discretion of those beneficiaries. The parents have a genuine nonreligious choice when all the choices available are considered, and, therefore, the voucher program is consistent with the Establishment Clause.

CONCURRENCE: (Thomas, J.) Although the voucher program easily passes muster under the Court's stringent test, this test should not be applied to the states. On its face, the Establishment Clause does not apply to the states; originally, it protected states and their citizens from the imposition of an established religion by the federal government. The use of the Fourteenth Amendment to protect religious liberty rights is acceptable, but to oppose neutral programs of school choice through the incorporation of the Establishment Clause is unacceptable. Religious schools, like other private schools, achieve far better educational results than their public counterparts. But, the success of religious and private schools is in the end beside the point, because the state has a constitutional right to experiment with a variety of different programs to promote educational opportunity. That Ohio's program includes successful schools simply indicates that such reform can in fact provide improved education to underprivileged urban children.

DISSENT: (Stevens, J.) The voluntary character of the private choice to prefer a parochial education to a public one is irrelevant to the question whether the government's choice to pay for religious indoctrination is constitutionally permissible. The removal of any safeguard of the separation between religion and government weakens the foundation of our democracy.

DISSENT: (Souter, J.) The dismal condition of Cleveland's public schools is no excuse for giving short shrift to the Establishment Clause. Most of the money spent under the program the majority approves will be spent not only on teaching students secular subjects but will also be spent on teaching religion in schools that are founded to teach religious doctrine and to imbue all subjects with a religious dimension. Under the Court's precedent, neutrality conceived of as evenhandedness toward aid recipients has never been treated as alone sufficient to satisfy the Establishment Clause. However, under the majority's decision, the substantial character of government aid has no significance, and the criteria of neutrality in offering aid and private choice in directing it, are nothing but examples of verbal formalism. The Court's logic could lead to a finding that there is "neutrality" in a voucher scheme where there are no secular private schools at all. This, indeed, is the only way the majority can gloss over the very nonneutral

Continued on next page.

feature of the total scheme covering "all schools": public tutors may receive from the state no more than $324 per child to support extra tutoring, whereas the tuition voucher schools (which turn out to be mostly religious) can receive up to $2,250. If, contrary to the majority, the question is posed in terms of choice regarding how to use the vouchers, the answer here is that something is influencing choices in a way that aims the money in a religious direction. It is not the particular religion of the school that is responsible for this effect, because two out of three families chose religious schools the religion of which they did not embrace. The fact is that nonreligious private schools are more expensive than the religious schools, and can afford to accommodate only a few voucher students. The obvious fix to this problem would be to increase the value of the vouchers. However, to get to the point where true choice is available would require such massive funding of religion as to disserve every goal of the Establishment Clause even more than the scheme here does.

DISSENT: (Breyer, J.) The Establishment Clause's concern for protecting the nation's social fabric from religious conflict outweighs the goals of the well-intentioned voucher program at issue here.

▶ *ANALYSIS*

The Court has traditionally been satisfied that a law has a neutral primary effect if the religious impact of the law is remote, indirect, and incidental. Here, the dissent seems to argue that the voucher program's impact was not remote or incidental, because by its very design, given the demographic realities of the school district, it encouraged enrollment in religious schools. The case leaves several constitutional questions unanswered, including whether provisions in voucher programs that prohibit discrimination by recipient schools are now constitutionally mandated, and whether state laws that expressly prohibit the use of aid for religious schools are themselves unconstitutional.

■═■

Quicknotes

ESTABLISHMENT CLAUSE The constitutional provision prohibiting the government from favoring any one religion over others, or engaging in religious activities or advocacy.

■═■

Roemer v. Board of Public Works of Maryland

Colleges (P) v. State (D)

426 U.S. 736 (1976).

NATURE OF CASE: Action for injunction.

FACT SUMMARY: The State of Maryland enacted a statute providing for the awarding of noncategorical grants in aid to religiously affiliated institutions.

🏛 RULE OF LAW
"Religious institutions need not be quarantined from public benefits that are neutrally available to all"; and, as such, noncategorical grants in aid to religiously affiliated colleges do not offend the First Amendment as long as they have "a secular purpose, a primary effect other than the advancement of religion, and no tendency to entangle the state excessively in church affairs."

FACTS: The State of Maryland enacted a statute providing for the awarding of annual noncategorical grants in aid to religiously affiliated institutions. Four of the institutions affected were Roman Catholic colleges. Though these schools conducted religious exercises, taught "mandatory theology courses," favored members of religious orders in hiring decisions, they nevertheless enjoyed a high degree of autonomy from the church hierarchy, did not compel attendance at religious exercises, pursued a policy of intellectual freedom in their "mandatory" classes, and used "academic quality" as the principle yardstick in making hiring decisions. Roemer (P) and others seek an injunction against the grants in question on the ground that they violate the First Amendment. This appeal followed denial.

ISSUE: Do annual noncategorical grants from the state to religiously affiliated institutions violate the Establishment Clause of the First Amendment?

HOLDING AND DECISION: (Blackmun, J.) No. "Religious institutions need not be quarantined from public benefits that are neutrally available to all"; and, as such, noncategorical state grants in aid to religiously affiliated colleges do not offend the First Amendment as long as they have "a secular purpose, a primary effect other than the advancement of religion, and no tendency to entangle the state excessively in church affairs." The secular purpose (encouraging private education) here is unquestioned. The primary effect can be determined by determining whether the institutions are "pervasively sectarian" (the emphasis on intellectual freedom and academic quality protects them from such charge), and whether secular activities can be "separated out" so they alone can be funded (it must be assumed that college officials will perform their statutory duties to do so). Finally, the prevention of excessive state entanglement is to be determined by the character of the

institution (the same factors as above)—not the character of the grant. As such, even though this court prefers "one-time, single-purpose" grants, the annual grants here are not impermissible. Affirmed.

CONCURRENCE: (White, J.) The third test (excessive entanglement) is redundant with the second and should be discarded.

DISSENT: (Brennan, J.) Grants which are unmarked as to purpose must necessarily create excessive entanglement or the state cannot assure they are not being employed for purely secular purposes.

DISSENT: (Stewart, J.) The fact that theology was mandatory here makes advancement of religion inevitable.

▶ ANALYSIS

This case reinforces the so-called *Lemon v. Kurtzman*, 403 U.S. 602 (1971), three-pronged test for whether state aid to religious institutions violates the First Amendment's Establishment Clause. Note that it is consistent with the recurrent Burger court theme of expanding state discretion in areas in which fundamental rights are involved. It also reinforces, however, the basic rule that "neutrality" is the ultimate goal of the state in any relations with the church. This rule results from the long recognized fact that total separation of church and state—to the point of no contact whatsoever—is practically impossible.

■══■

Quicknotes

ESTABLISHMENT CLAUSE The constitutional provision prohibiting the government from favoring any one religion over others, or engaging in religious activities or advocacy.

FIRST AMENDMENT Prohibits Congress from enacting any law respecting an establishment of religion, prohibiting the free exercise of religion, abridging freedom of speech or the press, the right of peaceful assembly and the right to petition for a redress of grievances.

FUNDAMENTAL RIGHT A liberty that is either expressly or impliedly provided for in the United States Constitution, the deprivation or burdening of which is subject to a heightened standard of review.

GRANT-IN-AID Money given by a governmental or other institutional body to an individual or group for a specific use.

■══■

School District of Abington Township v. Schempp

School district (D) v. Families (P)

374 U.S. 203 (1963).

NATURE OF CASE: Suit to obtain injunctive relief; action seeking the issuance of a writ of mandamus.

FACT SUMMARY: Both Schempp (P) and Murray (P) challenged provisions which mandated the reading of Bible verses at the beginning of each day of public school.

🏛 RULE OF LAW
A statute or rule that has as its purpose or primary effect either the advancement or the inhibition of religion is contrary to the Establishment Clause of the First Amendment and therefore invalid.

FACTS: In separate cases, the Schempps (P) and the Murrays (P) attacked the constitutionality of provisions which required that the Bible be read at the beginning of each public school day. The Schempp (P) family brought suit to enjoin enforcement of a Pennsylvania statute mandating that at least ten verses from the Bible be read, without comment, every morning. Upon written request of their parent or guardian, students were entitled to be excused from the classroom while the verses were read. A three-judge district court ruled that the statute violated the Establishment Clause of the First Amendment, and ordered injunctive relief. The School District of Abington (D) appealed to the Supreme Court, and the suit was joined with that of Mrs. Madalyn Murray (P) and her son (P), avowed atheists, who objected to a rule which the Baltimore Board of School Commissioners (D) had adopted pursuant to a Maryland statute. The rule required schools to hold opening ceremonies which included the reading, without comment, of a chapter from the Bible. The Murrays (P) sought mandamus to compel the rescission and cancellation of the rule, but the trial court sustained the Board's (D) demurrer without leave to amend. The Maryland Court of Appeals affirmed, and it was from the order of that court that the Murrays (P) appealed.

ISSUE: Does the Establishment Clause of the First Amendment to the Constitution permit compulsory Bible reading in the public schools?

HOLDING AND DECISION: (Clark, J.) No. A statute or rule that has as its purpose or primary effect either the advancement or the inhibition of religion is contrary to the Establishment Clause of the First Amendment and is therefore invalid. Although religion has historically played a major role in this and other countries, ours is a nation imbued with a strong sense of religious freedom and tolerance. Whenever an enactment does not have a secular purpose and effect, there is a danger that either the Establishment Clause, the Free Exercise Clause, or both will be violated. In these cases, the religious neutrality that the Constitution mandates has been compromised. The Bible reading in both cases takes place within schools that children are legally obliged to attend, and is carried out by or under the supervision of teachers hired by the schools. The state is thus imposing religious training, and it matters little that students may absent themselves from the ceremonies or that the intrusion upon personal liberties may be minimal. Official hostility toward religion is impermissible, but the concept of neutrality does not interfere with anyone's right to practice the religion of his choice. Thus, while Bible reading for secular purposes, e.g., as literature, may be condoned, the mandatory provisions presented by these cases must both be struck down as violative of the Establishment Clause.

CONCURRENCE: (Brennan, J.) It has been vigorously debated whether the Framers of the First Amendment intended that the Establishment Clause prohibit devotional exercises in public schools. I doubt that the view of even the Framers themselves would produce a dispositive answer. Rather we should inquire as to whether the practices here questioned threatened to result in the consequence feared by the Framers of the First Amendment.

DISSENT: (Stewart, J.) If exercises of the type here complained of were held before or after the official school day, the exercises would do no more than provide an opportunity to voluntarily express religious beliefs.

▶ ANALYSIS

The First Amendment to the Constitution proclaims that Congress shall make no law which relates to the establishment of religion or prevents the free exercise of religion. Both the Establishment Clause and the Free Exercise Clause have, of course, been applied to the states as well by virtue of the Fourteenth Amendment. During the 19th and early 20th century, constitutional protections relating to religious freedom were enforced only haphazardly. However, since the 1930s, the Supreme Court has applied those provisions conscientiously, thus eliminating many long-standing examples of religious doctrines being imposed upon unwilling individuals. As a result, it is now an accepted proposition that the Constitution guarantees all people the right to practice any religion of their choosing or no religion at all, free of state interference.

■■■

Continued on next page.

Quicknotes

ESTABLISHMENT CLAUSE The constitutional provision prohibiting the government from favoring any one religion over others, or engaging in religious activities or advocacy.

FIRST AMENDMENT Prohibits Congress from enacting any law respecting an establishment of religion, prohibiting the free exercise of religion, abridging freedom of speech or the press, the right of peaceful assembly and the right to petition for a redress of grievances.

FREE EXERCISE CLAUSE The guarantee of the First Amendment to the United States Constitution prohibiting Congress from enacting laws regarding the establishment of religion or prohibiting the free exercise thereof.

Epperson v. Arkansas

Teacher (P) v. State (D)

393 U.S. 97 (1968).

NATURE OF CASE: Suit seeking declaratory relief.

FACT SUMMARY: Epperson (P) attacked the validity of an Arkansas (D) statute which prohibited the teaching of any doctrine based on the theory that mankind has evolved from a lower order of animals.

🏛 **RULE OF LAW**
The First Amendment prevents state governments from enacting laws that promote any one religion or the concept of religion in general.

FACTS: A 1928 Arkansas (D) statute made it illegal for any teacher in a state-supported school or university to teach the theory that man evolved from a lower order of animals or to utilize a textbook which included that theory. Violation of the statute was punishable as a misdemeanor and subjected the offending teacher to dismissal. In 1965, Central High School in Little Rock planned to use for the first time a biology textbook which contained a chapter setting forth the theory of evolution. Susan Epperson (P), a teacher at Central who claimed that compliance with her orders to utilize the book would place her in violation of the state statute, sued for an order declaring the Arkansas (D) law invalid and enjoining officials from dismissing her from her teaching position. The challenged statute had not been invoked on a single occasion since its enactment. The chancery court granted the relief sought, holding that the statute violated the First and Fourteenth Amendments to the Constitution since it amounted to a restriction upon freedom of speech and thought. The Supreme Court of Arkansas reversed, noting in its two-sentence opinion that the statute did not specify whether or not a teacher at least could lawfully describe the theory of evolution without advocating it or asserting its accuracy, but holding that the law was a valid exercise of the state's authority to control the curriculum taught in its schools. Epperson (P), together with a parent (P) who had intervened in the suit, appealed to the U.S. Supreme Court.

ISSUE: May a state legislature prohibit the teaching of the theory of evolution in the public schools?

HOLDING AND DECISION: (Fortas, J.) No. The First Amendment prevents state governments from enacting laws that promote any one religion or the concept of religion in general. Obviously, the disputed statute is intended to bar the teaching of any theory contrary to that endorsed by those who ascribe to a literal reading of the account of creation set forth in the Book of Genesis. Whether or not the statute is unconstitutionally vague in that it does not state whether the mere teaching of the

theory of evolution is itself criminal even without advocacy, the law violates the Establishment Clause of the First Amendment. Government must be neutral in its attitude toward religion. It cannot favor one faith to the exclusion of other faiths or of no religion at all. This law is designed to preserve the beliefs of one religious group. No other motive for the statute's passage has ever been suggested. In view of this circumstance, it plainly violates the Constitution and cannot be permitted to stand. Reversed.

CONCURRENCE: (Black, J.) Probably the case presents no justiciable controversy since the State (D) has no plans to enforce the statute and none of those challenging it remains in a position to be adversely affected by it. But if the statute must be dealt with at all, it should be struck down on the ground that it is too vague because it does not clarify whether or not a teacher can be punished merely for neutral description of the theory, without advocating it. The decision should not be based upon the Establishment Clause, because there is no proof that the statute was passed solely for the benefit of any one religious group. It might have been enacted merely to forestall the controversy which it was feared would be generated by a free discussion of man's origins. In any event, it is at least arguable that to force the state to permit the teaching of evolution is more offensive to the Constitution than to prohibit its teaching, because the doctrine is obviously contrary to the religious beliefs of Fundamentalists. Perhaps most importantly, the majority opinion deprives school officials of their right to prescribe a curriculum of their choosing, and forces them to permit the teaching of a theory which is itself subject to scientific challenge. Either the statute should be struck down on vagueness grounds, or the case should be remanded to the Supreme Court of Arkansas.

▌ *ANALYSIS*

Since the American colonies were first established as a haven for religious dissenters, it is not surprising that freedom of religion was a privilege much cherished by the Framers of the Bill of Rights. The Establishment Clause is frequently invoked in the context of school administration. In addition to curriculum matters such as that involved in *Epperson*, the clause has been cited as a bar to Bible reading in the classroom, state aid to parochial schools, and tax benefits for the parents of students who attend religiously affiliated secondary schools. However, the Establishment Clause has also been the basis for attacks upon other types of official action, e.g., the

Continued on next page.

enforcement of Sunday "blue laws," which require that businesses be closed on the Christian sabbath day.

■═■

Quicknotes

FOURTEENTH AMENDMENT Declares that no state shall make or enforce any law which shall abridge the privileges and immunities of citizens of the United States.

VAGUENESS Doctrine that a statute that does not clearly or definitely inform an individual as to what conduct is unlawful is unconstitutional, in violation of the Due Process Clause.

■═■

Lynch v. Donnelly

City (D) v. Residents (P)

465 U.S. 668 (1984).

NATURE OF CASE: Appeal from order enjoining a city-sponsored nativity scene.

FACT SUMMARY: The district court held that Pawtucket's (D) inclusion of a nativity scene in its Christmas display violated the Establishment Clause.

🏛 RULE OF LAW
A nativity scene does not constitute a benefit to religion by a city displaying it and therefore such display does not violate the Establishment Clause.

FACTS: For over 40 years, Pawtucket (D) included a nativity scene in its Christmas display. Donnelly (P) and other residents sued, contending the inclusion of the scene violated the Establishment Clause. The district court held the scene benefitted the Christian religion and, therefore, violated the clause. The court of appeals affirmed, and the Supreme Court granted certiorari.

ISSUE: Does the inclusion of a nativity scene in a city display violate the Establishment Clause?

HOLDING AND DECISION: (Burger, C.J.) No. A nativity scene does not benefit the Christian religion to any greater extent that other governmental uses of religious symbols, such as the use of "In God We Trust" on currency. The display depicted the historical origin of a holiday and, therefore, had a recognizable secular purpose. Thus, its inclusion did not violate the Constitution. Reversed.

CONCURRENCE: (O'Connor, J.) Absent city endorsement of a particular religion, the display of religious symbols does not violate the Constitution.

DISSENT: (Brennan, J.) The nativity scene lies at the heart of the Christian religion and its display by a governmental unit was unconstitutional.

▶ ANALYSIS

The trend in recent years in cases involving the Establishment Clause is to make ad hoc decisions based on the circumstances of the case. Prior to this trend, the Court routinely followed a three-prong analysis articulated in *Lemon v. Kurtzman*, 403 U.S. 602 (1970). This test requires a determination that the government action had no secular purpose, it neither advanced nor inhibited religion, and it did not create excessive governmental entanglement in religion.

Quicknotes

AD HOC DECISION An appointment or determination made for a specific purpose; e.g., an attorney appointed to represent a client for a particular action in a limited circumstance.

ESTABLISHMENT CLAUSE The constitutional provision prohibiting the government from favoring any one religion over others, or engaging in religious activities or advocacy.

Wallace v. Jaffree

Parties not identified.

472 U.S. 38 (1985).

NATURE OF CASE: Appeal from grant of injunctive relief from school prayer statute.

FACT SUMMARY: Plaintiff contended that an Alabama statute authorizing a period of silence for meditation or voluntary prayer was invalid as violative of the Establishment Clause of the First Amendment.

🏛 RULE OF LAW
A state statute allowing for voluntary prayer in public school violates the First Amendment.

FACTS: Alabama enacted a statute allowing public schools to observe a period of silence to allow meditation or voluntary prayer. Plaintiff sought to enjoin such activity on the basis it impermissibly mixed government and religion. The district court held the statute unconstitutional, the court of appeals affirmed, and the Supreme Court granted certiorari.

ISSUE: Does a state statute allowing for voluntary prayer in public school violate the Establishment Clause of the First Amendment?

HOLDING AND DECISION: (Stevens, J.) Yes. A state statute allowing for voluntary prayer in school violates the First Amendment. Statutes involving religion are unconstitutional if they have a nonsecular legislative purpose, their primary effect is to advance or inhibit religion, and it fosters excessive governmental entanglement in religion. The legislative history of the statute clearly indicates that the sole purpose was to put religion back in the schools. The only conclusion is a nonsecular purpose and an advancement of religion. Thus the statute is unconstitutional. Affirmed.

DISSENT: (Burger, C.J.) A moment of silence clearly does not advance religion, nor does it entangle the government in religious actions.

DISSENT: (White, J.) The legislative history alone does not invalidate the statute.

DISSENT: (Rehnquist, J.) The endorsement of prayer by state law is not unconstitutional.

▌ ANALYSIS

This case applies the traditional Establishment Clause analysis involving a three-prong approach. This approach has evolved through the decisions in *Board of Education v. Allen*, 392 U.S. 236 (1968), and *Waly v. Tax Commission*, 397 U.S. 664 (1970). This analysis has been used in every recent Establishment Clause case and was last affirmed in *Lemon v. Kurtzman*, 403 U.S. 602 (1971).

■■■

Quicknotes

ESTABLISHMENT CLAUSE The constitutional provision prohibiting the government from favoring any one religion over others, or engaging in religious activities or advocacy.

FIRST AMENDMENT Prohibits Congress from enacting any law respecting an establishment of religion, prohibiting the free exercise of religion, abridging freedom of speech or the press, the right of peaceful assembly and the right to petition for a redress of grievances.

■■■

Capitol Square Review and Advisory Board v. Pinette

State agency (D) v. Applicant (P)

515 U.S. 753 (1995).

NATURE OF CASE: Review of order mandating a state to allow a religious symbol to be placed on public property.

FACT SUMMARY: A state agency refused to allow the erection of a religious symbol on property traditionally used for public displays.

🏛 **RULE OF LAW**
Unattended religious displays in public forums do not violate the Establishment Clause.

FACTS: A ten-acre plaza known as Capitol Square was adjacent to the Ohio Statehouse. It had traditionally been a forum for public expression, both verbal and symbolic. To erect a display, all that an applicant had to do was meet certain content-neutral safety standards. The local chapter of the Ku Klux Klan (KKK) (P) applied to erect a cross. This was denied by the Capitol Square Review and Advisory Board (Board) (D) on grounds that the display would violate the Establishment Clause. The KKK (P) filed suit. The district court issued an injunction and the Board (D) appealed. The Supreme Court granted review.

ISSUE: Do unattended religious displays in public forums violate the Establishment Clause?

HOLDING AND DECISION: (Scalia, J.) No. Unattended religious displays in public forums do not violate the Establishment Clause. Private religious speech is protected by the First Amendment. Just as nonreligious speech may not be unduly abridged, neither may religious expression. Not all public property, of course, is a forum for private speech. But public forums must be available for private religious expression no less than political expression. Here, Capitol Square was clearly a traditional forum for public expression. The State (D) argues that allowing an unattended religious symbol to be placed so close to the seat of government would be an unconstitutional endorsement of religion. However, proximity is not favoritism, and only favoritism is prohibited by the Establishment Clause. Here, no such favoritism existed. Affirmed.

CONCURRENCE: (O'Connor, J.) The scope of the Establishment Clause is broader than the opinion of the plurality suggests.

CONCURRENCE: (Souter, J.) An unattended display on public property could be interpreted by observers as an endorsement of religion by the state.

DISSENT: (Stevens, J.) The Establishment Clause creates a strong presumption against allowing unattended religious symbols on public property.

DISSENT: (Ginsburg, J.) The Establishment Clause exists to uncouple government and church and cannot permit displays such as that at issue here.

▶ **ANALYSIS**

Not all of Justice Scalia's opinion was on behalf of the Court. Part IV was only a plurality opinion. This was the portion of the opinion dealing with proximity, so that part of the opinion is of uncertain precendential value.

■━■

Quicknotes

ESTABLISHMENT CLAUSE The constitutional provision prohibiting the government from favoring any one religion over others, or engaging in religious activities or advocacy.

PUBLIC FORUM Public area so associated with freedom of speech so that restriction of access to it for that purpose is unconstitutional (e.g., sidewalks, streets, parks, etc.).

■━■

Rosenberger v. Rector and Visitors of the University of Virginia

Magazine (P) v. University (D)

515 U.S. 819 (1995).

NATURE OF CASE: Review of order holding a college funding decision constitutional.

FACT SUMMARY: The University of Virginia (D) refused to fund a student organization on the grounds that it had religious purposes.

🏛 RULE OF LAW
State universities may not deny funding to otherwise qualifying student organizations on the grounds that the organization has religious purposes.

FACTS: The University of Virginia (D), a state institution, had a program wherein student organizations' funding needs were met by the University (D), provided certain criteria were met. Wide Awake Productions (WAP) (P) was formed to publish a small-circulation magazine with a decidedly pro-Christian slant. The organization qualified for funding. The application was denied on the grounds that such funding violated the Establishment Clause. The court of appeals agreed, and rejected WAP's (P) claim of a First Amendment violation. The Supreme Court granted review.

ISSUE: May a state university deny funding to an otherwise qualifying organization on the grounds that the organization has religious purposes?

HOLDING AND DECISION: (Kennedy, J.) No. State universities may not deny funding to otherwise qualifying organizations on the grounds that the organization has religious purposes. A state is not necessarily obligated to provide a forum for expression. Having done so, however, it cannot favor one speaker over another based on the content of his speech. The mere fact that speech has a religious content does not remove it from this analysis. While a state apparatus may not endorse a religious point of view, it may not prohibit a religious point of view from being expressed. Here, the way that the University of Virginia's (D) funding structure was set up made it clear that any organization receiving funding was to be considered private and connected to the University (D) only in that its students had to be organization members. To refuse to supply WAP (P) with funds constituted a de facto act of speaker favoritism, something the First Amendment cannot allow. Reversed.

CONCURRENCE: (O'Connor, J.) The analysis here of necessity must be done on a case-by-case basis.

CONCURRENCE: (Thomas, J.) This case stands for the proposition that the Establishment Clause does not compel exclusion of religious groups from benefits available at large.

DISSENT: (Souter, J.) The Court has essentially countenanced the use of public funds to underwrite preaching, which is fundamentally at odds with the First Amendment.

▌ANALYSIS

Perhaps more than any other provision in the Constitution, the Free Exercise Clause and the Establishment Clause are at odds with each other. The free speech guarantee only further muddies the issue. The Court has never been able to sort out these competing provisions in a consistent manner; perhaps this cannot be done.

■══■

Quicknotes

ESTABLISHMENT CLAUSE The constitutional provision prohibiting the government from favoring any one religion over others, or engaging in religious activities or advocacy.

FIRST AMENDMENT Prohibits Congress from enacting any law respecting an establishment of religion, prohibiting the free exercise of religion, abridging freedom of speech or the press, the right of peaceful assembly and the right to petition for a redress of grievances.

FREE EXERCISE CLAUSE The guarantee of the First Amendment to the United States Constitution prohibiting Congress from enacting laws regarding the establishment of religion or prohibiting the free exercise thereof.

■══■

McGowan v. Maryland

Employee (D) v. State (P)

366 U.S. 420 (1961).

NATURE OF CASE: Action to determine the constitutionality of a state Sunday "blue law."

FACT SUMMARY: McGowan (D) and others were indicted for violating a Maryland law prohibiting the Sunday sale of all merchandise, except the retail sale of certain goods.

🏛 RULE OF LAW
State laws that were motivated by religious forces, but that now have a purpose and effect that do not aid religion, are not laws respecting an establishment of religion in violation of the First Amendment.

FACTS: McGowan (D) and other employees of a large retail store in Anne Arundel County, Maryland, were indicted for selling a loose-leaf binder, floor wax, and other articles in violation of a certain Maryland statute. This law prohibited the Sunday sale of all merchandise except the retail sale of certain goods such as tobacco, milk, and gasoline, or the sale of any goods by any retail establishment in Anne Arundel County that does not employ more than one person besides the owner. The Maryland State Supreme Court found the statute constitutional, and McGowan (D) and the others appealed.

ISSUE: Are state laws that were motivated by religious forces, but that now have a purpose and effect that do not aid religion, laws respecting an establishment of religion in violation of the First Amendment?

HOLDING AND DECISION: (Warren, C.J.) No. It is true that the original Sunday labor laws were motivated by religious interests, but this does not necessarily mean the present form of Sunday laws has retained a religious character. The purpose and effect of most Sunday closing legislation these days is to provide a uniform day of rest for all laborers. That the day chosen by the state has special significance to Christian sects does not prevent the state from achieving secular goals. Thus, although state laws may have been motivated by religious forces, laws that do not presently have a purpose and effect that aid religion are not in violation of the First Amendment's Establishment Clause. The Maryland statute in question, though it does talk in terms of "profaning the Lord's day," has undergone extensive changes which decay its religious character. The State's (P) purpose is to set aside one particular day a week as a day of repose which the community can share and enjoy. The purpose and effect of the statute do not aid religion. Affirmed.

SEPARATE OPINION: (Frankfurter, J.) To determine what interest a piece of legislation serves, a court may look at the statute's necessary effects, but it may not inquire into the hidden motives that may have moved the legislature to use its constitutionally conferred powers.

DISSENT: (Douglas, J.) The state cannot make criminal the performing of innocent acts during the day that Christians revere, as this would serve to penalize a person for not observing a religious custom, which is plainly prohibited by the Establishment Clause.

▶ ANALYSIS

McGowan was one of four companion decisions in which the Court upheld various "Sunday closing laws" over objections based on the Free Exercise and Establishment Clauses of the First Amendment, and the Due Process and Equal Protection Clauses of the Fourteenth Amendment. The Court's analysis of the Establishment Clause issue turned on the change in character of the laws from religious to nonreligious. Modern statutes appeared to be designed to provide a uniform day of rest and had the support of the labor and trade organization. While the laws made attendance of religious services easier for Christians, this was viewed as a coincidental effect and not a real aid to those religions. To hold otherwise would require the state to select a day when the fewest people might want to attend religious services, a result the Court saw as hostile to the public welfare without promoting the separation of church and state.

Quicknotes

BLUE LAWS Laws that restrict certain types of activities (such as commerce) that can occur on Sundays.

DUE PROCESS CLAUSE Clauses found in the Fifth and Fourteenth Amendments to the United States Constitution providing that no person shall be deprived of "life, liberty, or property, without due process of law."

ESTABLISHMENT CLAUSE The constitutional provision prohibiting the government from favoring any one religion over others, or engaging in religious activities or advocacy.

FIRST AMENDMENT Prohibits Congress from enacting any law respecting an establishment of religion, prohibiting the free exercise of religion, abridging freedom of speech

Continued on next page.

or the press, the right of peaceful assembly and the right to petition for a redress of grievances.

FREE EXERCISE CLAUSE The guarantee of the First Amendment to the United States Constitution prohibiting Congress from enacting laws regarding the establishment of religion or prohibiting the free exercise thereof.

■══■

Braunfeld v. Brown

Orthodox Jews (P) v. State (D)

366 U.S. 599 (1961).

NATURE OF CASE: Appeal from a ruling upholding the constitutionality of a Sunday closing law.

FACT SUMMARY: Braunfeld (P) and other Orthodox Jews brought this action to challenge the constitutionality of a Pennsylvania criminal statute which proscribes the Sunday retail sale of certain enumerated commodities.

🏛 RULE OF LAW
If a state regulates conduct by enacting a general law within its power, the purpose and effect of which is to advance the state's secular goals, the statute is valid despite its indirect effect on religious observation unless there is an alternative means which does not impose such a burden.

FACTS: A Pennsylvania criminal statute proscribed the Sunday retail sale of certain enumerated commodities. Braunfeld (P) and others were merchants in Philadelphia who engaged in the retail sale of clothing and home furnishings within the proscription of the statute. Braunfeld (P) and the others were also members of the Orthodox Jewish faith, which required the closing of their places of business and a total abstention from all manner of work from nightfall each Friday until nightfall each Saturday. Braunfeld (P) alleged that he and the others had previously kept their places of business open on Sunday, had done a substantial amount of business on Sunday, compensating somewhat for their closing on Saturday, and that Sunday closing resulted in impairing their ability to earn a livelihood and that the statute is an unconstitutional violation of the free exercise of their religion. The lower court upheld the statute and Braunfeld (P) appealed.

ISSUE: If a state regulates conduct by enacting a general law within its power, the purpose and effect of which is to advance the state's secular goals, is the statute valid despite its indirect effect on religion?

HOLDING AND DECISION: (Warren, C.J.) Yes. Certain aspects of religious exercise cannot, in any way, be restricted of or burdened by either federal or state legislation. Compulsion by law of the acceptance of any creed or the practice of any form of worship is strictly forbidden. The freedom to hold religious beliefs and opinions is absolute. However, the freedom to act, even when the action is in accord with one's religious convictions, is not totally free from legislative restrictions. If a state regulates conduct by enacting a general law within its power, the purpose and effect of which is to advance the state's secular goals, the statute is valid despite its indirect effect on religious obser-

vation unless the state may accomplish its purpose by means which do not impose such a burden. In the case at bar the statute does not make unlawful any religious practices of Braunfeld (P) and the others; the Sunday law simply regulates a secular activity and, as applied to the plaintiffs operates so as to make the practice of their religion more expensive. Therefore, the statute is not violative of the Free Exercise Clause. Affirmed.

CONCURRENCE AND DISSENT: (Brennan, J.) The Court today has exalted administrative convenience to a high enough level to justify making one religion less economically advantageous than another. I would reverse and remand for trial on the free exercise of religion issues only.

▶ ANALYSIS

In *Reynold v. United States,* 98 U.S. 145 (1879), the First Amendment's guarantee of religious freedom received its first extensive consideration. There the Court upheld the polygamy convictions of a member of the Mormon faith despite the fact that an accepted doctrine of his church then imposed upon its male members the duty to practice polygamy. And, in *Prince v. Massachusetts,* 321 U.S. 158 (1944), the Court upheld a statute making it a crime for a girl under 18 years of age to sell any newspapers, periodicals, or merchandise in public places despite the fact that a child of the Jehovah's Witnesses faith believed that it was her religious duty to perform this work. The Court in *Braunfeld* cited these cases to point out that the freedom to act in accord with one's religious beliefs is not free from legislative restraints.

■=■

Quicknotes

FREE EXERCISE CLAUSE The guarantee of the First Amendment to the United States Constitution prohibiting Congress from enacting laws regarding the establishment of religion or prohibiting the free exercise thereof.

POLYGAMY The offense of having several wives or husbands at the same time, or more than one wife or husband at the same time.

■=■

Sherbert v. Verner

Employee (P) v. State (D)

374 U.S. 398 (1963).

NATURE OF CASE: Action arising out of the Employment Security Commission's (D) denial of Sherbert's (P) claim for unemployment compensation benefits.

FACT SUMMARY: Sherbert (P) was discharged by her employer because she would not work on her religion's sabbath.

RULE OF LAW
It is an unconstitutional burden on a worker's free exercise of religion for a state to apply eligibility requirements for unemployment benefits so as to force a worker to abandon her religious principles respecting her religion's sabbath.

FACTS: Sherbert (P) was discharged by her employer because she refused to work on Saturday, her religion's sabbath. The Employment Security Commission (D) found Sherbert (P) ineligible for benefits because her refusal to work on Saturday was failure without good cause to accept available work. The state law provides that no employee shall be required to work on Sunday.

ISSUE: Is it unconstitutional for a state to refuse unemployment benefits to a worker who was discharged because of her refusal to work on her religion's sabbath?

HOLDING AND DECISION: (Brennan, J.) Yes. Sherbert (P) is forced to choose between following her religion or obtaining unemployment benefits. Such a choice puts the same kind of burden on her free exercise of religion as would a fine imposed for Saturday worship. Further, by expressly providing that no one will be compelled to work on Sunday, the state saves the Sunday worshipper from having to make such a choice. The state has shown no compelling state interest to justify this burden on Sherbert's (P) free exercise of religion. Hence, the burden is unconstitutional. This case is distinguishable from *Braunfeld v. Brown*, 366 U.S. 599 (1961). There, the state showed a strong state interest in providing one uniform day of rest for all workers. Constraining a worker to abandon his religious convictions respecting the day of rest is unconstitutional.

DISSENT: (Harlan, J.) The purpose of unemployment benefits was to tide people over while work was unavailable. It was not to provide relief for those who for personal reasons became unavailable for work. Secondly, this decision is in conflict with and overrules *Braunfeld*.

▶ ANALYSIS

The Court has encountered many situations not unlike *Sherbert*'s, in which the individual's right to freedom of religious belief and practices is subordinated to other community interests. Freedom of religion is not absolute, and does not extend to situations where its practice would jeopardize public health, safety, or morals, or the rights of third persons. Hence, laws prohibiting polygamy and bigamy have been upheld, as well as those requiring compulsory vaccination and X-rays, in spite of allegations that such laws required action in violation of the Mormon and Christian Science religions. The conscientious objector's right to avoid military service has been said to rest upon legislative grace rather than constitutional right.

■■■

Quicknotes

COMPELLING STATE INTEREST Defense to an alleged Equal Protection Clause violation that a state action was necessary in order to protect an interest that the government is under a duty to protect.

FREE EXERCISE CLAUSE The guarantee of the First Amendment to the United States Constitution prohibiting Congress from enacting laws regarding the establishment of religion or prohibiting the free exercise thereof.

■■■

Wisconsin v. Yoder

State (P) v. Amish parents (D)

406 U.S. 205 (1972).

NATURE OF CASE: Appeal from conviction for violating state compulsory school attendance law.

FACT SUMMARY: Amish parents (D), in violation of state law, refused to send their children to public school after the eighth grade.

🏛 RULE OF LAW
The state's interest in universal education is subject to a balancing test when it infringes on other fundamental rights, such as those specifically protected by the First Amendment (Congress shall make no law prohibiting the free exercise of religion) as applied to the states through the Fourteenth Amendment, and the right of parents to handle the religious upbringing of their children.

FACTS: Amish parents (D), who refused to send their children to public school after the eighth grade, were convicted of violating a Wisconsin statute which required all children under the age of 16 to attend public school. The Amish believe that formal high school education places Amish children in an environment that emphasizes competition, sports, and non-Amish practices and removes the children from the Amish community during their formative years. At the trial, experts testified that high school attendance could only result in great psychological harm to the Amish children, that Amish education is more relevant than public schooling to the Amish way of life, and that the Amish are generally self-sufficient and law-abiding citizens. The Wisconsin Supreme Court overturned the convictions.

ISSUE: Is a state's interest in universal education totally free from a balancing process when it impinges on other fundamental rights and interests?

HOLDING AND DECISION: (Burger, C.J.) No. For the state's law to prevail against the claims of the Amish (D), it must appear that there is no abridgment of the free exercise of religious belief, or that there is a state interest of sufficient magnitude to override the interest protected by the First Amendment. Initially, it must be determined whether the Amish way of life is rooted in religious belief. From the record, it is clear that compulsory formal education would greatly endanger if not destroy the free exercise of the Amish's religious beliefs. Wisconsin's justifications for its system—to prepare citizens to effectively and intelligently perform in our political system, and to be self-reliant and self-sufficient—are legitimate. However, requiring an additional one or two years in public school would not greatly advance the state's interests particularly in light of the destructive effect on the Amish

community. It is too speculative to assume that those children who will eventually leave the Amish community will be ill-equipped for life. Since only the parents (D) are subject to prosecution, it is their right of free exercise, and not the children's, that is at issue here. This is a special case, unlikely to be often repeated, with considerable weight given to the Amish's long history and distinct culture. The decision of the Wisconsin Supreme Court is affirmed.

DISSENT IN PART: (Douglas, J.) The right of the Amish children to religious freedom is an issue in this case. The child's opinion should be canvassed, if he is of sufficient maturity, to determine if he wants to attend public high school. While the parents normally speak for the entire family, the child may have decided views on the subject of education. Finally, the Court should not concern itself with the "law and order" record of a religious group.

▶ ANALYSIS

In dealing with the freedom of religion section of the First Amendment, the Court is faced with the problem of neither restricting nor encouraging religion. This is a narrow tightrope to walk. This problem must then be considered in the context of the state's interest in the regulation it seeks to promote. But once the Court carves out an exception to a state regulation based on religious convictions there is a strong possibility of an implicit encouragement of religion.

▬▬▮

Quicknotes

COMPULSORY ATTENDANCE LAWS State laws mandating school attendance for children of specified ages.

FIRST AMENDMENT Prohibits Congress from enacting any law respecting an establishment of religion, prohibiting the free exercise of religion, abridging freedom of speech or the press, the right of peaceful assembly and the right to petition for a redress of grievances.

FUNDAMENTAL RIGHT A liberty that is either expressly or impliedly provided for in the United States Constitution, the deprivation or burdening of which is subject to a heightened standard of review.

▬▬▮

Estate of Thornton v. Caldor, Inc.

Employee's estate (P) v. Employer (D)

472 U.S. 703 (1985).

NATURE OF CASE: Review of order invalidating state law as violative of the Establishment Clause of the First Amendment.

FACT SUMMARY: Connecticut enacted a law mandating that employers permit employees to observe their chosen Sabbath days.

🏛 RULE OF LAW
A law mandating that employers allow employees to observe their Sabbath day violates the Establishment Clause.

FACTS: In 1977 Connecticut enacted a law compelling employers to allow employees to observe their Sabbath day, whatever day it might be. No hardship provisions or other exceptions were made. Thornton (P) was an employee of Caldor, Inc. (D), which had mandated that employees in his position work every other Sunday. Thornton (P) announced that he would no longer work on Sundays. Caldor (D) responded by demoting him. He filed an administrative claim. The administrative authorities ordered Caldor (D) to reinstate him, with back pay. On appeal, the state supreme court voided the law as a violation of the Establishment Clause of the First Amendment. The U.S. Supreme Court granted review.

ISSUE: Does a law mandating that employers allow employees to observe their Sabbath day violate the Establishment Clause?

HOLDING AND DECISION: (Burger, C.J.) Yes. A law mandating that employers allow employees to observe their Sabbath day violates the Establishment Clause. To survive an Establishment Clause challenge, a law must have a secular purpose, not foster excessive governmental entanglement in religion, and neither inhibit nor advance religion. Here, the law at issue provides that a person may decline to work any day of the week out of religious conviction. The statute contains no exception for special circumstances, no matter what the burden on the employer. This unyielding weighing in favor of a Sabbath observer over all other interests makes it clear that the law's primary effect is to advance religion. This is a violation of the Establishment Clause. Affirmed.

CONCURRENCE: (O'Connor, J.) It should be emphasized that this decision in no way affects Title VII of the Civil Rights Act as it pertains to the prohibition against discrimination on the basis of religion.

▶ ANALYSIS

This case is yet another illustration of how the Free Exercise and Establishment Clauses can clash. Connecticut's law was an attempt at promoting the exercise of religion. Nonetheless, the Court saw it as an attempt to promote religion, in violation of the Establishment Clause.

■==■

Quicknotes

ESTABLISHMENT CLAUSE The constitutional provision prohibiting the government from favoring any one religion over others, or engaging in religious activities or advocacy.

FREE EXERCISE CLAUSE The guarantee of the First Amendment to the United States Constitution prohibiting Congress from enacting laws regarding the establishment of religion or prohibiting the free exercise thereof.

■==■

Employment Division, Department of Human Resources v. Smith

State agency (D) v. Employee (P)

494 U.S. 872 (1990).

NATURE OF CASE: Appeal from judgment awarding unemployment compensation benefits.

FACT SUMMARY: Alfred Smith and Galen Black (P) were fired from their jobs as drug counselors after they ingested peyote for sacramental purposes during a Native American Church ceremony.

🏛 RULE OF LAW
An individual's religious beliefs do not excuse his compliance with an otherwise valid law prohibiting conduct that the state is free to regulate.

FACTS: Alfred Smith (P) was fired from his job with a drug rehabilitation organization because he ingested peyote for sacramental purposes during a Native American Church religious ceremony. Smith's (P) application for unemployment benefits from the Employment Division (D) was denied on the basis that Smith (P) was terminated for work-related misconduct. The Oregon Court of Appeals reversed, holding that the denial of the benefits violated Smith's (P) free exercise of religion rights guaranteed by the First Amendment. The Oregon Supreme Court affirmed. The Employment Division (D) appealed, contending that the First Amendment is not violated by the incidental burdening of a religious activity through the prosecution of a valid criminal provision.

ISSUE: Do an individual's religious beliefs excuse compliance with an otherwise valid law prohibiting conduct that the state is free to regulate?

HOLDING AND DECISION: (Scalia, J.) No. An individual's religious beliefs do not excuse compliance with an otherwise valid law prohibiting conduct that the state is free to regulate. To permit the violation of laws because of religious beliefs would make the professed doctrines of religious belief superior to the law of the land. The Court in the past has only barred application of neutral, generally applicable laws that involve the Free Exercise Clause in conjunction with some other constitutional protection such as freedom of speech or parental rights. Here, Smith's (P) free exercise claim is unconnected with any communicative activity or parental right. Reversed.

CONCURRENCE: (O'Connor, J.) To say that a person's right to free exercise has been burdened does not mean that he has an absolute right to engage in the conduct. The critical question is whether exempting Smith (P) from the state's general criminal prohibition will unduly interfere with fulfillment of the governmental interest. In view of the societal interest in preventing the trafficking in controlled substances, uniform application of the criminal prohibition at issue is essential to the effectiveness of Oregon's stated interest in preventing any possession of peyote.

DISSENT: (Blackmun, J.) The state proclaims an interest in protecting the health and safety of its citizens from the dangers of unlawful drugs. It offers, however, no evidence that the religious use of peyote has ever harmed anyone.

▶ ANALYSIS

It is interesting to note that the majority opinion rejects the contention espoused in the concurring and dissenting opinions, that all laws burdening religious practices should be subject to compelling state interest scrutiny. The majority opinion cited precedents where race-neutral laws that had the effect of disadvantaging a particular group were not subject to compelling interest analysis. See *Washington v. Davis*, 426 U.S. 229 (1976) (concerning the effect of a racially neutral police employment examination).

Quicknotes

COMPELLING STATE INTEREST Defense to an alleged Equal Protection Clause violation that a state action was necessary in order to protect an interest that the government is under a duty to protect.

FIRST AMENDMENT Prohibits Congress from enacting any law respecting an establishment of religion, prohibiting the free exercise of religion, abridging freedom of speech or the press, the right of peaceful assembly and the right to petition for a redress of grievances.

FREE EXERCISE CLAUSE The guarantee of the First Amendment to the United States Constitution prohibiting Congress from enacting laws regarding the establishment of religion or prohibiting the free exercise thereof.

CHAPTER 12

The Procedural Context of Constitutional Litigation

Quick Reference Rules of Law

International Longshoremen's and Warehousemen's Union, Local 37 v. Boyd

Union (P) v. Director of Immigration (D)

347 U.S. 222 (1954).

NATURE OF CASE: Action for injunction.

FACT SUMMARY: The International Long-shoremen's and Warehousemen's Union (Union) (P) seeks to prevent Boyd (D), District Director of the Immigration and Naturalization Service (INS) in Seattle, Washington, from applying a certain federal law in a manner which would prejudice certain of its members.

RULE OF LAW
"Determination of the scope and constitutionality of legislation in advance of its immediate adverse effect in the context of a concrete case involves too remote and abstract an inquiry for the proper exercise of the judicial function."

FACTS: Boyd (D), District Director of the Immigration and Naturalization Service (INS) in Seattle, Washington, ordered his agents to treat all resident alien members of the International Longshoremen's and Warehousemen's Union (Union) (P), who returned from temporary work in Alaska, as if they were aliens entering the U.S. for the first time. As a result, Union (P) filed this action to enjoin Boyd (D) and the INS from carrying out these orders and for a declaratory judgment on the question of whether Boyd (D) was legally empowered to act as he did. The case was dismissed on the merits, so Union (P) appealed. In addition to praying that the dismissal on the merits be upheld, Boyd (D) also prays on appeal that Union's (P) action be dismissed for lack of requisite judicial ripeness.

ISSUE: Should the courts undertake to determine the constitutionality of legislation prior to the occurrence of a concrete dispute between adverse parties over it?

HOLDING AND DECISION: (Frankfurter, J.) No. "Determination of the scope and constitutionality of legislation in advance of its immediate adverse effect in the context of a concrete case involves too remote and abstract an inquiry for the proper exercise of the judicial function." Lawsuits properly exist to enforce the rights of parties, not to pose abstract questions of law. Since no threat of enforcement here was made against any member of Union (P), no justiciable "case or controversy" arose for the Court's determination. Dismissal on the merits vacated, with instructions to dismiss for want of a case or controversy.

DISSENT: (Black, J.) The true test of whether a case or controversy has arisen is whether one of the parties to a dispute faces irreparable injury unless the courts act to protect him. Here, it appears that those members of Union (P) who regularly travel to Alaska for seasonal work face just such irreparable injury unless the courts act not to determine whether Boyd's (D) actions are constitutional.

ANALYSIS

This case points up the doctrine of "ripeness," which is one component of the general constitutional doctrine of "case or controversy." In *United Public Workers of America v. Mitchell*, 330 U.S. 75 (1947), the Supreme Court set out the broad definition of "ripeness" as arising when the judicial power is necessary to protect defined rights between adverse parties. As *Boyd* points out, this generally requires some specific threat particularly directed against the plaintiff in the lawsuit. Note, here, that Union (P) sought a declaratory judgment on an issue. Although it is true that a declaratory judgment may be obtained in order to avoid irreparable harm in the future, the Supreme Court in *Poe v. Ullmen*, 367 U.S. 497 (1961) made it clear that declaratory relief "does not permit litigants to invoke the power of this court . . . in advance of necessity."

Quicknotes

ALIEN An individual who is a citizen of a foreign country.

CASE OR CONTROVERSY Constitutional requirement in order to invoke federal court jurisdiction that the matter present a justiciable issue.

RIPENESS A doctrine precluding a federal court from hearing or determining a matter, unless it constitutes an actual and present controversy warranting a determination by the court.

DeFunis v. Odegaard

Law school applicant (P) v. School (D)

416 U.S. 312 (1974).

NATURE OF CASE: Appeal from reversal of injunction compelling law school admission.

FACT SUMMARY: DeFunis (P) contended that the procedures employed by the University of Washington Law School Admissions Committee violated the Equal Protection Clause of the Fourteenth Amendment.

RULE OF LAW

Federal courts are without power to decide cases which are moot.

FACTS: In 1971, DeFunis (P) was denied admission to the University of Washington Law School. De Funis (P) then brought suit, contending that the procedures and criteria employed by the Law School Admissions Committee invidiously discriminated against him on account of his race in violation of the Equal Protection Clause of the Fourteenth Amendment. The trial court issued a mandatory injunction compelling the school to admit him. Although the Washington Supreme Court later reversed this decision, a stay was granted so that DeFunis (P) could remain in school. At the time this case was argued to the Supreme Court, DeFunis (P) was in his last quarter in law school, and the school indicated that it would not seek to abrogate his registration. The primary issue then revolved around whether a case or controversy was ripe for adjudication.

ISSUE: Are federal courts without power to decide cases which are moot?

HOLDING AND DECISION: (Per curiam) Yes. Under Article III of the Constitution, federal courts are without power to decide questions that cannot affect the rights of litigants in the case before them. All parties agree that DeFunis (P) is now entitled to complete his legal studies at the University of Washington. A determination of the legal issues tendered by the parties is no longer necessary to compel that result and could not serve to prevent it. The controversy between the parties has thus clearly ceased to be definitive and concrete and no longer touches the legal relations of parties having adverse legal interests. Vacated and remanded.

DISSENT: (Brennan, J.) If DeFunis (P) were to fall ill or fail to pass all his classes, it is possible that he would not graduate at the end of the present term. Because there is the possibility that DeFunis (P) would once again be subject to the challenged admissions policy, the case is ripe for decision, on a fully developed factual record, with sharply defined and fully canvassed legal issues.

ANALYSIS

In this case, DeFunis (P) sued as an individual and not as the named representative of a particular class. In a class action, the action will not be rendered moot so long as the issue is alive as to the class of person whom the named plaintiff has been certified to represent.

Quicknotes

CLASS ACTION A suit commenced by a representative on behalf of an ascertainable group that is too large to appear in court, who shares a commonality of interests and who will benefit from a successful result.

EQUAL PROTECTION CLAUSE A constitutional guarantee that no person should be denied the same protection of the laws enjoyed by other persons in like circumstances.

MOOTNESS Judgment on the particular issue would not resolve the controversy.

RIPENESS A doctrine precluding a federal court from hearing or determining a matter, unless it constitutes an actual and present controversy warranting a determination by the court.

STAY An order by a court requiring a party to refrain from a specific activity until the happening of an event or upon further action by the court.

Massachusetts v. Mellon/Frothingham v. Mellon

State/Taxpayer (P) v. Federal government (D)

262 U.S. 447 (1923).

NATURE OF CASE: Constitutional challenge to federal law.

FACT SUMMARY: The federal government offered a voluntary federal-state plan under the Maternity Act.

RULE OF LAW

A state has no standing to challenge a voluntary federal-state program on the ground that it is an unconstitutional encroachment on the state's sovereignty.

FACTS: The Maternity Act provided for funds for a voluntary federal-state program to protect the health of mothers and infants. To qualify for the federal funds a state had to conform that portion of its aid program to federal standards and report on how the money was being expended. If the state failed to use the money properly, i.e., according to the federal standards, the aid would be terminated. Massachusetts (P) accepted the aid program, but it subsequently brought suit alleging that this and other similar aid programs were being used to force states to yield a portion of their sovereign rights since all of the programs concerned strictly local problems. Massachusetts (P) alleged that this violated the Tenth Amendment. Frothingham (P), a taxpayer, filed suit challenging the validity of the Act, alleging that it took her property, under the guise of taxation, without due process of law. The U.S. (Mellon) (D) alleged that neither Massachusetts (P) nor Frothingham (P) had standing to maintain the suit.

ISSUE: Does a state have standing to challenge a voluntary federal-state participation plan on the ground that it violates the Tenth Amendment?

HOLDING AND DECISION: (Sutherland, J.) No. A state has no standing to challenge a voluntary federal-state program on the ground that it is an unconstitutional encroachment on sovereignty in violation of the Tenth Amendment. Massachusetts (P) has not been injured in its own right or as parens patriae for its citizens. The program is voluntary. Massachusetts (P) has not been forced to join it. Merely because a state is a party to a suit does not confer power on federal courts. Massachusetts (P) has failed to establish any injury, i.e., a justiciable controversy. A state may not seek a declaratory judgment absent a case or controversy which is not present herein. Massachusetts (P) has no standing to challenge the statute. Frothingham (P) also has no standing. Frothingham (P) has suffered no personal injury. Frothingham's (P) comparative share of the federal funds for this program which are from taxes and other sources is de minimus. The effect on future tax rates is so remote, speculative, and minute as to be beyond the powers of equity to afford relief. The administration of any federal program is likely to produce some effect on taxation. The statute itself has not caused any personal harm to Frothingham (P). The suit would require us to restrain the actions of a coequal branch of the government on the ground that a statute might be unconstitutional solely to protect an interest Frothingham (P) bears with every other taxpayer. We cannot act in such matters without a showing of personal injury. No. 24, Original, dismissed. No. 962 affirmed.

ANALYSIS

A state has standing in cases involving border disputes. *North Dakota v. Minnesota*, 263 U.S. 583 (1924). A state also has standing to assert its taxing power, to enforce its contracts, and to protect its public works, its quasi-public institutions, or its interest as a proprietor. *Texas v. Florida*, 306 U.S. 398 (1939). In *Pennsylvania v. West Virginia*, 262 U.S. 553 (1924), the state was deemed to have standing to sue to protect a natural gas supply for its schools and other residents of the state.

Quicknotes

PARENS PATRIAE Maxim that the government as sovereign is conferred with the duty to act as guardian on behalf of those citizens under legal disability.

STANDING Whether a party possesses the right to commence suit against another party by having a personal stake in the resolution of the controversy.

TENTH AMENDMENT The tenth amendment to the United States Constitution reserving those powers therein, not expressly delegated to the federal government or prohibited to the states, to the states or to the people.

Flast v. Cohen

Taxpayer (P) v. Federal government (D)

392 U.S. 83 (1968).

NATURE OF CASE: Taxpayer action to enjoin federal expenditures.

FACT SUMMARY: Flast (P), a taxpayer, brought suit to enjoin the federal funding of a religious school.

🏛 **RULE OF LAW**
A taxpayer may only bring suit to enjoin fiscal expenditures if they exceed a specific constitutional limitation and it is part of a federal spending program.

FACTS: Flast (P), a taxpayer, brought suit in federal court to enjoin Cohen (D), a federal official, from using funds to finance religious school instruction and to provide them with teaching materials. These practices allegedly violated the Establishment Clause of the First Amendment. The U.S. (D) challenged Flast's (P) standing to bring suit.

ISSUE: Does a taxpayer have standing to challenge federal expenditures?

HOLDING AND DECISION: (Warren, C.J.) Yes. The taxpayer must establish that the expenditures exceed a specific constitutional limitation on the taxing and spending power and that it is part of a specific federal spending program. It is not sufficient to merely allege that unauthorized expenditures increase the general tax burden. The taxpayer must show that the expenditures are unconstitutional under the Taxing and Spending Clause, Art. 1 § 8 and they must not be incidental to the administration of an essentially regulatory scheme. The expenditures must exceed specific constitutional limitations. Since no expenditures are allowed under the Establishment Clause and the expenditures herein were enacted pursuant to the "general welfare" provisions of Art. 1 § 8, Flast (P) is deemed to have standing to maintain this action. Reversed.

CONCURRENCE: (Douglas, J.) Courts no longer sit in judgment of the wisdom of legislation. The less the judiciary does the better because participation by the judiciary in the legislative process tends to dwarf the political capacity of the people and to deaden its sense of moral responsibility.

CONCURRENCE: (Fortas, J.) The status of taxpayers should not be accepted as a launching pad for an attack upon any target other than legislation affecting the Establishment Clause.

DISSENT: (Harlan, J.) Taxpayer suits should only be allowed where they represent public interests recognized by Congress as having standing to bring such suits. Absent such a showing, I would dismiss because there is no specific injury to the taxpayer.

▶ *ANALYSIS*

At issue in *Frothingham*, 262 U.S. 447 (1923), was a maternity act providing grants-in-aid for states willing to participate in a federal program to protect the health of mothers and their infants. The Court there held that the plaintiff-taxpayer must be able to show not only that the state statute is invalid but that he has sustained a direct injury different from most taxpayers. Congress subsequently enacted legislation granting taxpayers, citizens, and institutions standing to challenge alleged First Amendment violations under certain spending acts.

■═■

Quicknotes

ESTABLISHMENT CLAUSE The constitutional provision prohibiting the government from favoring any one religion over others, or engaging in religious activities or advocacy.

FIRST AMENDMENT Prohibits Congress from enacting any law respecting an establishment of religion, prohibiting the free exercise of religion, abridging freedom of speech or the press, the right of peaceful assembly and the right to petition for a redress of grievances.

STANDING Whether a party possesses the right to commence suit against another party by having a personal stake in the resolution of the controversy.

■═■

Duke Power Co. v. Carolina Environmental Study Group, Inc.

Public utility (D) v. Citizens (P)

438 U.S. 59 (1978).

NATURE OF CASE: Appeal from judgment finding the Price-Anderson Act unconstitutional.

FACT SUMMARY: The Carolina Environmental Study Group, Inc. (Study Group) (P), who sued Duke Power Co. (D) to prevent the construction of a nuclear power plant, first faced the test of whether It had standing to bring suit.

> 🏛 **RULE OF LAW**
> The test for standing requires both a distinct and palpable injury to the plaintiff, and a fairly traceable causal connection between the claimed injury and the challenged conduct.

FACTS: In 1957, Congress passed the Price-Anderson Act, to limit liability for nuclear accidents resulting from the operation of private nuclear power plants. In 1973, the Carolina Environmental Study Group, Inc. (Study Group) (P) and other citizens, sued Duke Power Co. (D), an investor-owned public utility, to prevent the construction of a nuclear power plant, and to obtain a declaration that the Price-Anderson Act was unconstitutional. The district court held that the Price-Anderson Act was unconstitutional because it violated the Due Process Clause of the Fifth Amendment in that it allowed injuries to occur without assuring adequate compensation to the victims; and the Act violated the equal protection component of the Fifth Amendment by forcing the victims of nuclear incidents to bear the burden of injury. The initial issue was whether Study Group (P) had standing to sue.

ISSUE: Does the test for standing require both a distinct and palpable injury to the plaintiff and a fairly traceable causal connection between the claimed injury and the challenged conduct?

HOLDING AND DECISION: (Burger, C.J.) Yes. The essence of the standing inquiry is whether the parties have alleged a sufficient personal stake in the outcome of the controversy. The test for standing requires not only a distinct and palpable injury to the plaintiff, but also a fairly traceable causal connection between the claimed injury and the challenged conduct. Here, the environmental and aesthetic consequences of the thermal pollution of the two lakes in the vicinity of the disputed power plant is the type of harmful effect which has been deemed adequate to satisfy the injury-in-fact standard. Further, the requisite causal connection is present because there is a substantial likelihood that the nuclear power plants in question would have neither been completed nor operated absent the Price-Anderson Act. Where a party champions his own rights,

and where the injury alleged is a concrete and particularized one which will be prevented or redressed by the relief requested, the basic practical and prudential concerns underlying the standing requirement are generally satisfied when the constitutional requisites are met. Accordingly, Study Group (P) has standing to challenge the constitutionality of the Price-Anderson Act. Standing of appellees affirmed.

CONCURRENCE: (Stevens, J.) The string of contingencies supposedly holding this litigation together is insufficient either to make this litigation ripe for decision, or to establish the Study Group's (P) standing.

▶ **ANALYSIS**

In an earlier decision, Justice Douglas established a two-pronged test for standing to challenge the validity of statutes. "The first question is whether the plaintiff alleges that the challenged action has caused him injury in fact, economic or otherwise." Second, it must be determined "whether the interest sought to be protected or regulated by the statute or constitutional guarantee is in question." See *Association of Data Processing Serv. Organizations, Inc. v. Camp*, 397 U.S. 150 (1970).

■═■

Quicknotes

DUE PROCESS CLAUSE Clauses found in the Fifth and Fourteenth Amendments to the United States Constitution providing that no person shall be deprived of "life, liberty, or property, without due process of law."

RIPENESS A doctrine precluding a federal court from hearing or determining a matter, unless it constitutes an actual and present controversy warranting a determination by the court.

STANDING Whether a party possesses the right to commence suit against another party by having a personal stake in the resolution of the controversy.

■═■

Singleton v. Wulff

State (D) v. Doctors (P)

428 U.S. 106 (1976).

NATURE OF CASE: Action challenging constitutionality of state abortion statute.

FACT SUMMARY: Wulff (P) and other physicians who performed nonmedically indicated abortions, challenged the constitutionality of a Missouri anti-abortion statute.

🏛 RULE OF LAW
A physician may be allowed to assert the rights of women patients against governmental interference with one woman's decision to have an abortion.

FACTS: Wulff (P) and other physicians who performed nonmedically indicated abortions, challenged the constitutionality of a Missouri statute excluding abortions that were not "medically indicated" from the purposes for which Medicaid benefits are available to needy persons. The district court dismissed the action for lack of standing. The court of appeals held that Wulff (P) and the other physicians had standing to assert the rights of their female patients. The issue of standing, as well as the substantive constitutional issues, were then appealed to the Supreme Court.

ISSUE: Is a physician allowed to assert the rights of women patients against governmental interference with an abortion decision?

HOLDING AND DECISION: (Blackmun, J.) Yes. Ordinarily, one may not claim standing to vindicate the constitutional rights of some third party. The right to assert the rights of third parties depends upon two factors. First, the relationship between the litigant and the third party must be such that the former is fully, or very nearly, as effective a proponent of the right as the latter. Here, the confidential nature of the relationship between physician and patient supports the notion that physicians should be permitted to assert the rights of their patients. The second factor is the ability of the third party to assert his own rights. If there is some genuine obstacle to such assertion, the party who is in court becomes by default the right's best available proponent. Here, the combination of privacy concerns and imminent mootness combine to support the notion that many women patients cannot effectively assert their own rights. Therefore, it generally is appropriate to allow a physician to assert the rights of women patients as against governmental interference with the abortion decision. The case is remanded to the district court.

CONCURRENCE: (Stevens, J.) Wulff (P) and the others have standing because they have a financial stake in the outcome of the litigation, and they claim that the statute impairs their own constitutional rights.

CONCURRENCE AND DISSENT: (Powell, J.) A plaintiff may assert the rights of a third party when litigation by the third party is in all practicable terms impossible. Here, it seems wholly inappropriate, as a matter of judicial self-governance, to reach unnecessarily to decide a difficult constitutional issue in a case in which nothing more is at stake than remuneration for professional services.

▶ *ANALYSIS*

The Supreme Court takes a more flexible approach to third party standing issues in the First Amendment area. In attacking an allegedly overbroad statute, there is no requirement that the person making the attack demonstrate that the statute necessarily restricted their own free speech rights. Litigants "are permitted to challenge a statute not because their own rights of free expression are violated, but because of a judicial . . . assumption that the statute's very existence may cause others . . . to refrain from constitutionally protected speech or expression." *Broadrick v. Oklahoma*, 413 U.S. 602 (1973).

Quicknotes

MOOTNESS Judgment on the particular issue would not resolve the controversy.

OVERBROAD Refers to a statute that proscribes lawful as well as unlawful conduct.

STANDING Whether a party possesses the right to commence suit against another party by having a personal stake in the resolution of the controversy.

Raines v. Byrd

Parties not identified.

521 U.S. 811 (1997).

NATURE OF CASE: Expedited direct appeal of judgment striking down the Line Item Veto Act.

FACT SUMMARY: Four senators (P) and two congressmen (P) who had voted against the Line Item Veto Act of 1996 filed an action alleging that the Act was unconstitutional.

🏛 RULE OF LAW
Members of Congress whose votes for or against a bill have been given full effect do not have standing to bring a suit challenging the bill's constitutionality.

FACTS: The Line Item Veto Act of 1996 provided that the president may cancel certain items appropriated for expenditure in any bill or joint resolution after he has signed it into law. Such cancellation would take effect upon receipt in both Houses of Congress of a "special message" from the president specifying the canceled item, and the Congress could undo the cancellation only by passage of a "disapproval bill" signed by the president or reenacted by two-thirds of each House over his veto. The Act also specifically provided that "any Member of Congress" may bring an action challenging the constitutionality of the Act. Four senators (P) and two congressmen (P) who had voted against the bill brought an action challenging the Act's constitutionality. The district court granted the members' (P) motion for summary judgment, holding that the Act was an unconstitutional delegation of legislative power to the president and a violation of the Presentment Clause. The court noted that standing to challenge the validity of the Act was justified because the members' (P) voting power had been severely diluted by the Act. The Supreme Court granted review.

ISSUE: Do members of Congress whose votes for or against a bill have been given full effect have standing to bring a suit challenging the bill's constitutionality?

HOLDING AND DECISION: (Rehnquist, C.J.) No. Members of Congress whose votes for or against a bill have been given full effect do not have standing to bring a suit challenging the bill's constitutionality. Federal courts have jurisdiction over a dispute only if there exists a genuine case or controversy and a legally cognizable injury. Although this Court had previously upheld standing for legislators claiming an institutional injury in *Coleman v. Miller*, 307 U.S. 433 (1939), the legislators in *Coleman* were deprived of their votes' validity. The members (P) here were simply on the losing side of a fair vote. There is a vast difference between the vote nullification at issue in

Coleman and the abstract dilution of institutional legislative power that is alleged here. The injuries alleged by the members (P) are merely abstract and impersonal, and therefore they lack standing to sue. Nevertheless, this holding does not prevent them from repealing the Act, or foreclose the Act from a constitutional challenge brought by someone who truly suffers a judicially cognizable injury as a result of the Act. Vacated and remanded with instructions for dismissal.

DISSENT: (Stevens, J.) The Act deprives all members of Congress of any opportunity to vote for or against the truncated measure that survives the exercise of the president's cancellation authority. Because the opportunity to cast such votes is a right guaranteed by the text of the Constitution, it is clear that the six members (P) in this case have standing to sue. Furthermore, the constant threat of the partial veto power has an immediate impact on their current legislative choices.

DISSENT: (Breyer, J.) The members' (P) roles in the lawmaking procedure has immediately been affected. This harm seems more serious, immediate, and pervasive than the harm at issue in *Coleman*. It seems impossible for the Court to find this case nonjusticiable without overruling *Coleman*.

▶ ANALYSIS

Although the language of the Act explicitly authorizes the type of challenge that was brought, this point was ignored by the Court. While the majority stated that there was no true "injury" suffered by the members (P), this ignores Justice Steven's point that their voting rights had been dramatically altered and restricted. Nevertheless, as Justice Souter indicated, the validity of the Act will undoubtedly be revisited in a private suit in the near future.

■=■

Quicknotes

PRESENTMENT The act of bringing a congressional decision before the President for his approval or veto.

STANDING Whether a party possesses the right to commence suit against another party by having a personal stake in the resolution of the controversy.

■=■

Warth v. Seldin

Individuals/organizations (P) v. Municipality (D)

422 U.S. 490 (1975).

NATURE OF CASE: Appeal from dismissal of complaint on grounds of lack of standing.

FACT SUMMARY: Various organizations and individuals challenged the town of Penfield's (D) zoning ordinance which allegedly excluded persons of low and moderate income from living in the town.

🏛 RULE OF LAW
The question of standing (whether the litigant is entitled to have the court decide the merits of the dispute or of particular issues) has two limitations: (1) when the asserted harm is a "generalized grievance" shared substantially by all or a large class of citizens, that harm alone does not normally warrant exercise of jurisdiction; and (2) even when plaintiff presents "a case or controversy," generally he still must assert his own legal rights and interests, and cannot rest his claim to relief on the legal rights or interests of third parties.

FACTS: Warth (P) and other individuals and various organizations residing in the Rochester, New York, metropolitan area, sued the town of Penfield (D), adjacent to Rochester, and the members (D) of its zoning, planning, and town boards. Warth (P) claimed that the town's zoning ordinance effectively excluded persons of low and moderate income from living in Penfield (D) in violation of the First, Ninth, and Fourteenth Amendments, and federal statutes. The district court, the court of appeals affirming, dismissed the complaint for lack of standing. Warth (P) appealed.

ISSUE: Does the question of standing (whether the litigant is entitled to have the court decide the merits of the dispute or of particular issues) have any limitations?

HOLDING AND DECISION: (Powell, J.) Yes. The question of standing (whether the litigant is entitled to have the court decide the merits of the dispute or of particular issues) has two limitations: (1) when the asserted harm is a "general grievance" shared substantially by all or a large class of citizens, that harm alone does not normally warrant exercise of jurisdiction; and (2) even when plaintiff presents a "case or controversy," generally he must still assert his own legal rights and interests, and cannot rest in his claim to relief on the legal rights or interests of third parties. As for the claims of the individual petitioners who assert standing as persons of low or moderate income and as members of minority groups, the fact that they share attributes common to persons who may have been excluded from Penfield (D) is an insufficient fact from which to conclude that they themselves have been excluded, or that Penfield (D) has violated their rights. There has been no personal injury alleged. They have not alleged that their inability to find housing in Penfield (D) reasonably resulted from Penfield's (D) alleged constitutional and statutory violations, or that if the court affords relief, their inability will be removed. As for the petitioners who assert standing on the basis of their Rochester taxpayer status on grounds that Penfield's (D) failure to offer lower cost housing places the burden on Rochester, their asserted injury is conjectural and lacks any apparent line of causation between Penfield's (D) actions and the alleged injury. Any increase in Rochester taxes results from decisions of Rochester officials, non-parties, not from Penfield's (D) actions. The Rochester individuals assert no personal right, but the rights of third parties. The only relationship existing between them and the excluded prospective Penfield (D) residents is an incidental congruity of interest. As for the petitioning associations, Metro-Act (P), Home Builders (P), and Housing Council (P), an association may have standing to seek relief from injury or as its members' representative, but it must allege that they, or any one member, are suffering immediate or threatened injury. Metro-Act (P), as to its claim of standing as a Rochester taxpayer and as a representative of members who are Rochester taxpayers or lower income persons, lacks standing for the same reasons as do those same individuals previously discussed. As to Metro-Act's (P) claim based on its representing the 9% of its members who are Penfield (D) residents, the harm was indirect, and thus Metro-Act (P) was only raising the rights of third parties. As for Home Builders (P), it can only have standing if it alleged facts sufficient to make out a case or controversy had the members themselves brought suit, but its claim that various members lost business opportunities and profits by not being able to build is not a common claim, and requires individual proof of injury and damages. Finally, Housing Council (P), which includes 17 groups involved in development of lower cost housing fails for the same reasons as did Home Builders (P). Affirmed.

DISSENT: (Douglas, J.) "It would be a better practice to decide the question of standing only when the merits have been developed."

DISSENT: (Brennan, J.) It was a "glaring defect" to view each set of plaintiffs as if it were bringing a separate lawsuit. The interests were intertwined. The facts which the Court says must be alleged in order to get into court reverts to a form of fact-pleading, long dispensed within federal court.

Continued on next page.

▶ *ANALYSIS*

Note that had any party alleged that a zoning ordinance of the town was blocking a pending construction project, the question as to whether all administrative remedies had first been exhausted would have arisen. Generally the standing question is whether the constitutional or statutory provision on which the claim rests properly can be understood to grant persons in the plaintiff's position a right to judicial relief. An additional limitation on standing is whether the interest sought to be protected by the complainant is arguably within the zone of interests to be protected or regulated by this statute or constitutional guarantee in question, *Data Processing Service v. Camp,* 397 U.S. 150, 153 (1970).

■══■

Quicknotes

CASE OR CONTROVERSY Constitutional requirement in order to invoke federal court jurisdiction that the matter present a justiciable issue.

ZONING Municipal statutory scheme dividing an area into districts in order to regulate the use or building of structures within those districts.

■══■

Glossary

Common Latin Words and Phrases Encountered in the Law

A FORTIORI: Because one fact exists or has been proven, therefore a second fact that is related to the first fact must also exist.

A PRIORI: From the cause to the effect. A term of logic used to denote that when one generally accepted truth is shown to be a cause, another particular effect must necessarily follow.

AB INITIO: From the beginning; a condition which has existed throughout, as in a marriage which was void ab initio.

ACTUS REUS: The wrongful act; in criminal law, such action sufficient to trigger criminal liability.

AD VALOREM: According to value; an ad valorem tax is imposed upon an item located within the taxing jurisdiction calculated by the value of such item.

AMICUS CURIAE: Friend of the court. Its most common usage takes the form of an amicus curiae brief, filed by a person who is not a party to an action but is nonetheless allowed to offer an argument supporting his legal interests.

ARGUENDO: In arguing. A statement, possibly hypothetical, made for the purpose of argument, is one made arguendo.

BILL QUIA TIMET: A bill to quiet title (establish ownership) to real property.

BONA FIDE: True, honest, or genuine. May refer to a person's legal position based on good faith or lacking notice of fraud (such as a bona fide purchaser for value) or to the authenticity of a particular document (such as a bona fide last will and testament).

CAUSA MORTIS: With approaching death in mind. A gift causa mortis is a gift given by a party who feels certain that death is imminent.

CAVEAT EMPTOR: Let the buyer beware. This maxim is reflected in the rule of law that a buyer purchases at his own risk because it is his responsibility to examine, judge, test, and otherwise inspect what he is buying.

CERTIORARI: A writ of review. Petitions for review of a case by the United States Supreme Court are most often done by means of a writ of certiorari.

CONTRA: On the other hand. Opposite. Contrary to.

CORAM NOBIS: Before us; writs of error directed to the court that originally rendered the judgment.

CORAM VOBIS: Before you; writs of error directed by an appellate court to a lower court to correct a factual error.

CORPUS DELICTI: The body of the crime; the requisite elements of a crime amounting to objective proof that a crime has been committed.

CUM TESTAMENTO ANNEXO, ADMINISTRATOR (ADMINISTRATOR C.T.A.): With will annexed; an administrator c.t.a. settles an estate pursuant to a will in which he is not appointed.

DE BONIS NON, ADMINISTRATOR (ADMINISTRATOR D.B.N.): Of goods not administered; an administrator d.b.n. settles a partially settled estate.

DE FACTO: In fact; in reality; actually. Existing in fact but not officially approved or engendered.

DE JURE: By right; lawful. Describes a condition that is legitimate "as a matter of law," in contrast to the term "de facto," which connotes something existing in fact but not legally sanctioned or authorized. For example, de facto segregation refers to segregation brought about by housing patterns, etc., whereas de jure segregation refers to segregation created by law.

DE MINIMIS: Of minimal importance; insignificant; a trifle; not worth bothering about.

DE NOVO: Anew; a second time; afresh. A trial de novo is a new trial held at the appellate level as if the case originated there and the trial at a lower level had not taken place.

DICTA: Generally used as an abbreviated form of obiter dicta, a term describing those portions of a judicial opinion incidental or not necessary to resolution of the specific question before the court. Such nonessential statements and remarks are not considered to be binding precedent.

DUCES TECUM: Refers to a particular type of writ or subpoena requesting a party or organization to produce certain documents in their possession.

EN BANC: Full bench. Where a court sits with all justices present rather than the usual quorum.

EX PARTE: For one side or one party only. An ex parte proceeding is one undertaken for the benefit of only one party, without notice to, or an appearance by, an adverse party.

EX POST FACTO: After the fact. An ex post facto law is a law that retroactively changes the consequences of a prior act.

EX REL.: Abbreviated form of the term ex relatione, meaning upon relation or information. When the state brings an action in which it has no interest against an individual at the instigation of one who has a private interest in the matter.

FORUM NON CONVENIENS: Inconvenient forum. Although a court may have jurisdiction over the case, the action should be tried in a more conveniently located court, one to which parties and witnesses may more easily travel, for example.

GUARDIAN AD LITEM: A guardian of an infant as to litigation, appointed to represent the infant and pursue his/her rights.

HABEAS CORPUS: You have the body. The modern writ of habeas corpus is a writ directing that a person (body) being detained (such as a prisoner) be brought before the court so that the legality of his detention can be judicially ascertained.

IN CAMERA: In private, in chambers. When a hearing is held before a judge in his chambers or when all spectators are excluded from the courtroom.

IN FORMA PAUPERIS: In the manner of a pauper. A party who proceeds in forma pauperis because of his poverty is one who is allowed to bring suit without liability for costs.

INFRA: Below, under. A word referring the reader to a later part of a book. (The opposite of supra.)

IN LOCO PARENTIS: In the place of a parent.

IN PARI DELICTO: Equally wrong; a court of equity will not grant requested relief to an applicant who is in pari delicto, or as much at fault in the transactions giving rise to the controversy as is the opponent of the applicant.

IN PARI MATERIA: On like subject matter or upon the same matter. Statutes relating to the same person or things are said to be in pari materia. It is a general rule of statutory construction that such statutes should be construed together, i.e., looked at as if they together constituted one law.

IN PERSONAM: Against the person. Jurisdiction over the person of an individual.

IN RE: In the matter of. Used to designate a proceeding involving an estate or other property.

IN REM: A term that signifies an action against the res, or thing. An action in rem is basically one that is taken directly against property, as distinguished from an action in personam, i.e., against the person.

INTER ALIA: Among other things. Used to show that the whole of a statement, pleading, list, statute, etc., has not been set forth in its entirety.

INTER PARTES: Between the parties. May refer to contracts, conveyances or other transactions having legal significance.

INTER VIVOS: Between the living. An inter vivos gift is a gift made by a living grantor, as distinguished from bequests contained in a will, which pass upon the death of the testator.

IPSO FACTO: By the mere fact itself.

JUS: Law or the entire body of law.

LEX LOCI: The law of the place; the notion that the rights of parties to a legal proceeding are governed by the law of the place where those rights arose.

MALUM IN SE: Evil or wrong in and of itself; inherently wrong. This term describes an act that is wrong by its very nature, as opposed to one which would not be wrong but for the fact that there is a specific legal prohibition against it (malum prohibitum).

MALUM PROHIBITUM: Wrong because prohibited, but not inherently evil. Used to describe something that is wrong because it is expressly forbidden by law but that is not in and of itself evil, e.g., speeding.

MANDAMUS: We command. A writ directing an official to take a certain action.

MENS REA: A guilty mind; a criminal intent. A term used to signify the mental state that accompanies a crime or other prohibited act. Some crimes require only a general mens rea (general intent to do the prohibited act), but others, like assault with intent to murder, require the existence of a specific mens rea.

MODUS OPERANDI: Method of operating; generally refers to the manner or style of a criminal in committing crimes, admissible in appropriate cases as evidence of the identity of a defendant.

NEXUS: A connection to.

NISI PRIUS: A court of first impression. A nisi prius court is one where issues of fact are tried before a judge or jury.

N.O.V. (NON OBSTANTE VEREDICTO): Notwithstanding the verdict. A judgment n.o.v. is a judgment given in favor of one party despite the fact that a verdict was returned in favor of the other party, the justification being that the verdict either had no reasonable support in fact or was contrary to law.

NUNC PRO TUNC: Now for then. This phrase refers to actions that may be taken and will then have full retroactive effect.

PENDENTE LITE: Pending the suit; pending litigation underway.

PER CAPITA: By head; beneficiaries of an estate, if they take in equal shares, take per capita.

PER CURIAM: By the court; signifies an opinion ostensibly written "by the whole court" and with no identified author.

PER SE: By itself, in itself; inherently.

PER STIRPES: By representation. Used primarily in the law of wills to describe the method of distribution where a person, generally because of death, is unable to take that which is left to him by the will of another, and therefore his heirs divide such property between them rather than take under the will individually.

PRIMA FACIE: On its face, at first sight. A prima facie case is one that is sufficient on its face, meaning that the evidence supporting it is adequate to establish the case until contradicted or overcome by other evidence.

PRO TANTO: For so much; as far as it goes. Often used in eminent domain cases when a property owner receives partial payment for his land without prejudice to his right to bring suit for the full amount he claims his land to be worth.

QUANTUM MERUIT: As much as he deserves. Refers to recovery based on the doctrine of unjust enrichment in those cases in which a party has rendered valuable services or furnished materials that were accepted and enjoyed by another under circumstances that would reasonably notify the recipient that the rendering party expected to be paid. In essence, the law implies a contract to pay the reasonable value of the services or materials furnished.

QUASI: Almost like; as if; nearly. This term is essentially used to signify that one subject or thing is almost analogous to another but that material differences between them do exist. For example, a quasi-criminal proceeding is one that is not strictly criminal but shares enough of the same characteristics to require some of the same safeguards (e.g., procedural due process must be followed in a parole hearing).

QUID PRO QUO: Something for something. In contract law, the consideration, something of value, passed between the parties to render the contract binding.

RES GESTAE: Things done; in evidence law, this principle justifies the admission of a statement that would otherwise be hearsay when it is made so closely to the event in question as to be said to be a part of it, or with such spontaneity as not to have the possibility of falsehood.

RES IPSA LOQUITUR: The thing speaks for itself. This doctrine gives rise to a rebuttable presumption of negligence when the instrumentality causing the injury was within the exclusive control of the defendant, and the injury was one that does not normally occur unless a person has been negligent.

RES JUDICATA: A matter adjudged. Doctrine which provides that once a court of competent jurisdiction has rendered a final judgment or decree on the merits, that judgment or decree is conclusive upon the parties to the case and prevents them from engaging in any other litigation on the points and issues determined therein.

RESPONDEAT SUPERIOR: Let the master reply. This doctrine holds the master liable for the wrongful acts of his servant (or the principal for his agent) in those cases in which the servant (or agent) was acting within the scope of his authority at the time of the injury.

STARE DECISIS: To stand by or adhere to that which has been decided. The common law doctrine of stare decisis attempts to give security and certainty to the law by following the policy that once a principle of law as applicable to a certain set of facts has been set forth in a decision, it forms a precedent which will subsequently be followed, even though a different decision might be made were it the first time the question had arisen. Of course, stare decisis is not an inviolable principle and is departed from in instances where there is good cause (e.g., considerations of public policy led the Supreme Court to disregard prior decisions sanctioning segregation).

SUPRA: Above. A word referring a reader to an earlier part of a book.

ULTRA VIRES: Beyond the power. This phrase is most commonly used to refer to actions taken by a corporation that are beyond the power or legal authority of the corporation.

Addendum of French Derivatives

IN PAIS: Not pursuant to legal proceedings.

CHATTEL: Tangible personal property.

CY PRES: Doctrine permitting courts to apply trust funds to purposes not expressed in the trust but necessary to carry out the settlor's intent.

PER AUTRE VIE: For another's life; during another's life. In property law, an estate may be granted that will terminate upon the death of someone other than the grantee.

PROFIT A PRENDRE: A license to remove minerals or other produce from land.

VOIR DIRE: Process of questioning jurors as to their predispositions about the case or parties to a proceeding in order to identify those jurors displaying bias or prejudice.

Casenote Legal Briefs